P9-DFA-099

THE WORLD'S GREAT THINKERS

MAN AND SPIRIT:

The Speculative Philosophers

THE WORLD'S GREAT THINKERS

Man and Spirit:

THE SPECULATIVE PHILOSOPHERS

Edited by SAXE COMMINS & ROBERT N. LINSCOTT

RANDOM HOUSE · NEW YORK

 PUBLISHED IN NEW YORK BY RANDOM HOUSE, INC., AND SIMULTANEOUSLY IN TORONTO, CANADA, BY RANDOM HOUSE OF CANADA, LIMITED, 1947. MANUFACTURED IN THE UNITED STATES OF AMERICA.

Designed by Oscar Ogg.

ACKNOWLEDGMENT ☙ FOR PERMISSION TO REPRINT COPYRIGHTED SECTIONS OF THIS VOLUME, ACKNOWLEDGMENT IS HERE MADE TO: *Paul R. Reynolds and Son for "Philosophy" from* THE VARIETIES OF RELIGIOUS EXPERIENCE *by William James.* COPYRIGHT, 1902, BY WILLIAM JAMES. *Allen & Unwin, Ltd., for "The Religious Mood" and "The Natural History of Morals" from* BEYOND GOOD AND EVIL *by Friedrich Nietzsche. On the Immortality of the Soul* BY ST. AUGUSTINE, TRANSLATED BY GEORGE G. LECKIE. COPYRIGHT, 1938, BY D. APPLETON-CENTURY COMPANY, INC. *G. Bell & Sons, Ltd., for* THE FOUNDATIONS OF THE MORAL LIFE *by Baruch Spinoza, translated by White and Elwes. Routledge & Kegan Paul, Ltd., for* THE WORLD AS IDEA *by Arthur Schopenhauer, translated by Haldane.*

CONTENTS

PAGE

St. Augustine

ON THE IMMORTALITY OF THE SOUL

Saint Augustine
[354–430]

Torn by the struggle between flesh and spirit, after an early life of incontinence, Saint Augustine became a convert to Christianity in his thirty-third year and was ordained a priest in 391. Consecrated Bishop of Hippo, his influence spread throughout the Christian world from his native Numidian Africa by means of sermons, letters, philosophical and theological essays, confessions, and his famous *City of God*, in all of which he reiterated the goodness and all-pervasiveness of God. Characteristic of the content and style of his thinking and writing is "On the Immortality of the Soul," given here in its entirety.

ON THE IMMORTALITY OF THE SOUL

ST. AUGUSTINE

The First Reason Why the Soul Is Immortal: It Is the Subject of Science Which Is Eternal

1 ☙ If science [*disciplina*] exists anywhere, and cannot exist except in that which lives; and if it is eternal, and nothing in which an eternal thing exists can be non-eternal; then that in which science exists lives eternally. If we exist who reason, that is, if our mind does, and if our mind cannot reason rightly without science, and if without science no mind can exist except as a mind without science, then science is in the mind of man. Science, moreover, is somewhere, for it exists, and whatever exists cannot be nowhere. Further, science cannot exist except in that which lives. For nothing which is not alive learns anything, and science cannot be in a thing which does not learn.

Again, science is eternal. For what exists and is unchangeable must be eternal. But no one denies that science exists. And whoever admits that it is impossible that a line drawn through the midpoint of a circle is not greater than all lines which are not drawn through the midpoint, and admits that this is a part of science, does not deny that science is unchangeable. Further, nothing in which an eternal thing exists can be non-eternal. For nothing which is eternal ever allows to be taken from it that in which it exists eternally.

Now, truly, when we reason it is the mind which reasons. For only he who thinks reasons. Neither does the body think, nor does the mind receive the help of the body in thinking, since when the mind wishes to think it turns away from the body. For what is thought is thus eternal, and nothing pertaining to the body is thus eternal, therefore the body cannot help the mind as it strives to understand; for it is sufficient if the body does not hamper the mind. Again, without science [*disciplina*] nobody reasons rightly. For thought is right reasoning moving from things certain to the investigation of things uncertain, and there is nothing certain in an ignorant mind. All that the mind knows, moreover, it contains within itself, nor does knowledge consist in anything which does not pertain to some science. For science is the knowledge of any things whatsoever. Therefore the human mind always lives.

Another Reason: It Is the Subject of Reason Which Is Not Changed

2 ☙ Surely, reason either is the mind or is in the mind. Our reason, moreover, is better than our body, and body is a substance, and it is better to be a substance than to be nothing. Therefore, reason is not nothing.

Again, whatever the harmony of the body is, it must be in the body inseparably as in a subject; and nothing may be held to be in the harmony unless it is also necessarily in that body inseparably as in a subject. But the human body is mutable and reason is immutable. For all which does not exist always in the same mode is mutable, but that two and two are four exists always in the same mode, and also that four contains two and two exists always in the same mode, but two does not contain four, therefore two is not four. This sort of reasoning, then, is immutable. Therefore, reason is immutable.

Moreover, if the subject is changed, there is no way in which that which is in the subject remains unchanged. Hence, it follows that the mind is not a harmony of the body. Nor can death befall unchangeable things. Consequently, the mind always lives, and either the mind is reason itself or has reason in it inseparably.

Mind Is Living Substance and Immutable; and if It Is in Some Mode Mutable, It Does Not on That Account Become Mortal

3 ☙ Some power [*virtus*] is constant, and all constancy is unchangeable, and all power can act, nor does it cease to be power when it acts. Further, all action is moved or moves. Therefore, not all which is moved, or surely not all which moves, is changeable. But all which is moved by another and does not move itself is a mortal thing. Nor is anything immutable which is mortal. Hence, certainly and without any disjunction, it is concluded that not all which moves is changed.

There is, moreover, no motion without substance, and any substance either is alive or is not alive, and all which does not live is inanimate. But no action is inanimate. Therefore, that which moves so as not to be changed can be only living substance. Any action, moreover, moves the body through a number of steps; therefore, not all which moves the body is changeable. The body, moreover, is not moved except in time; and to the body pertains being moved faster and slower; therefore, there is shown to be a certain thing which moves in time and is not changed. Moreover, every body which moves in time, although it tends towards one end, yet can neither accomplish simultaneously all the steps which lead to this end, nor can avoid the several steps. For by whatever impulse it is moved, a body cannot be perfectly one, because it can be divided into parts; and there is no body without parts, as there is no time without an interval of delay, even if it is expressed by a very short syllable of which you hear neither the beginning nor the end. Further, what occurs thus needs expectation that it may be accomplished and memory that it may be understood as much as possible. And expectation is of future things, while memory is of things past. But intention to act belongs to present time, through which the future moves into the past. And without memory we cannot expect the end of a motion which has begun. For how can that be expected to cease which forgets either that it has begun or that it is in motion? Again, the intention of accomplishing which is present cannot be without expectation of the end which is future: nor does anything exist which does not yet exist or which has already ceased to exist. Therefore, there can be something in acting which pertains to those things which do not yet exist. There can be several things simultaneously in the agent, although these several acts when executed cannot exist simultaneously. Likewise, they can exist simultaneously in the mover, although they cannot in the thing moved. But whatever things cannot exist simultaneously in time, and yet are transmitted from future into past, must of necessity be mutable.

4 ⸎ From the above we have already gathered that there can be a certain thing which is not changed when it moves changeable things. For when the intention of the mover to bring the body which it moves tc the end it desires is not changed, while the body which is acted upon is changed by this motion from moment to moment, and when that intention of accomplishment, which obvicusly remains unchanged, moves both the members of the artificer and the wood or stone which are

subject to the artificer, who may doubt that what we have said follows as a logical consequence? Therefore, if any change in bodies be effected by the mind as mover, however intent upon the change the mind may be, we should not think that the mind is changed necessarily by this, or that the mind dies. For along with this intention it can have memory of past things and expectation of future things, none of which can exist without life. And even if there be no destruction without change, and no change without motion, yet not all change is engaged in destruction, nor is all motion engaged in change. For we can say that this body of ours has been for the most part moved by an action, and that it has undoubtedly been changed especially by age; still it has not yet perished, that is, is not without life. Therefore, from this it follows immediately that the mind is not deprived of life, even though some change does perchance occur to it through motion.

Art and the Unchangeable Principle of Numbers, Which Do Not Inhere in the Mind Without Life

5 ☙ For if there persists anything in the mind unchangeable. which cannot exist without life, then life must also remain in the mind eternally. For indeed the mind is so constituted that if the antecedent is true, the consequent is true. Moreover, the antecedent is true. For who dares say, not to mention other things, either that the principle [*ratio*] of number is changeable or that there is any art which does not depend upon this principle [*ratio*]; or that an art is not in the artist even if he be not applying it; or that it is in him other than as being in the mind; or that it can be where there is no life; or that what is unchangeable cannot be anywhere; or that art is other than a principle [*ratio*]? For although an art is said to be a sort of assemblage of many principles [*rationes*], yet an art can in truth be called one principle [*ratio*] and

can be so thought. But whether it be the former or the latter, it follows none the less that art is unchangeable. Moreover, it is clear not only that an art is in the mind of the artist, but also that it is nowhere else except in the mind, and in it inseparably. For if art is separated from the mind it will be other than in the mind, or will be nowhere, or will pass immediately from the mind. But just as there is no seat of art without life, so there is no life according to a principle [*ratio*] anywhere except in the soul. Further, that which is cannot be nowhere nor can that which is immutable be non-existent at any time. But if art passes from mind to mind, it would leave one mind and abide in another; in this case nobody would teach an art except by losing it, or further, nobody would become skilled except through the forgetting of his teacher, or by the teacher's death. If these things are utterly absurd and false, as they are, then the human mind is immortal.

6 ☙ And if indeed art exists at some time, it does not so exist in a mind which is conspicuous for its forgetfulness and ignorance. The conclusion of this argument adds nothing to the mind's immortality unless the preceding be denied in the following way. Either there is something in the mind which is not in present thought or else the art of music is not in the educated mind when it thinks of geometry alone. And this latter is false. Hence the former is true. Moreover, the mind does not perceive that it contains anything except what comes into thought. Therefore, there can be something in the mind, which the mind itself does not perceive to be in it. But as long as it is there, this makes no difference. For if the mind has been occupied with other things too long to be able to turn its attention back to things thought of before, this is called forgetting or ignorance. But since, when we reason with ourselves or when we are skilfully questioned by another concerning certain liberal arts, we then discover the

things which we discover nowhere else but in the mind; and since to discover is not to make or to cause, as otherwise the mind would cause eternal things through temporal discovery (for it often discovers eternal things, as the principle [*ratio*] of the circle, or anything else of this sort in the arts, which is not understood either to have been non-existent at some time or ever to be about to be); hence it is also evident that the human mind is immortal, and all true principles [*rationes*] are in its hidden places, although, either because of ignorance or forgetting, it seems not to contain them or to have lost them.

Mind Is Not Changed So That It Ceases To Be Mind

7 ☙ But now let us see to what extent we should accept the statement that the mind changes. For if the mind is the subject, with art existing in the subject, and if a subject cannot be changed unless that which is in it as in a subject be changed also, who can hold that art and principle [*ratio*] are unchangeable in the mind if the mind in which they exist is shown to be changeable? Moreover, where is there greater change than that in contraries? And who denies that the mind is, to say the least, at times stupid and at other times wise? Therefore, let us see in how many ways that which is called change of the soul may be taken. Of these I think there are found two genera quite evident or at last quite clear to us, though there are found several species. For the soul is said to be changed either according to passions of the body or according to its own passions. According to the passions of the body, as through age, disease, sorrow, work, hatred, or carnal desires; according to its own passions, however, as by desiring, enjoying, fearing, worrying, striving, or learning.

8 ❧ All these changes, if they are not necessarily proof that the soul dies, ought not to be feared at all taken separately each by each; but it should be seen whether they oppose our reasoning in which we said that when a subject is changed all which is in the subject is necessarily changed. But they do not oppose it. For this is said of a subject according to such a change as makes the name change entirely. For if wax changes to a black color from white, it is none the less wax; and also if it assumes a round shape after being square, becomes hard when it has been soft, cools after being hot. These are all in the subject, and wax is the subject. But wax remains not more or less wax when these things are changed. Therefore, some change of the things in the subject can occur, when the subject itself is not changed with regard to what it is and is called. But if so much change occurs in those things which are in the subject that that which was said to be the subject cannot any longer be so called, as, for example, when from the heat of fire wax disappears into the air, and suffers such change that it may rightly be understood that the subject is changed, since it was wax, and is no longer wax; then by no reasoning of any kind whatever would we think that any of those things would remain, which were in that subject because it was what it was.

9 ❧ Consequently, if, as we said above, the soul is a subject in which reason is inseparably (by that necessity also by which it is shown to be in the subject), neither can there be any soul except a living soul, nor can reason be in a soul without life, and reason is immortal; hence, the soul is immortal. For in absolutely no way could the soul remain immutable if its subject did not exist. This would happen if so great a change should befall the soul as would make it not a soul, that is, would compel it to die. Moreover, not one of those changes which occur to the soul, either through the body or through itself (although there is not a little question whether

any occur through itself, that is, of which it is itself the cause), causes the soul not to be a soul. Therefore, they need not be feared *per se;* nor because they may oppose our reasoning.

Unchangeable Reason, Whether It Be in the Mind or with the Mind, or Whether the Mind Be in It, Cannot Be Separated from the Very Same Mind

10 ☙ Hence I see that all men of reason ought to take pains to know what reason is and in how many ways it can be defined, so that it may remain firm according to all modes and with regard to the immortality of the soul. Reason is the aspect of the mind which perceives the true *per se* and not through the body; or it is the contemplation of the true, not through the body; or it is the true itself which is contemplated. Nobody doubts that the first of these is in the mind. There can be a question about the second and third; but even the second cannot exist without the mind. Concerning the third the great question is whether the true which is perceived by the mind without the instrument of the body exists *per se,* and is not in the mind, or whether it can exist without the mind. Moreover, in whatever mode the true may be, the mind cannot contemplate it *per se* except through some connection with it. For all that we contemplate we either perceive through cogitation [*cogitatio*], or through a sense or through the intellect. But those things which are perceived through sense we also sense to be outside us, and to be contained in places apart from which it is established that they cannot be perceived. But those things which are thought are not thought as being in another place other than the very mind which thinks them: for at the same time they also are thought as not being contained in any place.

11 ☙ Consequently, the connection between the mind which perceives and the true which it perceives is either such that the mind is the subject with the true in it as in a subject; or on the other hand the true is the subject with the mind in it as in a subject; or else each is a substance. Moreover, if the connection is of the first sort, the mind is as immortal as reason, according to the preceding argument, since reason can be in nothing but a living thing. The same necessity lies in the second sort of connection. For if the true, which is called reason, contains nothing which is changeable, as it appears, then nothing can be changed which is in it as in a subject. Therefore, all the struggle is left to the third. For if mind is one substance and reason another substance to which it is joined, he is not absurd who would think it possible for the former to remain while the latter perishes. But it is evident that as long as the mind is not separated from reason and remains connected with it, the mind necessarily survives and lives. But by what force can it be separated? By bodily force, whose power is weaker, whose origin is inferior, whose order is more disparate? Not at all. Then by animate strength? But how so? Cannot a more powerful mind contemplate reason without separating another mind from it? Reason is not lacking in any mind which contemplates, if all minds contemplate; and since nothing is more powerful than reason itself, than which nothing is more immutable, by no means will there be a mind not joined to reason and yet more powerful than one which is so joined. It remains that either reason separates itself from mind, or else the mind itself is separated by will. But there is no envy in that nature, and, therefore, it offers itself for mind's enjoyment; and, what is more, whatever it joins to itself it causes to be, which is contrary to destruction. Moreover, it is too absurd for someone to say that the mind is separated from reason by the mind's own will, provided there can be any mutual separation of things which space does not contain. Indeed this can be said in contradiction to all we have argued above in meeting other opposition. What then? Should it be concluded that the mind

is immortal? Or, even though it cannot be separated, can it perhaps be extinguished? But if the very strength of reason affects the mind by its connection (and it cannot fail to affect it), then it at once causes being to be ascribed to mind. For it is in great measure reason itself in which the supreme immutability is thought. Therefore, that which reason affects by virtue of itself it causes to exist in a certain respect. Hence the mind cannot be extinguished unless it be separated from reason, and it cannot be separated, as we have proved above. Therefore it cannot perish.

And If the Mind Tends Through Substance Towards Defection, Still It Does Not On This Account Perish

12 But that very turning away from reason by which stupidity enters the mind cannot occur without a defect in the mind. For if the mind has more being when turned towards reason and inhering in it, thus adhering to the unchangeable thing which is truth, both greatest and first; so when turned away from reason it has less being, which constitutes a defection. Moreover, every defect tends towards nothing [non-being], nor do we ever speak more properly of destruction than when that which was something becomes nothing. Therefore, to tend towards nothing [non-being] is to tend towards destruction. It is hard to say why this does not occur to the soul in which defect occurs. We grant all the above, but we deny that it follows that what tends towards nothing [non-being] perishes, that is, that it reaches nothing. This can be observed in the body also. For any body is part of the sensible world, and for this reason the larger it is and the more space it occupies the nearer it is to the universe; and the more it does this, the greater it is. For the whole is greater than

the part. Hence, necessarily, it is less when it is diminished; that is, it suffers a defect when it is lessened. Moreover, it is lessened when something is taken from it by cutting away, and it follows from this that because of such subtraction it tends to nothing. But no cutting away leads to nothing as such. For every part which remains is a body, and whatever is a body occupies a place in some space. Nor would this be possible unless it were to have parts into which it might be cut again and again. Therefore, it can be infinitely diminished through infinite division, and hence can suffer defection and tend towards nothing, although it can never reach nothing. Further, this can be said and understood of space itself and of any interval whatever. For by taking, let us say, a half part from the limits, and always a half part from what is left, the interval is diminished and approaches a limit which yet it can in no mode attain. Accordingly, even less should it be feared that the mind may become nothing, for the mind is indeed better and more lively than the body.

Just as That Cannot Be Taken from Body by Which It Is Body, So Neither Can That Be Taken from Mind by Which It Is Mind

13 ☙ But if that which causes the body to be is not in the matter of the body but in the form, (which point is established by quite irrefutable reasoning, for a body is greater according as it has better form and is more excellent, and it is less according as it is uglier and is more deformed, which defect occurs not from a taking away of matter, about which enough has been said, but from a privation of form), then this should be questioned and discussed, lest someone assert that mind perishes through defect of form; for seeing that when it is stupid mind is deprived of some of its form, it may be be-

lieved that this privation can be increased so much as to deprive the mind of form in every mode, by this misfortune reducing it to nothing and causing it to perish. Hence, if we can succeed in showing that not even the body can be deprived of that by virtue of which it is body, perhaps we shall rightly maintain that the mind can much less have that taken from it by virtue of which it is mind. For whoever considers carefully will admit that any kind of mind whatever must be preferred to every body.

14 ⁂ Let this, then, be the beginning of our argument, namely, that no thing makes or begets itself, unless it was before it existed: if the latter is false, the former is true. Again, that which has not been made or begotten, and yet is, must be everlasting. Whoever attributes this nature and this excellence to any body, errs indeed greatly. But why do we dispute? For even were we to attribute it to body we should be forced to attribute it much more to the mind. Thus if any body is everlasting, there is no mind which is not everlasting; seeing that any mind is to be preferred to any body and eternal things to non-eternal things. But if it is truly said that the body is made, it was made by some maker, nor was the maker inferior to body. For an inferior maker would not have power to give to that which he was making whatever it is that makes it what it is. But the maker and the body are not equals, since it is necessary for a maker to have something better for making than that which he makes. For we do not make the absurd statement that the begetter is that thing which is begotten by him. Therefore, a whole body has been made by some force which is more powerful and better, or at least not corporeal. For if a body be made by a body, it cannot be made whole; for it is very true, as we stated in the beginning of this argument, that no thing can be made by itself. Moreover, this force or incorporeal nature being the producer of the whole body preserves the whole by its abiding power. For it did not make a thing and then vanish and desert the thing made. In-

deed that substance which is not body is not, if I may speak thus, moved in space so that it can be separated from that substance which is localized; and this effecting strength cannot be idle, but preserves that which it has made, and does not allow it to lack the form by virtue of which it is to whatever extent it is. For since the thing made does not exist *per se*, if it is abandoned by that through which it exists, it will immediately cease to exist, and we cannot say that when the body was made it received the power to be sufficient by virtue of itself when it is deserted by its maker.

15 ☙ And if this is so, the mind which clearly excels the body has power to a greater degree. And thus the mind is proved immortal, if it can exist *per se*. For whatever exists thus must be incorruptible, and therefore unable to perish, since nothing abandons itself. But the changeability of the body is manifest, which the whole motion of the entire body indicates adequately. Hence, it is found by those who investigate carefully, in so far as such a nature can be investigated, that ordered changeableness imitates that which is unchangeable. Moreover, that which exists *per se* has no need of anything, not even of motion, since it has all it needs existing in itself; for all motion is towards another thing which is that which is lacked by that which is moved. Therefore, form is present in the whole body while a better nature which made it provides for and sustains it, hence, that changeability does not take away from a body its being a body, but causes it to pass from one form to another by a well-ordered motion. For not one of its parts is allowed to be reduced to nothing, since that effective power with its force, neither striving nor inactive, aims at a whole, permitting the body to be all which through the power it is, in so far as it is. Consequently, there should be no one so devoid of reason as not to be certain that the mind is better than the body, or when this has been granted, to think that it does not happen to the body that the

body is not body, yet happens to the mind that it is not mind If this does not happen, and a mind cannot exist unless it lives, surely a mind can never die.

Mind Is Life, and Thus It Cannot Lack Life

16 ☙ If anyone asserts that the mind ought not to fear that destruction in which that which was something becomes nothing, but ought to fear that in which we call those things dead which lack life, let him notice that there is no thing which lacks itself. Moreover, mind is a certain life, so that all which is animated lives. But every inanimate thing which can be animated is understood to be dead, that is, deprived of life. Hence the mind cannot die. For if anything can lack life, this thing is not mind which animates, but a thing which has been animated. If this is absurd, this kind of destruction should be feared much less by the mind, since destruction of life is surely not to be feared. For if the mind dies wholly when life abandons it, that very life which deserts it is understood much better as mind, as now mind is not something deserted by life, but the very life itself which deserted. For whatever dead thing is said to be abandoned by life, is understood to be deserted by the soul. Moreover, this life which deserts the things which die is itself the mind, and it does not abandon itself: hence the mind does not die.

Mind Is Not the Organization of Body

17 ☙ Unless perhaps we ought to believe that life is some organization [*temperatio*] of the body, as some have held. It would never have seemed so to them if they had been able to

see those things which exist truly and which remain unchangeable when the same mind has been freed from the habit of bodies and cleansed. For who has looked well within himself without having experienced that the more earnestly he had thought something, the more he was able to move and draw the attention of the mind away from the senses of the body? If the mind were an organization of the body, this would absolutely not happen. For a thing which did not have a nature of its own and was not a substance, but which like color and shape was in the body inseparably as in a subject, would not try in any way to turn itself away from that same body in order to perceive intelligible things; and only inasmuch as it could do this would it be able to look upon intelligible things and be made by this vision better and more excellent. Indeed, in no way can shape or color, or the very organization of the body, which is a certain mixture of four natures in which the same body consists, turn from the thing in which they are inseparably as in a subject. In comparison with these things, those things which the mind thinks when it turns away from the body are not wholly corporeal, and yet they exist, and that in great degree, for they maintain themselves always in the same mode. For nothing more absurd can be said than that those things which we see with the eyes exist, while those things which we perceive by the intellect do not; for it is mad to doubt that the intellect is incomparably superior to the eyes. Moreover, while these things which are thought maintain themselves in the same mode, when the mind sees them it shows well enough that it is joined to them in a certain miraculous and likewise incorporeal way, that is, not locally. For either they are in it, or it is in them. And whichever one of these is true, either the one is in the other as in a subject, or each one is a substance. But if the first is true, the mind is not in the body as in a subject, as color and shape are, since either it is substance itself or it is in another substance which is not body. Moreover, if the second is true, mind is not in body as in a subject, as color is in body, because the mind is a substance. Further, the organization of a body is in the body as in a subject, just as color is; therefore, mind is not the organization of the body, but the mind is life. No thing deserts itself, and that dies which is deserted by life. Therefore, the mind cannot die.

Even Though Truth Is the Cause of the Mind, Mind Does Not Perish Through Falsehood, the Contrary of Truth

18 ☙ And so again, if anything should be feared, it is that the mind may perish by defection, that is, may be deprived of the very form of existence. Although I think enough has been said about this, and it has been shown by clear reasoning that this cannot be done, yet it should also be observed that there is no other reason for this fear except that we have admitted that the stupid mind exists defectively, while the wise mind exists in more certain and fuller essence. But if, as nobody doubts, the mind is most wise when it looks upon truth which is always in the same mode, and clings immovable to it, joined by divine love; and if all things which exist in any mode whatever exist by that essence which exists in the highest and greatest degree; then either the mind exists by virtue of that essence, inasmuch as it does exist, or it exists *per se*. But if it exists *per se*, since it is itself the cause of its existing and never deserts itself, it never perishes, as we also argued above. But if we exist from that essence there is need to inquire carefully what thing can be contrary to it, which may rob the mind of being the mind which the essence causes. So, then, what is it? Falsity, perhaps, because the essence is truth? But it is manifest and clearly established to what extent falsity can harm the mind. For can it do more than deceive? And except he live is any deceived? Therefore, falsity cannot destroy the mind. But if what is contrary to truth cannot rob the mind of that being mind which truth gave it (for truth is thus unconquerable), what else may be found which may take from the

mind that which is mind? Nothing, surely; for nothing is more able than a contrary to take away that which is made by its contrary.

There Is No Contrary to the Truth by Which Mind Exists in So Far as It Exists

19 ◆ But suppose we seek the contrary of truth, not inasmuch as it is truth as the contrary of falsity, but inasmuch as it exists in the greatest and highest degree (although truth exists thus to the extent that it is truth, if we call that truth by which all things are true, in whatever degree they may exist, they exist inasmuch as they are true); yet by no means shall I seek to avoid that which this suggests to me so clearly. For if there is no contrary to any essence inasmuch as it is an essence, then much less is there a contrary to that first essence inasmuch as it is essence. Moreover, the antecedent is true. For no essence exists for any other reason than that it exists. Being, moreover, has no contrary except non-being: hence nothing is the contrary of essence. Therefore, in no way can anything exist as a contrary to that substance which exists first and in highest degree. If the mind has its very essence from that essence (for since it does not have it from itself [*ex se*] it cannot have it otherwise than from that thing which is superior to the mind itself); then there is no thing by which it may lose its existence (being), because there is nothing contrary to that thing from which it has it. Hence the mind cannot cease to exist. But since the mind has wisdom because of turning to that by virtue of which it exists, so also when it turns away it can lose this wisdom. For turning away is the contrary of turning toward. But what it has from that to which there is no contrary is not a thing which it can lose. Therefore, it cannot perish.

Nor Is Mind Changed into Body

20 ◆§ Here perhaps some question may appear as to whether the mind which does not perish is not changed into a lower essence. For it can appear to some, and not unjustly, that this reasoning proves that the mind cannot reach nothing, yet can be perhaps changed into body. For if what was formerly mind becomes body it will not yet be wholly non-existent. But this is impossible unless the mind desires it or else is compelled by another. Yet mind will not necessarily be able to be body, even if it desires it, or if it is compelled. For if it is body it follows that it desires this or is compelled. But it does not follow that if it desires or is compelled, it is body. Moreover, it will never desire to be body: for all the mind desires in regard to body is that it may possess it, or make it live, or fashion it in a certain manner, or look out for it in some way or other. Moreover, none of these things is possible if mind is not better than body. But if mind is body, it follows that it will not be better than body. Therefore, it will not wish to be body. Nor is there any surer proof of this than when the mind questions itself about this point. For thus the mind easily discovers that it has no desire except for some action, either knowing or sensing, or only living to the fullest extent of its power.

21 ◆§ But if it is compelled to be body, by what, pray, is it compelled? Whatever it is it must surely be more powerful than mind, hence it cannot be compelled by body itself; for no body can in any way be more powerful than mind. Moreover, a more powerful mind compels only that which is set under its power, and no mind can in any way be set under the power of another mind except by the former's own desire. Hence, one mind does not compel another mind more than the desires of the other allow. Moreover, it has been said that mind cannot have desire to be body. Also it is clear that the mind attains no satisfaction of its desire while it loses all de-

sire, which happens when it is made body. Therefore, a mind cannot be compelled to become body by one whose only right to compel lies in the desires of the one compelled. Then whatever mind has another mind in its power must prefer having it to having a body in its power, and must wish to promote its goodness or to have power over evil. Therefore, it will not wish it to be body.

22 ☙ Finally, the mind which compels either is animal or it lacks body. But if it lacks body it is not in this world. And if it is thus, it is supremely good and cannot wish another to suffer such a wicked change. But if it is animal, either the mind it compels is animal or it is not. But if it is not, it cannot be compelled to anything by another. For none is more powerful than that which exists in the greatest degree. On the other hand, if it is body, again it is forced through body to whatever extent it is forced. But who believes that in any way such a change can be made in mind through body? For it would be made if the body were greater than it; although no matter what it is to which it is compelled by body it is not compelled wholly through body, but is compelled through its own desires, about which enough has been said. Moreover, that which is better than a rational soul is God, as all agree. He surely looks after the soul, and, therefore, the soul cannot be forced by Him to be changed into body.

Nor Is the Strength of the Mind Diminished by Sleep or Any Other Similar Affection of the Body

23 ☙ Hence, if the mind does not suffer this change by its own will, or because it is compelled by another, by what

means can it suffer it? Or, because sleep for the most part overtakes us against our will, should it be feared that by some such defect the mind may be changed to body? As if when our limbs are overwhelmed by sleep to say that the mind is made weaker in some sense. Sensible things only it does not sense, because whatever causes sleep pertains to the body and works in the body. Sleep lulls and shuts off the corporeal senses so soundly that the soul submits with pleasure to such a change of the body. Such a change is according to nature and refreshes the body after its labors, yet it does not take from the mind the power of sensing and thinking. For it still has images of sensible things at hand of such evident similarity that at the time they cannot be distinguished from the things of which they are the images. If the mind thinks anything, it is as true in sleeping as in waking. For, to give an example, if it should argue to itself in a dream, and following true principles in argument should learn something, when it is awakened the same principles remain immutable, although other things may be found false, such as the place where the argument seemed to have occurred, the person with whom it seemed to have been held, even, as far as sound is concerned, the words themselves by which it seemed the argument was made, and other things of this sort. Likewise when these things are perceived and discussed by those who are awake, they pass away and in no sense attain the eternal presence of true principles. From this it is inferred that when a body changes as in sleep the soul's use of that body can be diminished, but not its own life.

Again, Mind Cannot Be Changed into Body

24 ☙ Finally, however much the soul is joined to a body occupying space, still it is not joined locally. The soul is prior to the body in connection with those supreme and eternal

principles which survive unchangeably and are not contained in space; and the soul's connection is not only prior but also greater; as much prior as it is nearer, and for the same reason as much greater as it is better than body. And this nearness is not in place but in the order of nature. According to this order it is understood that the supreme essence bestows form upon the body through the soul by which it exists in whatever degree it does exist. Therefore, the body subsists through the soul, and it exists to the extent that it is animated, whether universally, as the world, or particularly, as some animal or other within the world. Therefore, the conclusion was that a soul would become body through a soul, or else not at all. Since it does not become body, and the soul remains soul in that in which it is the soul, the body subsists through the soul which gives it form and does not take this form away; hence the soul cannot be changed into body. For if it does not give up the form which it takes from the Supreme Good, it does not become body through that form; and if it does not become body through that, either it does not become body at all, or else takes a form as near the Supreme Good as soul. But if, when it became body, it assumed a form as near the Supreme Good as soul, that form would be a soul; for this is important, that the soul is better to the extent to which it takes a form nearer the Supreme Good. Moreover, body would take a form of the corporeal order even if it did not take its form through soul. For if nothing intervened it would still take a form in this order. Nor is there found anything which exists between the Supreme Life which is wisdom and truth unchangeable and that remote thing which is made alive (that is, body), except the soul which makes the body live. If the soul gives form to body, so that body may exist to the extent that it does exist, it does not take the form away by giving. Moreover, it takes the soul into the body by transmutation. Therefore, the soul does not become body, either *per se*, because body is not made by soul unless the soul remains, or through another, because not except by giving form is body made through soul, and by taking away form soul would be changed into body, if it were changed.

Nor Even Is the Rational Soul Changed into the Irrational. The Whole Soul Is in the Body as a Whole and in Each Part

25 ⸎ Likewise it can be said that the rational soul is not changed into the irrational soul or life. For the irrational soul, even were it not held in a lower order by the rational soul, would nevertheless assume the same form it does assume and be moved as it is. Therefore, more powerful things receive form from the Supreme Excellence and give it to things in the natural order. And when they give, surely, they do not take away. And to whatever extent the things which are inferior exist, they exist because the form in which they exist is given to them by those more powerful than they. And, indeed, the more powerful are also better. For to these natures it has been granted, not that through greater mass they have more power over things of lesser mass, but that without any increase of local magnitude they are more powerful than and better than the lower forms. In this way the soul is better than and greater than the body. Therefore, since the body, as has been said, subsists through the soul, the soul can in no way be changed into body; for no body is made except by receiving its form from the soul. The soul, if it became body, would become body through losing form, not through receiving it; therefore, it is not possible, unless perhaps the soul be contained in a place and joined locally to the body. For if this were true, although the soul is more perfect in form, perhaps a greater mass could change the soul into its lower form, just as the greater air changes the lesser fire. But it is not true. Indeed, every mass which occupies a place is not a separate whole in each of its parts, but the whole consists of all the parts. Consequently, one part of such a whole is in one place, and another in another. But the soul is present as a whole not only in the entire mass of a body, but also in every least part of the body at the same time. For the soul senses

the suffering of a part of the body as a whole, and yet not in the whole body. For when there is a pain in the foot the eye turns, the tongue speaks, the hand moves forward. This would not happen unless the soul which senses in these parts, also senses in the foot, nor could it while absent sense what was happening there. For it is not to be believed that it happens through any agent of communication which does not sense what it communicates; for the suffering which occurs does not run through the whole extent of the mass in such a way as to involve all the other parts of the soul which are elsewhere. Rather, the whole soul senses what happens to the foot in particular, and only senses it at the place at which it happens. The whole soul, therefore, is present simultaneously in each part, and simultaneously senses in each. Yet the soul is not wholly present in the way in which whiteness or any other quality of this sort is wholly present in each part of a body. For what a body suffers in one part by change of whiteness cannot pertain to the whiteness which is in another part. Hence, it is shown that a mass itself is differentiated according as its parts are differentiated. But we have proved above that this is not the case with the soul as it senses.

St. Thomas Aquinas

TREATISE ON THE DIVINE GOVERNMENT

Saint Thomas Aquinas

[1225–1274]

Prince of Scholastics and Doctor of the Church who systematized Catholic theology and provided the basic educational principles of the Roman Faith, Saint Thomas Aquinas has exercised a continuing and growing influence from the time of his death in 1274 until now, when his followers, champions of Thomism, have made his teachings a major force in philosophy, religion and education. His important works, *Summa Theologica* and *Summa Contra Gentiles*, epitomize Christian wisdom in the later Middle Ages and have remained through seven centuries among the most closely reasoned expressions of man's need for God. "Treatise on Divine Government" is from *Summa Theologica.*

TREATISE ON THE DIVINE GOVERNMENT

ST. THOMAS AQUINAS

The Government of Things In General

IN EIGHT ARTICLES

HAVING considered the creation of things and their distinction, we now consider in the third place the government thereof, and (1) the government of things in general; (2) in particular, the effects of this government. Under the first head there are eight points of inquiry: (1) Whether the world is governed by someone? (2) What is the end of this government? (3) Whether the world is governed by one? (4) On the effects of this government. (5) Whether all things are subject to the divine government? (6) Whether all things are immediately governed by God? (7) Whether the divine government is frustrated in anything? (8) Whether anything is contrary to the divine providence?

FIRST ARTICLE

WHETHER THE WORLD IS GOVERNED BY ANYONE?

We proceed thus to the First Article:—

Objection 1. It would seem that the world is not governed by anyone. For it belongs to those things to be governed which move or work for an end. But natural things which make up the greater part of the world do not move, or work for an end, for they have no knowledge of their end. Therefore the world is not governed.

Obj. 2. Further, those things are governed which are moved towards some object. But the world does not appear to be so directed, but has stability in itself. Therefore it is not governed.

Obj. 3. Further, what is necessarily determined by its own nature to one particular course does not require any external principle of government. But the principal parts of the world are by a certain necessity determined to something particular in their actions and movements. Therefore the world does not require to be governed.

On the contrary, It is written (*Wis.* xiv. 3): *But Thou, O Father, governest all things by Thy Providence.* And Boethius says: *Thou Who governest this universe by mandate eternal.*

I answer that, Certain ancient philosophers denied the government of the world, saying that all things happened by chance. But such an opinion can be refuted as impossible in two ways. First, by the observation of things themselves. For we observe that in nature things happen always or nearly always for the best; which would not be the case unless some sort of providence directed nature towards good as an end. And this is to govern. Therefore the unfailing order we observe in things is a sign of their being governed. For instance, if we were to enter a well-ordered house, we would gather from the order manifested in the house the notion of a governor, as Cicero says, quoting Aristotle. Secondly, this is clear from a consideration of the divine goodness, which, as we have said above, is the cause of the production of things in being. For as *it belongs to the best to produce the best*, it is not fitting that the supreme goodness of God should produce things without giving them their perfection. Now a thing's ultimate perfection consists in the attainment of its end. Therefore it belongs to the divine goodness, as it brought things into being, so to lead them to their end. And this is to govern.

Reply Obj. 1. A thing moves or operates for an end in two ways. First, in moving itself to the end, as do man and other rational creatures; and such beings have a knowledge of their end, and of the means to the end. Secondly, a thing is said to move or operate for an end, as though moved or directed thereto by another, as an arrow is directed to the target by the archer, who knows the end unknown to the arrow. Hence, as the movement of the arrow towards a definite end shows clearly that it is directed by someone with knowledge, so the unvarying course of natural things which are without knowledge shows clearly that the world is governed by some reason.

Reply Obj. 2. In all created things there is a stable element, even if this be only primary matter, and something belonging to movement, if under movement we include operation. Now things need governing as to both, because even that which is stable, since it is created from nothing, would return to nothingness were it not sustained by a governing hand, as will be explained later.

Reply Obj. 3. The natural necessity inherent in those beings which are determined to a particular course is a kind of impression from God, directing them to their end; just as the necessity whereby the arrow is moved so as to fly towards a certain point is an impression from the archer, and not from the arrow. But there is a difference, inasmuch as that which creatures receive from God is their nature, while that which natural things receive from man in addition to their nature is something violent. Therefore, just as the violent necessity in the movement of the arrow shows the action of the archer, so the natural necessity of things shows the government of divine providence.

SECOND ARTICLE

WHETHER THE END OF THE GOVERNMENT OF THE WORLD IS SOMETHING OUTSIDE THE WORLD?

We proceed thus to the Second Article:—

Objection 1. It would seem that the end of the government

of the world is not something existing outside the world. For the end of the government of a thing is that to which the thing governed is brought. But that to which a thing is brought is some good in the thing itself; and thus a sick man is brought back to health, which is something good in him. Therefore the end of the government of things is some good, not outside, but existing within the things themselves.

Obj. 2. Further, the Philosopher says: *Some ends are operations; some are works—i.e.*, products of operations. But nothing can be produced by the whole universe outside itself, and operation exists in the agent. Therefore nothing extrinsic can be the end of the government of things.

Obj. 3. Further, the good of a multitude seems to consist in order and peace, which is the *tranquillity of order*, as Augustine says. But the world is composed of a multitude of things. Therefore the end of the government of the world is a peaceful order in things themselves. Therefore the end of the government of the world is not an extrinsic good.

On the contrary, It is written (*Prov.* xvi. 4): *The Lord hath made all things for Himself*. But God is outside the entire order of the universe. Therefore the end of all things is something extrinsic to them.

I answer that, As the end of a thing corresponds to its beginning, it is not possible to be ignorant of the end of things if we know their beginning. Therefore, since the beginning of all things is something outside the universe, namely, God, as is clear from what has been said above, we must conclude that the end of all things is some extrinsic good. This can be proved by reason. For it is clear that good has the nature of an end. And so the particular end of anything consists in some particular good, while the universal end of all things is a universal good. A universal good is good of itself by virtue of its essence, which is the very essence of goodness; whereas a particular good is good by participation. Now it is manifest that in the whole created universe there is not a good which is not such by participation. Therefore that good which is the end of the whole universe must be a good outside the universe.

Reply Obj. 1. We may acquire some good in many ways: first, as a form existing in us, such as health or knowledge; secondly, as something done by us, as a builder attains his end by building a house; thirdly, as something good possessed or acquired by us, as the buyer of a field attains his end when he enters into possession. Therefore nothing prevents something outside the universe from being the good to which it is directed.

Reply Obj. 2. The Philosopher is speaking of the ends of various arts. For the end of some arts consists in the operation itself, as the end of a harpist is to play the harp; whereas the end of other arts consists in something produced, as the end of a builder is not the act of building, but the house he builds. Now it may happen that something extrinsic is the end not only as made, but also as possessed or acquired, or even as represented, as if we were to say that Hercules is the end of the statue made to represent him. Therefore we may say that some good outside the whole universe is the end of the government of the universe, as something possessed and represented; for each thing tends to participate in it, and to assimilate itself to it, as far as is possible.

Reply Obj. 3. The end of the universe, namely, the order of the universe itself, is a good existing in it. This good, however, is not its ultimate end, but is ordered to an extrinsic good as to an ultimate end; just as the order in an army is ordered to the general, as is stated in *Metaph.* xii.

THIRD ARTICLE

WHETHER THE WORLD IS GOVERNED BY ONE?

We proceed thus to the Third Article:—

Objection 1. It would seem that the world is not governed by one. For we judge the cause by the effect. Now, we see in the government of the universe that things are not moved and do not operate uniformly, but some contingently and some of necessity, and according to other and various differences. Therefore the world is not governed by one.

Obj. 2. Further, things which are governed by one do not act against each other, except by the inexperience, the incapacity or the unskilfulness of the ruler; which cannot apply to God. But created things do not harmonize, and act against each other; as is evident in the case of contraries. Therefore the world is not governed by one.

Obj. 3. Further, in nature we always find what is the better. But it *is better that two should be together than one* (*Eccles.* iv. 9). Therefore the world is not governed by one, but by many.

On the contrary, We confess one God and one Lord, according to the words of the *Apostle* (*1 Cor.* viii. 6): *To us there is but one God, the Father . . . and one Lord;* and both of these pertain to government. For to the Lord belongs dominion over subjects; and the name *God* is taken from providence, as was stated above. Therefore the world is governed by one.

I answer that, We must of necessity say that the world is governed by one. For since the end of the government of the world is that which is essentially good, which is the greatest good, the government of the world must be the best kind of government. Now the best government is government by one. The reason for this is that government is nothing but the directing of the things governed to the end; which consists in some good. But unity belongs to the notion of goodness, as Boethius proves from this, that, as all things desire good, so do they desire unity, without which they would cease to exist. For a thing so far exists as it is one. Whence we observe that things resist division, as far as they can, and that the dissolution of a thing arises from some defect in the thing. Therefore the intention of a ruler over a multitude is unity, or peace. Now the proper cause of unity is that which is one. For it is clear that several cannot be the cause of unity or concord, except so far as they are united. Furthermore, what is one in itself is a more apt and a better cause of unity than several things united. Therefore a multitude is better governed by one than by several. From this it follows that the government of the world, being the best form of government, must be by one. This is expressed by the Philosopher: *Things refuse to be ill governed; and multiplicity of authorities is a bad thing. Therefore there should be one ruler.*

Reply Obj. 1. Movement is *the act of a thing moved, caused by the mover.* Therefore dissimilarity of movements is caused by the diversity of things moved, which is essential to the perfection of the universe, and not by a diversity of governors.

Reply Obj. 2. Although contraries do not agree with each other in their proximate ends, nevertheless they agree in the ultimate end, so far as they are included in the one order of the universe.

Reply Obj. 3. If we consider individual goods, then two are better than one. But if we consider the essential good, then no addition of good is possible.

FOURTH ARTICLE

WHETHER THE EFFECT OF GOVERNMENT IS ONE OR MANY?

We proceed thus to the Fourth Article:—

Objection 1. It would seem that there is but one effect of the government of the world, and not many. For the effect of government is that which is caused in the things governed. This is one, namely, the good which consists in order, as may be seen in the example of an army. Therefore the government of the world has but one effect.

Obj. 2. Further, from one there naturally proceeds but one. But the world is governed by one, as we have proved. Therefore the effect of this government is but one.

Obj. 3. Further, if the effect of government is not one by reason of the unity of the governor, it must be many by reason of the many things governed. But these are too numerous to be counted. Therefore we cannot assign any definite number to the effects of government.

On the contrary, Dionysius says: *God contains all and fills all by His providence and perfect goodness.* But government belongs to providence. Therefore there are certain definite effects of the divine government.

I answer that, The effect of any action may be judged from its end, because it is by action that the attainment of the end is effected. Now the end of the government of the world is the essential good, to the participation and similarity of which all things tend. Consequently the effect of the government of the world may be taken in three ways. First, on the part of the end itself, and in this way there is but one effect, that is, assimilation to the highest good. Secondly, the effect of the government of the world may be considered on the part of those things by means of which the creature is made like to God. Thus there are, in general, two effects of government. For the creature is assimilated to God in two respects. First, with regard to this, that God is good, and thus the creature becomes like Him by being good; and secondly, with regard to this, that God is the cause of goodness in others, and thus the creature becomes like God by moving others to be good. Therefore there are two effects of government, the preservation of things in their goodness, and the moving of things to good. Thirdly, we may consider the effects of the government of the world in particular instances, and in this way they are without number.

Reply Obj. 1. The order of the universe includes both the preservation of the things created by God and their movement. For it is in reference to these two things that we find order among things, namely, inasmuch as one is better than another, and one is moved by another.

From what has been said above, we can gather the replies to the other two objections.

FIFTH ARTICLE

WHETHER ALL THINGS ARE SUBJECT TO THE DIVINE GOVERNMENT?

We proceed thus to the Fifth Article:—

Objection 1. It would seem that not all things are subject to the divine government. For it is written (*Eccles.* ix. 11): *I saw that under the sun the race is not to the swift, nor the battle to the strong, nor bread to the wise, nor riches to the learned, nor favor to the skilful, but time and chance in all.* But things subject to the divine government are not ruled by chance. Therefore those things which are under the sun are not subject to the divine government.

Obj. 2. Further, the Apostle says (*1 Cor.* ix. 9): *God hath no care for oxen.* But he that governs has care for the things he governs. Therefore all things are not subject to the divine government.

Obj. 3. Further, what can govern itself needs not to be governed by another. But the rational creature can govern itself. For it is master of its own act, and acts of itself; nor is it made to act by another, which seems proper to things which are governed. Therefore all things are not subject to the divine government.

On the contrary, Augustine says: *Not only heaven and earth, not only man and angel, but even the bowels of the lowest animal, even the wing of the bird, the flower of the plant, the leaf of the tree, hath God endowed with every fitting detail of their nature.* Therefore all things are subject to His government.

I answer that, For the same reason is God the ruler of things as He is their cause, because the same cause gives being that gives perfection; and this belongs to government. Now God is the cause, not of some particular kind of being, but of the whole universal being, as was proved above. Therefore, as there can be nothing which is not created by God, so there can be nothing which is not subject to His government. This can also be proved from the nature of the end of government. For a man's government extends over all those things which come under the end of his government. Now the end of the divine government is the divine goodness, as we have shown. Therefore, as there can be nothing that is not ordered to the divine goodness as its end, as is clear from what we have said above, it is impossible for anything to escape from the divine government.

Foolish therefore was the opinion of those who said that the corruptible lower world, or individual things, or that even human affairs, were not subject to the divine government. These are represented as saying, *God hath abandoned the earth* (*Ezech.* ix. 9).

Reply Obj. 1. Those things are said to be under the sun which are generated and corrupted according to the sun's movement. In all such things we find chance; not that everything is by chance which occurs in such things, but that in each one there is an element of chance. And the very fact that an element of chance is found in these things proves that they are subject to government of some kind. For unless corruptible things were governed by a higher being, they would tend to nothing definite, especially those which possess no kind of knowledge. So nothing in them would happen unintentionally; which constitutes the nature of chance. Therefore to show how things happen by chance and yet according to the ordering of a higher cause, he does not say absolutely that he observes chance in all things, but *time and chance*, that is to say, that defects may be found in these things according to some order of time.

Reply Obj. 2. Government implies a certain change effected by the governor in the things governed. Now every movement is the act of a movable thing, caused by the moving principle, as is laid down in *Physics* iii. Now every act is proportioned to that of which it is an act. Consequently, diverse movable things must be moved diversely, even as regards movement by one and the same mover. Thus, by the one art of the divine governor things are diversely governed according to their diversity. Some, according to their nature, act of themselves, having dominion over their actions; and these are governed by God, not only in this, that they are moved by God Himself, Who works in them interiorly, but also in this, that they are induced by Him to do good and to fly from evil, by precepts and prohibitions, rewards and punishments. But irrational creatures, which do not act but are only acted upon, are not thus governed by God. Hence, when the Apostle says that *God hath no care for oxen*, he does not wholly withdraw them from the divine government, but only as regards the way in which rational creatures are governed.

Reply Obj. 3. The rational creature governs itself by its intellect and will, both of which require to be governed and perfected by the divine intellect and will. Therefore, above the government whereby the rational creature governs itself as master of its own act, it requires to be governed by God.

SIXTH ARTICLE

WHETHER ALL THINGS ARE IMMEDIATELY GOVERNED BY GOD?

We proceed thus to the Sixth Article:—

Objection 1. It would seem that all things are governed by God immediately. For Gregory of Nyssa reproves the opinion of Plato who divides providence into three parts. The first he ascribes to the supreme god, who watches over heavenly things and all universal realities; the second providence he attributes to the secondary deities, who go the round of the heavens to watch over generation and corruption; while he ascribes a third providence to certain demons who are guardians on earth of human actions. Therefore it seems that all things are immediately governed by God.

Obj. 2. Further, it is better that a thing be done by one, if possible, than by many, as the Philosopher says. But God can by Himself govern all things without any intermediary cause. Therefore it seems that He governs all things immediately.

Obj. 3. Further, in God nothing is defective or imperfect. But it seems to be imperfect in a ruler to govern by means of others; and thus an earthly king, by reason of not being able to do everything himself, and because he cannot be everywhere at the same time, requires to govern by means of ministers. Therefore God governs all things immediately.

On the contrary, Augustine says: *As the lower and grosser bodies are ruled in a certain orderly way by bodies of greater subtlety and power, so all bodies are ruled by the rational spirit of life; and the sinful and unfaithful spirit is ruled by the good and just spirit of life, and this spirit by God Himself.*

I answer that, In government there are two things to be considered: the nature of government, which is providence itself; and the execution of government. As to the nature of government, God governs all things immediately; whereas in its execution, He governs some things by means of others.

The reason for this is that, since God is the very essence of goodness, everything must be attributed to God in its highest degree of goodness. Now the highest degree of goodness in any practical order, function or knowledge (and such is the nature of government) consists in knowing the individuals within whose domain the action takes place. Thus, the best physician is not the one who gives his attention only to general principles, but who can consider the least details; and so on in other things. Therefore we must say that God possesses, in its very essence, the government of all things, even of the very least.

But since things which are governed should be brought to perfection by government, this government will be so much the better in the degree that the things governed are brought to perfection. Now it is a greater perfection for a thing to be good in itself and also the cause of goodness in others, than only to be good in itself. Therefore God so governs things that He makes some of them to be causes of others in government; as in the case of a teacher, who not only imparts knowledge to his pupils, but also makes some of them to be the teachers of others.

Reply Obj. 1. Plato's opinion is to be rejected, because he held that God did not govern all things immediately, even as concerns the nature of government; and this is clear from the fact that he divided providence, which is the nature of government, into three parts.

Reply Obj. 2. If God governed alone, things would be deprived of the perfection of causality. Therefore all that is effected by many would not be accomplished by one.

Reply Obj. 3. That an earthly king should have ministers to execute his laws is a sign not only of his imperfection, but also of his dignity; because from the array of ministers the kingly power is brought into greater evidence.

SEVENTH ARTICLE

WHETHER ANYTHING CAN HAPPEN OUTSIDE THE ORDER OF THE DIVINE GOVERNMENT?

We proceed thus to the Seventh Article:—

Objection 1. It would seem possible that something may occur outside the order of the divine government. For Boethius says that *God disposes all by good.* Therefore, if nothing happens outside the order of the divine government, it would follow that no evil exists.

Obj. 2. Further, nothing that is in accordance with the preordination of a ruler occurs by chance. Therefore, if nothing occurs outside the order of the divine government, it follows that there is nothing fortuitous and by chance.

Obj. 3. Further, the order of divine providence is certain and unchangeable, because it is in accord with an eternal design. Therefore, if nothing happens outside the order of the divine government, it follows that all things happen by necessity, and nothing is contingent; which is false. Therefore it is possible for something to occur outside the order of the divine government.

On the contrary, It is written (*Esth.* xiii. 9): *O Lord, Lord, almighty King, all things are in Thy power, and there is none that can resist Thy will.*

I answer that, It is possible for an effect to happen outside the order of some particular cause, but not outside the order of the universal cause. The reason for this is that no effect happens outside the order of a particular cause, except through some other and impeding cause; which other cause must itself be reduced to the first universal cause. Thus, indigestion may occur outside the order of the nutritive power by some such impediment as the coarseness of the food, which again is to be ascribed to some other cause, and so on till we come to the first universal cause. Therefore, as God is the first universal cause, not of one genus only, but of all being, it is impossible for anything to occur outside the order of the divine government; but from the very fact that from one point of view something seems to evade the order of divine providence considered in regard to one particular cause, it must necessarily come back to that order as regards some other cause.

Reply Obj. 1. There is nothing wholly evil in the world, for evil is always founded on good, as was shown above. Therefore something is said to be evil because it escapes from the order of some particular good. If it escaped wholly from the order of the divine government, it would wholly cease to exist.

Reply Obj. 2. Things are said to be by chance as regards some particular cause from whose order they escape. But as to the order of divine providence, *nothing in the world happens by chance*, as Augustine declares.

Reply Obj. 3. Certain effects are said to be contingent as compared to their proximate causes, which may fail in their effects; and not as though anything could happen entirely outside the order of divine government. The very fact that something occurs outside the order of some proximate cause is owing to some other cause, itself subject to the divine government.

EIGHTH ARTICLE

WHETHER ANYTHING CAN RESIST THE ORDER OF THE DIVINE GOVERNMENT?

We proceed thus to the Eighth Article:—

Objection 1. It would seem possible that some resistance can be made to the order of the divine government. For it is written (*Isa.* iii. 8): *Their tongue and their devices are against the Lord.*

Obj. 2. Further, a king does not justly punish those who do not rebel against his commands. Therefore if no one rebelled against God's commands, no one would be justly punished by God.

Obj. 3. Further, everything is subject to the order of the divine government. But some things oppose others. Therefore some things rebel against the order of the divine government.

On the contrary, Boethius says: *There is nothing that can desire or is able to resist this sovereign good. It is this sovereign good therefore that ruleth all mightily and ordereth all sweetly*, as is said (*Wis.* viii. 1) of divine wisdom.

I answer that, We may consider the order of divine providence in two ways: in general, inasmuch as it proceeds from the governing cause of all; and in particular, inasmuch as it proceeds from some particular cause which executes the order of the divine government.

Considered in the first way, nothing can resist the order of the divine government. This can be proved in two ways: First, from the fact that the order of the divine government is wholly directed to good, and everything by its own operation and effort tends to good only; *for no one acts intending evil*, as Dionysius says. Secondly, from the fact that, as we have said above, every inclination of anything, whether natural or voluntary, is nothing but a kind of impression from the first mover; just as the inclination of the arrow towards a fixed point is nothing but an impulse received from the archer. Hence, every agent, whether natural or voluntary, attains to its divinely appointed end, as though of its own accord. For this reason God is said *to order all things sweetly* (*Wis.* viii. 1).

Reply Obj. 1. Some are said to think, speak or act against God, not because they entirely resist the order of the divine government (for even the sinner intends the attainment of a certain good), but because they resist some particular good, which belongs to their nature or state. Therefore they are justly punished by God.

Reply Obj. 2 is clear from the above.

Reply Obj. 3. From the fact that one thing opposes another, it follows that some one thing can resist the order of a particular cause, but not that order which depends on the universal cause of all things.

The Special Effects of the Divine Government

IN FOUR ARTICLES

We next consider the effects of the divine government in particular, concerning which four points of inquiry arise: (1) Whether creatures need to be kept in being by God? (2) Whether they are immediately conserved by God? (3) Whether God can reduce anything to nothingness? (4) Whether anything is reduced to nothingness?

FIRST ARTICLE

WHETHER CREATURES NEED TO BE KEPT IN BEING BY GOD?

We proceed thus to the First Article:—

Objection 1. It would seem that creatures do not need to be kept in being by God. For what cannot not-be does not need to be kept in being, just as that which cannot depart does not need to be kept from departing. But some creatures by their very nature cannot not-be. Therefore not all creatures need to be kept in being by God. The middle proposition is proved thus. That which of itself is included in the nature of a thing is necessarily in that thing, and its contrary cannot be in it; and thus a multiple of two must necessarily be even, and cannot possibly be an odd number. Now being follows necessarily upon a form, because everything is a being actually in so far as it has a form. But some creatures are subsistent forms, as we have said of the angels. Hence, to be belongs to them of themselves. The same reasoning applies to those creatures whose matter is in potentiality to one form only, as was explained above of the heavenly bodies. Hence such creatures as these have in their nature to be necessarily, and cannot not-be. For there can be no potentiality to not-being, either in the form which has being of itself, or in matter existing under a form which it cannot lose, since it is not in potentiality to any other form.

Obj. 2. Further, God is more powerful than any created agent. But a created agent, even after ceasing to act, can cause its effect to be preserved in being. Thus, the house continues to stand after the builder has ceased to build; and water remains hot for some time after the fire has ceased to heat. Much more, therefore, can God cause His creature to be kept in being, after He has ceased to create it.

Obj. 3. Further, nothing violent can occur, except it have some active cause. But tendency to not-being is unnatural and violent to any creature, since all creatures naturally desire to be. Therefore no creature can tend to not-being, except through some active cause of corruption. Now there are creatures of such a nature that nothing can cause them to be corrupted. Such are spiritual substances and heavenly bodies. Therefore such creatures cannot tend to not-being, even if God were to withdraw His action.

Obj. 4. Further, if God keeps creatures in being, this is done by some action. Now every action of an agent, if that action be efficacious, produces something in the effect. Therefore the conserving power of God must produce something in the creature. But this is not so, because this action does not give being to the creature, since being is not given to that which already is; nor does it add anything new to the creature, because either God would not keep the creature in being continually, or He would be continually adding something new to the creature,—either of which is unreasonable. Therefore creatures are not kept in being by God.

On the contrary, It is written (*Heb.* i. 3): *Upholding all things by the word of His power.*

I answer that, Both reason and faith require us to say that creatures are kept in being by God. To make this clear, we must consider that a thing is conserved by another in two ways. First, indirectly and accidentally, and thus a person is said to conserve anything by removing the cause of its corruption; as a man may be said to conserve a child, whom he guards from falling into the fire. In this way God conserves some things, but not all, for there are some things of such a nature that nothing can corrupt them, so that it is not necessary to keep them from corruption. Secondly, a thing is said to conserve another essentially and directly, namely, in so far as what is conserved depends on the conserver in such a way that it cannot exist without it. In this manner all creatures need to be conserved by God. For the being of every creature depends on God, so that not for a moment could it subsist, but would fall into nothingness, were it not kept in being by the operation of the divine power, as Gregory says.

This is made clear as follows. Every effect depends on its cause, so far as it is its cause. But we must observe that an agent may be the cause of the *becoming* of its effect, but not directly of its *being*. This may be seen both in artificial and in natural things. For the builder causes the house in its *becoming*, but he is not the direct cause of its *being*. For it is clear that the *being* of the house is a result of its form, which consists in the putting together and arrangement of the materials, and which results from the natural qualities of certain things. Thus a cook prepares the food by applying the natural activity of fire; and in the same way a builder constructs a house, by making use of cement, stones and wood, which are able to be put together in a certain order and to conserve it. Therefore the *being* of the house depends on the nature of these materials, just as its *becoming* depends on the action of the builder. The same principle applies to natural things. For if an agent is not the cause of a form as such, neither will it be directly the cause of the *being* which results from that form; but it will be the cause of the effect only in its *becoming*.

Now it is clear that of two things in the same species one cannot be essentially the cause of the other's form as such, since it would then be the cause of its own form, since both forms have the same nature; but it can be the cause of this form inasmuch as it is in matter—in other words, it may be the cause that *this matter* receives *this form*. And this is to be the cause of *becoming*, as when man begets man, and fire causes fire. Thus, whenever a natural effect is such that it has an aptitude to receive from its active cause an impression specifically the same as in that active cause, then the *becoming* of the effect depends on the agent, but not its *being*. Sometimes, however, the effect has not this aptitude to receive the impression of its cause in the same way as it exists in the agent; as may be seen clearly in all agents which do not produce an effect of the same species as themselves. Thus, the heavenly bodies cause the generation of inferior bodies which differ from them in species. Such an agent can be the cause of a form as such, and not merely as being joined to this matter; and consequently it is not merely the cause of *becoming* but also the cause of *being*.

Therefore, as the becoming of a thing cannot continue when the action of the agent, which causes the *becoming* of the effect, ceases, so neither can the *being* of a thing continue after the action of the agent, which is the cause of the effect not only in *becoming* but also in *being*, has ceased. This is why hot water retains heat after the cessation of the fire's action; while, on the contrary, the air does not continue to be lit up, even for a moment, when the sun ceases to act upon it. For water is a matter susceptive of the fire's heat in the same way as it exists in the fire. Therefore, if it were to be reduced to the perfect form of fire, it would retain that form always; whereas if it has the form of fire imperfectly and inchoately, the heat will remain for a time only, by reason of the imperfect participation in the principle of heat. On the other hand, air is not of such a nature as to receive light in the same way as it exists in the sun, namely, to receive the form of the sun, which is the principle of light. Therefore, since it has no root in the air, the light ceases with the action of the sun.

Now every creature may be compared to God as the air is to the sun which illumines it. For as the sun possesses light by its nature, and as the air is illumined by participating light from the sun, though not participating in the sun's nature, so God alone is Being by virtue of His own essence (since His essence is His being), whereas every creature has being by participation, so that its essence is not its being. Therefore, as Augustine says: *If the ruling power of God were withdrawn from His creatures, their nature would at once cease, and all nature would collapse.* In the same work he says: *As the air becomes light by the presence of the sun, so is man illumined by the presence of God, and in His absence returns at once to darkness.*

Reply Obj. 1. *Being* necessarily results from the form of a creature, given the influence of the divine action; just as light results from the diaphanous nature of the air, given the action of the sun. Hence, the potentiality to not-being in spiritual creatures and heavenly bodies is rather something in God, Who can withdraw His influence, than in the form or matter of those creatures.

Reply Obj. 2. God cannot communicate to a creature that it be conserved in being after the cessation of the divine influence; as neither can He make it not to have received its being from Himself. For the creature needs to be conserved by God in so far as the being of an effect depends on the cause of its being. Hence, there is no comparison with an agent that is not the cause of *being*, but only of *becoming*.

Reply Obj. 3. This argument holds in regard to that conservation which consists in the removal of corruption; but all creatures do not need to be conserved thus, as was stated above.

Reply Obj. 4. The conservation of things by God is not by a new action, but by a continuation of that action whereby He gives being, which action is without either motion or time; so also the conservation of light in the air is by the continual influence of the sun.

SECOND ARTICLE

WHETHER GOD CONSERVES EVERY CREATURE IMMEDIATELY?

We proceed thus to the Second Article:—

Objection 1. It would seem that God conserves every creature immediately. For God creates and conserves things by the same action, as was stated above. But God created all things immediately. Therefore He conserves all things immediately.

Obj. 2. Further, a thing is nearer to itself than to another. But it cannot be given to a creature to conserve itself. Much less therefore can it be given to a creature to conserve another. Therefore God conserves all things without any intermediate conserving cause.

Obj. 3. Further, an effect is kept in being by the cause, not only of its *becoming*, but also of its *being*. But all created causes do not seem to cause their effects except in their becoming, for they cause only by moving, as was stated above. Therefore they are not causes that keep their effects in being.

On the contrary, A thing is kept in being by that which gives it being. But God gives being to things by means of certain intermediate causes. Therefore He also keeps things in being by means of certain causes.

I answer that, As was stated above, a thing keeps another in being in two ways: first, indirectly and accidentally, by removing or hindering the action of a corrupting cause; secondly, directly and essentially, by the fact that on it depends the other's being, as the being of the effect depends on the cause. And in both ways a created thing keeps another in being. For it is clear that even in corporeal things there are many causes which hinder the action of corrupting agents, and for that reason are called *conserving;* just as salt preserves meat from putrefaction, and in like manner with many other things. It happens also that an effect depends on a creature as to its being. For when we have many ordered causes, it necessarily follows that, while the effect depends first and principally on the first cause, it also depends in a secondary way on all the intermediate causes. Therefore the first cause is the principal cause of the conservation of the effect, which is to be referred to all the intermediate causes in a secondary way; and all the more so, as the intermediate cause is higher and nearer to the first cause.

For this reason, even in corporeal things, the conservation and endurance of things is ascribed to higher causes. Thus, the Philosopher says that the first, namely the diurnal, movement is the cause of the continuation of things generated; whereas the second movement, which is according to the zodiac, is the cause of diversity owing to generation and corruption. In like manner, astronomers ascribe to Saturn, the highest of the planets, those things which are permanent and fixed. So we conclude that God keeps certain things in being, by means of certain causes.

Reply Obj. 1. God created all things immediately, but in the creation itself He established an order among things, so that some depend on others, by which they are conserved in being; though He remains the principal cause of their conservation.

Reply Obj. 2. An effect is conserved by its proper cause, on which it depends. Hence, just as no effect can be its own cause, but can produce another effect, so no effect can be endowed with the power of self-conservation, but only with the power of conserving another.

Reply Obj. 3. No created being can cause another to acquire a new form or disposition, except by virtue of some change; for the created being acts always on something presupposed. But after causing the form or disposition in the effect, without any fresh change in the effect, the cause conserves that form or disposition; as in the air, when it is lit up anew, we must allow some change to have taken place, while the conservation of the light is without any further change in the air due to the presence of the source of light.

THIRD ARTICLE

WHETHER GOD CAN ANNIHILATE ANYTHING?

We proceed thus to the Third Article:—

Objection 1. It would seem that God cannot annihilate anything. For Augustine says that *God is not the cause of anything tending to not-being*. But He would be such a cause if He were to annihilate anything. Therefore He cannot annihilate anything.

Obj. 2. Further, by His goodness God is the cause why things exist, since, as Augustine says, *because God is good, we exist*. But God cannot cease to be good. Therefore He cannot cause things to cease to exist; which would be the case were He to annihilate anything.

Obj. 3. Further, if God were to annihilate anything, it would be by His action. But this cannot be, because the term of every action is some being. Thus, the action of a corrupting cause has its term in something generated; for when one thing is generated another undergoes corruption. Therefore God cannot annihilate anything.

On the contrary, It is written (*Jer.* x. 24): *Correct me, O Lord, but yet with judgment; and not in Thy fury, lest Thou bring me to nothing.*

I answer that, Some have held that God, in giving being to creatures, acted from natural necessity. Were this true, God could not annihilate anything, since His nature cannot change. But, as we have said above, such an opinion is entirely false, and absolutely contrary to the Catholic Faith, which confesses that God created things freely, according to *Ps.* cxxxiv. 6: *Whatsoever the Lord pleased, He hath done.* Therefore that God gives being to a creature depends on His will; nor does He conserve things in being otherwise than by continually giving being to them, as we have said. Therefore, just as before things existed, God was free not to give them being, and so not to make them, so, after they have been made, He is free not to give them being, and thus they would cease to exist. This would be to annihilate them.

Reply Obj. 1. Not-being has no essential cause; for nothing is a cause except inasmuch as it is a being, and a being essentially as such is a cause of being. Therefore, God cannot cause a thing to tend to not-being, but a creature has this tendency of itself, since it is produced from nothing. But indirectly God can cause things to be reduced to not-being by withdrawing His action from them.

Reply Obj. 2. God's goodness is the cause of things, not as though by natural necessity, because the divine goodness does not depend on creatures; but by a free will. Therefore, just as without prejudice to His goodness He might not have brought things into being, so, without prejudice to His goodness, He might not conserve things in being.

Reply Obj. 3. If God were to annihilate anything, this

would not imply an action on God's part, but a mere cessation of His action.

FOURTH ARTICLE

WHETHER ANYTHING IS ANNIHILATED?

We proceed thus to the Fourth Article:—

Objection 1. It would seem that something is annihilated. For the end corresponds to the beginning. But in the beginning there was nothing but God. Therefore all things must tend to this end, that there shall be nothing but God. Therefore creatures will be reduced to nothing.

Obj. 2. Further, every creature has a finite power. But no finite power extends to the infinite. Therefore the Philosopher proves that a *finite power cannot move in infinite time.* Therefore a creature cannot last for an infinite duration; and so at some time it will be reduced to nothing.

Obj. 3. Further, forms and accidents have no matter as part of themselves. But at some time they cease to exist. Therefore they are reduced to nothing.

On the contrary, It is written (*Eccles.* iii. 14): *I have learned that all the works that God hath made continue forever.*

I answer that, Some of the things which God does in creatures occur in accordance with the natural course of things; others happen miraculously, and not in accordance with the natural order, as will be explained. Now whatever God wills to do according to the natural order of things may be observed from the natures themselves of things; but those things which occur miraculously are ordered to the manifestation of grace, according to the Apostle, *To each one is given the manifestation of the Spirit, unto profit* (*1 Cor.* xii. 7). He goes on to mention, among other things, the working of miracles.

Now the nature of creatures shows that none of them is annihilated. For, either they are immaterial, and therefore have no potentiality to not-being, or they are material, and then they continue to exist, at least in matter, which is incorruptible, since it is the subject of generation and corruption. Moreover, the annihilation of things does not pertain to the manifestation of grace, since the power and goodness of God are rather manifested by the conservation of things in being. Therefore we must conclude by denying absolutely that anything at all will be annihilated.

Reply Obj. 1. That things were brought into being from not-being clearly shows the power of Him Who made them; but that they should be reduced to nothing would hinder that manifestation, since the power of God is conspicuously shown in His preserving all things in being, according to the Apostle: *Upholding all things by the word of His power* (*Heb.* i. 3).

Reply Obj. 2. A creature's potentiality to being is merely receptive; the active power belongs to God Himself, from Whom being is derived. Therefore, the infinite duration of things is a consequence of the infinity of the divine power. To some things, however, is given a determinate power of duration for a certain time, in that they may be hindered from receiving the influx of being, which comes from Him, by some contrary agent to which a finite power cannot offer resistance for an infinite time, but only for a limited time. So things which have no contrary, though they have a finite power, continue to exist forever.

Reply Obj. 3. *Forms* and *accidents* are not complete beings, since they do not subsist, but each one of them is something *of a being;* for each is called a being, because something is by it. Yet according to their mode of being, they are not entirely reduced to nothingness; not that any part of them survives, but that they remain in the potentiality of the matter, or of the subject.

The Movement of God In Creatures

IN EIGHT ARTICLES

WE now consider the second effect of the divine government, *i.e.*, the moving of creatures by God: and first whether God moves creatures; secondly, the movement of one creature by another.

Under the first head there are eight points of inquiry: (1) Whether God can move immediately the matter to the form? (2) Whether He can immediately move a body? (3) Whether He can move the intellects? (4) Whether He can move the will? (5) Whether God works in every agent? (6) Whether He can do anything outside the order imposed on things? (7) Whether all that God thus does is miraculous? (8) On the diversity of miracles.

FIRST ARTICLE

WHETHER GOD CAN MOVE THE MATTER IMMEDIATELY TO THE FORM?

We proceed thus to the First Article:—

Objection 1. It would seem that God cannot move the matter immediately to receive the form. For, as the Philosopher proves, nothing can bring a form into any particular matter, except that form which is in matter; because like begets like. But God is not a form in matter. Therefore He cannot cause a form in matter.

Obj. 2. Further, any agent inclined to several effects will produce none of them, unless it is determined to a particular one by some other cause. As the Philosopher says, a universal judgment does not move except by means of some particular apprehension. But the divine power is the universal cause of all things. Therefore it cannot produce any particular form, except by means of a particular agent.

Obj. 3. As universal being depends on the first universal cause, so determinate being depends on determinate particular causes, as we have seen above. But the determinate being of a particular thing is from its own form. Therefore the forms of things are produced by God only by means of particular causes.

On the contrary, It is written (*Gen.* ii. 7): *God formed man of the slime of the earth.*

I answer that, God can move matter immediately to a form. For whatever is in passive potentiality can be reduced to act by the active power which extends over that potentiality. Therefore, since the divine power extends over matter, as having been produced by God, matter can be reduced to act by the divine power; and this is what is meant by matter being moved to a form, for a form is nothing else but the act of matter.

Reply Obj. 1. An effect is assimilated to the active cause in two ways. First, according to the same species, as man is generated by man, and fire by fire. Secondly, by being virtually contained in the cause, as the form of the effect is virtually contained in its cause. Thus animals, produced by putrefaction, and plants and minerals are like the sun and stars, by whose power they are produced. In this way the effect is like its active cause as regards all that over which the power of that cause extends. Now the power of God extends to both matter and form, as we have said above. Therefore, if a composite thing be produced, it is likened to God by way of a virtual inclusion; and it is likened to the composite generator by a likeness of species. Therefore, just as the composite generator can move matter to a form by generating a composite thing like itself, so also can God. But no other form not existing in matter can do this, because the power of no other separate substance extends over matter. Hence angels and demons act on visible matter, not by imprinting forms in matter, but by making use of corporeal seminal principles.

Reply Obj. 2. This argument would hold if God acted from

natural necessity. But since He acts by His will and intellect, which knows the particular and not only the universal natures of all forms, it follows that He can determinately imprint this or that form on matter.

Reply Obj. 3. The fact that secondary causes are ordered to determinate effects is due to God; and so, since God ordains other causes to determinate effects, He can also produce determinate effects by Himself without any other cause.

SECOND ARTICLE

WHETHER GOD CAN MOVE A BODY IMMEDIATELY?

We proceed thus to the Second Article:—

Objection 1. It would seem that God cannot move a body immediately. For *as the mover and the moved must exist simultaneously*, as the Philosopher says, it follows that there must be some contact between the mover and the moved. But there can be no contact between God and a body, for Dionysius says: *There is no contact with God.* Therefore God cannot move a body immediately.

Obj. 2. Further, God is an unmoved mover. But such also is the desirable object when apprehended. Therefore God moves as the object of desire and apprehension. But He cannot be apprehended except by the intellect, which is neither a body nor a corporeal power. Therefore God cannot move a body immediately.

Obj. 3. Further, the Philosopher proves that an infinite power moves instantaneously. But it is impossible for a body to be moved in one instant, for since every movement is between opposites, it would follow that two opposites would exist at once in the same subject; which is impossible. Therefore a body cannot be moved immediately by an infinite power. But God's power is infinite, as we have explained above. Therefore God cannot move a body immediately.

On the contrary, God produced the works of the six days

immediately, among which is included the movement of bodies, as is clear from *Gen.* i. 9: *Let the waters be gathered together into one place.* Therefore God can move a body immediately.

I answer that, It is erroneous to say that God cannot Himself produce all the determinate effects which are produced by any created cause. Therefore, since bodies are moved immediately by created causes, we cannot possibly doubt that God can move immediately any bodies whatever. This follows from what is stated above. For every movement of any body whatever either results from a form, as the movements of things heavy and light result from the form which they have from their generating cause, for which reason the generator is called the mover; or else it tends to a form, as heating tends to the form of heat. Now it belongs to the same cause to imprint a form, to dispose to that form, and to give the movement which results from that form; for fire not only generates fire, but it also heats and moves things upwards. Therefore, since God can imprint a form immediately in matter, it follows that He can move any body whatever in respect of any movement whatever.

Reply Obj. 1. There are two kinds of contact: corporeal contact (when two bodies touch each other) and virtual contact (as the cause of sadness is said to touch the one made sad). According to the first kind of contact, God, as being incorporeal, neither touches, nor is touched. But according to virtual contact, He touches creatures by moving them, but He is not touched, because the natural power of no creature can reach up to Him. Thus did Dionysius understand the words, *There is no contact with God;* that is, so that God Himself be touched.

Reply Obj. 2. God moves as the object of desire and apprehension, but it does not follow that He always moves as being desired and apprehended by that which is moved; but rather as being desired and known by Himself, for He does all things because of His own goodness.

Reply Obj. 3. The Philosopher intends to prove that the power of the first mover is not a power in a magnitude. This is his argument. The power of the first mover is infinite (which he proves from the fact that the first mover can move in infinite time). Now an infinite power, if it were a power in any magnitude, would move without time, which is impossible. Therefore the infinite power of the first mover must be in something which is without magnitude. Whence it is clear that for a body to be moved without time can be the result only of an infinite power. The reason is that every power in a magnitude moves in its entirety, since it moves by a necessity of nature. But an infinite power surpasses out of all proportion any finite power. Now the greater the power of the mover, the greater is the velocity of the movement. Therefore, since a finite power moves in a determinate time, it follows that an infinite power does not move in any time; for between one time and any other time there is some proportion. On the other hand, a power which is not in a magnitude is the power of an intelligent being, which operates in its effects according to what is fitting to them; and therefore, since it cannot be fitting for a body to be moved without time, it does not follow that it moves without time.

THIRD ARTICLE

WHETHER GOD MOVES THE CREATED INTELLECT IMMEDIATELY?

We proceed thus to the Third Article:—

Objection 1. It would seem that God does not immediately move the created intellect. For the action of the intellect is from the being in which it resides, since it does not pass into external matter, as is stated in *Metaph.* ix. But the action of what is moved by another does not proceed from that wherein it is, but from the mover. Therefore the intellect is not moved by another; and so apparently God cannot move the created intellect.

Obj. 2. Further, anything which in itself has a sufficient principle of movement is not moved by another. But the movement of the intellect is its act of understanding. Thus, we say that to understand or to sense is a kind of movement, as the Philosopher says. But the intelligible light with which the intellect is endowed is a sufficient principle of understanding. Therefore it is not moved by another.

Obj. 3. Further, as the senses are moved by the sensible, so the intellect is moved by the intelligible. But God is not intelligible to us, but exceeds the capacity of our intellect. Therefore God cannot move our intellect.

On the contrary, The teacher moves the intellect of the one taught. But it is written (*Ps.* xciii. 10) that God *teaches man knowledge.* Therefore God moves the human intellect.

I answer that, As in corporeal movement that is called the mover which gives the form that is the principle of movement, so that is said to move the intellect which is the cause of the form that is the principle of the intellectual operation called the movement of the intellect. Now there is a twofold principle of intellectual operation in the intelligent being: one is the intellectual power itself, which principle exists also in the one who understands in potentiality; while the other is the principle of actual understanding, namely, the likeness of the thing understood. So a thing is said to move the intellect, whether it gives to him who understands the power of understanding, or impresses on him the likeness of the thing understood.

Now God moves the created intellect in both ways. For He is the first and immaterial being; and as intellectuality is a result of immateriality, it follows that He is the first intelligent being. Therefore, since in each order the first is the cause of all that follows, we must conclude that from Him proceeds all intellectual power. In like manner, since He is the first being, and all other beings pre-exist in Him as in their first cause, it follows that they exist intelligibly in Him, after the mode of His own nature. For as the intelligible exemplars of everything exist first of all in God, and are derived from Him by other intellects in order that these may actually understand, so also are they derived by creatures that they may subsist. Therefore God so moves the created intellect that He gives it the power of understanding, whether natural, or superadded; and He impresses on the created intellect the intelligible species, and maintains and preserves both power and species in being.

Reply Obj. 1. The intellectual operation is performed by the intellect in which it exists as by a secondary cause; but it proceeds from God as from its first cause. For by Him the power to understand is given to the one who understands.

Reply Obj. 2. The intellectual light together with the likeness of the thing understood is a sufficient principle of understanding; but it is a secondary principle, and depends upon the first principle.

Reply Obj. 3. The intelligible object moves our human intellect in so far as it somehow impresses on it its own likeness, by means of which the intellect is able to understand it. But the likenesses which God impresses on the created intellect are not sufficient to enable the created intellect to understand God through His Essence, as we have seen above. Hence He moves the created intellect, and yet He cannot be intelligible to it, as we have explained.

FOURTH ARTICLE

WHETHER GOD CAN MOVE THE CREATED WILL?

We proceed thus to the Fourth Article:—

Objection 1. It would seem that God cannot move the created will. For whatever is moved from without, is forced. But the will cannot be forced. Therefore it is not moved from without. Therefore it cannot be moved by God.

Obj. 2. Further, God cannot make two contradictories to be true at the same time. But this would follow if He moved the will; for to be voluntarily moved means to be moved from within, and not by another. Therefore God cannot move the will.

Obj. 3. Further, movement is attributed to the mover rather than to the one moved; and so homicide is not ascribed to the stone, but to the thrower. Therefore, if God moves the will, it follows that voluntary actions are not imputed to man for reward or blame. But this is false. Therefore God does not move the will.

On the contrary, It is written (*Phil.* ii. 13): *It is God who worketh in us both to will and to accomplish.*

I answer that, Just as the intellect is moved by the object and by the giver of the power of understanding, as was stated above, so the will is moved by its object, which is the good, and by Him who creates the power of willing. Now the will can be moved by any good as its object, but by God alone is it moved sufficiently and efficaciously. For nothing can move a movable thing sufficiently unless the active power of the mover surpasses or at least equals the potentiality of the movable thing. Now the potentiality of the will extends to the universal good, for its object is the universal good, just as the object of the intellect is universal being. But every created good is some particular good, and God alone is the universal good. Therefore He alone fills the capacity of the will, and moves it sufficiently as its object. In like manner, the power of willing is caused by God alone. For to will is nothing but to be inclined towards the object of the will, which is the universal good. But to incline towards the universal good belongs to the first mover, to whom the ultimate end is proportioned; just as in human affairs to him that presides over the community belongs the directing of his subjects to the common weal. Therefore in both ways it belongs to God to move the will; but especially in the second way by an interior inclination of the will.

Reply Obj. 1. A thing moved by another is forced if it is moved against its natural inclination. But if it is moved by another which gives to it its natural inclination, it is not forced. Thus, a heavy body, made to move downward by that which produced it, is not forced. In like manner God, while moving the will, does not force it, because He gives the will its own natural inclination.

Reply Obj. 2. To be moved voluntarily is to be moved from within, that is, by an interior principle. But this interior principle may be caused by an exterior principle; and so to be moved from within is not repugnant to being moved by another.

Reply Obj. 3. If the will were so moved by another as in no way to be moved from within itself, the act of the will would not be imputed for reward or blame. But since its being moved by another does not prevent its being moved from within itself, as we have stated, it does not thereby forfeit the motive for merit or demerit.

FIFTH ARTICLE

WHETHER GOD WORKS IN EVERY AGENT?

We proceed thus to the Fifth Article:—

Objection 1. It would seem that God does not work in every agent. For we must not attribute any insufficiency to God. If therefore God works in every agent, He works sufficiently in each one. Hence it would be superfluous for the created agent to work at all.

Obj. 2. Further, the same work cannot proceed at the same time from two sources, just as neither can one and the same movement belong to two movable things. Therefore if the creature's operation is from God operating in the creature, it cannot at the same time proceed from the creature; and so no creature works at all.

Obj. 3. Further, the maker is the cause of the operation of the thing made, as giving it the form whereby it operates. Therefore, if God is the cause of the operation of the things made by Him, this would be inasmuch as He gives them the power of operating. But this is in the beginning, when He makes them. Thus it seems that God does not operate any further in the operating creature.

On the contrary, It is written (*Isa.* xxvi. 12): *Lord, Thou hast wrought all our works in us.*

I answer that, Some have understood God to work in every agent in such a way that no created power has any effect in things, but that God alone is the immediate cause of everything wrought; for instance, that it is not fire that gives heat, but God in the fire, and so forth. But this is impossible. First, because the order of cause and effect would be taken away from created things, and this would imply a lack of power in the Creator; for it is due to the power of the cause, that it bestows active power on its effect. Secondly, because the operative powers which are seen to exist in things would be bestowed on things to no purpose, if things produced nothing through them. Indeed, all things created would seem, in a way, to be purposeless, if they lacked an operation proper to them; since the purpose of everything is its operation. For the less perfect is always for the sake of the more perfect. Consequently, just as the matter is for the sake of the form, so the form which is the first act is for the sake of its operation, which is the second act; and thus operation is the end of the creature. We must therefore understand that God works in things in such a manner that things have also their proper operation.

In order to make this clear, we must observe that of the four causes matter is not a principle of action, but the subject that receives the effect of action. On the other hand, the end, the agent and the form are principles of action, but in a certain order. For the first principle of action is the end which moves the agent, the second is the agent, and the third is the form of that which the agent applies to action (although the agent also acts through its own form). This may be clearly seen in things made by art. For the craftsman is moved to action by the end, which is the thing wrought, for instance a chest or a bed, and he applies to action the axe which cuts because it is sharp.

Thus then does God work in every agent, according to these three things. First, as an end. For since every operation is for the sake of some good, real or apparent, and since nothing is good, either really or apparently, except in so far as it participates in a likeness to the highest good, which is God, it follows that God Himself is the cause of every operation as its end. Again, it is to be observed that where there are several agents in order, the second always acts in virtue of the first; for the first agent moves the second to act. And thus all agents act in virtue of God Himself; and so, He is the cause of action in every agent. Thirdly, we must observe that God not only moves things to operate, as it were applying their forms and powers to operation, just as the workman applies the axe to cutting (who nevertheless did not himself give the axe its form), but He also gives created agents their forms and preserves them in being. Therefore He is the cause of action not only by giving the form which is the principle of action, as the generator is said to be the cause of movement in things heavy and light, but also as conserving the forms and powers of things; just as the sun is said to be the cause of the manifestation of colors, inasmuch as it gives and conserves the light by which colors are made manifest. And since the form of a thing is within the thing, and all the more so, as it approaches nearer to the first and universal cause; and because in all things God Himself is properly the cause of universal being which is innermost in all things:—it follows that God works intimately in all things. For this reason in Holy Scripture the operations of nature are attributed to God as operating in nature, according to *Job* x. 11: *Thou hast clothed me with skin and flesh: Thou hast put me together with bones and sinews.*

Reply Obj. 1. God works sufficiently in things as a first cause, but it does not follow from this that the operation of secondary agents is superfluous.

Reply Obj. 2. One action does not proceed from two agents of the same order. But nothing hinders the same action from proceeding from a primary and a secondary agent.

Reply Obj. 3. God not only gives things their forms, but He also conserves them in being, and applies them to act, and is moreover the end of every action, as was explained above.

SIXTH ARTICLE

WHETHER GOD CAN DO ANYTHING OUTSIDE THE ESTABLISHED ORDER OF NATURE?

We proceed thus to the Sixth Article:—

Objection 1. It would seem that God cannot do anything outside the established order of nature. For Augustine says: *God, the Maker and Creator of each nature, does nothing against nature.* But that which is outside the natural order seems to be against nature. Therefore God can do nothing outside the natural order.

Obj. 2. Further, as the order of justice is from God, so is the order of nature. But God cannot do anything outside the order of justice, for then He would be doing something unjust. Therefore He cannot do anything outside the order of nature.

Obj. 3. Further, God established the order of nature. Therefore, if God does anything outside the order of nature, it would seem that He is changeable; which cannot be said.

On the contrary, Augustine says: *God sometimes does things which are contrary to the wonted course of nature.*

I answer that, From each cause there results a certain order to its effects, since every cause is a principle; and so, according to the multiplicity of causes, there results a multiplicity of orders, subject one to the other, just as cause is subject to cause. Hence, a higher cause is not subject to a cause of a lower order, but conversely. An example of this may be seen in human affairs. On the father of a family depends the order of the household; which order is contained in the order of the city; which order again depends on the ruler of the city; while this last order depends on that of the king, by whom the whole kingdom is ordered.

If, therefore, we consider the order of things according as it depends on the first cause, God cannot do anything against this order; for, if He did so, He would act against His foreknowledge, or His will, or His goodness. But if we consider the order of things according as it depends on any secondary cause, thus God can do something outside such order. For He is not subject to the order of secondary causes, but, on the contrary, this order is subject to Him, as proceeding from Him, not by a natural necessity, but by the choice of His own will; for He could have created another order of things. Therefore God can do something outside this order created by Him, when He chooses,—for instance, by producing the effects of secondary causes without them, or by producing certain effects to which secondary causes do not extend. So Augustine says: *God acts against the wonted course of nature, but by no means does He act against the supreme law; because He does not act against Himself.*

Reply Obj. 1. In natural things something may happen outside this natural order, in two ways. It may happen by the action of an agent which did not give them their natural inclination, as, for example, when a man moves a heavy body upwards, which does not owe to him its natural inclination to move downwards. Now this would be against nature. It may also happen by the action of the agent on whom the natural inclination depends, and this is not against nature, as is clear in the ebb and flow of the tide, which is not against nature, although it is against the natural movement of water, which is moved downward; for it is owing to the influence of a heavenly body, on which the natural inclination of lower bodies depends. Therefore since the order of nature is given to things by God, if He does anything outside this order, it is not against nature. Hence Augustine says: *That is natural to each thing which is caused by Him from Whom is all limit, number and order in nature.*

Reply Obj. 2. The order of justice arises by relation to the first cause, which is the rule of all justice; and that is why God can do nothing against such an order.

Reply Obj. 3. God fixed a certain order in things in such a way that at the same time He reserved to Himself whatever

He intended to do otherwise than by a particular cause. So when He acts outside this order, He does not change.

SEVENTH ARTICLE

WHETHER WHATEVER GOD DOES OUTSIDE THE NATURAL ORDER IS MIRACULOUS?

We proceed thus to the Seventh Article:—

Objection 1. It would seem that not everything which God does outside the natural order of things is miraculous. For the creation of the world and of souls, and the justification of the unrighteous, are done by God outside the natural order; for these effects are not accomplished by the action of any natural cause. Yet these things are not called miracles. Therefore not everything that God does outside the natural order is a miracle.

Obj. 2. Further, a miracle is *something difficult, which seldom occurs, surpassing the faculty of nature, and going so far beyond our hopes as to compel our astonishment.* But some things outside the order of nature are not arduous, for they occur in small things, such as the recovery of some precious stone or the healing of the sick. Nor are they of rare occurrence, since they happen frequently; as when the sick were placed in the streets, to be healed by the shadow of Peter (*Acts* v. 15). Nor do they surpass the ability of nature; as when people are cured of a fever. Nor are they beyond our hopes, since we all hope for the resurrection of the dead, which nevertheless will be outside the course of nature. Therefore not all things that are outside the course of nature are miraculous.

Obj. 3. Further, the term *miracle* is derived from admiration. Now admiration concerns things manifest to the senses. But sometimes things happen outside the order of nature which are not manifest to the senses; as when the Apostles were endowed with knowledge without studying or being taught. Therefore not everything that occurs outside the order of nature is miraculous.

On the contrary, Augustine says: *Where God does anything against that order of nature which we know and are accustomed to observe, we call it a miracle.*

I answer that, The term *miracle* is derived from admiration, which arises when an effect is manifest, whereas its cause is hidden; as when a man sees an eclipse without knowing its cause, as the Philosopher says in the beginning of his *Metaphysics*. Now the cause of a manifest effect may be known to one, but unknown to others. Hence a thing is wonderful to one man, and not at all to others; as an eclipse is to a rustic, but not to an astronomer. Now a miracle is so called as being full of wonder, in other words, as having a cause absolutely hidden from all. This cause is God. Therefore those things which God does outside the causes which we know are called miracles.

Reply Obj. 1. Creation, and the justification of the unrighteous, though done by God alone, are not, properly speaking, miracles, because they are not of a nature to proceed from any other cause; so they do not occur outside the order of nature, since they do not belong to the capacity of nature.

Reply Obj. 2. An arduous thing is called a miracle, not because of the excellence of the thing wherein it is done, but because it surpasses the ability of nature. So, too, a thing is called unusual, not because it does not often happen, but because it is outside the usual natural course of things. Furthermore, a thing is said to be above the ability of nature, not only by reason of the substance of the thing done, but also because of the manner and order in which it is done. Again, a miracle is said to go beyond the hope *of nature*, not above the hope *of grace*, which hope comes from faith, whereby we believe in the future resurrection.

Reply Obj. 3. The knowledge of the Apostles, although not manifest in itself, yet was made manifest in its effect, from which it was shown to be wonderful.

EIGHTH ARTICLE

WHETHER ONE MIRACLE IS GREATER THAN ANOTHER?

We proceed thus to the Eighth Article:—

Objection 1. It would seem that one miracle is not greater than another. For Augustine says: *In miraculous deeds, the whole measure of the deed is the power of the doer.* But by the same power of God all miracles are done. Therefore one miracle is not greater than another.

Obj. 2. Further, the power of God is infinite. But the infinite exceeds the finite beyond all proportion; and therefore no more reason exists to wonder at one effect thereof than at another. Therefore one miracle is not greater than another.

On the contrary, The Lord says, speaking of miraculous works (*Jo.* xiv. 12): *The works that I do, he also shall do, and greater than these shall he do.*

I answer that, Nothing is called a miracle by comparison with the divine power, because no action is of any account compared with the power of God, according to *Isa.* xl. 15: *Behold the Gentiles are as a drop from a bucket, and are counted as the smallest grain of a balance.* But a thing is called a miracle by comparison with the power of nature, which it surpasses. So the more the power of nature is surpassed, the greater is the miracle. Now the power of nature is surpassed in three ways: first, in the substance of the deed, for instance, if two bodies occupy the same place, or if the sun goes backwards, or if a human body is glorified. Such things nature is absolutely unable to do; and these hold the highest rank among miracles. Secondly, a thing surpasses the power of nature, not in the deed, but in that wherein it is done; as the raising of the dead, and giving sight to the blind, and the like. For nature can give life, but not to the dead, and it can give sight, but not to the blind. Such hold the second rank in miracles. Thirdly, a thing surpasses nature's power in the measure and order in which it is done; as when a man is cured of a fever suddenly by God, without treatment or the usual process of nature, or as when by divine power the air is suddenly condensed into rain, without a natural cause, as occurred at the prayers of Samuel and Elias. These hold the lowest place in miracles. Moreover, each of these kinds has various degrees, according to the different ways in which the power of nature is surpassed.

From this it is clear how to reply to the objections, arguing as they do from the power of God.

How One Creature Moves Another

IN FOUR ARTICLES

WE next consider how one creature moves another. This consideration will be threefold: (1) How the angels move, who are purely spiritual creatures; (2) how bodies move; (3) how man moves, who is composed of a spiritual and a corporeal nature.

Concerning the first point, there are three things to be considered: (1) how an angel acts on an angel; (2) how an angel acts on a corporeal creature; (3) how an angel acts on man.

The first of these raises the question of the illumination and speech of the angels; and of their mutual co-ordination, both of the good and of the bad angels.

Concerning their illumination, there are four points of inquiry: (1) Whether one angel moves the intellect of another by illumination? (2) Whether one angel moves the will of another? (3) Whether an inferior angel can illumine a superior angel? (4) Whether a superior angel illumines an inferior angel in all that he himself knows?

FIRST ARTICLE

WHETHER ONE ANGEL ILLUMINES ANOTHER?

We proceed thus to the First Article:—

Objection 1. It would seem that one angel does not illumine another. For the angels possess now the same beatitude which we hope to obtain. But one man will not then illumine another, according to *Jer.* xxxi. 34: *They shall teach no more every man his neighbor, and every man his brother.* Therefore neither does an angel illumine another now.

Obj. 2. Further, light in the angels is threefold: of nature, of grace, and of glory. But an angel is illumined with the light of nature by the Creator, with the light of grace by the Justifier, with the light of glory by the Beatifier; all of which comes from God. Therefore one angel does not illumine another.

Obj. 3. Further, light is a form in the mind. But the rational mind is *informed by God alone, without created intervention,* as Augustine says. Therefore one angel does not illumine the mind of another.

On the contrary, Dionysius says that *the angels of the second hierarchy are cleansed, illumined and perfected by the angels of the first hierarchy.*

I answer that, One angel illumines another. To make this clear, we must observe that intellectual light is nothing else than a manifestation of truth, according to *Ephes.* v. 13: *All that is made manifest is light.* Hence to illumine means nothing else than to communicate to others the manifestation of known truth. As the Apostle says (*Ephes.* iii. 8): *To me the least of all the saints is given this grace . . . to enlighten all men, that they may see what is the dispensation of the mystery which hath been hidden from eternity in God.* Therefore one angel is said to illumine another by manifesting the truth which he knows himself. Hence Dionysius says: *Theologians plainly show that the orders of the heavenly beings are taught divine science by the highest minds.*

Now since two things concur in understanding, as we have said, namely, the intellectual power, and the likeness of the thing understood, in both of these one angel can manifest a known truth to another. First, by strengthening his intellectual power. For just as the power of an imperfect body is strengthened by the proximity of a more perfect body,—for instance, the less hot is made hotter by the presence of what is hotter, so the intellectual power of an inferior angel is strengthened by the turning of a superior angel to him. For in spiritual beings, for one to turn to another corresponds to proximity in corporeal things. Secondly, one angel manifests the truth to another as regards the likeness of the thing understood. For the superior angel receives the knowledge of truth by a kind of universal conception, to receive which the inferior angel's intellect is not sufficiently powerful; for it is natural to him to receive truth in a more particular manner. Therefore the superior angel particularizes, in a way, the truth which he conceives universally, so that it can be grasped by the inferior angel; and thus he proposes it to his knowledge. Thus it is among men that the teacher, in order to adapt himself to others, divides into many points the knowledge which he possesses in the universal. This is thus expressed by Dionysius: *Every intellectual substance with provident power divides and multiplies the uniform knowledge bestowed on it by one nearer to God, so as to lead its inferiors upwards by analogy.*

Reply Obj. 1. All the angels, both inferior and superior, see the essence of God immediately, and in this respect one does not teach another. It is of this truth that the prophet speaks; wherefore he adds: *They shall teach no more every man his brother, saying: Know the Lord, for all shall know Me, from the least of them even to the greatest.* But all the exemplars of the divine works, which are known in God as in their cause, God knows in Himself, because He comprehends Himself; but of others who see God, each one knows the more exemplars, the more perfectly he sees God. Hence a superior angel knows more about the exemplars of the divine works than an inferior angel, and concerning these the former illumines the latter; and as to this Dionysius says that the angels *are illumined by the exemplars of existing things.*

Reply Obj. 2. An angel does not illumine another by giving him the light of nature, grace, or glory, but by strengthening his natural light, and by manifesting to him truths concerning the state of nature, of grace, and of glory, as was explained above.

Reply Obj. 3. The rational mind is formed immediately by God, either as the image from the exemplar, inasmuch as it is made to the image of God alone, or as a subject by the ultimate perfecting form. For the created mind is always considered to be unformed, except it adhere to the first truth; while other kinds of illumination that proceed from man or angel are, as it were, dispositions to this ultimate form.

SECOND ARTICLE

WHETHER ONE ANGEL MOVES ANOTHER ANGEL'S WILL?

We proceed thus to the Second Article:—

Objection 1. It would seem that one angel can move another angel's will. Because, according to Dionysius quoted above, just as one angel illumines another, so does he cleanse and perfect another. But cleansing and perfecting seem to belong to the will; for the former seems to point to the stain of sin which pertains to the will, while to be perfected is to obtain an end, which is the object of the will. Therefore an angel can move another angel's will.

Obj. 2. Further, as Dionysius says: *The names of the angels designate their properties.* Now the Seraphim are so called because they are *aflame* or *ablaze;* and this is by love, which belongs to the will. Therefore one angel moves another angel's will.

Obj. 3. Further, the Philosopher says that the higher appetite moves the lower. But as the intellect of the superior angel is higher, so also is his will. It seems, therefore, that the superior angel can change the will of another angel.

On the contrary, To him it belongs to change the will, to whom it belongs to justify it, for justice is the rectitude of the will. But God alone justifies. Therefore one angel cannot change another angel's will.

I answer that, As was said above, the will is changed in two ways: on the part of the object, and on the part of the power. On the part of the object, both the good itself, which is the object of the will, moves the will, as the appetible moves the appetite; and he who points out the object, as, for instance, one who proves something to be good. But as we have said above, other goods in a measure incline the will, yet nothing sufficiently moves the will save the universal good, and that is God. And this good He alone shows, that it may be seen by the blessed, Who, when Moses asked: *Show me Thy glory,* answered: *I will show thee all good* (*Exod.* xxxiii. 18, 19). Therefore an angel does not move the will sufficiently, either as the object or as showing the object. But he inclines the will as something lovable, and as manifesting some created good ordered to God's goodness. And thus he can incline the will to the love of the creature or of God, by way of persuasion.

But on the part of the power, the will cannot be moved at all save by God. For the operation of the will is a certain inclination of the one who wills to the thing willed. And He alone can change this inclination, Who bestowed on the creature the power to will; just as that agent alone can change the natural inclination, that can give the power which the natural inclination follows. Now God alone gave to the creature the power to will, because He alone is the author of the intellectual nature. Therefore an angel cannot move another angel's will.

Reply Obj. 1. Cleansing and perfecting are to be understood as illuminations. And since God illumines by changing the intellect and will, He cleanses by removing defects of intellect and will, and perfects unto the end of the intellect and will. But the illumination caused by an angel concerns the intellect, as was explained above: and therefore an angel is to be understood as cleansing from the defect of nescience in the intellect, and as perfecting unto the consummate end of the intellect, which is the known truth. Thus Dionysius says that *in the heavenly hierarchy the chastening of the inferior essence is an illumination of things unknown, that leads them to more perfect knowledge.* For instance, we might say that corporeal sight is cleansed by the removal of darkness, illumined by the diffusion of light, and perfected by being brought to the perception of the colored thing.

Reply Obj. 2. One angel can induce another by persuasion to love God, as was explained above.

Reply Obj. 3. The Philosopher is speaking of the lower sensitive appetite, which can be moved by the superior intellectual appetite, because it belongs to the same nature of the soul, and because the inferior appetite is a power in a corporeal organ. But this does not apply to the angels.

THIRD ARTICLE

WHETHER AN INFERIOR ANGEL CAN ILLUMINE A SUPERIOR ANGEL?

We proceed thus to the Third Article:—

Objection 1. It would seem that an inferior angel can illumine a superior angel. For the ecclesiastical hierarchy is derived from, and represents, the heavenly hierarchy; and hence the heavenly Jerusalem is called *our mother* (*Gal.* iv. 26). But in the Church even superiors are illumined and taught by their inferiors, as the Apostle says (*1 Cor.* xiv. 31): *You may all prophesy one by one, that all may learn and all may be exhorted.* Therefore, likewise in the heavenly hierarchy, the superiors can be illumined by inferiors.

Obj. 2. Further, as the order of corporeal substances depends on the will of God, so also does the order of spiritual substances. But, as was said above, God sometimes acts outside the order of corporeal substances. Therefore he also sometimes acts outside the order of spiritual substances, by illumining inferiors otherwise than through their superiors. Therefore in that way the inferiors illumined by God can illumine superiors.

Obj. 3. Further, one angel illumines the other to whom he turns, as was above explained. But since this turning to another is voluntary, the highest angel can turn to the lowest passing over the others. Therefore he can illumine him immediately; and thus the latter can illumine his superiors.

On the contrary, Dionysius says that *this is the divine unalterable law, that inferior things are led to God by the superior.*

I answer that, The inferior angels never illumine the superior, but are always illumined by them. The reason is, because, as was above explained, one order is under another, as cause is under cause; and hence as cause is ordered to cause, so is order to order. Therefore there is no incongruity if sometimes anything is done outside the order of the inferior cause, that it be ordered to a superior cause, as in human affairs the command of the governor is passed over from obedience to the prince. So it happens that God works miraculously outside the order of corporeal nature, in order that men may be ordered to the knowledge of Him. But the passing over of the order that belongs to spiritual substances in no way belongs to the ordering of men to God, since the angelic operations are not made known to us, as are the operations of sensible bodies. Thus the order which belongs to spiritual substances is never passed over by God; so that the inferiors are always moved by the superior, and not conversely.

Reply Obj. 1. The ecclesiastical hierarchy imitates the heavenly in some degree, but not by a perfect likeness. For in the heavenly hierarchy the perfection of the order is in proportion to its nearness to God. Hence, those who are the nearer to God are the more sublime in grade, and more clear in knowledge; and on that account the superiors are never illumined by the inferiors. But in the ecclesiastical hierarchy, sometimes those who are the nearer to God in sanctity are in the lowest grade, and are not conspicuous for science; and some also are eminent in one kind of science, and fail in another. On this account superiors may be taught by inferiors.

Reply Obj. 2. As was above explained, there is no similarity between what God does outside the order of corporeal nature, and that of spiritual nature. Hence the argument does not hold.

Reply Obj. 3. An angel turns voluntarily to illumine another angel, but the angel's will is always regulated by the divine law which established the order in the angels.

FOURTH ARTICLE

WHETHER THE SUPERIOR ANGEL ILLUMINES THE INFERIOR AS REGARDS ALL HE HIMSELF KNOWS?

We proceed thus to the Fourth Article:—

Objection 1. It would seem that the superior angel does not illumine the inferior concerning all he himself knows. For Dionysius says that the superior angels have a more universal knowledge, and the inferior a more particular and individual knowledge. But more is contained under a universal knowledge than under a particular knowledge. Therefore not all that the superior angels know is known by the inferior, through the illuminations of the superior.

Obj. 2. Further, the Master of the *Sentences* says that the superior angels had long known the mystery of the Incarnation, whereas the inferior angels did not know it until it was accomplished. Thus we find that on some of the angels inquiring, as it were, in ignorance: *Who is this King of glory?* other angels, who knew, answered: *The Lord of Hosts, He is the King of glory*, as Dionysius expounds. But this would not apply if the superior angels illumined the inferior concerning all they know themselves. Therefore they do not do so.

Obj. 3. Further, if the superior angels illumine the inferior about all they know, nothing that the superior angels know would be unknown to the inferior angels. Therefore the superior angels could communicate nothing more to the inferior; which appears open to objection. Therefore the superior angels illumine the inferior in all things.

On the contrary, Gregory says: *In that heavenly country, though there are some excellent gifts, yet nothing is held individually*. And Dionysius says: *Each heavenly essence communicates to the inferior the gift derived from the superior*, as was quoted above.

I answer that, Every creature participates in the divine goodness, so as to diffuse the good it possesses to others; for it is of the nature of good to communicate itself to others. Hence corporeal agents also give their likeness to others so far as they can. Hence, the more an agent is established in the share of the divine goodness, so much the more does it strive to transmit its perfections to others as far as possible. Hence the Blessed Peter admonishes those who by grace share in the divine goodness, saying: *As every man hath received grace, ministering the same one to another, as good stewards of the manifold grace of God* (*1 Pet.* iv. 10). Much more therefore do the holy angels, who enjoy the plenitude of participation of the divine goodness, impart the same to those below them.

Nevertheless this gift is not received so excellently by the inferior as by the superior angels. Therefore the superior always remain in a higher order, and have a more perfect knowledge; just as the teacher understands the same thing better than the pupil who learns from him.

Reply Obj. 1. The knowledge of the superior angels is said to be more universal with reference to the more eminent mode of understanding.

Reply Obj. 2. The Master's words are not to be so understood as if the inferior angels were entirely ignorant of the mystery of the Incarnation; but that they did not know it as fully as the superior angels, and that they progressed in the knowledge of it afterwards when the mystery was accomplished.

Reply Obj. 3. Till the Judgment Day some new things are always being revealed by God to the highest angels, concerning the course of the world, and especially the salvation of the elect. Hence there is always something for the superior angels to make known to the inferior.

From The Upanishads

DIALOGUE WITH DEATH

THE BRAHMANA

From *The Upanishads*

DIALOGUE WITH DEATH

The Upanishads antedate the birth of Buddha in the fifth century, B.C. They are a mystical interpretation of man and God and the universe. Known as the "Vedanta," because they constitute the end of the "Veda," or that whole body of philosophic development from 1500 to 600 B.C., they are in a sense an anthology of transcendental thinking on man's search beyond logic and reality for infinite bliss. "Dialogue with Death" and "Brahmana" are typical of the emphasis throughout *The Upanishads* on the world as illusion and the spirit as the highest perfection.

DIALOGUE WITH DEATH

Vagasravasa, desirous of heavenly rewards, surrendered at a sacrifice all that he possessed. He had a son of the name of Nakiketas.

When the promised presents were being given to the priests, faith entered into the heart of Nakiketas, who was still a boy, and he thought:

"Unblessed, surely, are the worlds to which a man goes by giving, as his promised present at a sacrifice, cows which have drunk water, eaten hay, given their milk, and are barren."

He, knowing that his father had promised to give up all that he possessed, and therefore his son also, said to his father: "Dear father, to whom wilt thou give me?"

He said it a second and a third time. Then the father replied angrily:

"I shall give thee unto Death."

The father, having once said so, though in haste, had to be true to his word and to sacrifice his son.

The son said: "I go as the first, at the head of many who have still to die; I go in the midst of many who are now dying. What will be the work of Yama the ruler of the departed which to-day he has to do unto me?

"Look back how it was with those who came before, look forward how it will be with those who come hereafter. A mortal ripens like corn, like corn he springs up again."

Nakiketas enters into the abode of Yama Vaivasvata, and there is no one to receive him. Thereupon one of the attendants of Yama is supposed to say: "Fire enters into the houses, when a Brahmana enters as a guest. That fire is quenched by this peace-offering;—bring water, O Vaivasvata!

"A Brahmana that dwells in the house of a foolish man without receiving food to eat, destroys his hopes and expectations, his possessions, his righteousness, his sacred and his good deeds, and all his sons and cattle."

Yama, returning to his house after an absence of three nights, during which time Nakiketas had received no hospitality from him, says:

"O Brahmana, as thou, a venerable guest, hast dwelt in my house three nights without eating, therefore choose now three boons. Hail to thee! and welfare to me!"

Nakiketas said: "O Death, as the first of the three boons I choose that Gautama, my father, be pacified, kind, and free from anger towards me; and that he may know me and greet me, when I shall have been dismissed by thee."

Yama said: "Through my favour Auddalaki Aruni, thy father, will know thee, and be again towards thee as he was before. He shall sleep peacefully through the night, and free from anger, after having seen thee freed from the mouth of death."

Nakiketas said: "In the heaven-world there is no fear; thou art not there, O Death, and no one is afraid on account of old age. Leaving behind both hunger and thirst, and out of the reach of sorrow, all rejoice in the world of heaven."

"Thou knowest, O Death, the fire-sacrifice which leads us to heaven; tell it to me, for I am full of faith. Those who live in the heaven-world reach immortality,—this I ask as my second boon."

Yama said: "I tell it thee, learn it from me, and when thou understandest that fire-sacrifice which leads to heaven, know, O Nakiketas, that it is the attainment of the endless worlds, and their firm support, hidden in darkness."

Yama then told him that fire-sacrifice, the beginning of all the worlds, and what bricks are required for the altar, and how many, and how they are to be placed. And Nakiketas repeated all as it had been told to him. Then Mrityu, being pleased with him, said again:

The generous, being satisfied, said to him: "I give thee now another boon; that fire-sacrifice shall be named after thee, take also this many-coloured chain."

"He who has three times performed this Nakiketa rite, and has been united with the three, father, mother, and teacher, and has performed the three duties, study, sacrifice, almsgiving, overcomes birth and death. When he has learnt and understood this fire, which knows or makes us know all that is born of Brahman, which is venerable and divine, then he obtains everlasting peace."

"He who knows the three Nakiketa fires, and knowing the three, piles up the Nakiketa sacrifice, he, having first thrown off the chains of death, rejoices in the world of heaven, beyond the reach of grief."

"This, O Nakiketas, is thy fire which leads to heaven, and which thou hast chosen as thy second boon. That fire all men will proclaim. Choose now, O Nakiketas, thy third boon."

Nakiketas said: "There is that doubt, when a man is dead —some saying, he is; others, he is not. This I should like to know, taught by thee; this is the third of my boons."

Death said: "On this point even the gods have doubted formerly; it is not easy to understand. That subject is subtle. Choose another boon, O Nakiketas, do not press me, and let me off that boon."

Nakiketas said: "On this point even the gods have doubted indeed, and thou, Death, hast declared it to be not easy to understand, and another teacher like thee is not to be found —surely no other boon is like unto this."

Death said: "Choose sons and grandsons who shall live a hundred years, herds of cattle, elephants, gold, and horses. Choose the wide abode of the earth, and live thyself as many harvests as thou desirest."

"If you can think of any boon equal to that, choose wealth, and long life. Be king, Nakiketas, on the wide earth. I make thee the enjoyer of all desires."

"Whatever desires are difficult to attain among mortals, ask for them according to thy wish—these fair maidens with their chariots and musical instruments—such are indeed not to be obtained by men—be waited on by them whom I give to thee, but do not ask me about dying."

Nakiketas said: "These things last till tomorrow, O Death, for they wear out this vigour of all the senses. Even the whole of life is short. Keep thou thy horses, keep dance and song for thyself."

"No man can be made happy by wealth. Shall we possess wealth, when we see thee? Shall we live, as long as thou rulest? Only that boon (which I have chosen) is to be chosen by me."

"What mortal, slowly decaying here below, and knowing, after having approached them, the freedom from decay enjoyed by the immortals, would delight in a long life, after he has pondered on the pleasures which arise from beauty and love?"

"No, that on which there is this doubt, O Death, tell us what there is in that great Hereafter. Nakiketas does not choose another boon but that which enters into the hidden world."

Death said: "The good is one thing, the pleasant another; these two, having different objects, chain a man. It is well with him who clings to the good; he who chooses the pleasant, misses his end."

"The good and the pleasant approach man: the wise goes round about them and distinguishes them. Yea, the wise prefers the good to the pleasant, but the fool chooses the pleasant through greed and avarice."

"Thou, O Nakiketas, after pondering all pleasures that are or seem delightful, hast dismissed them all. Thou hast not gone into the road that leadeth to wealth, in which many men perish."

"Wide apart and leading to different points are these two, ignorance, and what is known as wisdom. I believe Nakiketas to be one who desires knowledge, for even many pleasures did not tear thee away."

"Fools dwelling in darkness, wise in their own conceit, and puffed up with vain knowledge, go round and round, staggering to and fro, like blind men led by the blind."

"The Hereafter never rises before the eyes of the careless child, deluded by the delusion of wealth. 'This is the world,' he thinks, 'there is no other;'—thus he falls again and again under my sway."

"He (the Self) of whom many are not even able to hear, whom many, even when they hear of him, do not comprehend; wonderful is a man, when found, who is able to teach him the Self; wonderful is he who comprehends him, when taught by an able teacher."

"That Self, when taught by an inferior man, is not easy to be known, even though often thought upon; unless it be taught by another, there is no way to it, for it is inconceivably smaller than what is small."

"That doctrine is not to be obtained by argument, but when it is declared by another, then, O dearest, it is easy to understand. Thou hast obtained it now; thou art truly a man of true resolve. May we have always an inquirer like thee!"

Nakiketas said: "I know that what is called a treasure is transient, for that eternal is not obtained by things which are not eternal. Hence the Nakiketa fire-sacrifice has been laid by me first; then, by means of transient things, I have obtained what is not transient (the teaching of Yama)."

Yama said: "Though thou hadst seen the fulfilment of all desires, the foundation of the world, the endless rewards of good deeds, the shore where there is no fear, that which is magnified by praise, the wide abode, the rest, yet being wise thou hast with firm resolve dismissed it all."

"The wise who, by means of meditation on his Self, recognises the Ancient, who is difficult to be seen, who has entered into the dark, who is hidden in the cave, who dwells in the abyss, as God, he indeed leaves joy and sorrow far behind."

"A mortal who has heard this and embraced it, who has separated from it all qualities, and has thus reached the subtle Being, rejoices, because he has obtained what is a cause for rejoicing. The house of Brahman is open, O Nakiketas."

Nakiketas said: "That which thou seest as neither this nor that, as neither effect nor cause, as neither past nor future, tell me that."

Yama said: "That word or place which all the Vedas record, which all penances proclaim, which men desire when they live as religious students, that word I tell thee briefly, it is Om."

"That imperishable syllable means Brahman, that syllable means the highest Brahman; he who knows that syllable, whatever he desires, is his."

"This is the best support, this is the highest support; he who knows that support is magnified in the world of Brahma."

"The knowing Self is not born, it dies not; it sprang from nothing, nothing sprang from it. The Ancient is unborn, eternal, everlasting; he is not killed, though the body is killed."

"If the killer thinks that he kills, if the killed thinks that he is killed, they do not understand; for this one does not kill, nor is that one killed."

"The Self, smaller than small, greater than great, is hidden in the heart of that creature. A man who is free from desires and free from grief, sees the majesty of the Self by the grace of the Creator."

"Though sitting still, he walks far; though lying down, he goes everywhere. Who, save myself, is able to know that God who rejoices and rejoices not?"

"The wise who knows the Self as bodiless within the bodies, as unchanging among changing things, as great and omnipresent, does never grieve."

"That Self cannot be gained by the Veda, nor by understanding, nor by much learning. He whom the Self chooses, by him the Self can be gained. The Self chooses him (his body) as his own."

"But he who has not first turned away from his wickedness, who is not tranquil, and subdued, or whose mind is not at rest, he can never obtain the Self even by knowledge."

"Who then knows where He is, He to whom the Brahmans and Kshatriyas are but food, and death itself a condiment?"

"There are the two, drinking their reward in the world of their own works, entered into the cave of the heart, dwelling on the highest summit, the ether in the heart. Those who know Brahman call them shade and light; likewise, those householders who perform the Trinakiketa sacrifice."

"May we be able to master that Nakiketa rite which is a bridge for sacrificers; also that which is the highest, imperishable Brahman for those who wish to cross over to the fearless shore."

"Know the Self to be sitting in the chariot, the body to be the chariot, the intellect the charioteer, and the mind the reins."

"The senses they call the horses, the objects of the senses their roads. When he (the Highest Self) is in union with the body, the senses, and the mind, then wise people call him the Enjoyer."

"He who has no understanding and whose mind (the reins) is never firmly held, his senses (horses) are unmanageable, like vicious horses of a charioteer."

"But he who has understanding and whose mind is always firmly held, his senses are under control, like good horses of a charioteer."

"He who has no understanding, who is unmindful and always impure, never reaches that place, but enters into the round of births."

"But he who has understanding, who is mindful and always pure, reaches indeed that place, from whence he is not born again."

"But he who has understanding for his charioteer, and who holds the reins of the mind, he reaches the end of his journey, and that is the highest place of Vishnu."

"Beyond the senses there are the objects, beyond the objects there is the mind, beyond the mind there is the intellect, the Great Self is beyond the intellect."

"Beyond the Great there is the Undeveloped, beyond the Undeveloped there is the Person (purusha). Beyond the Person there is nothing—this is the goal, the highest road."

"That Self is hidden in all beings and does not shine forth, but it is seen by subtle seers through their sharp and subtle intellect."

"A wise man should keep down speech and mind; he should keep them within the Self which is knowledge; he should keep knowledge within the Self which is the Great; and he should keep that (the Great) within the Self which is the Quiet."

"Rise, awake! having obtained your boons, understand them! The sharp edge of a razor is difficult to pass over; thus the wise say the path to the Self is hard."

"He who has perceived that which is without sound, without touch, without form, without decay, without taste, eternal, without smell, without beginning, without end, beyond the Great, and unchangeable, is freed from the jaws of death."

"A wise man who has repeated or heard the ancient story of Nakiketas told by Death, is magnified in the world of Brahman."

"And he who repeats this greatest mystery in an assembly of Brahmans, or full of devotion at the time of the Sraddha sacrifice, obtains thereby infinite rewards."

Death said: "The Self-existent pierced the openings of the senses so that they turn forward: therefore man looks forward, not backward into himself. Some wise man, however, with his eyes closed and wishing for immortality, saw the Self behind."

"Children follow after outward pleasures, and fall into the snare of wide-spread death. Wise men only, knowing the nature of what is immortal, do not look for anything stable here among things unstable."

"That by which we know form, taste, smell, sounds, and loving touches, by that also we know what exists besides. This is that which thou hast asked for."

"The wise, when he knows that that by which he perceives all objects in sleep or in waking is the great omnipresent Self, grieves no more."

"He who knows this living soul which eats honey (perceives objects) as being the Self, always near, the Lord of the past and the future, henceforward fears no more. This is that."

"He who knows him who was born first from the brooding heat, for he was born before the water, who, entering into the heart, abides therein, and was perceived from the elements. This is that."

"He who knows Aditi also, who is one with all deities, who arises with Prana (breath or Hiranyagarbha), who, entering into the heart, abides therein, and was born from the elements. This is that."

"There is Agni, fire, the all-seeing, hidden in the two fire-sticks, well-guarded like a child in the womb by the mother, day after day to be adored by men when they awake and bring oblations. This is that."

"And that whence the sun rises, and whither it goes to set, there all the Devas are contained, and no one goes beyond. This is that."

"What is here visible in the world, the same is there invisible in Brahman; and what is there, the same is here. He who sees any difference here between Brahman and the world goes from death to death."

"Even by the mind this Brahman is to be obtained, and then there is no difference whatsoever. He goes from death to death who sees any difference here."

"The person, of the size of a thumb, stands in the middle of the Self (body?), as lord of the past and the future, and henceforward fears no more. This is that."

"That person, of the size of a thumb, is like a light without smoke, lord of the past and the future, he is the same to-day and to-morrow. This is that."

"As rain-water that has fallen on a mountain-ridge runs down the rocks on all sides, thus does he, who sees a difference between qualities, run after them on all sides."

"As pure water poured into pure water remains the same, thus, O Gautama, is the Self of a thinker who knows."

"There is a town with eleven gates belonging to the Unborn (Brahman), whose thoughts are never crooked. He who approaches it, grieves no more, and liberated from all bonds of ignorance becomes free. This is that."

"He (Brahman) is the swan (sun), dwelling in the bright heaven; he is the Vasu (air), dwelling in the sky; he is the sacrificer (fire), dwelling on the hearth; he is the guest (Soma), dwelling in the sacrificial jar; he dwells in men, in gods (vara), in the sacrifice (rita), in heaven; he is born in the water, on earth, in the sacrifice (rita), on the mountains; he is the True and the Great."

"He (Brahman) it is who sends up the breath (prana), and who throws back the breath (apana). All the Devas (senses) worship him, the adorable (or the dwarf), who sits in the centre."

"When that incorporated (Brahman), who dwells in the body, is torn away and freed from the body, what remains then? This is that."

"No mortal lives by the breath that goes up and by the breath that goes down. We live by another, in whom these two repose."

"Well then, O Gautama, I shall tell thee this mystery, the old Brahman, and what happens to the Self, after reaching death."

"Some enter the womb in order to have a body, as organic beings, others go into inorganic matter, according to their work and according to their knowledge."

"He, the highest Person, who is awake in us while we are asleep, shaping one lovely sight after another, that indeed is the Bright, that is Brahman, that alone is called the Immortal. All worlds are contained in it, and no one goes beyond. This is that."

"As the one fire, after it has entered the world, though one, becomes different according to whatever it burns, thus the one Self within all things becomes different, according to whatever it enters, and exists also without."

"As the one air, after it has entered the world, though one, becomes different according to whatever it enters, thus the one Self within all things becomes different, according to whatever it enters, and exists also without."

"As the sun, the eye of the whole world, is not contaminated by the external impurities seen by the eyes, thus the one Self within all things is never contaminated by the misery of the world, being himself without."

"There is one ruler, the Self within all things, who makes the one form manifold. The wise who perceive him within their Self, to them belongs eternal happiness, not to others."

"There is one eternal thinker, thinking noneternal thoughts, who, though one, fulfils the desires of many. The wise who perceive him within their Self, to them belongs eternal peace, not to others."

"They perceive that highest indescribable pleasure, saying, This is that. How then can I understand it? Has it its own light, or does it reflect light?"

"The sun does not shine there, nor the moon and the stars, nor these lightnings, and much less this fire. When he shines, everything shines after him; by his light all this is lighted."

"There is that ancient tree, whose roots grow upward and whose branches grow downward—that indeed is called the Bright, that is called Brahman, that alone is called the Immortal. All worlds are contained in it, and no one goes beyond. This is that."

"Whatever there is, the whole world, when gone forth from the Brahman, trembles in its breath. That Brahman is a great terror, like a drawn sword. Those who know it become immortal."

"From terror of Brahman fire burns, from terror the sun burns, from terror Indra and Vayu, and Death, as the fifth, run away."

"If a man could not understand it before the falling asunder of his body, then he has to take body again in the worlds of creation."

"As in a mirror, so Brahman may be seen clearly here in this body; as in a dream, in the world of the Fathers; as in the water, he is seen about in the world of the Gandharvas; as in light and shade, in the world of Brahma."

"Having understood that the senses are distinct (from the Atman), and that their rising and setting (their waking and sleeping) belongs to them in their distinct existence (and not to the Atman), a wise man grieves no more."

"Beyond the senses is the mind, beyond the mind is the highest created Being, higher than that Being is the Great Self, higher than the Great, the highest Undeveloped."

"Beyond the Undeveloped is the Person, the all-pervading and entirely imperceptible. Every creature that knows him is liberated, and obtains immortality."

"His form is not to be seen, no one beholds him with the eye. He is imagined by the heart, by wisdom, by the mind. Those who know this, are immortal."

"When the five instruments of knowledge stand still together with the mind, and when the intellect does not move, that is called the highest state."

"This, the firm holding back of the senses, is what is called Yoga. He must be free from thoughtlessness then, for Yoga comes and goes."

"He (the Self) cannot be reached by speech, by mind, or by the eye. How can it be apprehended except by him who says: 'He is?' "

"By the words 'He is,' is he to be apprehended, and by admitting the reality of both the invisible Brahman and the visible world, as coming from Brahman. When he has been apprehended by the words 'He is,' then his reality reveals itself."

"When all desires that dwell in his heart cease, then the mortal becomes immortal, and obtains Brahman."

"When all the ties of the heart are severed here on earth, then the mortal becomes immortal—here ends the teaching."

"There are a hundred and one arteries of the heart, one of them penetrates the crown of the head. Moving upwards by it, a man at his death reaches the Immortal; the other arteries serve for departing in different directions."

"The Person not larger than a thumb, the inner Self, is always settled in the heart of men. Let a man draw that Self forth from his body with steadiness, as one draws the pith from a reed. Let him know that Self as the Bright, as the Immortal; yes, as the Bright, as the Immortal."

Having received this knowledge taught by Death and the whole rule of Yoga (meditation), Nakiketas became free from passion and death, and obtained Brahman. Thus it will be with another also who knows thus what relates to the Self.

May He protect us both! May He enjoy us both! May we acquire strength together! May our knowledge become bright! May we never quarrel! Om! Peace! peace! peace! Harih, Om!

THE BRAHMANA

Yagnavalkya came to Ganaka Vaideha, and he did not mean to speak with him. But when formerly Ganaka Vaideha and Yagnavalkya had a disputation on the Agnihotra, Yagnavalkya had granted him a boon, and he chose for a boon that he might be free to ask him any question he liked. Yagnavalkya granted it, and thus the King was the first to ask him a question.

"Yagnavalkya," he said, "what is the light of man?"

Yagnavalkya replied: "The sun, O King; for, having the sun alone for his light, man sits, moves about, does his work, and returns."

Ganaka Vaideha said: "So indeed it is, O Yagnavalkya."

Ganaka Vaideha said: "When the sun has set, O Yagnavalkya, what is then the light of man?"

Yagnavalkya replied: "The moon indeed is his light; for, having the moon alone for his light, man sits, moves about, does his work, and returns."

Ganaka Vaideha said: "So indeed it is, O Yagnavalkya."

Ganaka Vaideha said: "When the sun has set, O Yagnavalkya, and the moon has set, what is the light of man?"

Yagnavalkya replied: "Fire indeed is his light; for, having fire alone for his light, man sits, moves about, does his work, and returns."

Ganaka Vaideha said: "When the sun has set, O Yagnavalkya, and the moon has set, and the fire is gone out, what is then the light of man?"

Yagnavalkya replied: "Sound indeed is his light; for, having sound alone for his light, man sits, moves about, does his work, and returns. Therefore, O King, when one cannot see even one's own hand, yet when a sound is raised, one goes towards it."

Ganaka Vaideha said: "So indeed it is, O Yagnavalkya."

Ganaka Vaideha said: "When the sun has set, O Yagnavalkya, and the moon has set, and the fire is gone out, and the sound hushed, what is then the light of man?"

Yagnavalkya said: "The Self indeed is his light; for, having the Self alone as his light, man sits, moves about, does his work, and returns."

Ganaka Vaideha said: "Who is that Self?"

Yagnavalkya replied: "He who is within the heart, surrounded by the Pranas (senses), the person of light, consisting of knowledge. He, remaining the same, wanders along the two worlds, as if thinking, as if moving. During sleep (in dream) he transcends this world and all the forms of death (all that falls under the sway of death, all that is perishable).

"On being born that person, assuming his body, becomes united with all evils; when he departs and dies, he leaves all evils behind.

"And there are two states for that person, the one here in this world, the other in the other world, and as a third an intermediate state, the state of sleep. When in that intermediate state, he sees both those states together, the one here in this world, and the other in the other world. Now whatever his admission to the other world may be, having gained that admission, he sees both the evils and the blessings.

"And when he falls asleep, then after having taken away

with him the material from the whole world, destroying and building it up again, he sleeps (dreams) by his own light. In that state the person is self-illuminated.

"There are no real chariots in that state, no horses, no roads, but he himself sends forth (creates) chariots, horses, and roads. There are no blessings there, no happiness, no joys, but he himself sends forth (creates) blessings, happiness, and joys. There are no tanks there, no lakes, no rivers, but he himself sends forth (creates) tanks, lakes, and rivers. He indeed is the maker.

"On this there are these verses:

"After having subdued by sleep all that belongs to the body, he, not asleep himself, looks down upon the sleeping senses. Having assumed light, he goes again to his place, the golden person, the lonely bird.

"Guarding with the breath (prana, life) the lower nest, the immortal moves away from the nest; that immortal one goes wherever he likes, the golden person, the lonely bird.

"Going up and down in his dream, the god makes manifold shapes for himself, either rejoicing together with women, or laughing with his friends, or seeing terrible sights.

"People may see his playground, but himself no one ever sees. Therefore they say, 'Let no one wake a man suddenly, for it is not easy to remedy, if he does not get back rightly to his body.'

"Here some people object and say: 'No, this sleep is the same as the place of waking, for what he sees while awake, that only he sees when asleep.' No, here (in sleep) the person is self-illuminated (as we explained before)."

Ganaka Vaideha said: "I give you, Sir, a thousand. Speak on for the sake of my emancipation."

Yagnavalkya said: "That person having enjoyed himself in that state of bliss (samprasâda, deep sleep), having moved about and seen both good and evil, hastens back again as he came, to the place from which he started (the place of sleep), to dream. And whatever he may have seen there, he is not followed (affected) by it, for that person is not attached to anything."

Ganaka Vaideha said: "So it is indeed, Yagnavalkya. I give you, Sir, a thousand. Speak on for the sake of emancipation."

Yagnavalkya said: "That person having enjoyed himself in that sleep (dream), having moved about and seen both good and evil, hastens back again as he came, to the place from which he started, to be awake. And whatever he may have seen there, he is not followed (affected) by it, for that person is not attached to anything."

Ganaka Vaideha said: "So it is indeed, Yagnavalkya. I give you, Sir, a thousand. Speak on for the sake of emancipation."

Yagnavalkya said: "That person having enjoyed himself in that state of waking, having moved about and seen both good and evil, hastens back again as he came, to the place from which he started, to the state of sleeping (dream).

"In fact, as a large fish moves along the two banks of a river, the right and the left, so does that person move along these two states, the state of sleeping and the state of waking.

"And as a falcon, or any other swift bird, after he has roamed about here in the air, becomes tired, and folding his wings is carried to his nest, so does that person hasten to that state where, when asleep, he desires no more desires, and dreams no more dreams.

"There are in his body the veins called Hita, which are as small as a hair divided a thousandfold, full of white, blue, yellow, green, and red. Now when, as it were, they kill him, when, as it were, they overcome him, when, as it were, an elephant chases him, when, as it were, he falls into a well, he fancies, through ignorance, that danger which he commonly sees in waking. But when he fancies that he is, as it were, a god, or that he is, as it were, a king, or 'I am this altogether,' that is his highest world.

"This indeed is his true form, free from desires, free from evil, free from fear. Now as a man, when embraced by a beloved wife, knows nothing that is without, nothing that is within, thus this person, when embraced by the intelligent (pragna) Self, knows nothing that is without, nothing that is within. This indeed is his true form, in which his wishes are fulfilled, in which the Self only is his wish, in which no wish is left,—free from any sorrow.

"Then a father is not a father, a mother not a mother, the worlds not worlds, the gods not gods, the Vedas not Vedas. Then a thief is not a thief, a murderer not a murderer, a Kandala not a Kandala, a Paulkasa not a Paulkasa, a Sramana not a Sramana, a Tapasa not a Tapasa. He is not followed by good, not followed by evil, for he has then overcome all the sorrows of the heart.

"And when it is said that there in the Sushupti he does not see, yet he is seeing, though he does not see. For sight is inseparable from the seer, because it cannot perish. But there is then no second, nothing else different from him that he could see.

"And when it is said that there in the Sushupti he does not smell, yet he is smelling, though he does not smell. For smelling is inseparable from the smeller, because it cannot perish. But there is then no second, nothing else different from him that he could smell.

"And when it is said that there in the Sushupti he does not taste, yet he is tasting, though he does not taste. For tasting is inseparable from the taster, because it cannot perish. But there is then no second, nothing else different from him that he could taste.

"And when it is said that there in the Sushupti he does not speak, yet he is speaking, though he does not speak. For speaking is inseparable from the speaker, because it cannot perish. But there is then no second, nothing else different from him that he could speak.

"And when it is said that there in the Sushupti he does not hear, yet he is hearing, though he does not hear. For hearing is inseparable from the hearer, because it cannot perish. But there is then no second, nothing else different from him that he could hear.

"And when it is said that there in the Sushupti he does not think, yet he is thinking, though he does not think. For thinking is inseparable from the thinker, because it cannot perish.

But there is then no second, nothing else different from him that he could think.

"And when it is said that there in the Sushupti he does not touch, yet he is touching, though he does not touch. For touching is inseparable from the toucher, because it cannot perish. But there is then no second, nothing else different from him that he could think.

"And when it is said that there in the Sushupti he does not know, yet he is knowing, though he does not know. For knowing is inseparable from the knower, because it cannot perish. But there is then no second, nothing else different from him that he could know.

"When in waking and dreaming there is, as it were, another, then can one see the other, then can one smell the other, then can one speak to the other, then can one hear the other, then can one think the other, then can one touch the other, then can one know the other.

"An ocean is that one seer, without any duality; this is the Brahma-world, O King." Thus did Yagnavalkya teach him. This is his highest goal, this is his highest success, this is his highest world, this is his highest bliss. All other creatures live on a small portion of that bliss.

"If a man is healthy, wealthy, and lord of others, surrounded by all human enjoyments, that is the highest blessing of men. Now a hundred of these human blessings make one blessing of the fathers who have conquered the world (of the fathers). A hundred blessings of the fathers who have conquered this world make one blessing in the Gandharva world. A hundred blessings in the Gandharva world make one blessing of the Devas by merit (work, sacrifice), who obtain their godhead by merit. A hundred blessings of the Devas by merit make one blessing of the Devas by birth, also of a Srotriya who is without sin, and not overcome by desire. A hundred blessings of the Devas by birth make one blessing in the world of Pragapati, also of a Srotriya who is without sin, and not overcome by desire. A hundred blessings in the world of Pragapati make one blessing in the world of Brahman, also of a Srotriya who is without sin, and not overcome by desire. And this is the highest blessing.

"This is the Brahma-world, O king," thus spake Yagnavalkya.

Ganaka Vaideha said: "I give you, Sir, a thousand. Speak on for the sake of my emancipation."

Then Yagnavalkya was afraid lest the King, having become full of understanding, should drive him from all his positions.

And Yagnavalkya said: "That person, having enjoyed himself in that state of sleeping (dream), having moved about and seen both good and bad, hastens back again as he came, to the place from which he started, to the state of waking.

"Now as a heavy-laden carriage moves along groaning, thus does this corporeal Self, mounted by the intelligent Self, move along groaning, when a man is thus going to expire.

"And when the body grows weak through old age, or becomes weak through illness, at that time that person, after separating himself from his members, as an Amra (mango), or Udumbara (fig), or Pippala-fruit is separated from the stalk, hastens back again as he came, to the place from which he started, to new life.

"And as policemen, magistrates, equerries, and governors wait for a king who is coming back, with food and drink, saying, 'He comes back, he approaches,' thus do all the elements wait on him who knows this, saying, 'That Brahman comes, that Brahman approaches.'

"And as policemen, magistrates, equerries, and governors gather round a king who is departing, thus do all the senses (pranas) gather round the Self at the time of death, when a man is thus going to expire."

Yagnavalkya continued: "Now when that Self, having sunk into weakness, sinks, as it were, into unconsciousness, then gather those senses (pranas) around him, and he, taking with him those elements of light, descends into the heart. When that person in the eye turns away, then he ceases to know any forms.

" 'He has become one,' they say, 'he does not see.' 'He has

become one,' they say, 'he does not smell.' 'He has become one,' they say, 'he does not taste.' 'He has become one,' they say, 'he does not speak.' 'He has become one,' they say, 'he does not hear.' 'He has become one,' they say, 'he does not think.' 'He has become one,' they say, 'he does not touch.' 'He has become one,' they say, 'he does not know.' The point of his heart becomes lighted up, and by that light the Self departs, either through the eye, or through the skull, or through other places of the body. And when he thus departs, life (the chief prana) departs after him, and when life thus departs, all the other vital spirits (pranas) depart after it. He is conscious, and being conscious he follows and departs.

"Then both his knowledge and his work take hold of him, and his acquaintance with former things."

"And as a caterpillar, after having reached the end of a blade of grass, and after having made another approach to another blade, draws itself together towards it, thus does this Self, after having thrown off this body and dispelled all ignorance, and after making another approach to another body, draw himself together towards it.

"And as a goldsmith, taking a piece of gold, turns it into another, newer and more beautiful shape, so does this Self, after having thrown off this body and dispelled all ignorance, make unto himself another, newer and more beautiful shape, whether it be like the Fathers, or like the Gandharvas, or like the Devas, or like Pragapati, or like Brahman, or like other beings.

"That Self is indeed Brahman, consisting of knowledge, mind, life, sight, hearing, earth, water, wind, ether, light and no light, desire and no desire, anger and no anger, right or wrong, and all things. Now as a man is like this or like that, according as he acts and according as he behaves, so will he be—a man of good acts will become good, a man of bad acts, bad. He becomes pure by pure deeds, bad by bad deeds.

"And here they say that a person consists of desires. And as is his desire, so is his will; and as is his will, so is his deed; and whatever deed he does, that he will reap.

"And here there is this verse: 'To whatever object a man's own mind is attached, to that he goes strenuously together with his deed; and having obtained the end (the last results) of whatever deed he does here on earth, he returns again from that world (which is the temporary reward of his deed) to this world of action.'

"So much for the man who desires. But as to the man who does not desire, who, not desiring, freed from desires, is satisfied in his desires, or desires the Self only, his vital spirits do not depart elsewhere,—being Brahman, he goes to Brahman.

"On this there is this verse: 'When all desires which once entered his heart are undone, then does the mortal become immortal, then he obtains Brahman.'

"And as the slough of a snake lies on an ant-hill, dead and cast away, thus lies this body; but that disembodied immortal spirit (prana, life) is Brahman only, is only light."

Ganaka Vaideha said: "Sir, I give you a thousand."

"On this there are these verses:

"The small, old path stretching far away has been found by me. On it sages who know Brahman move on to the Svarga-loka (heaven), and thence higher on, as entirely free.

"On that path they say that there is white, or blue, or yellow, or green, or red; that path was found by Brahman, and on it goes whoever knows Brahman, and who has done good, and obtained splendour.

"All who worship what is not knowledge (avidya) enter into blind darkness: those who delight in knowledge, enter, as it were, into greater darkness.

"There are indeed those unblessed worlds, covered with blind darkness. Men who are ignorant and not enlightened go after death to those worlds.

"If a man understands the Self, saying, 'I am He,' what could he wish or desire that he should pine after the body.

"Whoever has found and understood the Self that has entered into this patched-together hiding-place, he indeed is the creator, for he is the maker of everything, his is the world, and he is the world itself.

"While we are here, we may know this; if not, I am ignorant, and there is great destruction. Those who know it, become immortal, but others suffer pain indeed.

"If a man clearly beholds this Self as God, and as the lord of all that is and will be, then he is no more afraid.

"He behind whom the year revolves with the days, him the gods worship as the light of lights, as immortal time.

"He in whom the five beings and the ether rest, him alone I believe to be the Self—I who know, believe him to be Brahman; I who am immortal, believe him to be immortal.

"They who know the life of life, the eye of the eye, the ear of the ear, the mind of the mind, they have comprehended the ancient, primeval Brahman.

"By the mind alone it is to be perceived, there is in it no diversity. He who perceives therein any diversity, goes from death to death.

"This eternal being that can never be proved, is to be perceived in one way only; it is spotless, beyond the ether, the unborn Self, great and eternal.

"Let a wise Brahmana, after he has discovered him, practise wisdom. Let him not seek after many words, for that is mere weariness of the tongue.

"And he is that great unborn Self, who consists of knowledge, is surrounded by the Pranas, the ether within the heart. In it there reposes the ruler of all, the lord of all, the king of all. He does not become greater by good works, nor smaller by evil works. He is the lord of all, the king of all things, the protector of all things. He is a bank and a boundary, so that these worlds may not be confounded. Brahmanas seek to know him by the study of the Veda, by sacrifice, by gifts, by penance, by fasting, and he who knows him, becomes a Muni. Wishing for that world for Brahman only, mendicants leave their homes.

"Knowing this, the people of old did not wish for offspring. What shall we do with offspring, they said, we who have this Self and this world of Brahman? And they, having risen above the desire for sons, wealth, and new worlds, wander about as mendicants. For desire for sons is desire for wealth.

and desire for wealth is desire for worlds. Both these are indeed desires only. He, the Self, is to be described by No, no! He is incomprehensible, for he cannot be comprehended; he is imperishable, for he cannot perish; he is unattached, for he does not attach himself; unfettered, he does not suffer, he does not fail. Him (who knows), these two do not overcome, whether he says that for some reason he has done evil, or for some reason he has done good—he overcomes both, and neither what he has done, nor what he has omitted to do, burns (affects) him.

"This has been told by a verse (*Rik*): 'This eternal greatness of the Brahmana does not grow larger by work, nor does it grow smaller. Let man try to find (know) its trace, for having found (known) it, he is not sullied by any evil deed.'

"He therefore that knows it, after having become quiet, subdued, satisfied, patient, and collected, sees self in Self, sees all as Self. Evil does not overcome him, he overcomes all evil. Evil does not burn him, he burns all evil. Free from evil, free from spots, free from doubt, he becomes a (true) Brahmana; this is the Brahma-world, O King"—thus spoke Yagnavalkya.

Ganaka Vaideha said: "Sir, I give you the Videhas, and also myself, to be together your slaves."

This indeed is the great, the unborn Self, the strong, the giver of wealth. He who knows this obtains wealth.

This great, unborn Self, undecaying, undying, immortal, fearless, is indeed Brahman. Fearless is Brahman, and he who knows this becomes verily the fearless Brahman.

From The Bhagavadgita

THE WAY TO PURITY

From *The Bhagavadgita*

THE WAY TO PURITY

Krishna, the "Blessed Lord," god of peace and salvation, is personified in *The Bhagavadgita* and speaks to the warrior Arguna on the importance of the denial of materialism and the affirmation of the spirit as the ultimate truth. The teachings in *The Bhagavadgita*, or "The Lord's Song," are basic in all Hindu religious belief. Written in the second century, B.C., during what is known as the Epic Period, these dialogues embody the Vedic wisdom and faith.

THE WAY TO PURITY

Sangaya said: "To him, who was overcome with pity, and dejected, and whose eyes were full of tears and turbid, the destroyer of Madhu spoke these words."

The Deity said: "How comes it that this delusion, O Arguna! which is discarded by the good, which excludes from heaven, and occasions infamy, has overtaken you in this place of peril? Be not effeminate, O son of Pritha! it is not worthy of you. Cast off this base weakness of heart, and arise, O terror of (your) foes!"

Arguna said: "How, O destroyer of Madhu! shall I encounter with arrows in the battle Bhishma and Drona—both, O destroyer of enemies! entitled to reverence? Not killing my preceptors—men of great glory—it is better to live even on alms in this world. But killing them, though they are avaricious of worldly goods, I should only enjoy blood-tainted enjoyments. Nor do we know which of the two is better for us—whether that we should vanquish them, or that they should vanquish us. Even those, whom having killed, we do not wish to live—even those sons of Dhritarashtra stand arrayed against us. With a heart contaminated by the taint of helplessness, with a mind confounded about my duty, I ask you. Tell me what is assuredly good for me. I am your disciple; instruct me, who have thrown myself on your indulgence. For I do not perceive what is to dispel that grief which will dry up my organs after I shall have obtained a prosperous kingdom on earth without a foe, or even the sovereignty of the gods."

Sangaya said: "Having spoken thus to Hrishikesa, O terror

of your foes! Gudakesa said to Govinda, 'I shall not engage in battle;' and verily remained silent. To him thus desponding between the two armies, O descendant of Bharata! Hrishikesa spoke these words with a slight smile."

The Deity said: "You have grieved for those who deserve no grief, and you talk words of wisdom. Learned men grieve not for the living nor the dead. Never did I not exist, nor you, nor these rulers of men; nor will any one of us ever hereafter cease to be. As in this body, infancy and youth and old age come to the embodied self, so does the acquisition of another body; a sensible man is not deceived about that. The contacts of the senses, O son of Kunti! which produce cold and heat, pleasure and pain, are not permanent, they are ever coming and going. Bear them, O descendant of Bharata! For, O chief of men! that sensible man whom they (pain and pleasure being alike to him) afflict not, he merits immortality. There is no existence for that which is unreal; there is no non-existence for that which is real. And the correct conclusion about both is perceived by those who perceive the truth. Know that to be indestructible which pervades all this; the destruction of that inexhaustible principle none can bring about. These bodies appertaining to the embodied self which is eternal, indestructible, and indefinable, are said to be perishable; therefore do engage in battle, O descendant of Bharata! He who thinks it to be the killer and he who thinks it to be killed, both know nothing. It kills not, is not killed. It is not born, nor does it ever die, nor, having existed, does it exist no more. Unborn, everlasting, unchangeable, and primeval, it is not killed when the body is killed. O son of Pritha! how can that man who knows it thus to be indestructible, everlasting, unborn, and inexhaustible, how and whom can he kill, whom can he cause to be killed? As a man, casting off old clothes, puts on others and new ones, so the embodied self casting off old bodies, goes to others and new ones. Weapons do not divide it into pieces; fire does not burn it; waters do not moisten it; the wind does not dry it up. It is not divisible; it is not combustible; it is not to be moistened; it is not to be dried up. It is everlasting, all-pervading, stable, firm, and eternal. It is said to be unperceived, to be unthinkable, to be unchangeable. Therefore knowing it to be such, you ought not to grieve. But even if you think that it is constantly born, and constantly dies, still, O you of mighty arms! you ought not to grieve thus. For to one that is born, death is certain; and to one that dies, birth is certain. Therefore about this unavoidable thing, you ought not to grieve. The source of things, O descendant of Bharata! is unperceived; their middle state is perceived; and their end again is unperceived. What occasion is there for any lamentation regarding them? One looks upon it as a wonder; another similarly speaks of it as a wonder; another too hears of it as a wonder; and even after having heard of it, no one does really know it. This embodied self, O descendant of Bharata! within every one's body is ever indestructible. Therefore you ought not to grieve for any being. Having regard to your own duty also, you ought not to falter, for there is nothing better for a Kshatriya than a righteous battle. Happy those Kshatriyas, O son of Pritha! who can find such a battle to fight—come of itself—an open door to heaven! But if you will not fight this righteous battle, then you will have abandoned your own duty and your frame, and you will incur sin. All beings, too, will tell of your everlasting infamy; and to one who has been honoured, infamy is a greater evil than death. Warriors who are masters of great cars will think that you abstained from the battle through fear, and having been highly thought of by them, you will fall down to littleness. Your enemies, too, decrying your power, will speak much about you that should not be spoken. And what, indeed, more lamentable than that? Killed, you will obtain heaven; victorious, you will enjoy the earth. Therefore arise, O son of Kunti! resolved to engage in battle. Looking alike on pleasure and pain, on gain and loss, on victory and defeat, then prepare for battle, and thus you will not incur sin. The knowledge here declared to you is that relating to the Sankhya. Now hear that relating to the Yoga. Possessed of this knowledge, O son of Pritha! you will cast off the bonds of action. In this path to final emancipation nothing that is commenced becomes abortive;

no obstacles exist; and even a little of this form of piety protects one from great danger. There is here, O descendant of Kuru! but one state of mind consisting in firm understanding. But the states of mind of those who have no firm understanding are many-branched and endless. The state of mind consisting in firm understanding regarding steady contemplation does not belong to those, O son of Pritha! who are strongly attached to worldly pleasures and power, and whose minds are drawn away by that flowery talk which is full of ordinances of specific acts for the attainment of those pleasures and that power, and which promises birth as the fruit of acts—(that flowery talk) which those unwise ones utter, who are enamoured of Vedic words, who say there is nothing else, who are full of desires, and whose goal is heaven. The Vedas merely relate to the effects of the three qualities; do you, O Arguna! rise above those effects of the three qualities, and be free from the pairs of opposites, always preserve courage, be free from anxiety for new acquisitions or protection of old acquisitions, and be self-controlled. To the instructed Brahmana, there is in all the Vedas as much utility as in a reservoir of water into which waters flow from all sides. Your business is with action alone; not by any means with fruit. Let not the fruit of action be your motive to action. Let not your attachment be fixed on inaction. Having recourse to devotion, O Dhanangaya! perform actions, casting off all attachment, and being equable in success or ill-success; such equability is called devotion. Action, O Dhanangaya! is far inferior to the devotion of the mind. In that devotion seek shelter. Wretched are those whose motive to action is the fruit of action. He who has obtained devotion in this world casts off both merit and sin. Therefore apply yourself to devotion; devotion in all actions is wisdom. The wise who have obtained devotion cast off the fruit of action; and released from the shackles of repeated births, repair to that seat where there is no unhappiness. When your mind shall have crossed beyond the taint of delusion, then will you become indifferent to all that you have heard or will hear. When your mind, confounded by what you have heard, will stand firm and steady in contemplation, then will you acquire devotion."

Arguna said: "What are the characteristics, O Kesava! of one whose mind is steady, and who is intent on contemplation? How should one of steady mind speak, how sit, how move?"

The Deity said: "When a man, O son of Pritha! abandons all the desires of his heart, and is pleased in his self only and by his self, he is then called one of steady mind. He whose heart is not agitated in the midst of calamities, who has no longing for pleasures, and from whom the feelings of affection, fear, and wrath have departed, is called a sage of steady mind. His mind is steady, who, being without attachments anywhere, feels no exultation and no aversion on encountering the various agreeable and disagreeable things of this world. A man's mind is steady, when he withdraws his senses from all objects of sense, as the tortoise withdraws its limbs from all sides. Objects of sense draw back from a person who is abstinent; not so the taste for those objects. But even the taste departs from him, when he has seen the Supreme. The boisterous senses, O son of Kunti! carry away by force the mind even of a wise man, who exerts himself for final emancipation. Restraining them all, a man should remain engaged in devotion, making me his only resort. For his mind is steady whose senses are under his control. The man who ponders over objects of sense forms an attachment to them; from that attachment is produced desire; and from desire anger is produced; from anger results want of discrimination; from want of discrimination, confusion of the memory; from confusion of the memory, loss of reason; and in consequence of loss of reason he is utterly ruined. But the self-restrained man who moves among objects with senses under the control of his own self, and free from affection and aversion, obtains tranquillity. When there is tranquillity, all his miseries are destroyed, for the mind of him whose heart is tranquil soon becomes steady. He who is not self-restrained has no steadiness of mind; nor has he who is not self-restrained perseverance in the pursuit of self-knowledge; there is no tranquillity for him who does not persevere in the pursuit of self-knowledge; and whence can there be happiness for one who is not tranquil? For the heart which follows the rambling senses leads away his judgment, as the wind leads a boat astray upon the waters. Therefore, O you of mighty arms! his mind is steady whose senses are restrained on all sides from objects of sense. The self-restrained man is awake, when it is night for all beings; and when all beings are awake, that is the night of the right-seeing sage. He into whom all objects of desire enter, as waters enter the ocean, which, though replenished, still keeps its position unmoved—he only obtains tranquillity; not he who desires those objects of desire. The man who, casting off all desires, lives free from attachments, who is free from egoism, and from the feeling that this or that is mine, obtains tranquillity. This, O son of Pritha! is the Brahmic state; attaining to this, one is never deluded; and remaining in it in one's last moments, one attains (brahma-nirvana) the Brahmic bliss."

Arguna said: "If, O Ganardana! devotion is deemed by you to be superior to action, then why, O Kesava! do you prompt me to this fearful action? You seem, indeed, to confuse my mind by equivocal words. Therefore, declare one thing determinately, by which I may attain the highest good."

The Deity said: "O sinless one! I have already declared, that in this world there is a twofold path—that of the Sankhyas by devotion in the shape of true knowledge; and that of the Yogins by devotion in the shape of action. A man does not attain freedom from action merely by not engaging in action; nor does he attain perfection by mere renunciation. For nobody ever remains even for an instant without performing some action; since the qualities of nature constrain everybody, not having free-will in the matter, to some action. The deluded man who, restraining the organs of action, continues to think in his mind about objects of sense, is called a hypocrite. But he, O Arguna! who restraining his senses by his mind, and being free from attachments, engages in devotion in the shape of action, with the organs of action, is far superior. Do you perform prescribed action, for action is better than inaction, and the support of your body, too, cannot be accomplished with inaction. This world is fettered by all action other than action for the purpose of the sacrifice. Therefore, O son of Kunti! do you, casting off attachment, perform action for that purpose. The Creator, having in olden times created men together with the sacrifice, said: 'Propagate with this. May it be the giver to you of the things you desire. Please the gods with this, and may those gods please you. Pleasing each other, you will attain the highest good. For pleased with the sacrifices, the gods will give you the enjoyments you desire. And he who enjoys himself without giving them what they have given, is, indeed, a thief.' The good, who eat the leavings of a sacrifice, are released from all sins. But the unrighteous ones, who prepare food for themselves only, incur sin. From food are born all creatures; from rain is the production of food; rain is produced by sacrifices; sacrifices are the result of action; know that action has its source in the Vedas; the Vedas come from the Indestructible. Therefore the all-comprehending Vedas are always concerned with sacrifices. He who in this world does not turn round the wheel revolving thus, is of sinful life, indulging his senses, and, O son of Pritha! he lives in vain. But the man who is attached to his self only, who is contented in his self, and is pleased with his self, has nothing to do. He has no interest at all in what is done, and none whatever in what is not done, in this world; nor is any interest of his dependent on any being. Therefore always perform action, which must be performed, without attachment. For a man, performing action without attachment, attains the Supreme. By action alone, did Ganaka and the rest work for perfection. And having regard also to the keeping of people to their duties you should perform action. Whatever a great man does, that other men also do. And people follow whatever he receives as authority. There is nothing, O son of Pritha! for me to do in all the three worlds, nothing to acquire which has not been acquired. Still I do engage in action. For should I at any time not engage without sloth in action, men would follow in my path from all sides, O son of Pritha! If I did not perform actions, these worlds would be destroyed, I should be the cause of caste-interminglings; and I should be ruining these people. As the ignorant act, O descendant of Bharata! with attachment to action, so should a wise man act without attachment, wishing to keep the people to their duties. A wise man should not shake the convictions of the ignorant who are attached to action, but acting with devotion himself should make them apply themselves to all action. He whose mind is deluded by egoism thinks himself the doer of the actions, which, in every way, are done by the qualities of nature. But he, O you of mighty arms! who knows the truth about the difference from qualities and the difference from actions, forms no attachments, believing that qualities deal with qualities. But those who are deluded by the qualities of nature form attachments to the actions of the qualities. A man of perfect knowledge should not shake these men of imperfect knowledge (in their convictions). Dedicating all actions to me with a mind knowing the relation of the supreme and individual self, engage in battle without desire, without any feeling that this or that is mine, and without any mental trouble. Even those men who always act on this opinion of mine, full of faith, and without carping, are released from all actions. But those who carp at my opinion and do not act upon it, know them to be devoid of discrimination, deluded as regards all knowledge, and ruined. Even a man of knowledge acts consonantly to his own nature. All beings follow nature. What will restraint effect? Every sense has its affections and aversions towards its objects fixed. One should not become subject to them, for they are one's opponents. One's own duty, though defective, is better than another's duty well performed. Death in performing one's own duty is preferable; the performance of the duty of others is dangerous."

Arguna said: "But by whom, O descendant of Vrishni! is man impelled, even though unwilling, and, as it were, constrained by force, to commit sin?"

The Deity said: "It is desire, it is wrath. born from the

quality of passion; it is very ravenous, very sinful. Know that that is the foe in this world. As fire is enveloped by smoke, a mirror by dust, the fœtus by the womb, so is this enveloped by desire. Knowledge, O son of Kunti! is enveloped by this constant foe of the man of knowledge, in the shape of desire, which is like a fire and insatiable. The senses, the mind, and the understanding are said to be its seat; with these it deludes the embodied self after enveloping knowledge. Therefore, O chief of the descendants of Bharata! first restrain your senses, then cast off this sinful thing which destroys knowledge and experience. It has been said, Great are the senses, greater than the senses is the mind, greater than the mind is the understanding. What is greater than the understanding is that. Thus knowing that which is higher than the understanding, and restraining yourself by yourself, O you of mighty arms! destroy this unmanageable enemy in the shape of desire."

The Deity said: "This everlasting system of devotion I declared to the sun, the sun declared it to Manu, and Manu communicated it to Ikshvaku. Coming thus by steps, it became known to royal sages. But, O terror of your foes! that devotion was lost to the world by long lapse of time. That same primeval devotion I have declared to you to-day, seeing that you are my devotee and friend, for it is the highest mystery."

Arguna said: "Later is your birth; the birth of the sun is prior. How then shall I understand that you declared this first?"

The Deity said: "I have passed through many births, O Arguna! and you also. I know them all, but you, O terror of your foes! do not know them. Even though I am unborn and inexhaustible in my essence, even though I am lord of all beings, still I take up the control of my own nature, and am born by means of my delusive power. Whensoever, O descendant of Bharata! piety languishes, and impiety is in the ascendant, I create myself. I am born age after age, for the protection of the good, for the destruction of evil-doers, and the establishment of piety. Whoever truly knows thus my divine birth and work, casts off this body and is not born again. He comes to me, O Arguna! Many from whom affection, fear, and wrath have departed, who are full of me, who depend on me, and who are purified by the penance of knowledge, have come into my essence. I serve men in the way in which they approach me. In every way, O son of Pritha! men follow in my path. Desiring the success of actions, men in this world worship the divinities, for in this world of mortals, the success produced by action is soon obtained. The fourfold division of castes was created by me according to the apportionment of qualities and duties. But though I am its author, know me to be inexhaustible, and not the author. Actions defile me not. I have no attachment to the fruit of actions. He who knows me thus is not tied down by actions. Knowing this, the men of old who wished for final emancipation, performed action. Therefore do you, too, perform action as was done by men of old in olden times. Even sages are confused as to what is action, what inaction. Therefore I will speak to you about action, and learning that, you will be freed from this world of evil. One must possess knowledge about action; one must also possess knowledge about prohibited action; and again one must possess knowledge about inaction. The truth regarding action is abstruse. He is wise among men, he is possessed of devotion, and performs all actions, who sees inaction in action, and action in inaction. The wise call him learned, whose acts are all free from desires and fancies, and whose actions are burnt down by the fire of knowledge. Forsaking all attachment to the fruit of action, always contented, dependent on none, he does nothing at all, though he engages in action. Devoid of expectations, restraining the mind and the self, and casting off all belongings, he incurs no sin, performing actions merely for the sake of the body. Satisfied with earnings coming spontaneously, rising above the pairs of opposites, free from all animosity, and equable on success or ill-success, he is not fettered down, even though he performs actions. The acts of one who is devoid of attachment, who is free, whose mind is fixed on knowledge, and who performs action for the purpose of the sacrifice are all destroyed. Brahman is the oblation; with Brahman as a sacrificial instrument it is offered up; Brahman is in the fire; and by Brahman it is thrown; and Brahman, too, is the goal to which he proceeds who meditates on Brahman in the action. Some devotees perform the sacrifice to the gods, some offer up the sacrifice by the sacrifice itself in the fire of Brahman. Others offer up the senses, such as the sense of hearing and others, in the fires of restraint; others offer up the objects of sense, such as sound and so forth, into the fires of the senses. Some again offer up all the operations of the senses and the operations of the life-breaths into the fire of devotion by self-restraint, kindled by knowledge. Others perform the sacrifice of wealth, the sacrifice of penance, the sacrifice of concentration of mind, the sacrifice of Vedic study, and of knowledge, and others are ascetics of rigid vows. Some offer up the upward life-breath into the downward life-breath, and the downward life-breath into the upper life-breath, and stopping up the motions of the upward and downward life-breaths, devote themselves to the restraint of the life-breaths. Others, who take limited food, offer up the life-breaths into the life-breaths. All of these, conversant with the sacrifice, have their sins destroyed by the sacrifice. Those who eat the nectar-like leavings of the sacrifice repair to the eternal Brahman. This world is not for those who perform no sacrifice, whence then the other, O best of the Kauravas! Thus sacrifices of various sorts are laid down in the Vedas. Know them all to be produced from action, and knowing this you will be released from the fetters of this world. The sacrifice of knowledge, O terror of your foes! is superior to the sacrifice of wealth, for action, O son of Pritha! is wholly and entirely comprehended in knowledge. That you should learn by salutation, question, and service. The men of knowledge who perceive the truth will teach knowledge to you. Having learnt that, O son of Pandu! you will not again fall thus into delusion; and by means of it, you will see all beings, without exception, first in yourself, and then in me. Even if you are the most sinful of all sinful men, you will cross over all trespasses by means of the boat of knowledge alone. As a fire well kindled, O Arguna! reduces fuel to ashes, so the fire of knowledge reduces all actions to ashes. For there is in this world no means of sanctification like knowledge, and that one perfected by devotion finds within one's self in time. He who has faith, whose senses are restrained, and who is assiduous, obtains knowledge. Obtaining knowledge, he acquires, without delay, the highest tranquillity. He who is ignorant and devoid of faith, and whose self is full of misgivings, is ruined. Not this world, not the next, nor happiness, is for him whose self is full of misgivings. Actions, O Dhanangaya! do not fetter one who is self-possessed, who has renounced action by devotion, and who has destroyed misgivings by knowledge. Therefore, O descendant of Bharata! destroy, with the sword of knowledge, these misgivings of yours which fill your mind, and which are produced from ignorance. Engage in devotion. Arise!"

Arguna said: "O Krishna! you praise renunciation of actions and also the pursuit (of them). Tell me determinately which one of these two is superior."

The Deity said: "Renunciation and pursuit of action are both instruments of happiness. But of the two, pursuit of action is superior to renunciation of action. He should be understood to be always an ascetic, who has no aversion and no desire. For, O you of mighty arms! he who is free from the pairs of opposites is easily released from all bonds. Children—not wise men—talk of sâñkhya and yoga as distinct. One who pursues either well obtains the fruit of both. The seat which the sâñkhyas obtain is reached by the yogas also. He sees truly who sees the sâñkhya and yoga as one. Renunciation, O you of mighty arms! is difficult to reach without devotion; the sage possessed of devotion attains Brahman without delay. He who is possessed of devotion, whose self is pure, who has restrained his self, and who has controlled his senses, and who identifies his self with every being, is not tainted though he performs actions. The man of devotion, who knows the truth, thinks he does nothing at all, when he sees, hears, touches, smells, eats, moves, sleeps, breathes, talks, throws out, takes, opens or closes the eyelids; he holds that the senses deal with the objects of the senses. He who, casting off all attachment, performs actions dedicating them to Brahman, is not tainted by sin, as the lotus-leaf is not tainted by water. Devotees, casting off attachment, perform actions for attaining purity of self, with the body, the mind, the understanding, or even the senses—all free from egoistic notions. He who is possessed of devotion, abandoning the fruit of actions, attains the highest tranquillity. He who is without devotion, and attached to the fruit of action, is tied down by reason of his acting in consequence of some desire. The self-restrained, embodied self lies at ease within the city of nine portals, renouncing all actions by the mind, not doing nor causing anything to be done. The Lord is not the cause of actions, or of the capacity of performing actions amongst men, or of the connexion of action and fruit. But nature only works. The Lord receives no one's sin, nor merit either. Knowledge is enveloped by ignorance, hence all creatures are deluded. But to those who have destroyed that ignorance by knowledge of the self, such knowledge, like the sun, shows forth that supreme principle. And those whose mind is centred on it, whose very self it is, who are thoroughly devoted to it, and whose final goal it is, go never to return, having their sins destroyed by knowledge. The wise look upon a Brahmana possessed of learning and humility, on a cow, an elephant, a dog, and a Svapaka, as alike. Even here, those have conquered the material world, whose mind rests in equability; since Brahman is free from defects and equable, therefore they rest in Brahman. He who knows Brahman, whose mind is steady, who is not deluded, and who rests in Brahman, does not exult on finding anything agreeable, nor does he grieve on finding anything disagreeable. One whose self is not attached to external objects, obtains the happiness that is in one's self; and by means of concentration of mind, joining one's self with the Brahman, one obtains indestructible happiness. For the enjoyments born of contact between senses and their objects are, indeed, sources of misery; they have a beginning as well as an end. O son of Kunti! a wise man feels no pleasure in them. He who even in this world, before his release from the body, is able to bear the agitations produced from desire and wrath, is a devoted man, he is a happy man. The devotee whose happiness is within himself, whose recreation is within himself, and whose light of knowledge also is within himself, becoming one with the Brahman, obtains the Brahmic bliss. The sages whose sins have perished, whose misgivings are destroyed, who are self-restrained, and who are intent on the welfare of all beings, obtain the Brahmic bliss. To the ascetics, who are free from desire and wrath, and whose minds are restrained, and who have knowledge of the self, the Brahmic bliss is on both sides of death. The sage who excludes from his mind external objects, concentrates the visual power between the brows, and making the upward and downward life-breaths even, confines their movements within the nose, who restrains senses, mind, and understanding, whose highest goal is final emancipation, from whom desire, fear, and wrath have departed, is, indeed, for ever released from birth and death. He knowing me to be the enjoyer of all sacrifices and penances, the great Lord of all worlds, and the friend of all beings, attains tranquillity."

The Deity said: "He who, regardless of the fruit of actions, performs the actions which ought to be performed, is the devotee and renouncer; not he who discards the sacred fires, nor he who performs no acts. Know, O son of Pandu! that what is called renunciation is devotion; for nobody becomes a devotee who has not renounced all fancies. To the sage who wishes to rise to devotion, action is said to be a means, and to him, when he has risen to devotion, tranquillity is said to be a means. When one does not attach oneself to objects of sense, nor to action, renouncing all fancies, then is one said to have risen to devotion. A man should elevate his self by his self; he should not debase his self, for even a man's own self is his friend, a man's own self is also his enemy. To him who has subjugated his self by his self, his self is a friend; but to him who has not restrained his self, his own self behaves inimically, like an enemy. The self of one who has subjugated his self and is tranquil, is absolutely concentrated on itself, in the midst of cold and heat, pleasure and pain, as well as honour and dishonour. The devotee whose self is contented with knowledge and experience, who is unmoved, who has restrained his senses, and to whom a sod, a stone, and gold are alike, is said to be devoted. And he is esteemed highest, who thinks alike about well-wishers, friends, and enemies, and those who are indifferent, and those who take part with both sides, and those who are objects of hatred, and relatives, as well as about the good and the sinful. A devotee should constantly devote his self to abstraction, remaining in a secret place, alone, with his mind and self restrained, without expectations, and without belongings. Fixing his seat firmly in a clean place, not too high nor too low, and covered over with a sheet of cloth, a deerskin, and blades of Kusa (grass)—and there seated on that seat, fixing his mind exclusively on one point, with the workings of the mind and senses restrained, he should practice devotion for purity of self. Holding his body, head, and neck even and unmoved, remaining steady, looking at the tip of his own nose, and not looking about in all directions, with a tranquil self, devoid of fear, and adhering to the rules of Brahmakarins, he should restrain his mind, and concentrate it on me, and sit down engaged in devotion, regarding me as his final goal. Thus constantly devoting his self to abstraction, a devotee whose mind is restrained, attains that tranquillity which culminates in final emancipation, and assimilation with me. Devotion is not his, O Arguna! who eats too much, nor his who eats not at all; not his who is addicted to too much sleep, nor his who is ever awake. That devotion which destroys all misery is his, who takes due food and exercise, who toils duly in all works, and who sleeps and awakes in due time. When a man's mind well restrained becomes steady upon the self alone, then he being indifferent to all objects of desire, is said to be devoted. As a light standing in a windless place flickers not, that is declared to be the parallel for a devotee, whose mind is restrained, and who devotes his self to abstraction. That mental condition, in which the mind restrained by practice of abstraction, ceases to work; in which too, one seeing the self by the self, is pleased in the self; in which one experiences that infinite happiness which transcends the senses, and which can be grasped by the understanding only; and adhering to which, one never swerves from the truth; acquiring which, one thinks no other acquisition higher than it; and adhering to which, one is not shaken off even by great misery; that should be understood to be called devotion in which there is a severance of all connexion with pain. That devotion should be practised with steadiness and with an undesponding heart. Abandoning, without exception, all desires, which are produced from fancies, and restraining the whole group of the senses on all sides by the mind only, one should by slow steps become quiescent, with a firm resolve coupled with courage; and fixing his mind upon the self, should think of nothing. Wherever the active and unsteady mind breaks forth, there one should ever restrain it, and fix it steadily on the self alone. The highest happiness comes to such a devotee, whose mind is fully tranquil, in whom the quality of passion has been suppressed, who is free from sin, and who is become one with the Brahman. Thus constantly devoting his self to abstraction, a devotee, freed from sin, easily obtains that supreme happiness—contact with the Brahman. He who has devoted his self to abstraction, by devotion, looking alike on everything, sees the self abiding in all beings, and all beings in the self. To him who sees me in everything, and everything in me, I am never lost, and he is not lost to me. The devotee who worships me abiding in all beings, holding that all is one, lives in me, however he may be living. That devotee, O Arguna! is deemed to be the best, who looks alike on pleasure or pain, whatever it may be, in all creatures, comparing all with his own pleasure or pain."

Arguna said: "I cannot see, O destroyer of Madhu! how the sustained existence is to be secured of this devotion by means of equanimity which you have declared—in consequence of fickleness. For, O Krishna! the mind is fickle, boisterous, strong, and obstinate; and I think that to restrain it is as difficult as (to restrain) the wind."

The Deity said: "Doubtless, O you of mighty arms! the mind is difficult to restrain, and fickle. Still, O son of Kunti! it may be restrained by constant practice and by indifference to worldly objects. It is my belief, that devotion is hard to obtain for one who does not restrain his self. But by one who is self-restrained and assiduous, it can be obtained through proper expedients."

Arguna said: "What is the end of him, O Krishna! who does not attain the consummation of his devotion, being not assiduous, and having a mind shaken off from devotion, though full of faith? Does he, fallen from both paths, go to ruin like a broken cloud, being, O you of mighty arms! without support, and deluded on the path leading to the Brahman? Be pleased, O Krishna! to entirely destroy this doubt of mine, for none else than you can destroy this doubt."

The Deity said: "O son of Pritha! neither in this world nor the next, is ruin for him; for, O dear friend! none who performs good deeds comes to an evil end. He who is fallen from devotion attains the worlds of those who perform meritorious acts, dwells there for many a year, and is afterwards born into a family of holy and illustrious men. Or he is even born into a family of talented devotees; for such a birth as that in this world is more difficult to obtain. There he comes into contact with the knowledge which belonged to him in his former body, and then again, O descendant of Kuru! he works for perfection. For even though reluctant, he is led away by the self-same former practice, and although he only wishes to learn devotion, he rises above the fruits of action laid down in the divine word. But the devotee working with great efforts, and cleared of his sins, attains perfection after many births, and then reaches the supreme goal. The devotee is esteemed higher than the performers of penances, higher even than the men of knowledge, and the devotee is higher than the men of action; therefore, O Arguna! become a devotee. And even among all devotees, he who, being full of faith, worships me, with his inmost self intent on me, is esteemed by me to be the most devoted."

From The Surangama Sutra

THE ESSENCE OF MIND

From *The Surangama Sutra*

THE ESSENCE OF MIND

To the Western mind the exposition of Buddhist ideas is frequently obscured by metaphysical locutions. Such expressions as "essence-mind," "all-inclusive unity," "the attainment of Nirvana" create for us problems of semantics as well as of philosophy which our own Greek and Anglican heritage rejects as incomprehensible or accepts as poetical and symbolic. *The Surangama Sutra*, written in Sanskrit about the first century, A.D., interprets the search by dialectical method for the meaning of ultimate reality as taught by Buddha.

THE ESSENCE OF MIND

When Ananda came into the presence of the Lord Buddha, he bowed down to the ground in great humanity, blaming himself that he had not yet fully developed the potentialities of Enlightenment, because from the beginning of his previous lives, he had too much devoted himself to study and learning. He earnestly pleaded with the Lord Buddha and with all the other Tathagatas from the ten quarters of the Universe, to support him in attaining perfect Enlightenment, that is, to support him in his practice of the Three Excellencies of Dhyana, Samadhi and Samapatti,[1] by some most fundamental and expedient means.

At the same time, all of the Bodhisattvas-Mahasattva, as numerous as the sands of the river Ganges, together with all the Arhats, Pratyaka-Buddhas, from all the ten quarters, with one accord and with gladness of heart, prepared to listen to the instruction to be given to Ananda by the Lord Buddha. With one accord they paid homage to the Lord and then resuming their seats, waited in perfect quietness and patience to receive the sacred teaching.

Then the Lord Buddha spoke to Ananda, saying:—Ananda, you and I are from the same ancestral blood and we have always cherished a fraternal affection for each other. Let me ask you a few questions and you answer me spontaneously and freely. When you first began to be interested in Buddhism what was it that impressed you in our Buddhist way of life and most influenced you to forsake all worldly pleasures and enabled you to cut asunder your youthful sexual cravings?

---

[1] *Dhyana*, meditation; *Samadhi*, a state of superconsciousness; *Samapatti*, a further state of heightened exaltation and spiritual powers.

Ananda replied:—Oh, my Lord! The first thing that impressed me were the thirty-two marks of excellency in my Lord's personality. They appeared to me so fine, as tender and brilliant, and transparent as a crystal.

From that time I have constantly thought about them and have been more and more convinced that these marks of excellence would be impossible for anyone who was not free from all sexual passion and desire. And why? Because when anyone becomes inflamed by sexual passion, his mind becomes disturbed and confused, he loses self-control and becomes reckless and crude. Besides, in sexual intercourse, the blood becomes inflamed and impure and adulterated with impure secretions. Naturally from such a source, there can never originate an aureole of such transcendently pure and golden brightness as I have seen emanating from the person of my Lord. It was because of this that I admired my Lord and it was this that influenced me to become one of thy true followers.

The Lord Buddha then said:—Very good, Ananda! All of you in this Great Dharma Assembly ought to know and appreciate that the reason why sentient beings by their previous lives since beginningless time have formed a succession of deaths and rebirths, life after life, is because they have never realized the true Essence of Mind and its self-purifying brightness. On the contrary they have been absorbed all the time busying themselves with their deluding and transient thoughts which are nothing but falsity and vanity. Hence they have prepared for themselves the conditions for this ever returning cycle of deaths and rebirths.

Ananda, if you are now desirous of more perfectly understanding Supreme Enlightenment and the enlightening nature of pure Mind-Essence, you must learn to answer questions spontaneously with no recourse to discriminating thinking. For the Tathagatas in the ten quarters of the universes have been delivered from the ever returning cycle of deaths and rebirths by this same single way, namely, by reliance upon their intuitive minds.

It is because of the straight-forwardness of their minds and the spontaneity of their mentations that the Tathagatas have ever remained, from beginningless time to endless time, of one pure Suchness, undisturbed by any complexity within their minds nor any rising thoughts of discrimination.

Then the Lord Buddha said:—Ananda, I want to question you; please listen carefully. You have just said that at the time your faith in me was awakened, that it was due to seeing the thirty-two marks of excellence. Let me ask you: What was it that gave you the sensation of seeing? What was it that experienced the sensation? And who was it that experienced the feeling of being pleased?

Ananda replied:—My Lord! At the time I experienced the sensation of being pleased, it was both through my eyes and my mind. When my eyes saw my Lord's excellencies, my mind immediately experienced a feeling of being pleased. It was then that I made up my mind to become thy disciple so that I might be delivered from the cycle of deaths and re-births.

The Lord said:—From what you have just said, Ananda, your feeling of being pleased originated in your eyes and mind. But if you do not know where lies the perception of sight and where the activities of the mind originate, you will never be able to subjugate your worldly attachments and con-taminations. It is like a king whose city was pestered by rob-bers and who tried to put an end to the thieving but was unsuccessful because he could not locate the secret hiding place of the robbers. So it is in the lives of human beings who are always being troubled by worldly attachments and con-taminations, causing their perception of sight to become in-verted and unreliable and seducing their thoughts and causing them to wander about ignorantly and uncontrolled. Ananda, let me ask you? Referring to your eyes and mind, do you know their secret hiding place?

Ananda replied:—Noble Lord! In all the ten different or-ders of life, the eyes are in the front of the face, as are my Lord's clear lotus eyes, and mine also. The same is true of the other sense organs, they are on the surface of the body, but the mind is hidden within the body.

The Lord Buddha interrupted:—Ananda, you are now sitting in the lecture hall, are you not? And when you are looking out to the Jetavana Grove, can you tell me where the hall and the grove are situated?

Certainly, my Lord. This quiet and splendid lecture hall and the Jetavana Grove are both situated in Anathapindika's beautiful park.

Now, Ananda, what do you see first, the people in this hall or the park outside?

I first see my Lord, then I see the noble audience, and other things in turn, and only afterward do I see the grove and the lovely park outside.

True, Ananda! Now tell me, while you are looking outside at the grove and park, what is it that enables you to distinguish the different views that your eyes see?

Noble Lord! It is because the windows and doors of the lecture hall are open wide. That is why I can see the distant views from inside the hall.

Then the Blessed Lord, in view of the great audience, reached out his golden hand and softly stroked Ananda's head, at the same time speaking to both him and the great assembly, saying:—

There is a particular Samadhi called, The Highest Samadhi, which was the Lord Buddha's Crowning Experience, and by it he attained a perfect realization of all manifestations and transformations. It was a wonderful door that opened to the mysterious Path that all the Tathagatas of all the ten quarters of all the universes have followed. It is of this Highest Samadhi that I am going to speak. Listen very carefully.

Then Ananda and the great audience bowed to the ground in deep adoration and then resumed their seats and waited humbly for the Master's solemn teaching.

The Lord Buddha then addressed Ananda and the great assembly, saying:—

Ananda, you have just said that from the inside of the lecture hall you can look out to the grove and the distant park because the windows and doors are open wide. It is possible that there are some within this very audience that only see these outside things and who are unable to see the Lord Tathagata within.[1]

Ananda interrupted:—But my Lord, how can it be that anyone in this hall who can see the grove and streams without can fail to see the Lord within?

It does seem absurd, Ananda, but it is just that way with you. You say that your mind exists within your body and that it is quite clear of all obstructions, but if this clear mind really exists within your body, then you ought to see the inside of your body first of all. But there are no sentient beings who can do this, that is, see both the inside and outside of their bodies. Though they may not see all the inside things—such as the heart, stomach, liver, kidneys, etc.—but at least they ought to see the growth of the finger-nails, the lengthening of the hair, the knotting of the sinews, the throbbing of the pulse. If the mind is within the body, why does it not see these things? But if the mind is within the body and can not see the things within, how can it see the things without the body? So you must see that what you have said about the perceiving mind, abiding within the body, is untrue.

With a respectful bow, Ananda said to the Lord:—Listening to the words of my Lord, I begin to realize that my mind, after all, may be outside my body. It may be like a lamp. If the lamp is within the room, it will certainly illumine the room first and then shining through the open door and windows will illumine the yard outside. If it was like that, why is it that one seeing only outside objects does not see the things within? It must be that the mind is like a lamp placed outside of a room, for then it would be dark within. If one can clearly understand what his mind is, he would no longer be puzzled, but would have the same intelligence and understanding that the Buddhas have. Would it not be so, my Lord?

The Lord replied:—Ananda, this morning all of the Bhikshus followed me to the city of Sravasti begging for food in

---

[1] Here it is particularly clear that "Buddha" is not a particular god, but is that indefinable entity or state of perfect wisdom achieved by the godly

regular order and afterwards all returned to this Grove. I was fasting at the time, but the others ate the food. What think you, Ananda? If only one of the Bhikshus ate the food, would the others be satisfied of their hunger?

Ananda replied:—No, my Lord, and why? Because, although all of these Bhikshus are Arahats, yet their physical bodies are individually separated. How could it be, that one Bhikshu eating, could satisfy the hunger of all?

The Lord Buddha replied:—Ananda if your perceiving, understanding mind is really outside your body, then what the mind perceives could not be felt by the body, and what the body feels could not be perceived by the mind. Look at my hand, Ananda. When your eyes are looking at it, does your mind make any discriminations about it?

Yes, my Lord, it makes discriminations.

The Lord continued:—But if your mind and body are in mutual correspondence, how can it possibly be said, that the mind exists outside the body? Therefore, Ananda, you ought to know that what you have just said about the mind existing outside the body is impossible.

Then Ananda said:—According to what my Lord says, the perceiving mind does not exist within the body because it does not see the things within, neither does it exist outside the body, because the mind and body are in mutual correspondence and therefore cannot be isolated from each other. Yet it seems to be that the perceiving mind must be in some locality.

Then the Lord Buddha questioned Ananda further:—But Ananda, where is its abiding place?

Ananda replied:—My Lord, since this perceiving mind cannot know the inside of its own body, but can see outside objects, it seems to me now, that it must be concealed in the sense organ itself. It may be like a man covering his eyes with a crystal bowl; though his eyes are covered yet there is no hindrance to his sight—the eye can still see clearly and make distinctions as usual. The reason that it does not see the inside of the body is because it is a part of the organ of the eye, and the reason it can see outside objects clearly is because it is hidden in the organ of the eye.

But, Ananda, you have just said that this perceiving mind concealed within the organ of the eye is like a crystal bowl covering the eyes. Now suppose a man has covered his eyes with a crystal bowl, but is still able to see outer objects such as mountains, rivers, etc., tell me, does he see the crystal bowl, also?

Yes, my Lord, while the man is covering his eyes with the crystal bowl, he sees the crystal bowl, also.

The Lord said:—Ananda, if your mind is just the same as the crystal bowl covering the eyes, why does your mind, while seeing the outside mountains and rivers, not see your own eyes, too? Or, supposing your mind does see your eyes, then your eyes will be regarded as any other objective thing and they will no longer be regarded as a dependent organ. Or, if the mind cannot see everything, then how can it be said of the perceiving mind, that it is concealed within the organ of the eyes in the resemblance of a crystal bowl covering the eyes? Therefore, Ananda, what you have asserted, that this perceiving mind is concealed within the organ of the eyes like a crystal bowl covering the eyes, is impossible also.

Then Ananda said to the Lord Buddha:—Honored of the worlds! It may be like this:—As all sentient beings have their intestines inside the body and the opening outside the body, the intestines are hidden to their sight but the opening is visible. While I am standing before you and open my eyes, I see your brightness—this means to see the outside. When my eyes are closed, I see the hiddenness—this means to see the inside.

The Lord interrupted:—Ananda, when you close your eyes, you say you see the hiddenness, but this hidden condition, is it in an opposing direction to your eyes, or is it not? If it is directly opposed to your eyes, then the hiddenness must be in front of your eyes and then it cannot be thought of as a part of your inside. Or suppose it is meant as part of your inside, then when in any dark room, without the light of any such thing as sun, moon, or lamp, the whole dark space of the room might be regarded as your intestines or your heart. Or, if it is in a direction not opposite to your eyes, then how does it happen that the sight of your eyes is being affected at all?

Or, if you put aside this outside perception of sight and say that it is to be regarded as being in an inside opposite direction to your eyes, so that when you shut your eyes, you see darkness only, which would mean to see your inside body. But when you open your eyes and see the brightness, why do you not see your own face, also? If you do not see your own face, it would mean that the face is not in an inside opposite direction to your eyes. Or, supposing you can see your own face, then both this perceiving mind and the organ of sight must be in the open space, or they can no longer be thought of as being in an inside opposite direction.

If your perceptive mind is supposed to be in the open space, naturally it cannot belong to the body, and then, when the Lord Tathagata is in sight of your face which would mean that he is a part of your body, your eyes will, of course, get the perception, but the other parts of your body could not get into consciousness at the same time.

Or, if you persistently claim that the body and the eyes have each a separate consciousness, then there would be two perceiving minds, which would mean that your single personality would see two Buddhas. Therefore you should understand that it is utterly absurd for you to say that to see into the dimness of the eyes is the same as seeing into the inside of the body.

Then Ananda said to the Lord Buddha:—I have constantly learned from the instruction of my Lord and from the teaching of all four classes of Thy disciples that all the existences of phenomena are simply the manifestation of the mind itself and vice versa that all the existences of mind are the manifestation of phenomena. Now it seems to me that this thinking mind is really the essence of my mind, and that wherever it happens to meet outer objects, there is a manifestation of mind. That is, the perceiving mind is neither inside, nor outside, nor between the body.

The Lord interrupted, saying:—What you are just saying—that all the manifestations of thought are simply meant as all the existences of phenomena and that wherever the mind happens to meet outer objects, there is its manifestations. But if your mind has no substantiality of its own, how can it meet any outer objects? Or, if it should be that in spite of the mind having no substantiality of its own, it might happen to meet outer objects, then there would be another newly assumed datum of nineteen spheres of mentation, namely, the six objects, the six sense organs, the six perceptions, plus this newly assumed normality of thought considered as a "thing in itself." And then there must be assumed a new datum of seven objects,—the object of sight, the object of hearing, of smelling, of tasting, of touching, of the unified object of thought, plus this outer "thing of itself." No, your suggestion is by no means the right interpretation.

Ananda, your interpretation that the perceiving mind has a substantiality of its own at the point where the object and thought meet, would put fetters to your mind, like putting fetters to your hands and feet. Let me ask you in this way: does your mental consciousness arise within or without your body? If it arises within, you should be able to know the inside of your body; if it comes from outside your body, you should be able to first see your own face.

Ananda replied:—My Lord! I see with my eyes and I perceive with my mind. That does not mean that they are interchangeable.

The Lord Buddha continued:—Ananda, if your eyes can see by themselves, then supposing you are within a room, can the door share the perception of seeing? If the door shares with the eyes this perception of seeing, then all dead bodies that still have eye organs intact, should continue to see things. If they can still perceive, how can it be said that they are dead bodies.

Ananda, if we grant that your perceiving mind has some

kind of substantiality, is it one body or many bodies? Is it located in one place in your body or is it distributed all over the body? If it is one body, then if you bind one limb the others will feel bound. If they all feel bound, then there can be no sure knowledge of the exact place of the binding. Or, if the perception of being bound is located in one place, then the perceiving mind cannot be considered as one localized body. Or if the perceiving mind is considered to be many bodies or involved in many bodies, it would mean that there must be as many personalities, and the question would arise, which of these localized perceiving minds rightly belongs to you. Or if your mind is considered as being uniformally distributed over all parts of your body, then if your limb was tightly bound, then the whole body would feel the suffering. Or if not uniformally distributed, but only on some parts of the body, then if you touch your head and at the same touch your feet, one would know it and the other would not. We know that this is not so. Therefore, Ananda, you must see that your suggestion that wherever the mind happens to meet outer objects, there is localized a manifestation of mind is unreasonable.

Then Ananda said to the Lord Buddha:—Now I recall hearing my Lord Buddha say, at a time when he was teaching Brother Manjusri and other princes of the Dharma, that the mind neither abides inside nor outside the body. It seems to me, if it is inside and we cannot see the inside, and if it was outside we ought not to feel the outside. We know that we cannot see the inside of the body, so it must mean that the mind is not abiding inside the body; it must mean that in some way our mind and body are in mutual correspondence with each other through the faculty of perception, and that would mean that it is not abiding outside the body. Now, My Lord, I see that since our mind and body are in mutual correspondence and yet we cannot see the inside of our body, it must be that the perceiving understanding mind must be abiding between these things.

The Lord Buddha resumed:—Ananda, now you think that the mind must be abiding between somethings. Let us consider it. If it is abiding between somethings, there must be some particular place where it is abiding. We can not conceive of an indefinite abiding place. Now Ananda, supposing you guess between what things it is located. Is it located between outside things and our bodies? Then it would be on the surface of the body and could not mean any place within the body. If it is located between parts of our body, then it would be within the body. Or, if it is between external things, what is its standard of direction? Suppose we take the case of a man: if he is standing between things looking toward the east, he must be standing in the west; or if he is looking toward the west, he must be standing in the east; or if he is looking toward the south, he must be standing in the north. If the mind is between things but has no standard of direction, it is the same as saying that it has no existence; or even if it has some standard of direction, there can be no certainty about it (if by just turning he can be either in east or west or north or south). If the standard is uncertain, the mind will be confused naturally.

Ananda replied:—What I said of the mind being "between somethings," is not meant in that sense. On one occasion my Lord has said:—"As causal conditions, eyes and sights are mutually attracted," but there must be something that is manifested in the consciousness that is dependent upon the eyes. That is what I meant by the mind being "between somethings." The eyes note discriminations while objects and sights are insensible things. As consciousness develops between them, the conceiving mind must be localized between them.

The Lord Buddha interrupted, saying:—Ananda, if it is stated that the mind is existing between the sense organ and the object, then, let me ask, is the essence of mind separated into two parts or not? If it is, the object and essential mind will be confusingly mingled, and as the object can not be exactly the same as essential mind which possesses the consciousness, they must be opposite to each other. How then can you say, that the mind exists between them?

If the statement that the mind is separated into two parts

has no ground, then the statement that the insensible object is imperceptive, means just the same as saying that it has no essence itself and must be, therefore, imperceptible. So the expression "between somethings," has no meaning. Therefore, Ananda, you must admit that the statement that the mind exists between somethings, is an absurd statement that is incapable of interpretation.

Ananda then addressed the Lord Buddha, saying:—Noble Lord! Some time ago when my Lord was discussing the intrinsic Dharma with the four great Bodhisattva-Mahasattvas, Maudgalyayana, Subhuti, Purna, and Sariputra, I overheard my Lord to say, that the essence of the discerning, perceiving, conscious mind existed neither inside nor outside, nor between, in fact, that it had no location of existence. Since my Lord has interpreted this in his teachings just now, I have ceased to grasp any arbitrary conception as to the location of mind, but if this is true, and it is something intangible, in what sense can it be thought of as "my mind."

The Lord Buddha replied:—Ananda, as to what you have just said that the essence of the discerning, perceptive, conscious mind has no definite location anywhere, the meaning is clear; it is neither in this world, in the vast open spaces, neither in water, nor on land, neither flying with wings, nor walking, nor is it anywhere. But when you say that your mind no longer grasps any arbitrary conception of the existence of the phenomena of mind, what do you mean by it? Do you mean that the phenomena have no true existence, or that they have no tangible existence? If you mean that they have no true existence, that would mean that they are like hair on a tortoise, or like horns on a rabbit. But so long as you retain this notion of not grasping, you cannot mean perfect non-existence. But what do you mean? Of course if your mind is perfectly blank, it must mean, as far as you are concerned, absolute non-existence, but if you are still cherishing some arbitrary conception of phenomena, you must mean some kind of existence. How is it then, that so long as the notion of not-grasping of anything, as for instance, the notion of "my mind," that you mean its non-existence? Therefore.

Ananda, you ought to see that what you have just said concerning the non-existence of anything just because you no longer cherish a conception of it within your mind, and that would mean the non-existence of a discerning, perceptive, conscious mind, would be quite absurd, would it not?

Thereupon, Ananda rose from his place in the midst of the assembly, adjusted his ceremonial scarf, knelt upon his right knee, placed the palms of his hands together, and respectfully addressed the Lord Buddha, saying:—

My Noble Lord! I have the honor of being thy youngest relative and thou hast always treated me with affectionate kindness. Although I am now only one of your many converts, thou dost still continue to show thy affection for me. But in spite of all I have gained mentally, I have not become liberated from contaminations and attachments and consequently I could not overcome the magic spell at the home of a harlot. My mind became confused and I was at the point of drowning in its defilement. I can see now that it was wholly due to my ignorance as to the right realization of what is true and essential Mind. I pray thee, Oh my Lord, to have pity and mercy upon me and show me the right Path to the spiritual graces of the Samapatti so that I may attain to self-mastery and become emancipated from the lure of evil myself, and be able to free all heretics from the bonds of their false ideas and craft.

When Ananda had finished his plea, he bowed humbly before the Lord Buddha, with hands and forehead touching the ground, and the whole audience, awed into intense excitement, waited with earnest and reverential hearts for the response of the Blessed One.

Suddenly in the Meditation Hall, filled with its awed and expectant throng, there appeared a most marvelous sight that transcended everything that had ever been seen before. The Hall was filled with a radiant splendor that emanated from the moon-like face of the Blessed One, like hundreds of thousands of sunbeams scintillating everywhere, and wherever the rays reached immediately there were seen celestial Buddha-lands. Moreover, the person of the Lord Buddha was vibrant with the six transcendental motions simultaneously manifesting and embracing all the Buddha-lands of the ten quarters of all the universes, as numerous as the finest particles of dust in the sunlight. And this all-embracing, blessed and transcendent glory united all these innumerable Buddha-lands into one single whole, and all the great Bodhisattvas of all these innumerable Buddha-lands were seen to be each in his own place with hands raised and pressed together expectantly waiting for the words of the Blessed One.

Then the Lord Buddha addressed the assembly, saying:—Ananda, from beginningless time, from life to life, all sentient beings have had their disturbing illusions that have been manifested in their natural development each under the conditioning power of his own individual karma, such as the seed-pod of the okra which when opening always drops three seeds in each group. The reason why all devoted disciples do not at once attain to supreme enlightenment is because they do not realize two primary principles and because of it some attain only to Arhatship, or to Pratyakaship, and some to even lower attainments, to the state of devas and heretics, and some to Mara kings and their dependents. The reason for these great differences is because, not knowing these two basic principles, they become confused in mind and fall into wrong practices. It is as if they were trying to cook fine delicacies by boiling stones or sand, which of course they could never do if they tried for countless kalpas.

What are these two fundamental principles, Ananda? The First Fundamental Principle is the primary cause of the succession of deaths and rebirths from beginningless time. [It is the Principle of Ignorance, the outgoing principle of individuation, manifestation, transformation, succession and discrimination.] From the working out of this Principle there has resulted the various differentiation of minds of all sentient beings, and all the time they have been taking these limited and perturbed and contaminated minds to be their true and natural Essence of Mind.

The Second Fundamental Principle is the primary cause of the pure unity of Enlightenment and Nirvana that has existed from beginningless time. [It is the Principle of integrating compassion, the in-drawing, unifying principle of purity, harmony, likeness, rhythm, permanency and peace.] By the in-drawing of this Principle within the brightness of your own nature, its unifying spirit can be discovered and developed and realized under all varieties of conditions. The reason why this unifying spirit is so quickly lost amongst the conditions is because you so quickly forget the brightness and purity of your own essential nature, and amid the activities of the day, you cease to realize its existence. That is why, Ananda, you and all sentient beings have fallen through ignorance into misfortune and into different realms of existence.

Now, Ananda, you wish to know the right road to Samapatti, so as to escape from the cycle of deaths and rebirths. Is it not so, Ananda? Then let me ask you some more questions. The Lord Tathagata raised one of his arms with hand and fingers clenched, saying:—Ananda, do you see this?

Yes, I see it, my Lord.

What do you see, Ananda?

I see my Lord raising one of his arms with hand clenched and its brightness blinds my eyes and warms my heart.

With what do you see it, Ananda?

I see it with my eyes, of course.

Then the Lord Buddha said:—Ananda, you have just answered me by saying that when the Tathagata by clenching his fingers made a shining fist, that its brightness shone into your eyes and warmed your heart. Very good. Now I will ask you:—While my fist is shining brightly and while you are looking at it closely, what is it that reveals the existence of your mind?

Ananda replied:—You are now asking me about the existence of my mind. To answer that question I must use my thinking and reasoning faculty to search and find an answer.

Yes, now I understand. This thinking and reasoning being is what is meant as "my mind."

The Lord Buddha rebuked Ananda sharply and said:—Surely that is nonsense, to assert that your being is your mind.

Ananda stood up with hands pressed together and said with astonishment:—Why, my Lord, if my being is not my mind, what else can be my mind?

The Lord Buddha replied:—The notion that your being is your mind is simply one of the false conceptions that arises from reflecting about the relations of yourself and outside objects, and which obscures your true and essential Mind. It is because, since from beginningless time down to the present life, you have been constantly misunderstanding your true and essential Mind. It is like treating a petty thief as your own son. By so doing you have lost consciousness of your original and permanant Mind and because of it have been forced to undergo the sufferings of successive deaths and rebirths.

Ananda, in dismay and confusion, said to the Lord:—I am your beloved cousin and owing to my appreciation of your marks of excellence, you have permitted me to become your disciple. So, in regard to my mind, it is not simply that my mind has offered adoration to my Lord Tathagata, but it has also offered praise to all the Buddhas and learned Masters of all the innumerable Buddha-lands. More than that, it is my mind that has been attempting all manner of difficult practices with great resolution and courage. These are all activities of my mind as well as of myself. How can they be separated? Even my evil acts of slandering the Dharma, neglecting good practices, these also are activities of my mind as well as of myself. Myself is my mind. If these acts can be shown to be not the activities of my mind, then I would be mindless, just like any other image made from a log or from earth. Oh, if I should give up my perceptions and consciousness, there would be nothing left that could be regarded as my self or as my mind. What do you mean, my Lord, when you say that my being is not my mind? As you can see, I am astonished and confused. And this audience, they are also in doubt. Pray have mercy upon us all and explain yourself clearly for we are only ignorant disciples.

Thereupon the Blessed Lord laid his hand affectionately upon the head of Ananda and proceeded to explain the true and Essence nature of Mind, desiring to awaken in them a consciousness of that which transcended phenomena. He explained to them how necessary it was to keep the mind free from all discriminating thoughts of self and not-self if they were to correctly understand it.

He continued:—Ananda and all my Disciples! I have always taught you that all phenomena and their developments are simply manifestations of mind. All causes and effects, from great universes to the fine dust only seen in the sunlight come into apparent existence only by means of the discriminating mind. If we examine the origin of anything in all the universe, we find that it is but a manifestation of some primal essence. Even the tiny leaves of herbs, knots of thread, everything, if we examine them carefully we find that there is some essence in its originality. Even open space is not nothingness. How can it be then that the wonderful, pure, tranquil and enlightened Mind, which is the source of all conceptions of manifested phenomena, should have no essence of itself.

If you must niggardly grasp this perceptive mind of discriminating consciousness that is dependent upon the different sense organs as being the same as Essential Mind, then the discriminative mind would have to forsake all those activities responding to any kind of form, sight, sound. odor, taste, touch, and seek for another and more perfect self-nature. You are now listening to my teaching and your minds are making discriminations by means of the sounds rising from my speaking, but when the sounds cease and all the perceptions arising from the sounds come to an end, still the mind goes on discriminating the memory of those sounds and you find it difficult to keep your mind in emptiness and tranquillity. This does not mean that I am instructing you not to grasp at these following activities, but I am instructing you to study their nature more closely. If your mind, after the object is removed from sight, still has its discriminating nature, does it necessarily mean that your discriminating mind has lost its substantiality? Does it not rather mean that you are now discriminating merely the shadows and reflections of unreal things which had their origin in objects in the presence of your sight? Objects certainly are not permanent; as they vanish, does your mind vanish, also, and become like hair on a tortoise, or a horn on a rabbit? If mind vanishes, then the Dharmakaya would be exterminated and who would be devoted to the practice of attaining perseverence in getting rid of the developments arising from the conceptions of phenomena? At this, Ananda and the great audience became more confused and speechless.

The Lord Buddha continued:—Ananda, if in this world disciples practiced meditation assiduously, though they attained all the nine stages of calmness in Dhyana, yet do not accomplish the attainment of Arhats free from the intoxicants arising from worldly contaminations and attachments, it is wholly due to their grasping this deceiving conception of discriminative thinking that is based on unrealities and mistaking the delusion as being a reality. Ananda, although you have learned a great deal, you are not yet ready for the maturity of Buddhahood.

When Ananda heard this solemn teaching, he became very sorrowful and with tears falling, with forehead, hands and feet touching the ground, he paid homage to the Lord. Then kneeling, he said:—

Noble Lord! Since I determined to follow thee and become thy disciple, I have always thought that I could rely upon thy supernormal strength and that it would not be difficult to put thy teachings into practice. I expected that the Lord would favor me with an experience of Samadhi in this body; I did not appreciate that the body and mind were different and could not be substituted for each other, so I have likely lost my own mind. Although I have become a disciple of Buddha, my heart is not yet absorbed in Enlightenment. I am like a prodigal son who has forsaken his father. I now see that in spite of my learning, if I am not able to put it into practice, I am no better than an unlearned man. It is like a man talking about food, but never eating and becoming satisfied. We are all entangled in these two hindrances: knowledge and learning, and vexation and suffering. I can now see that it is all due to our ignorance of the eternal and tranquil nature of true Mind. Pray, my Lord Tathagata, have mercy upon us all; show us clearly the mysterious, enlightening Mind, and open our true eye of Enlightenment.

Suddenly from the holy symbol on the breast of the Lord Tathagata, there shown forth a glorious, blazing brightness, which radiated forth brilliantly into hundreds and thousands of colored rays reaching to the ten quarters of the universes, which were instantly turned into innumerable Buddha-lands, and glorified all the holy shrines of the Tathagata, in all the ten quarters of the universes. And, finally, the scintillating splendor returned to rest on the crown of Ananda and upon the crown of each one in the assembly.

Then the Lord Buddha addressed Ananda, saying:—For the sake of all I will lift the luminous beacon of the Dharma so that by its light all sentient beings may realize the wonderful, mysterious nature of the pure enlightening Mind and acquire its true intrinsic Eye.

First, let me question you, Ananda. You saw my fist and it seemed bright to you. By what means did its brightness manifest itself? By what means was it seen, and by what means was the thought of brightness conceived?

Ananda replied:—My Lord, the brightness comes from the whole luminous body of my Lord which is as brightly shining as a valley filled with rubies. Your holy body, shining as it does, could not have originated except from Purity itself. Your hand being clenched was in the form of a fist. I saw it with my eyes, my mind conceived its brightness.

The Buddha said:—You say that it takes the movement of my fingers and the seeing of your eyes to give you the conception of a fist. Does that mean that the nature of the movement of the fingers and the seeing of the eyes and the thinking of the mind are all alike?

Ananda replied:—Yes, my Lord. If you had no hand, or I had no eyes, there could be no conception of a fist. There must be the meeting of the two conditions.

The Lord Buddha interrupted:—You state that the movement of the hand and the seeing of the eyes being in agreement, the mind conceives a fist. Is that wholly true? If a man loses his hand he loses it forever, but if a man loses his eyes, he does not wholly lose the sense of sight, nor does he lose the conception of a fist. Suppose you meet a blind man on the road and you ask him, "In your blindness, what do you see?" He will give you some such answer as this:—"I can only see darkness, nothing else." This means that the objects within the range of his former sight have become darkened; there is no loss of his conception of sight but the conception is of darkness.

Ananda asked:—My Lord, if the blind man can only perceive darkness, how can it mean that he still possesses the perception of sight?

The Buddha replied:—Ananda, this blind man of no eyes simply sees darkness just as any seeing man who is shut up in a dark room sees darkness. Close your eyes, Ananda, what do you perceive but darkness?

Ananda had to admit that as far as perceiving darkness was concerned there was no difference between the blind man, the man in a dark room and himself with his eyes closed.

The Buddha resumed:—If the blind man seeing only darkness suddenly recovers his sight and again sees objects, we say that he sees them by means of his eyes. A lamp is suddenly brought into the dark room and we say that the man again sees objects by means of the lamp. That is not strictly true for while the lamp does reveal objects, it is the eyes that perceive them. If it were otherwise and the seeing belonged to the lamp then it would no longer be a lamp and the seeing would have no relation to him. In a true sense, however, it is neither the lamp nor the eyes that perceives objects.

Although this was the second instruction that Ananda had

had on this subject, he did not yet understand it and sat dazed hoping for a clearer interpretation of it in the kind and gentle tones of the Master and he waited with a pure and expectant heart for the Blessed One's further explanation.

The Lord Buddha, in great kindness, let his hand rest kindly on the head of Ananda and said to him:—Ananda, at the beginning of my perfect Enlightenment I went to the Deer Forest at Sarnath where Kaundinya and his four disciples were staying and gave them my first teaching. The teaching was this:—The reason why all sentient beings fail to attain enlightenment and Arhatship is because they have been led astray by false conceptions regarding phenomena and objects, which defiled their minds. Since that time they have understood the import of that teaching and have become enlightened.

Then Kaundinya rose from his seat and addressed the Lord, saying:—Blessed Lord I am now the oldest in this assembly and am credited with having the best understanding of the Dharma. I attained Arhatship by realizing the significance of objective things. I was like a traveler seeking lodgings where I could satisfy my hunger and take my rest, but, like a traveler after he had satisfied his hunger and taken his rest, he could no longer stay there for a comfortable rest but must set out on another day's journey. If he was the inn-keeper he could do so, but the traveler is the symbol of impermanency. We may also draw a lesson from the sky. After a rain it is fresh and clear and the sun's rays penetrating the clouds light up the dust particles moving about in the air. We think of open space as a symbol of motionlessness and permanency, while we think of dust particles as symbols of motion and impermanency.

The Lord Buddha was much pleased by the words of Kaundinya and said:—So it is, it is, Kaundinya! Then raising his hand, he opened his fingers and then closed them, saying: —What do you see, Ananda?

Ananda replied:—I see my Lord standing before the assembly opening and closing his beautiful fingers.

The Lord resumed:—As you watch the fingers of my hand

opening and closing, does the perception of motion belong to my hand or to your eyes?

Ananda replied:—My Lord, while thy precious hand is opening and closing I recognize the motion as belonging to thy hand and not to my eyes.

The Lord enquired:—Ananda, what is in motion and what is still?

Ananda replied:—My Lord, it is thy fingers that are in motion, but as to the perception of my eyes, while it can not be said that it possesses the nature of absolute stillness, it can hardly be said that it is in motion.

The Lord Buddha was pleased with this reply and said: So it is, Ananda. Then the Lord Buddha caused a bright beam of light to dart from his hand and fall on Ananda's right side. Ananda quickly turned his head to look at it. Then the Lord caused another beam of light to fall on Ananda's left, and Ananda quickly turned his head to look at that. Then the Lord Buddha questioned Ananda, saying:—Ananda, what caused you to turn your heard about?

My Lord, it was because I saw a shining beam of light springing from my Lord's hand and darting first to my right and then to my left, and I turned my head to look at it.

Ananda, you say that when your eyes followed the light, you turned your head from right to left. Tell me was it your head or the perception of your sight that moved?

My Lord, it was my head that moved. As to the perception of sight, while it can not be said that it has the nature of motionlessness, neither can it be said that it has no motion.

The Lord was pleased with this reply and said:—So it is, Ananda. When I was looking at you as sentient beings do, it was your head that was moving about but my perception of sight did not move, and when you were looking at me, it was my hand opening and closing, not your "seeing" that moved. Ananda, can you not see the difference in nature in that which moves and changes, and that which is motionless and unchanging? It is body which moves and changes, not Mind. Why do you so persistently look upon motion as appertaining to both body and mind? Why do you permit your thoughts to rise and fall, letting the body rule the mind, instead of Mind ruling the body? Why do you let your senses deceive you as to the true unchanging nature of Mind and then to do things in a reversed order which leads to motion and confusion and suffering? As one forgets the true nature of Mind, so he mistakes the reflections of objects as being his own mind, thus binding him to the endless movements and changes and suffering of the recurring cycles of deaths and rebirths that are of his own causing. You should regard all that changes as "dust-particles" and that which is unchanging as being your own true Nature of Mind.

Then Ananda and all the assembly realized that from beginningless time, they had forgotten and ignored their own true nature, had misinterpreted conditional objects, and had confused their minds by false discriminations and illusive reflections. They felt like a little baby that had found its mother's breast, and became calm and peaceful in spirit. In this spirit they pressed their hands together and made devout obeisance to the Blessed One. They besought the Lord Tathagata to teach them how to make distinctions between body and mind, between the real and the unreal, between that which is true and that which is false, between the manifested natures of deaths and rebirths on the one hand, and the intrinsic nature of that which is un-born and never dies on the other hand; the one appearing and disappearing, the other forever abiding within the essence of their own mind.

From The Dhammapada

From *The Dhammapada*

Ascribed to Buddha himself, *The Dhammapada* is a collection of aphorisms and parables which underline man's moral struggle with his own nature: evil can only be overcome by good; virtue and happiness are inseparable; the conquest of self is man's noblest triumph. Uttered more than 500 years before the birth of Christ and transcribed a century or more later, these are teachings comparable in spirit and substance to the doctrines of Christianity. For the Indian people their influence has been as profound as the Gospels have been in the West.

FROM THE DHAMMAPADA

The Twin-Verses

All that we are is the result of what we have thought: it is founded on our thoughts, it is made up of our thoughts. If a man speaks or acts with an evil thought, pain follows him, as the wheel follows the foot of the ox that draws the carriage.

All that we are is the result of what we have thought: it is founded on our thoughts, it is made up of our thoughts. If a man speaks or acts with a pure thought, happiness follows him, like a shadow that never leaves him.

"He abused me, he beat me, he defeated me, he robbed me" —in those who harbour such thoughts hatred will never cease.

"He abused me, he beat me, he defeated me, he robbed me" —in those who do not harbour such thoughts hatred will cease.

For hatred does not cease by hatred at any time: hatred ceases by love, this is an old rule.

The world does not know that we must all come to an end here—but those who know it, their quarrels cease at once.

He who lives looking for pleasures only, his senses uncontrolled, immoderate in his food, idle, and weak, Mara (the tempter) will certainly overthrow him, as the wind throws down a weak tree.

He who lives without looking for pleasures, his senses well controlled, moderate in his food, faithful and strong, him

Mara will certainly not overthrow, any more than the wind throws down a rocky mountain.

He who wishes to put on the yellow dress without having cleansed himself from sin, who disregards also temperance and truth, is unworthy of the yellow dress.

But he who has cleansed himself from sin, is well grounded in all virtues, and regards also temperance and truth, he is indeed worthy of the yellow dress.

They who imagine truth in untruth, and see untruth in truth, never arrive at truth, but follow vain desires.

They who know truth in truth, and untruth in untruth, arrive at truth, and follow true desires.

As rain breaks through an ill-thatched house, passion will break through an unreflecting mind.

As rain does not break through a well-thatched house, passion will not break through a well-reflecting mind.

The evil-doer mourns in this world, and he mourns in the next; he mourns in both. He mourns and suffers when he sees the evil of his own work.

The virtuous man delights in this world, and he delights in the next; he delights in both. He delights and rejoices, when he sees the purity of his own work.

The evil-doer suffers in this world, and he suffers in the next; he suffers in both. He suffers when he thinks of the evil he has done; he suffers more when going on the evil path.

The virtuous man is happy in this world, and he is happy in the next; he is happy in both. He is happy when he thinks of the good he has done; he is still more happy when going on the good path.

The thoughtless man, even if he can recite a large portion of the law, but is not a doer of it, has no share in the priesthood, but is like a cowherd counting the cows of others.

The follower of the law, even if he can recite only a small portion (of the law), but, having forsaken passion and hatred and foolishness, possesses true knowledge and serenity of mind, he, caring for nothing in this world or that to come, has indeed a share in the priesthood.

On Earnestness

Earnestness is the path of immortality (Nirvana), thoughtlessness the path of death. Those who are in earnest do not die, those who are thoughtless are as if dead already.

Those who are advanced in earnestness, having understood this clearly, delight in earnestness, and rejoice in the knowledge of the Ariyas (the elect).

These wise people, meditative, steady, always possessed of strong powers, attain to Nirvana, the highest happiness.

If an earnest person has roused himself, if he is not forgetful, if his deeds are pure, if he acts with consideration, if he restrains himself, and lives according to law—then his glory will increase.

By rousing himself, by earnestness, by restraint and control, the wise man may make for himself an island which no flood can overwhelm.

Fools follow after vanity, men of evil wisdom. The wise man keeps earnestness as his best jewel.

Follow not after vanity, nor after the enjoyment of love and lust! He who is earnest and meditative, obtains ample joy.

When the learned man drives away vanity by earnestness, he, the wise, climbing the terraced heights of wisdom, looks down upon the fools, serene he looks upon the toiling crowd, as one that stands on a mountain looks down upon them that stand upon the plain.

Earnest among the thoughtless, awake among the sleepers, the wise man advances like a racer, leaving behind the hack.

By earnestness did Maghavan (Indra) rise to the lordship of the gods. People praise earnestness; thoughtlessness is always blamed.

A Bhikshu (mendicant) who delights in earnestness, who looks with fear on thoughtlessness, moves about like fire, burning all his fetters, small or large.

A Bhikshu who delights in reflection, who looks with fear

on thoughtlessness, cannot fall away from his perfect state—he is close upon Nirvana.

Thought

As a fletcher makes straight his arrow, a wise man makes straight his trembling and unsteady thought, which is difficult to guard, difficult to hold back,

As a fish taken from his watery home and thrown on the dry ground, our thought trembles all over in order to escape the dominion of Mara (the tempter).

It is good to tame the mind, which is difficult to hold in and flighty, rushing wherever it listeth; a tamed mind brings happiness.

Let the wise man guard his thoughts, for they are difficult to perceive, very artful, and they rush wherever they list: thoughts well guarded bring happiness.

Those who bridle their mind which travels far, moves about alone, is without a body, and hides in the chamber of the heart, will be free from the bonds of Mara.

If a man's thoughts are unsteady, if he does not know the true law, if his peace of mind is troubled, his knowledge will never be perfect.

If a man's thoughts are not dissipated, if his mind is not perplexed, if he has ceased to think of good or evil, then there is no fear for him while he is watchful.

Knowing that this body is fragile like a jar, and making this thought firm like a fortress, one should attack Mara with the weapon of knowledge, one should watch him when conquered, and should never rest.

Before long, alas! this body will lie on the earth, despised, without understanding, like a useless log.

Whatever a hater may do to a hater, or an enemy to an enemy, a wrongly-directed mind will do us greater mischief.

Not a mother, not a father will do so much, nor any other relative; a well-directed mind will do us greater service.

Flowers

Who shall overcome this earth, and the world of Yama (the lord of the departed), and the world of the gods? Who shall find out the plainly shown path of virtue, as a clever man finds out the right flower?

The disciple will overcome the earth, and the world of Yama, and the world of the gods. The disciple will find out the plainly shown path of virtue, as a clever man finds out the right flower.

He who knows that this body is like froth, and has learnt that it is as unsubstantial as a mirage, will break the flower-pointed arrow of Mara, and never see the king of death.

Death carries off a man who is gathering flowers and whose mind is distracted, as a flood carries off a sleeping village.

Death subdues a man who is gathering flowers, and whose mind is distracted, before he is satiated in his pleasures.

As the bee collects nectar and departs without injuring the flower, or its colour or scent, so let a sage dwell in his village.

Not the perversities of others, not their sins of commission or omission, but his own misdeeds and negligences should a sage take notice of.

Like a beautiful flower, full of colour, but without scent, are the fine but fruitless words of him who does not act accordingly.

But, like a beautiful flower, full of colour and full of scent, are the fine and fruitful words of him who acts accordingly.

As many kinds of wreaths can be made from a heap of flowers, so many good things may be achieved by a mortal when once he is born.

The scent of flowers does not travel against the wind, nor

that of sandal-wood, or of Tagara and Mallika flowers; but the odour of good people travels even against the wind; a good man pervades every place.

Sandal-wood or Tagara, a lotus-flower, or a Vassiki, among these sorts of perfumes, the perfume of virtue is unsurpassed.

Mean is the scent that comes from Tagara and sandal-wood —the perfume of those who possess virtue rises up to the gods as the highest.

Of the people who possess these virtues, who live without thoughtlessness, and who are emancipated through true knowledge, Mara, the tempter, never finds the way.

As on a heap of rubbish cast upon the highway the lily will grow full of sweet perfume and delight, thus the disciple of the truly enlightened Buddha shines forth by his knowledge among those who are like rubbish, among the people that walk in darkness.

The Thousands

Even though a speech be a thousand (of words), but made up of senseless words, one word of sense is better, which if a man hears, he becomes quiet.

Even though a Gatha (poem) be a thousand (of words), but made up of senseless words, one word of a Gatha is better, which if a man hears, he becomes quiet.

Though a man recite a hundred Gathas made up of senseless words, one word of the law is better, which if a man hears, he becomes quiet.

If one man conquer in battle a thousand times thousand men, and if another conquer himself, he is the greatest of conquerors.

One's own self conquered is better than all other people; not even a god, a Gandharva, not Mara with Brahman could change into defeat the victory of a man who has vanquished himself, and always lives under restraint.

If a man for a hundred years sacrifice month after month with a thousand, and if he but for one moment pay homage to a man whose soul is grounded in true knowledge, better is that homage than a sacrifice for a hundred years.

If a man for a hundred years worship Agni (fire) in the forest, and if he but for one moment pay homage to a man whose soul is grounded in true knowledge, better is that homage than sacrifice for a hundred years.

Whatever a man sacrifice in this world as an offering or as an oblation for a whole year in order to gain merit, the whole of it is not worth a quarter (a farthing); reverence shown to the righteous is better.

He who always greets and constantly reveres the aged, four things will increase to him, viz. life, beauty, happiness, power.

But he who lives a hundred years, vicious and unrestrained, a life of one day is better if a man is virtuous and reflecting.

And he who lives a hundred years, ignorant and unrestrained, a life of one day is better if a man is wise and reflecting.

And he who lives a hundred years, idle and weak, a life of one day is better if a man has attained firm strength.

And he who lives a hundred years, not seeing beginning and end, a life of one day is better if a man sees beginning and end.

And he who lives a hundred years, not seeing the immortal place, a life of one day is better if a man sees the immortal place.

And he who lives a hundred years, not seeing the highest law, a life of one day is better if a man sees the highest law.

The Way

The best of ways is the eightfold; the best of truths the four words; the best of virtues passionlessness; the best of men he who has eyes to see.

This is the way, there is no other that leads to the purifying of intelligence. Go on this way! Everything else is the deceit of Mara (the tempter).

If you go on this way, you will make an end of pain! The way was preached by me, when I had understood the removal of the thorns (in the flesh).

You yourself must make an effort. The Tathagatas (Buddhas) are only preachers. The thoughtful who enter the way are freed from the bondage of Mara.

"All created things perish," he who knows and sees this becomes passive in pain; this is the way to purity.

"All created things are grief and pain," he who knows and sees this becomes passive in pain; this is the way that leads to purity.

"All forms are unreal," he who knows and sees this becomes passive in pain; this is the way that leads to purity.

He who does not rouse himself when it is time to rise, who, though young and strong, is full of sloth, whose will and thought are weak, that lazy and idle man will never find the way to knowledge.

Watching his speech, well restrained in mind, let a man never commit any wrong with his body! Let a man but keep these three roads of action clear, and he will achieve the way which is taught by the wise.

Through zeal knowledge is gotten, through lack of zeal knowledge is lost; let a man who knows this double path of gain and loss thus place himself that knowledge may grow.

Cut down the whole forest (of lust), not a tree only! Danger comes out of the forest (of lust). When you have cut down both the forest (of lust) and its undergrowth, then, Bhikshus, you will be rid of the forest and free!

So long as the love of man towards women, even the smallest, is not destroyed, so long is his mind in bondage, as the calf that drinks milk is to its mother.

Cut out the love of self, like an autumn lotus, with thy hand! Cherish the road of peace. Nirvana has been shown by Sugata (Buddha).

"Here I shall dwell in the rain, here in winter and summer," thus the fool meditates, and does not think of his death.

Death comes and carries off that man, praised for his children and flocks, his mind distracted, as a flood carries off a sleeping village.

Sons are no help, nor a father, nor relations; there is no help from kinsfolk for one whom death has seized.

A wise and good man who knows the meaning of this, should quickly clear the way that leads to Nirvana.

The Downward Course

He who says what is not, goes to hell; he also who, having done a thing, says I have not done it. After death both are equal, they are men with evil deeds in the next world.

Many men whose shoulders are covered with the yellow gown are ill-conditioned and unrestrained; such evil-doers by their evil deeds go to hell.

Better it would be to swallow a heated iron ball, like flaring fire, than that a bad unrestrained fellow should live on the charity of the land.

Four things does a wreckless man gain who covets his neighbour's wife—a bad reputation, an uncomfortable bed, thirdly, punishment, and lastly, hell.

There is bad reputation, and the evil way (to hell), there is the short pleasure of the frightened in the arms of the frightened, and the king imposes heavy punishment; therefore let no man think of his neighbour's wife.

As a grass-blade, if badly grasped, cuts the arm, badly-practised asceticism leads to hell.

An act carelessly performed, a broken vow, and hesitating obedience to discipline, all this brings no great reward.

If anything is to be done, let a man do it, let him attack it vigorously! A careless pilgrim only scatters the dust of his passions more widely.

An evil deed is better left undone. for a man repents of it

afterwards; a good deed is better done, for having done it, one does not repent.

Like a well-guarded frontier fort, with defences within and without, so let a man guard himself. Not a moment should escape, for they who allow the right moment to pass, suffer pain when they are in hell.

They who are ashamed of what they ought not to be ashamed of, and are not ashamed of what they ought to be ashamed of, such men, embracing false doctrines, enter the evil path.

They who fear when they ought not to fear, and fear not when they ought to fear, such men, embracing false doctrines, enter the evil path.

They who forbid when there is nothing to be forbidden, and forbid not when there is something to be forbidden, such men, embracing false doctrines, enter the evil path.

They who know what is forbidden as forbidden, and what is not forbidden as not forbidden, such men, embracing the true doctrine, enter the good path.

The Brahmana

Stop the stream valiantly, drive away the desires, O Brahmana! When you have understood the destruction of all that was made, you will understand that which was not made.

If the Brahmana has reached the other shore in both laws (in restraint and contemplation), all bonds vanish from him who has obtained knowledge.

He for whom there is neither this nor that shore, nor both, him, the fearless and unshackled, I call indeed a Brahmana.

He who is thoughtful, blameless, settled, dutiful, without passions, and who has attained the highest end, him I call indeed a Brahmana.

The sun is bright by day, the moon shines by night, the warrior is bright in his armour, the Brahmana is bright in his meditation; but Buddha, the Awakened, is bright with splendour day and night.

Because a man is rid of evil, therefore he is called Brahmana; because he walks quietly, therefore he is called Samana; because he has sent away his own impurities, therefore he is called Pravragita (Pabbagita, a pilgrim).

No one should attack a Brahmana, but no Brahmana if attacked should let himself fly at his aggressor! Woe to him who strikes a Brahmana, more woe to him who flies at his aggressor!

It advantages a Brahmana not a little if he holds his mind back from the pleasures of life; when all wish to injure has vanished, pain will cease.

Him I call indeed a Brahmana who does not offend by body, word, or thought, and is controlled on these three points.

After a man has once understood the law as taught by the Well-awakened (Buddha), let him worship it carefully, as the Brahmana worships the sacrificial fire.

A man does not become a Brahmana by his platted hair, by his family, or by birth; in whom there is truth and righteousness, he is blessed, he is a Brahmana.

What is the use of platted hair, O fool! what of the raiment of goat-skins? Within thee there is ravening, but the outside thou makest clean.

The man who wears dirty raiments, who is emaciated and covered with veins, who lives alone in the forest, and meditates, him I call indeed a Brahmana.

I do not call a man a Brahmana because of his origin or of his mother. He is indeed arrogant, and he is wealthy: but the poor, who is free from all attachments, him I call indeed a Brahmana.

Him I call indeed a Brahmana who has cut all fetters, who never trembles, is independent and unshackled.

Him I call indeed a Brahmana who has cut the strap and the thong, the chain with all that pertains to it, who has burst the bar, and is awakened.

Him I call indeed a Brahmana who, though he has committed no offence, endures reproach, bonds, and stripes, who has endurance for his force, and strength for his army.

Him I call indeed a Brahmana who is free from anger, dutiful, virtuous, without appetite, who is subdued, and has received his last body.

Him I call indeed a Brahmana who does not cling to pleasures, like water on a lotus leaf, like a mustard seed on the point of a needle.

Him I call indeed a Brahmana who, even here, knows the end of his suffering, has put down his burden, and is unshackled.

Him I call indeed a Brahmana whose knowledge is deep, who possesses wisdom, who knows the right way and the wrong, and has attained the highest end.

Him I call indeed a Brahmana who keeps aloof both from laymen and from mendicants, who frequents no houses, and has but few desires.

Him I call indeed a Brahmana who finds no fault with other beings, whether feeble or strong, and does not kill nor cause slaughter.

Him I call indeed a Brahmana who is tolerant with the intolerant, mild with fault-finders, and free from passion among the passionate.

Him I call indeed a Brahmana from whom anger and hatred, pride and envy have dropt like a mustard seed from the point of a needle.

Him I call indeed a Brahmana who utters true speech, instructive and free from harshness, so that he offend no one.

Him I call indeed a Brahmana who takes nothing in the world that is not given him, be it long or short, small or large, good or bad.

Him I call indeed a Brahmana who fosters no desires for this world or for the next, has no inclinations, and is unshackled.

Him I call indeed a Brahmana who has no interests, and when he has understood (the truth) does not say How, how? and who has reached the depth of the Immortal.

Him I call indeed a Brahmana who in this world is above

good and evil, above the bondage of both, free from grief, from sin, and from impurity.

Him I call indeed a Brahmana who is bright like the moon, pure, serene, undisturbed, and in whom all gaiety is extinct.

Him I call indeed a Brahmana who has traversed this miry road, the impassable world and its vanity, who has gone through, and reached the other shore, is thoughtful, guileless, free from doubts, free from attachment, and content.

Him I call indeed a Brahmana who in this world, leaving all desires, travels about without a home, and in whom all concupiscence is extinct.

Him I call indeed a Brahmana who, leaving all longings, travels about without a home, and in whom all covetousness is extinct.

Him I call indeed a Brahmana who, after leaving all bondage to men, has risen above all bondage to the gods, and is free from all and every bondage.

Him I call indeed a Brahmana who has left what gives pleasure and what gives pain, who is cold, and free from all germs of renewed life, the hero who has conquered all the worlds.

Him I call indeed a Brahmana who knows the destruction and the return of beings everywhere, who is free from bondage, welfaring (Sugata), and awakened (Buddha).

Him I call indeed a Brahmana whose path the gods do not know, nor spirits (Gandharvas), nor men, whose passions are extinct, and who is an Arhat (venerable).

Him I call indeed a Brahmana who calls nothing his own, whether it be before, behind, or between, who is poor, and free from the love of the world.

Him I call indeed a Brahmana, the manly, the noble, the hero, the great sage, the conqueror, the impassible, the accomplished, the awakened.

Him I call indeed a Brahmana who knows his former abodes, who sees heaven and hell, has reached the end of births, is perfect in knowledge, a sage, and whose perfections are all perfect.

Baruch Spinoza

THE FOUNDATIONS OF THE MORAL LIFE

Baruch Spinoza
[1632–1677]

Born in Amsterdam of Jewish parents who had fled from the Spanish Inquisition, a prodigy of learning and the gentlest of men, Baruch Spinoza while still a student became a dissident against the orthodox teachings of the Synagogue and was excommunicated. For the rest of his life he devoted himself austerely to philosophy while earning his living as a lens grinder. His first major work, the *Ethics,* was not published until after his death, and his *Tractatus Theologica-Politicus* was issued anonymously. The philosopher of exaltation and reality, passionate in his love of God, the determinist, the teacher of universal interdependence, the fighter for freedom of thought, Spinoza found his philosophy and religion in the heart and mind of man.

THE FOUNDATIONS OF THE MORAL LIFE

BARUCH SPINOZA

Introductory

I HAVE briefly explained the causes of human impotence and want of stability, and why men do not obey the dictates of reason. It remains for me now to show what it is which reason prescribes to us, which emotions agree with the rules of human reason, and which, on the contrary, are opposed to these rules. Before, however, I begin to demonstrate these things by our full method, I should like briefly to set forth here these dictates of reason, in order that what I have in my mind about them may be easily comprehended by all.

Since reason demands nothing which is opposed to Nature, it demands, therefore, that every person should love himself, should seek his own profit—what is truly profitable to him—should desire everything that really leads man to greater perfection, and absolutely that every one should endeavor, as far as in him lies, to preserve his own being. This is all true as necessarily as that the whole is greater than its part. Again, since virtue means nothing but acting according to the laws of our own nature, and since no one endeavors to preserve his being except in accordance with the laws of his own nature, it follows: *Firstly,* That the foundation of virtue is that endeavor itself to preserve our own being, and that happiness consists in this—that a man can preserve his own being. *Secondly,* It follows that virtue is to be desired for its own sake, nor is there anything more excellent or more useful to us than virtue, for the sake of which virtue ought to be desired. *Thirdly,* It follows that all persons who kill themselves are impotent in mind, and have been thoroughly overcome by external causes opposed to their nature.

Again, we can never free ourselves from the need of something outside us for the preservation of our being, and we can never live in such a manner as to have no intercourse with objects which are outside us. Indeed, so far as the mind is concerned, our intellect would be less perfect if the mind were alone, and understood nothing but itself. There are many things, therefore, outside us which are useful to us, and which, therefore, are to be sought. Of all these, none more excellent can be discovered than those which exactly agree with our nature. If, for example, two individuals of exactly the same nature are joined together, they make up a single individual, doubly stronger than each alone. Nothing, therefore, is more useful to man than man. Men can desire, I say, nothing more excellent for the preservation of their being than that all should so agree at every point that the minds and bodies of all should form, as it were, one mind and one body; that all should together endeavor as much as possible to preserve their being, and that all should together seek the common good of all. From this it follows that men who are governed by reason—that is to say, men who, under the guidance of reason, seek their own profit—desire nothing for themselves which they do not desire for other men, and that, therefore, they are just, faithful, and honorable.

These are those dictates of reason which I purposed briefly to set forth before commencing their demonstration by a fuller method, in order that, if possible, I might win the attention of those who believe that this principle—that every one is bound to seek his own profit—is the foundation of impiety, and not of virtue and piety.

The Essence of Virtue

1 ☙ According to the laws of his own nature each person necessarily desires that which he considers to be good, and avoids that which he considers to be evil.

The more each person strives and is able to seek his own profit, that is to say, to preserve his being, the more virtue does he possess; on the other hand, in so far as each person neglects his own profit, that is to say, neglects to preserve his own being, is he impotent.

No one, therefore, unless defeated by external causes and those which are contrary to his nature, neglects to seek his own profit or preserve his being. No one, I say, refuses food or kills himself from a necessity of his nature, but only when forced by external causes. The compulsion may be exercised in many ways. A man kills himself under compulsion by another when that other turns the right hand, with which the man had by chance laid hold of a sword, and compels him to direct the sword against his own heart; or the command of a tyrant may compel a man, as it did Seneca, to open his own veins, that is to say, he may desire to avoid a greater evil by a less. External and hidden causes also may so dispose his imagination and may so affect his body as to cause it to put on another nature contrary to that which it had at first, and one whose idea cannot exist in the mind; but a very little reflection will show that it as impossible that a man, from the necessity of his nature, should endeavor not to exist, or to be changed into some other form, as it is that something should be begotten from nothing.

The endeavor after self-preservation is the essence itself of a thing. If, therefore, any virtue could be conceived prior to this of self-preservation, the essence itself of the thing would be conceived as prior to itself, which (as is self-evident) is absurd.

The endeavor after self-preservation is the primary and only foundation of virtue. For prior to this principle no other can be conceived, and without it no virtue can be conceived.

No one endeavors to preserve his own being for the sake of another object. For if a man endeavored to preserve his being for the sake of any other object, this object would then become the primary foundation of virtue (as is self-evident), which is an absurdity.

No one can desire to be happy, to act well and live well, who does not at the same time desire to be, to act, and to live, that is to say, actually to exist.

II ☙ To act absolutely in conformity with virtue is nothing but acting according to the laws of our own proper nature. But only in so far as we understand do we act. Therefore, to act in conformity with virtue is nothing but acting, living, and preserving our being as reason directs, and doing so from the ground of seeking our own profit.[1]

In so far as a man is determined to action because he has inadequate ideas he suffers, that is to say, he does something which through his essence alone cannot be perceived, that is

---

[1] . . . If it agreed better with a man's nature that he should hang himself, could any reasons be given for his not hanging himself? Can such a nature possibly exist? If so, I maintain (whether I do or do not grant free will), that such an one, if he sees that he can live more conveniently on the gallows than sitting at his own table, would act most foolishly, if he did not hang himself. So any one who clearly saw that, by committing crimes, he would enjoy a really more perfect and better life and existence, than he could attain by the practice of virtue, would be foolish if he did not act on his convictions. For, with such a perverse human nature as his, crime would become virtue. *From a letter to Wm. Blyenbergh* (March 13, 1665).

to say, which does not follow from his virtue. But in so far as he is determined to any action because he understands, he acts, that is to say he does something which is perceived through his essence alone, or which adequately follows from his virtue.

The Highest Virtue of Reason

All efforts which we make through reason are nothing but efforts to understand, and the mind, in so far as it uses reason, adjudges nothing as profitable to itself excepting that which conduces to understanding.

The mind, in so far as it reasons, desires nothing but to understand, nor does it adjudge anything to be profitable to itself excepting what conduces to understanding. But the mind possesses no certitude, unless in so far as it possesses adequate ideas, or in so far as it reasons. We do not know, therefore, that anything is certainly good, excepting that which actually conduces to understanding, and, on the other hand, we do not know that anything is evil excepting that which can hinder us from understanding.

The highest thing which the mind can understand is God, that is to say, Being absolutely infinite, and without whom nothing can be nor can be conceived, and therefore that which is chiefly profitable to the mind, or which is the highest good of the mind, is the knowledge of God. Again, the mind acts only in so far as it understands and only in so far can it be absolutely said to act in conformity with virtue. To understand, therefore, is the absolute virtue of the mind. But the highest thing which the mind can understand is God (as we have already demonstrated), and therefore the highest virtue of the mind is to understand or know God.

THE MORAL VALUE OF THE EMOTIONS

I: *General Principles*

That which so disposes the human body that it can be affected in many ways, or which renders it capable of affecting external bodies in many ways, is profitable to man, and is more profitable in proportion as by its means the body becomes better fitted to be affected in many ways, and to affect other bodies; on the other hand, that thing is injurious which renders the body less fitted to affect or be affected.

Whatever is effective to preserve the proportion of motion and rest which the parts of the human body bear to each other is good, and, on the contrary, that is evil which causes the parts of the human body to have a different proportion of motion and rest to each other.

In what degree these things may injure or profit the mind will be explained below. Here I observe merely that I understand the body to die when its parts are so disposed as to acquire a different proportion of motion and rest to each other. For I dare not deny that the human body, though the circulation of the blood and the other things by means of which it is thought to live be preserved, may, nevertheless, be changed into another nature altogether different from its own. No reason compels me to affirm that the body never dies unless it is changed into a corpse. Experience, indeed, seems to teach the contrary. It happens sometimes that a man undergoes such changes that he cannot very well be said to be the same man, as was the case with a certain Spanish poet of whom I have heard, who was seized with an illness, and although he recovered, remained, nevertheless, so oblivious of his past life that he did not believe the tales and tragedies he had composed were his own, and he might, indeed, have been taken for a grown-up child if he had also forgotten his native tongue. But if this seems incredible, what shall we say of children? The man of mature years believes the nature of children to be so different from his own, that it would be impossible to persuade him he had ever been a child, if he did not conjecture regarding himself from what he sees of others. But in order to avoid giving to the superstitious matter for new questions, I prefer to go no farther in the discussion of these matters.

II: *Value of Joy and Sorrow*

Joy is an emotion by which the body's power of action is increased or assisted. Sorrow, on the other hand, is an emotion by which the body's power of action is lessened or restrained, and therefore joy is not directly evil, but good; sorrow, on the other hand, is directly evil.

III: *The Good Emotions*

Cheerfulness is joy, which, in so far as it is related to the body, consists in this, that all the parts of the body are equally affected, that is to say, the body's power of action is increased or assisted, so that all the parts acquire the same proportion of motion and rest to each other. Cheerfulness, therefore, is always good, and can never be excessive. But melancholy is sorrow, which, in so far as it is related to the body consists in this, that the body's power of action is absolutely lessened or restrained, and melancholy, therefore, is always evil.

Pleasurable excitement is joy, which, in so far as it is related to the body, consists in this, that one or some of the parts of the body are affected more than others. The power of this emotion may, therefore, be so great as to overcome the other actions of the body. It may cling obstinately to the body; it may impede the body in such a manner as to render it less capable of being affected in many ways, and therefore may be evil. Again, pain, which, on the contrary, is sorrow, considered in itself alone cannot be good. But because its power and increase is limited by the power of an external cause compared with our own power, we can therefore conceive infinite degrees of strength of this emotion, and infinite kinds of it, and we can therefore conceive it to be such that it can restrain an excess of pleasurable excitement, and so far (by the first part of this proposition) preventing the body from becoming less capable. So far, therefore, will pain be good.

Love is joy with the accompanying idea of an external cause. Pleasurable excitement, therefore with the accompanying idea of an external cause, is love, and therefore love may be excessive. Again, desire is greater as the emotion from which it springs is greater. Inasmuch, therefore, as an emotion may overpower the other actions of a man, so also the desire which springs from this emotion may also overpower the other desires, and may therefore exist in the same excess which we have shown (in the preceding proposition) that pleasurable excitement possesses.

Cheerfulness, which I have affirmed to be good, is more easily imagined than observed; for the emotions by which we are daily agitated are generally related to some part of the body which is affected more than the others, and therefore it is that the emotions exist for the most part in excess, and so hold the mind down to the contemplation of one object alone, that it can think about nothing else; and although men are subject to a number of emotions, and therefore few are found who are always under the control of one and the same emotion, there are not wanting those to whom one and the same emotion obstinately cling. We see men sometimes so affected by one object, that although it is not present, they believe it to be before them; and if this happens to a man who is not asleep, we say that he is delirious or mad. Nor are those believed to be less mad who are inflamed by love, dreaming about nothing but a mistress or harlot day and night, for they excite our laughter. But the avaricious man who thinks of nothing else but gain or money, and the ambitious man who thinks of nothing but glory, inasmuch as they do harm, and are, therefore, thought worthy of hatred, are not believed to be mad. In truth, however, avarice, lust, etc., are a kind of madness, although they are not reckoned amongst diseases.

IV: *The Evil Emotions*

The man whom we hate we endeavor to destroy, that is to say we endeavor to do something which is evil. Therefore hatred can never be good.[1]

Envy, mockery, contempt, anger, revenge, and the other affects which are related to hatred or arise from it, are evil.

Everything which we desire because we are affected by hatred is base and unjust in the State.

I make a great distinction between mockery (which I have said is bad) and laughter; for laughter and merriment are nothing but joy, and therefore, provided they are not excessive, are in themselves good. Nothing but a gloomy and sad superstition forbids enjoyment. For why is it more seemly to extinguish hunger and thirst than to drive away melancholy? My reasons and my conclusions are these: No God and no human being, except an envious one, is delighted by my impotence or my trouble, or esteems as any virtue in us tears, sighs, fears, and others things of this kind, which are signs of mental impotence; on the contrary, the greater the joy with which we are affected, the greater the perfection to which we pass thereby, that is to say, the more do we necessarily partake of the divine nature. To make use of things, therefore, and to delight in them as much as possible (provided we do not disgust ourselves with them, which is not delighting in them), is the part of a wise man. It is the part of a wise man, I say, to refresh and invigorate himself with moderate and pleasant eating and drinking, with sweet scents and the beauty

---

[1] It is to be observed that here and in the following I understand by hatred, hatred towards men only.

of green plants, with ornament, with music, with sports, with the theater, and with all things of this kind which one man can enjoy without hurting another. For the human body is composed of a great number of parts of diverse nature, which constantly need new and varied nourishment, in order that the whole of the body may be equally fit for everything which can follow from its nature, and consequently that the mind may be equally fit to understand many things at once. This mode of living best of all agrees both with our principles and with common practice; therefore this mode of living is the best of all, and is to be universally commended. There is no need, therefore, to enter more at length into the subject.

All emotions of hatred are evil and therefore the man who lives according to the guidance of reason will strive as much as possible to keep himself from being agitated by the emotions of hatred and, consequently, will strive to keep others from being subject to the same emotions. But hatred is increased by reciprocal hatred, and, on the other hand, can be extinguished by love, so that hatred passes into love. Therefore he who lives according to the guidance of reason will strive to repay the hatred of another, etc., with love, that is to say, with generosity. He who wishes to avenge injuries by hating in return does indeed live miserably. But he who, on the contrary, strives to drive out hatred by love, fights joyfully and confidently, with equal ease resisting one man or a number of men, and needing scarcely any assistance from fortune. Those whom he conquers yield gladly, not from defect of strength, but from an increase of it. These truths, however, all follow so plainly from the definitions alone of love and the intellect, that there is no need to demonstrate them singly.

v: *Necessary Evils*

1 ☙ The emotions of hope and fear cannot exist without sorrow; for fear is sorrow, and hope cannot exist without fear.

Therefore these emotions cannot be good of themselves, but only in so far as they are able to restrain the excesses of joy.

We may here add that these emotions indicate want of knowledge and impotence of mind, and, for the same reason, confidence, despair, gladness, and remorse are signs of weakness of mind. For although confidence and gladness are emotions of joy, they nevertheless suppose that sorrow has preceded them, namely, hope or fear. In proportion, therefore, as we endeavor to live according to the guidance of reason, shall we strive as much as possible to depend less on hope, to liberate ourselves from fear, to rule fortune, and to direct our actions by the sure counsels of reason.

Humility is sorrow, which springs from this, that a man contemplates his own weakness. But in so far as a man knows himself by true reason is he supposed to understand his essence, that is to say, his power. If, therefore, while contemplating himself, he perceives any impotence of his, this is not due to his understanding himself, but, as we have shown, to the fact that his power of actions is restrained. But if we suppose that he forms a conception of his own impotence because he understands something to be more powerful than himself, by the knowledge of which he limits his own power of action, in this case we simply conceive that he understands himself distinctly, and his power of action is increased. Humility or sorrow, therefore, which arises because a man contemplates his own impotence, does not spring from true contemplation or reason, and is not a virtue, but a passion.

Repentance is not a virtue, that is to say, it does not spring from reason; on the contrary, the man who repents of what he has done is doubly wretched or impotent. For, in the first place, we allow ourselves to be overcome by a depraved desire, and, in the second place, by sorrow.

Inasmuch as men seldom live as reason dictates, therefore these two emotions, humility and repentance, together with hope and fear, are productive of more profit than disadvantage, and therefore, since men must sin, it is better that they should sin in this way. For if men impotent in mind were all equally proud, were ashamed of nothing, and feared nothing, by what bonds could they be united or constrained? The multitude becomes a thing to be feared if it has nothing to fear. It is not to be wondered at, therefore, that the prophets, thinking rather of the good of the community than of a few, should have commended so greatly humility, repentance and reverence. Indeed, those who are subject to these emotions can be led much more easily than others, so that, at last, they come to live according to the guidance of reason, that is to say, become free men, and enjoy the life of the blessed.

II ☙ Pity is sorrow, and therefore is in itself evil. The good, however, which issues from pity, namely, that we endeavor to free from misery the man we pity, we desire to do from the dictate of reason alone; nor can we do anything except by the dictate of reason alone, which we are sure is good. Pity, therefore, in a man who lives according to the guidance of reason is in itself bad and unprofitable.

Hence it follows that a man who lives according to the dictates of reason endeavors as much as possible to prevent himself from being touched by pity.

The man who has properly understood that everything follows from the necessity of the divine nature, and comes to pass according to the eternal laws and rules of Nature, will in truth discover nothing which is worthy of hatred, laughter, or contempt, nor will he pity any one, but, so far as human virtue is able, he will endeavor to *do well*, as we say, and to *rejoice*. We must add also, that a man who is easily touched by the emotion of pity, and is moved by the misery or tears of another, often does something of which he afterward repents, both because from an emotion we do nothing which we certainly know to be good, and also because we are so easily deceived by false tears. But this I say expressly of the man who lives according to the guidance of reason. For he who is moved neither by reason nor pity to be of any service to others is properly called inhuman; for he seems to be unlike a man.

VI: *Diseased Emotions*

The primary foundation of virtue is the preservation of our being according to the guidance of reason. The man, therefore, who is ignorant of himself is ignorant of the foundation of all the virtues, and consequently is ignorant of all the virtues. Again, to act in conformity with virtue is nothing but acting according to the guidance of reason, and he who acts according to the guidance of reason must necessarily know that he acts according to the guidance of reason. He, therefore, who is ignorant of himself, and consequently (as we have just shown) altogether ignorant of all the virtues, cannot in any way act in conformity with virtue, that is to say, is altogether impotent in mind. Therefore the greatest pride or despondency indicates the greatest impotence of mind.

Hence follows, with the utmost clearness, that the proud and the desponding are above all others subject to emotions.

Despondency, nevertheless, can be corrected more easily than pride, since the former is an emotion of sorrow, while the latter is an emotion of joy, and is therefore stronger than the former.

Pride is joy arising from a man's having too high an opinion of himself. This opinion a proud man will endeavor, as much as he can, to cherish, and therefore, will love the presence of parasites or flatterers (the definitions of these people are omitted, because they are too well known), and will shun that of the noble-minded who think of him as is right.

It would take too much time to enumerate here all the evils of pride, for the proud are subject to all emotions, but to none are they less subject than to those of love and pity. It is necessary, however, to observe here that a man is also called proud if he thinks too little of other people, and so, in this sense, pride is to be defined as joy which arises from the false opinion that we are superior to other people, while despondency, the contrary to this pride, would be defined as sorrow arising from the false opinion that we are inferior to other people. This being understood, it is easy to see that the proud man is necessarily envious, and that he hates those above all others who are the most praised on account of their virtues. It follows, too, that his hatred of them is not easily overcome by love or kindness and that he is delighted by the presence of those only who humor his weakness, and from a fool make him a madman.

Although despondency is contrary to pride, the despondent man is closely akin to the proud man. For since the sorrow of the despondent man arises from his judging his own impotence by the power of virtue of others, his sorrow will be mitigated, that is to say, he will rejoice, if his imagination be occupied in contemplating the vices of others. Hence the proverb— It is a consolation to the wretched to have bad companions in their misfortunes. On the other hand, the more the despondent man believes himself to be below other people, the more will he sorrow; and this is the reason why none are more prone to envy than the despondent; and why they, above all others, try to observe men's actions with a view to finding fault with them rather than correcting them, so that at last they praise nothing but despondency and glory in it; but in such a manner, however, as always to seem despondent.

These things follow from this emotion as necessarily as it follows from the nature of a triangle that its three angles are equal to two right angles. It is true, indeed, that I have said that I call these and the like emotions evil, in so far as I attend to human profit alone; but the laws of Nature have regard to the common order of Nature of which man is a part —a remark I desired to make in passing, lest it should be thought that I talk about the vices and absurdities of men rather than attempt to demonstrate the nature and properties of things. As I said, I consider human emotions and their properties precisely as I consider other natural objects; and, indeed, the emotions of man, if they do not show his power, show at least the power and workmanship of Nature, no less than many other things which we admire and delight to contemplate.

VII: *Reasonable Emotions*

If we live according to the guidance of reason, we shall desire for others the good which we seek for ourselves. Therefore if we see one person do good to another, our endeavor to do good is assisted, that is to say, we shall rejoice, and our joy (by hypothesis) will be accompanied with the idea of the person who does good to the other, that is to say, we shall favor him. Favor is not opposed to reason, but agrees with it, and may arise from it.

Indignation, as it is defined by us, is necessarily evil; but it is to be observed that when the supreme authority, constrained by the desire of preserving peace, punishes a citizen who injures another, I do not say that it is indignant with the citizen, since it is not excited by hatred to destroy him, but punishes him from motives of piety.

Self-satisfaction is the joy which arises from a man's contemplating himself and his power of action. But man's true power of action or his virtue is reason itself, which he contemplates clearly and distinctly. Self-satisfaction therefore arises from reason. Again, man, when he contemplates himself, perceives nothing clearly and distinctly or adequately, excepting those things which follow from his power of action, that is to say, those things which follow from his power of understanding; and therefore from this contemplation alone the highest satisfaction which can exist arises.

Self-satisfaction is indeed the highest thing for which we can hope, for (as we have shown), no one endeavors to preserve his being for the sake of any end. Again, because this self-satisfaction is more and more nourished and strengthened by praise, and, on the contrary more and more disturbed by blame, therefore we are principally led by glory; and can scarcely endure life with disgrace.

Self-exaltation is not opposed to reason, but may spring from it.

What is called vainglory is self-satisfaction, nourished by

nothing but the good opinion of the multitude, so that when that is withdrawn, the satisfaction, that is to say, the chief good which every one loves, ceases. For this reason those who glory in the good opinion of the multitude anxiously and with daily care strive, labor, and struggle to preserve their fame. For the multitude is changeable and fickle, so that fame, if it be not preserved, soon passes away. As every one, moreover, is desirous to catch the praises of the people, one person will readily destroy the fame of another; and consequently, as the object of contention is what is commonly thought to be the highest good, a great desire arises on the part of every one to keep down his fellows by every possible means, and he who at last comes off conqueror boasts more because he has injured another person than because he has profited himself. This glory of self-satisfaction, therefore, is indeed vain, for it is really no glory.

What is worthy of notice with regard to shame may easily be gathered from what has been said about compassion and repentance. I will only add that pity, like shame, although it is not a virtue, is nevertheless good in so far as it shows that a desire of living uprightly is present in the man who is possessed with shame, just as pain is called good in so far as it shows that the injured part has not yet putrefied. A man, therefore, who is ashamed of what he has done, although he is sorrowful, is nevertheless more perfect that the shameless man who has no desire of living uprightly.

These are the things which I undertook to establish with regard to the emotions of joy and sorrow. With reference to the desires, these are good or evil as they spring from good or evil emotions. All of them, however, in so far as they are begotten in us of emotions which are passions, are blind, as may easily be inferred from what has been said, nor would they be of any use if men could be easily persuaded to live according to the dictates of reason alone.

The Life of Virtue

I ◆§ All our efforts or desires follow from the necessity of our nature in such a manner that they can be understood either through it alone as their proximate cause, or in so far as we are a part of Nature, which part cannot be adequately conceived through itself and without the other individuals.

II ◆§ The desires which follow from our nature in such a manner that they can be understood through it alone, are those which are related to the mind, in so far as it is conceived to consist of adequate ideas. The remaining desires are not related to the mind, unless in so far as it conceives things inadequately, whose power and increase cannot be determined by human power, but by the power of objects which are without us. The first kind of desires, therefore, are properly called actions, but the latter passions; for the first always indicate our power, and the latter, on the contrary, indicate our impotence and imperfect knowledge.

III ◆§ Our actions, that is to say, those desires which are determined by man's power or reason, are always good; the others may be good as well as evil.

IV ◆§ It is therefore more profitable to us in life to make perfect the intellect or reason as far as possible, and in this one thing consists the highest happiness or blessedness of man; for blessedness is nothing but the peace of mind which springs from the intuitive knowledge of God, and to perfect the intellect is nothing but to understand God, together with the attributes and actions of God, which flow from the necessity of His nature. The final aim, therefore, of a man who is guided by reason, that is to say, the chief desire by which he strives to govern all his other desires, is that by which he is led adequately to conceive himself and all things which can be conceived by his intelligence.

V ☙ There is no rational life, therefore, without intelligence and things are good only in so far as they assist man to enjoy that life of the mind which is determined by intelligence. Those things alone, on the other hand, we call evil which hinder man from perfecting his reason and enjoying a rational life.

VI ☙ But because all those things of which man is the efficient cause are necessarily good, it follows that no evil can happen to man except from external causes, that is to say, except in so far as he is a part of the whole Nature, whose laws human nature is compelled to obey—compelled also to accommodate himself to this whole of Nature in almost an infinite number of ways.

VII ☙ It is impossible that a man should not be a part of nature and follow her common order; but if he be placed amongst individuals who agree with his nature, his power of action will by that very fact be assisted and supported. But if, on the contrary, he be placed amongst individuals who do not in the least agree with his nature, he will scarcely be able without great change on his part to accommodate himself to them.

VIII ☙ Anything that exists in Nature which we judge to be evil or able to hinder us from existing and enjoying a rational life, we are allowed to remove from us in that way which seems the safest; and whatever, on the other hand, we judge to be good or to be profitable for the preservation of our being or the enjoyment of a rational life, we are permitted to take for our use and use in any way we may think proper;

and absolutely, every one is allowed by the highest right of Nature to do that which he believes contributes to his own profit.

IX ☙ Nothing, therefore, can agree better with the nature of any object than other individuals of the same kind, and so (see § VII) there is nothing more profitable to man for the preservation of his being and the enjoyment of a rational life than a man who is guided by reason. Again, since there is no single thing we know which is more excellent than a man who is guided by reason, it follows that there is nothing by which a person can better show how much skill and talent he possesses than by so educating men that at last they will live under the direct authority of reason.

X ☙ In so far as men are carried away by envy or any emotion of hatred towards one another, so far are they contrary to one another, and consequently so much the more are they to be feared, as they have more power than other individuals of nature.

XI ☙ Minds, nevertheless, are not conquered by arms, but by love and generosity.

XII ☙ Above all things is it profitable to men to form communities and to unite themselves to one another by bonds which may make all of them as one man; and absolutely, it is profitable for them to do whatever may tend to strengthen their friendships.

XIII ☙ But to accomplish this skill and watchfulness are required; for men are changeable (those being very few who live according to the laws of reason), and nevertheless generally envious and more inclined to vengeance than pity. To bear with each, therefore, according to his disposition and to refrain from imitating his emotions requires a singular power of mind. But those, on the contrary, who know how to revile men, to denounce vices rather than teach virtues, and not to strengthen men's minds but to weaken them, are injurious both to themselves and others, so that many of them through an excess of impatience and a false zeal for religion prefer living with brutes rather than amongst men; just as boys or youths, unable to endure with equanimity the rebukes of their parents, fly to the army, choosing the discomforts of war and the rule of a tyrant rather than the comforts of home and the admonitions of a father, suffering all kinds of burdens to be imposed upon them in order that they may revenge themselves upon their parents.

XIV ☙ Although, therefore, men generally determine everything by their pleasure, many more advantages than disadvantages arise from their common union. It is better, therefore, to endure with equanimity the injuries inflicted by them, and to apply our minds to those things which subserve concord and the establishment of friendship.

XV ☙ The things which beget concord are those which are related to justice, integrity, and honor; for besides that which is unjust and injurious, men take ill also anything which is esteemed base, or that any one should despise the received customs of the State. But in order to win love, those things are chiefly necessary which have reference to religion and piety.

XVI ☙ Concord, moreover, is often produced by fear, but it is without good faith. It is to be observed, too, that fear arises from impotence of mind, and therefore is of no service to reason; nor is pity, although it seems to present an appearance of piety.

XVII ☙ Men also are conquered by liberality, especially those who have not the means wherewith to procure what is necessary for the support of life. But to assist every one who is needy far surpasses the strength or profit of a private person, for the wealth of a private person is altogether insufficient to supply such wants. Besides, the power of any one man is too limited for him to be able to unite every one with himself in friendship. The care, therefore, of the poor is incumbent on the whole of society and concerns only the general profit.

XVIII ☙ In the receipt of benefits and in returning thanks, care altogether different must be taken.

XIX ☙ The love of a harlot, that is to say, the lust of sexual intercourse, which arises from mere external form, and absolutely all love which recognizes any other cause than the freedom of the mind, easily passes into hatred, unless, which is worse, it becomes a species of delirium, and thereby discord is cherished rather than concord.

XX ☙ With regard to marriage, it is plain that it is in accordance with reason, if the desire of connection is engendered not merely by external form, but by a love of begetting children and wisely educating them; and if, in addition, the love both of the husband and wife has for its cause not external form merely, but chiefly liberty of mind.

XXI ☙ Flattery, too, produces concord, but only by means of the disgraceful crime of slavery or perfidy; for there are none who are more taken by flattery than the proud, who wish to be first and are not so.

XXII ☙ There is a false appearance of piety and religion in dejection; and although dejection is the opposite of pride, the humble dejected man is very near akin to the proud.

XXIII ☙ Shame also contributes to concord, but only with regard to those matters which cannot be concealed. Shame, too, inasmuch as it is a kind of sorrow, does not belong to the service of reason.

XXIV ☙ The remaining emotions of sorrow which have man for their object are directly opposed to justice, integrity, honor, piety, and religion; and although indignation may seem to present an appearance of equity, yet there is no law where it is allowed to every one to judge the deeds of another, and to vindicate his own or another's right.

XXV ☙ Affability, that is to say, the desire of pleasing men, which is determined by reason, is related to piety. But if affability arises from an emotion, it is ambition or desire, by which men, generally under a false pretense of piety, excite discords and seditions. For he who desires to assist other people, either by advice or by deed, in order that they may together enjoy the highest good, will strive, above all things, to win their love, and not to draw them into admiration, so that a doctrine may be named after him, nor absolutely to give any occasion for envy. In common conversation, too, he will avoid referring to the vices of men, and will take care only sparingly to speak of human impotence, while he will talk largely of human virtue or power, and of the way by which it may be made perfect, so that men being moved not by fear or aversion, but solely by the emotion of joy, may endeavor as much as they can to live under the rule of reason.

XXVI ☙ Excepting man, we know no individual thing in Nature in whose mind we can take pleasure, nor anything which we can unite with ourselves by friendship or any kind of intercourse, and therefore regard to our own profit does not demand that we should preserve anything which exists in Nature excepting men, but teaches us to preserve it or destroy it in accordance with its varied uses, or to adapt it to our own service in any way whatever.

XXVII ☙ The profit which we derive from objects without us, over and above the experience and knowledge which we obtain because we observe them and change them from their existing forms into others, is chiefly the preservation of the body, and for this reason those objects are the most profitable to us which can feed and nourish the body, so that all its parts are able properly to perform their functions. For the more capable the body is of being affected in many ways, and affecting external bodies in many ways, the more capable of thinking is the mind. But there seem to be very few things in Nature of this kind, and it is consequently necessary for the requisite nourishment of the body to use many different kinds of food; for the human body is composed of a great number of parts of different nature, which need constant and varied food in order that the whole of the body may be equally adapted for all those things which can follow from its nature, and consequently that the mind also may be equally adapted to conceive many things.

XXVIII ☙ The strength of one man would scarcely suffice to obtain these things if men did not mutually assist one another. As money has presented us with an abstract of everything, it has come to pass that its image above every other usually occupies the mind of the multitude, because they can imagine hardly any kind of joy without the accompanying idea of money as its cause.

XXIX ☙ This, however, is a vice only in those who seek money not from poverty or necessity, but because they have learned the arts of gain, by which they keep up a grand appearance. As for the body itself, they feed it in accordance with custom, but sparingly, because they believe that they lose so much of their goods as they spend upon the preservation of their body. Those, however, who know the true use of money, and regulate the measure of wealth according to their needs, live contented with few things.

XXX ◆ Since, therefore, those things are good which help the parts of the body to perform their functions, and since joy consists in this, that the power of man, in so far as he is made up of mind and body, is helped or increased, it follows that all things which bring joy are good. But inasmuch as things do not work to this end—that they may effect us with joy—nor is their power of action guided in accordance with our profit, and finally, since joy is generally related chiefly to some one part of the body, it follows that generally the emotions of joy (unless reason and watchfulness be present), and consequently the desires which are begotten from them, are excessive. It is to be added, that an emotion causes us to put that thing first which is sweet to us in the present, and that we are not able to judge the future with an equal emotion of the mind.

XXXI ◆ Superstition, on the contrary, seems to affirm that what brings sorrow is good, and, on the contrary, that what brings joy is evil. But, as we have already said, no one, excepting an envious man, is delighted at my impotence or disadvantage, for the greater the joy with which we are affected, the greater the perfection to which we pass, and consequently the more do we participate in the divine nature; nor can joy ever be evil which is controlled by a true consideration for our own profit. On the other hand, the man who is led by fear, and does what is good that he may avoid what is evil, is not guided by reason.

XXXII ◆§ But human power is very limited, and is infinitely surpassed by the power of external causes, so that we do not possess an absolute power to adapt to our service the things which are without us. Nevertheless we shall bear with equanimity those things which happen to us contrary to what a consideration of our own profit demands, if we are conscious that we have performed our duty, that the power we have could not reach so far as to enable us to avoid those things, and that we are a part of the whole of Nature, whose order we follow. If we clearly and distinctly understand this, the part of us which is determined by intelligence, that is to say, the better part of us, will be entirely satisfied therewith, and in that satisfaction will endeavor to persevere; for, in so far as we understand, we cannot desire anything excepting what is necessary, nor, absolutely, can we be satisfied with anything but the truth. Therefore in so far as we understand these things properly will the efforts of the better part of us agree with the order of the whole of Nature.

Blaise Pascal

PENSÉES

Blaise Pascal
[1623–1662]

In the thirty-nine years of his life, Blaise Pascal was a prodigy in mathematics at the age of eleven, a pioneer in the study of hydrostatics, founder of the science of pneumatics and discoverer of the famous law of pressure named for him. He was, in addition, a philosopher and a master of style, known and revered for three centuries for a collection of notes called, with complete simplicity, "Thoughts." They have become a kind of gospel to men of every variety of religious, aesthetic and speculative inclination. The profundity of the ideas, the lucidity of expression and the genuineness of the sentiment pervading the *Pensées* certainly provide a more convincing declaration of Christian faith than almost all the abstruse arguments of the theologians. Fragmentary as his thoughts are, they are integrated in their general patterns: they trace the universal search for God. Pascal is preeminently the religious writer who cuts across doctrine and into the very heart of the moral problem. Always persuasive, he appeals to the intellect by his passion for truth and his spiritual rectitude. Above all, he moves the emotions by his almost merciless description of the plight of man without God.

PENSÉES

BLAISE PASCAL

1 ☙ Let man contemplate the whole of nature in her full and grand majesty, and turn his vision from the low objects which surround him. Let him gaze on that brilliant light, set like an eternal lamp to illumine the universe; let the earth appear to him a point in comparison with the vast circle described by the sun; and let him wonder at the fact that this vast circle is itself but a very fine point in comparison with that described by the stars in their revolution round the firmament. But if our view be arrested there, let our imagination pass beyond; it will sooner exhaust the power of conception than nature that of supplying material for conception. The whole visible world is only an imperceptible atom in the ample bosom of nature. No idea approaches it. We may enlarge our conceptions beyond all imaginable space; we only produce atoms in comparison with the reality of things. It is an infinite sphere, the centre of which is everywhere, the circumference nowhere. In short it is the greatest sensible mark of the almighty power of God, that imagination loses itself in that thought.

Returning to himself, let man consider what he is in comparison with all existence; let him regard himself as lost in this remote corner of nature; and from the little cell in which he finds himself lodged, I mean the universe, let him estimate at their true value the earth, kingdoms, cities, and himself. What is a man in the Infinite?

But to show him another prodigy equally astonishing, let him examine the most delicate things he knows. Let a mite be given him, with its minute body and parts incomparably more minute, limbs with their joints, veins in the limbs, blood in the veins, humours in the blood, drops in the humours, vapours in the drops. Dividing these last things again, let him exhaust his powers of conception, and let the last object at which he can arrive be now that of our discourse. Perhaps he will think that here is the smallest point in nature. I will let him see therein a new abyss. I will paint for him not only the visible universe, but all that he can conceive of nature's immensity in the womb of this abridged atom. Let him see therein an infinity of universes, each of which has its firmament, its planets, its earth, in the same proportion as in the visible world; in each earth animals, and in the last mites, in which he will find again all that the first had, finding still in these others the same thing without end and without cessation. Let him lose himself in wonders as amazing in their littleness as the others in their vastness. For who will not be astounded at the fact that our body, which a little while ago was imperceptible in the universe, itself imperceptible in the bosom of the whole, is now a colossus, a world, or rather a whole, in respect to the nothingness which we cannot reach? He who regards himself in this light will be afraid of himself, and observing himself sustained in the body given him by nature between those two abysses of the Infinite and Nothing, will tremble at the sight of these marvels; and I think that, as his curiosity changes into admiration, he will be more disposed to contemplate them in silence than to examine them with presumption.

For in fact what is man in nature? A Nothing in comparison with the Infinite, an All in comparison with the Nothing, a mean between nothing and everything. Since he is infinitely removed from comprehending the extremes, the end of things and their beginning are hopelessly hidden from him in an impenetrable secret; he is equally incapable of seeing the Nothing from which he was made, and the Infinite in which he is swallowed up.

What will he do then, but perceive the appearance of the middle of things, in an eternal despair of knowing either their beginning or their end. All things proceed from the Nothing, and are borne towards the Infinite. Who will follow these marvellous processes? The Author of these wonders understands them. None other can do so.

Through failure to contemplate these Infinities, men have rashly rushed into the examination of nature, as though they bore some proportion to her. It is strange that they have wished to understand the beginnings of things, and thence to arrive at the knowledge of the whole, with a presumption as infinite as their object. For surely this design cannot be formed without presumption or without a capacity infinite like nature.

If we are well informed, we understand that, as nature has graven her image and that of her Author on all things, they almost all partake of her double infinity. Thus we see that all the sciences are infinite in the extent of their researches. For who doubts that geometry, for instance, has an infinite infinity of problems to solve? They are also infinite in the multitude and fineness of their premises; for it is clear that those which are put forward as ultimate are not self-supporting, but are based on others which, again having others for their support, do not permit of finality. But we represent some as ultimate for reason, in the same way as in regard to material objects we call that an indivisible point beyond which our senses can no longer perceive anything, although by its nature it is infinitely divisible.

Of these two Infinities of science, that of greatness is the most palpable, and hence a few persons have pretended to know all things. "I will speak of the whole," said Democritus.

But the infinitely little is the least obvious. Philosophers have much oftener claimed to have reached it, and it is here they have all stumbled. This has given rise to such common titles as *First Principles*, *Principles of Philosophy*, and the like, as ostentatious in fact, though not in appearance, as that one which blinds us, *De omni scibili*.

We naturally believe ourselves far more capable of reaching the centre of things than of embracing their circumference. The visible extent of the world visibly exceeds us; but as we exceed little things, we think ourselves more capable of knowing them. And yet we need no less capacity for attaining the Nothing than the All. Infinite capacity is required for both, and it seems to me that whoever shall have understood the ultimate principles of being might also attain to the knowledge of the Infinite. The one depends on the other, and one leads to the other. These extremes meet and reunite by force of distance, and find each other in God, and in God alone.

Let us then take our compass; we are something, and we are not everything. The nature of our existence hides from us the knowledge of first beginnings which are born of the Nothing; and the littleness of our being conceals from us the sight of the Infinite.

Our intellect holds the same position in the world of thought as our body occupies in the expanse of nature.

Limited as we are in every way, this state which holds the mean between two extremes is present in all our impotence. Our senses perceive no extreme. Too much sound deafens us; too much light dazzles us; too great distance or proximity hinders our view. Too great length and too great brevity of discourse tend to obscurity; too much truth is paralysing (I know some who cannot understand that to take four from nothing leaves nothing). First principles are too self-evident for us; too much pleasure disagrees with us. Too many concords are annoying in music; too many benefits irritate us; we wish to have the wherewithal to over-pay our debts. *Beneficia eo usque læta sunt dum videntur exsolvi posse; ubi multum antevenere, pro gratia odium redditur.* We feel neither extreme heat nor extreme cold. Excessive qualities are prejudicial to us and not perceptible by the senses; we do not feel but suffer them. Extreme youth and extreme age hinder the mind, as also too much and too little education. In short, extremes are for us as though they were not, and we are not within their notice. They escape us, or we them.

This is our true state; this is what makes us incapable of certain knowledge and of absolute ignorance. We sail within a vast sphere, ever drifting in uncertainty, driven from end to end. When we think to attach ourselves to any point and to fasten to it, it wavers and leaves us; and if we follow it, it eludes our grasp, slips past us, and vanishes for ever. Nothing stays for us. This is our natural condition, and yet most contrary to our inclination; we burn with desire to find solid ground and an ultimate sure foundation whereon to build a tower reaching to the Infinite. But our whole groundwork cracks, and the earth opens to abysses.

Let us therefore not look for certainty and stability. Our reason is always deceived by fickle shadows; nothing can fix the finite between the two Infinites, which both enclose and fly from it.

If this be well understood, I think that we shall remain at rest, each in the state wherein nature has placed him. As this sphere which has fallen to us as our lot is always distant from either extreme, what matters it that man should have a little more knowledge of the universe? If he has it, he but gets a little higher. Is he not always infinitely removed from the end, and is not the duration of our life equally removed from eternity, even if it lasts ten years longer?

In comparison with these Infinities all finites are equal, and I see no reason for fixing our imagination on one more than on another. The only comparison which we make of ourselves to the finite is painful to us.

If man made himself the first object of study, he would see how incapable he is of going further. How can a part know the whole? But he may perhaps aspire to know at least the parts to which he bears some proportion. But the parts of the world are all so related and linked to one another, that I believe it impossible to know one without the other and without the whole.

Man, for instance, is related to all he knows. He needs a place wherein to abide, time through which to live, motion in order to live, elements to compose him, warmth and food to nourish him, air to breathe. He sees light; he feels bodies; in short, he is in a dependent alliance with everything. To know man, then, it is necessary to know how it happens that he needs air to live, and, to know the air, we must know how it is thus related to the life of man, etc. Flame cannot exist without air; therefore to understand the one, we must understand the other.

Since everything then is cause and effect, dependent and supporting, mediate and immediate, and all is held together by a natural though imperceptible chain, which binds together things most distant and most different, I hold it equally impossible to know the parts without knowing the whole, and to know the whole without knowing the parts in detail.

[The eternity of things in itself or in God must also astonish our brief duration. The fixed and constant immobility of nature, in comparison with the continual change which goes on within us, must have the same effect.]

And what completes our incapability of knowing things, is the fact that they are simple, and that we are composed of two opposite natures, different in kind, soul and body. For it is impossible that our rational part should be other than spiritual; and if any one maintain that we are simply corporeal, this would far more exclude us from the knowledge of things, there being nothing so inconceivable as to say that matter knows itself. It is impossible to imagine how it should know itself.

So if we are simply material, we can know nothing at all; and if we are composed of mind and matter, we cannot know perfectly things which are simple, whether spiritual or corporeal. Hence it comes that almost all philosophers have confused ideas of things, and speak of material things in spiritual terms, and of spiritual things in material terms. For they say boldly that bodies have a tendency to fall, that they seek after their centre, that they fly from destruction, that they fear the void, that they have inclinations, sympathies, antipathies, all of which attributes pertain only to mind. And in speaking of minds, they consider them as in a place, and attribute to them movement from one place to another; and these are qualities which belong only to bodies.

Instead of receiving the ideas of these things in their purity, we colour them with our own qualities, and stamp with our composite being all the simple things which we contemplate.

Who would not think, seeing us compose all things of mind and body, but that this mixture would be quite intelligible to us? Yet it is the very thing we least understand. Man is to himself the most wonderful object in nature; for he cannot conceive what the body is, still less what the mind is, and least of all how a body should be united to a mind. This is the consummation of his difficulties, and yet it is his very being. *Modus quo corporibus adhærent spiritus comprehendi ab hominibus non potest, et hoc tamen homo est.*

2 ☙ *The vanity of the sciences*—Physical science will not console me for the ignorance of morality in the time of affliction. But the science of ethics will always console me for the ignorance of the physical sciences.

3 ☙ *Imagination*—It is that deceitful part in man, that mistress of error and falsity, the more deceptive that she is not always so; for she would be an infallible rule of truth, if she were an infallible rule of falsehood. But being most generally false, she gives no sign of her nature, impressing the same character on the true and the false.

I do not speak of fools, I speak of the wisest men; and it is among them that the imagination has the great gift of persuasion. Reason protests in vain; it cannot set a true value on things.

This arrogant power, the enemy of reason, who likes to rule and dominate it, has established in man a second nature to show how all-powerful she is. She makes men happy and sad, healthy and sick, rich and poor; she compels reason to believe, doubt, and deny; she blunts the senses, or quickens them; she has her fools and sages; and nothing vexes us more than to see that she fills her devotees with a satisfaction far more full and entire than does reason. Those who have a lively imagination are a great deal more pleased with themselves than the wise can reasonably be. They look down upon men with haughtiness; they argue with boldness and confidence, others with fear and diffidence; and this gaiety of countenance often gives them the advantage in the opinion of the hearers, such favour have the imaginary wise in the eyes of judges of like nature. Imagination cannot make fools wise; but she can make them happy, to the envy of reason which can only make its friends miserable; the one covers them with glory, the other with shame.

What but this faculty of imagination dispenses reputation, awards respect and veneration to persons, works, laws, and the great? How insufficient are all the riches of the earth without her consent!

Would you not say that this magistrate, whose venerable age commands the respect of a whole people, is governed by pure and lofty reason, and that he judges causes according to their true nature without considering those mere trifles which only affect the imagination of the weak? See him go to sermon, full of devout zeal, strengthening his reason with the ardour of his love. He is ready to listen with exemplary respect. Let the preacher appear, and let nature have given him a hoarse voice or a comical cast of countenance, or let his barber have given him a bad shave, or let by chance his dress be more dirtied than usual, then however great the truths he announces, I wager our senator loses his gravity.

If the greatest philosopher in the world find himself upon a plank wider than actually necessary, but hanging over a precipice, his imagination will prevail, though his reason convince him of his safety. Many cannot bear the thought without a cold sweat. I will not state all its effects.

Every one knows that the sight of cats or rats, the crushing of a coal, etc., may unhinge the reason. The tone of voice affects the wisest, and changes the force of a discourse or a poem.

Love or hate alters the aspect of justice. How much greater confidence has an advocate, retained with a large fee, in the justice of his cause! How much better does his bold manner make his case appear to the judges, deceived as they are by appearances! How ludicrous is reason, blown with a breath in every direction!

I should have to enumerate almost every action of men who scarce waver save under her assaults. For reason has been obliged to yield, and the wisest reason takes as her own principles those which the imagination of man has everywhere rashly introduced. [He who would follow reason only would be deemed foolish by the generality of men. We must judge by the opinion of the majority of mankind. Because it has pleased them, we must work all day for pleasures seen to be imaginary; and after sleep has refreshed our tired reason, we must forthwith start up and rush after phantoms, and suffer the impressions of this mistress of the world. This is one of the sources of error, but it is not the only one.]

Our magistrates have known well this mystery. Their red robes, the ermine in which they wrap themselves like furry cats, the courts in which they administer justice, the *fleurs-de-lis*, and all such august apparel were necessary; if the physicians had not their cassocks and their mules, if the doctors had not their square caps and their robes four times too wide, they would never have duped the world, which cannot resist so original an appearance. If magistrates had true justice, and if physicians had the true art of healing, they would have no occasion for square caps; the majesty of these sciences would of itself be venerable enough. But having only imaginary knowledge, they must employ those silly tools that strike the imagination with which they have to deal; and thereby in fact they inspire respect. Soldiers alone are not disguised in this manner, because indeed their part is the most essential; they establish themselves by force, the others by show.

Therefore our kings seek out no disguises. They do not mask themselves in extraordinary costumes to appear such; but they are accompanied by guards and halberdiers. Those armed and red-faced puppets who have hands and power for them alone, those trumpets and drums which go before them, and those legions round about them, make the stoutest tremble. They have not dress only, they have might. A very refined reason is required to regard as an ordinary man the Grand Turk, in his superb seraglio, surrounded by forty thousand janissaries.

We cannot even see an advocate in his robe and with his cap on his head, without a favourable opinion of his ability. The imagination disposes of everything; it makes beauty, justice, and happiness, which is everything in the world. I should much like to see an Italian work, of which I only know the title, which alone is worth many books, *Della opinione regina del mondo*. I approve the book without knowing it, save the evil in it, if any. These are pretty much the effects of that deceptive faculty, which seems to have been expressly given us to lead us into necessary error. We have, however, many other sources of error.

Not only are old impressions capable of misleading us; the charms of novelty have the same power. Hence arise all the disputes of men, who taunt each other either with following the false impressions of childhood or with running rashly after the new. Who keeps the due mean? Let him appear and prove it. There is no principle, however natural to us from infancy, which may not be made to pass for a false impression either of education or of sense.

"Because," say some, "you have believed from childhood that a box was empty when you saw nothing in it, you have believed in the possibility of a vacuum. This is an illusion of your senses, strengthened by custom, which science must correct." "Because," say others, "you have been taught at school that there is no vacuum, you have perverted your common sense which clearly comprehended it, and you must correct this by returning to your first state." Which has deceived you, your senses or your education?

We have another source of error in diseases. They spoil the judgment and the senses; and if the more serious produce a sensible change, I do not doubt that slighter ills produce a proportionate impression.

Our own interest is again a marvellous instrument for nicely putting out our eyes. The justest man in the world is not allowed to be judge in his own cause; I know some who, in order not to fall into this self-love, have been perfectly unjust out of opposition. The sure way of losing a just cause has been to get it recommended to these men by their near relatives.

Justice and truth are two such subtle points, that our tools are too blunt to touch them accurately. If they reach the point, they either crush it, or lean all round, more on the false than on the true.

[Man is so happily formed that he has no . . . good of the true, and several excellent of the false. Let us now see how much . . . But the most powerful cause of error is the war existing between the senses and reason.]

4 ☙ There are different kinds of right understanding; some have right understanding in a certain order of things, and not in others, where they go astray. Some draw conclusions well from a few premises, and this displays an acute judgment.

Others draw conclusions well where there are many premises.

For example, the former easily learn hydrostatics, where the premises are few, but the conclusions are so fine that only the greatest acuteness can reach them.

And in spite of that these persons would perhaps not be great mathematicians, because mathematics contain a great number of premises, and there is perhaps a kind of intellect that can search with ease a few premises to the bottom, and cannot in the least penetrate those matters in which there are many premises.

There are then two kinds of intellect: the one able to penetrate acutely and deeply into the conclusions of given premises, and this is the precise intellect; the other able to comprehend a great number of premises without confusing them, and this is the mathematical intellect. The one has force and exactness, the other comprehension. Now the one quality can exist without the other; the intellect can be strong and narrow, and can also be comprehensive and weak.

5 ☙ *Mathematics, intuition*—True eloquence makes light of eloquence, true morality makes light of morality; that is to say, the morality of the judgment, which has no rules, makes light of the morality of the intellect.

For it is to judgment that perception belongs, as science belongs to intellect. Intuition is the part of judgment, mathematics of intellect.

To make light of philosophy is to be a true philosopher.

6 ☙ The greater intellect one has, the more originality one finds in men. Ordinary persons find no difference between men.

7 ☙ People are generally better persuaded by the reasons which they have themselves discovered than by those which have come into the mind of others.

8 ☙ When a natural discourse paints a passion or an effect, one feels within oneself the truth of what one reads, which was there before, although one did not know it. Hence one is inclined to love him who makes us feel it, for he has not shown us his own riches, but ours. And thus this benefit renders him pleasing to us, besides that such community of intellect as we have with him necessarily inclines the heart to love.

9 ☙ Eloquence is an art of saying things in such a way—(1) that those to whom we speak may listen to them without pain and with pleasure; (2) that they feel themselves interested, so that self-love leads them more willingly to reflection upon it

It consists, then, in a correspondence which we seek to establish between the head and the heart of those to whom we speak, on the one hand, and, on the other, between the thoughts and the expressions which we employ. This assumes that we have studied well the heart of man so as to know all its powers, and then to find the just proportions of the discourse which we wish to adapt to them. We must put ourselves in the place of those who are to hear us, and make trial on our own heart of the turn which we give to our discourse in order to see whether one is made for the other, and whether we can assure ourselves that the hearer will be, as it were, forced to surrender. We ought to restrict ourselves, so far as possible, to the simple and natural, and not to magnify that which is little, or belittle that which is great. It is not enough that a thing be beautiful; it must be suitable to the subject, and there must be in it nothing of excess or defect.

10 ☙ Rivers are roads which move, and which carry us whither we desire to go.

When we do not know the truth of a thing, it is of advantage that there should exist a common error which determines the mind of man, as, for example, the moon, to which is attributed the change of seasons, the progress of diseases, etc. For the chief malady of man is restless curiosity about things which he cannot understand; and it is not so bad for him to be in error as to be curious to no purpose.

11 ☙ The manner in which Epictetus, Montaigne, and Salomon de Tultie wrote is the most usual, the most suggestive, the most remembered, and the oftenest quoted; because it is entirely composed of thoughts born from the common talk of life. As when we speak of the common error which exists among men that the moon is the cause of everything, we never fail to say that Salomon de Tultie says that when we do not

know the truth of a thing, it is of advantage that there should exist a common error, etc.; which is the thought above.

12 ◆ *First part*: Misery of man without God.
Second part: Happiness of man with God.
Or,
First part: That nature is corrupt. Proved by nature itself.
Second part: That there is a Redeemer. Proved by Scripture.

13 ◆ One must know oneself. If this does not serve to discover truth, it at least serves as a rule of life, and there is nothing better.

There is an universal and essential difference between the actions of the will and all other actions.

14 ◆ The will is one of the chief factors in belief, not that it creates belief, but because things are true or false according to the aspect in which we look at them. The will, which prefers one aspect to another, turns away the mind from considering the qualities of all that it does not like to see; and thus the mind, moving in accord with the will, stops to consider the aspect which it likes, and so judges by what it sees.

15 ◆ Between us and heaven or hell there is only life, which is the frailest thing in the world.

16 ◆ Two errors: 1. To take everything literally. 2. To take everything spiritually.

17 ☙§ On what shall man found the order of the world which he would govern? Shall it be on the caprice of each individual? What confusion! Shall it be on justice? Man is ignorant of it.

Certainly had he known it, he would not have established this maxim, the most general of all that obtain among men, that each should follow the custom of his own country. The glory of true equity would have brought all nations under subjection, and legislators would not have taken as their model the fancies and caprice of Persians and Germans instead of this unchanging justice. We would have seen it set up in all the States on earth and in all times; whereas we see neither justice nor injustice which does not change its nature with change in climate. Three degrees of latitude reverse all jurisprudence; a meridian decides the truth. Fundamental laws change after a few years of possession; right has its epochs; the entry of Saturn into the Lion marks to us the origin of such and such a crime. A strange justice that is bounded by a river! Truth on this side of the Pyrenees, error on the other side.

Men admit that justice does not consist in these customs, but that it resides in natural laws, common to every country. They would certainly maintain it obstinately, if reckless chance which has distributed human laws had encountered even one which was universal; but the farce is that the caprice of men has so many vagaries that there is no such law.

Theft, incest, infanticide, parricide, have all had a place among virtuous actions. Can anything be more ridiculous than that a man should have the right to kill me because he lives on the other side of the water, and because his ruler has a quarrel with mine, though I have none with him?

Doubtless there are natural laws; but good reason once corrupted has corrupted all. *Nihil amplius nostrum est; quod nostrum dicimus, artis est. Ex senatus—consultis et plebiscitis crimina exercentur. Ut olim vitiis, sic nunc legibus laboramus.*

The result of this confusion is that one affirms the essence of justice to be the authority of the legislator; another, the interest of the sovereign; another, present custom, and this is the most sure. Nothing, according to reason alone, is just in itself; all changes with time. Custom creates the whole of equity, for the simple reason that it is accepted. It is the mystical foundation of its authority; whoever carries it back to first principles destroys it. Nothing is so faulty as those laws which correct faults. He who obeys them because they are just, obeys a justice which is imaginary, and not the essence of law; it is quite self-contained, it is law and nothing more. He who will examine its motive will find it so feeble and so trifling that if he be not accustomed to contemplate the wonders of human imagination, he will marvel that one century has gained for it so much pomp and reverence. The art of opposition and of revolution is to unsettle established customs, sounding them even to their source, to point out their want of authority and justice. We must, it is said, get back to the natural and fundamental laws of the State, which an unjust custom has abolished. It is a game certain to result in the loss of all; nothing will be just on the balance. Yet people readily lend their ear to such arguments. They shake off the yoke as soon as they recognise it; and the great profit by their ruin, and by that of these curious investigators of accepted customs. But from a contrary mistake men sometimes think they can justly do everything which is not without an example. That is why the wisest of legislators said that it was necessary to deceive men for their own good; and another, a good politician, *cum veritatem qua liberetur ignoret, expedit quod fallatur.* We must not see the fact of usurpation; law was once introduced without reason, and has become reasonable. We must make it regarded as authoritative, eternal, and conceal its origin, if we do not wish that it should soon come to an end.

18 ☙ Let them at least learn what is the religion they attack, before attacking it. If this religion boasted of having a clear view of God, and of possessing it open and unveiled, it would be attacking it to say that we see nothing in the world

which shows it with this clearness. But since, on the contrary, it says that men are in darkness and estranged from God, that He has hidden Himself from their knowledge, that this is in fact the name which He gives Himself in the Scriptures, *Deus absconditus;* and finally, if it endeavours equally to establish these two things: that God has set up in the Church visible signs to make Himself known to those who should seek Him sincerely, and that He has nevertheless so disguised them that He will only be perceived by those who seek Him with all their heart; what advantage can they obtain, when, in the negligence with which they make profession of being in search of the truth, they cry out that nothing reveals it to them; and since that darkness in which they are, and with which they upbraid the Church, establishes only one of the things which she affirms, without touching the other, and, very far from destroying, proves her doctrine?

In order to attack it, they should have protested that they had made every effort to seek Him everywhere, and even in that which the Church proposes for their instruction, but without satisfaction. If they talked in this manner, they would in truth be attacking one of her pretensions. But I hope here to show that no reasonable person can speak thus, and I venture even to say that no one has ever done so. We know well enough how those who are of this mind behave. They believe they have made great efforts for their instruction, when they have spent a few hours in reading some book of Scripture, and have questioned some priest on the truths of the faith. After that, they boast of having made vain search in books and among men. But, verily, I will tell them what I have often said, that this negligence is insufferable. We are not here concerned with the trifling interests of some stranger, that we should treat it in this fashion; the matter concerns ourselves and our all.

The immortality of the soul is a matter which is of so great consequence to us, and which touches us so profoundly, that we must have lost all feeling to be indifferent as to knowing what it is. All our actions and thoughts must take such different courses, according as there are or are not eternal joys to hope for, that it is impossible to take one step with sense and judgment, unless we regulate our course by our view of this point which ought to be our ultimate end.

Thus our first interest and our first duty is to enlighten ourselves on this subject, whereon depends all our conduct. Therefore among those who do not believe, I make a vast difference between those who strive with all their power to inform themselves, and those who live without troubling or thinking about it.

I can have only compassion for those who sincerely bewail their doubt, who regard it as the greatest of misfortunes, and who, sparing no effort to escape it, make of this inquiry their principal and most serious occupation.

But as for those who pass their life without thinking of this ultimate end of life, and who, for this sole reason that they do not find within themselves the lights which convince them of it, neglect to seek them elsewhere, and to examine thoroughly whether this opinion is one of those which people receive with credulous simplicity, or one of those which, although obscure in themselves, have nevertheless a solid and immovable foundation, I look upon them in a manner quite different.

This carelessness in a matter which concerns themselves, their eternity, their all, moves me more to anger than pity; it astonishes and shocks me; it is to me monstrous. I do not say this out of the pious zeal of a spiritual devotion. I expect, on the contrary, that we ought to have this feeling from principles of human interest and self-love; for this we need only see what the least enlightened persons see.

We do not require great education of the mind to understand that here is no real and lasting satisfaction; that our pleasures are only vanity; that our evils are infinite; and, lastly, that death, which threatens us every moment, must infallibly place us within a few years under the dreadful necessity of being for ever either annihilated or unhappy.

There is nothing more real than this, nothing more terrible. Be we as heroic as we like, that is the end which awaits the noblest life in the world. Let us reflect on this, and then say whether it is not beyond doubt that there is no good in this life but in the hope of another; that we are happy only in proportion as we draw near it; and that, as there are no more woes for those who have complete assurance of eternity, so there is no more happiness for those who have no insight into it.

Surely then it is a great evil thus to be in doubt, but it is at least an indispensable duty to seek when we are in such doubt; and thus the doubter who does not seek is altogether completely unhappy and completely wrong. And if besides this he is easy and content, professes to be so, and indeed boasts of it; if it is this state itself which is the subject of his joy and vanity, I have no words to describe so silly a creature.

How can people hold these opinions? What joy can we find in the expectation of nothing but hopeless misery? What reason for boasting that we are in impenetrable darkness? And how can it happen that the following argument occurs to a reasonable man?

"I know not who put me into the world, nor what the world is, nor what I myself am. I am in terrible ignorance of everything. I know not what my body is, nor my senses, nor my soul, not even that part of me which thinks what I say, which reflects on all and on itself, and knows itself no more than the rest. I see those frightful spaces of the universe which surround me, and I find myself tied to one corner of this vast expanse, without knowing why I am put in this place rather than in another, nor why the short time which is given me to live is assigned to me at this point rather than at another of the whole eternity which was before me or which shall come after me. I see nothing but infinities on all sides, which surround me as an atom, and as a shadow which endures only for an instant and returns no more. All I know is that I must soon die, but what I know least is this very death which I cannot escape.

"As I know not whence I come, so I know not whither I go. I know only that, in leaving this world, I fall for ever either into annihilation or into the hands of an angry God, without knowing to which of these two states I shall be for ever assigned. Such is my state, full of weakness and uncertainty. And from all this I conclude that I ought to spend all the days of my life without caring to inquire into what must happen to me. Perhaps I might find some solution to my doubts, but I will not take the trouble, nor take a step to seek it; and after treating with scorn those who are concerned with this care, I will go without foresight and without fear to try the great event, and let myself be led carelessly to death, uncertain of the eternity of my future state."

Who would desire to have for a friend a man who talks in this fashion? Who would choose him out from others to tell him of his affairs? Who would have recourse to him in affliction? And indeed to what use in life could one put him?

In truth, it is the glory of religion to have for enemies men so unreasonable; and their opposition to it is so little dangerous that it serves on the contrary to establish its truths. For the Christian faith goes mainly to establish these two facts: the corruption of nature, and redemption by Jesus Christ. Now I contend that if these men do not serve to prove the truth of the redemption by the holiness of their behaviour, they at least serve admirably to show the corruption of nature by sentiments so unnatural.

Nothing is so important to man as his own state, nothing is so formidable to him as eternity; and thus it is not natural that there should be men indifferent to the loss of their existence, and to the perils of everlasting suffering. They are quite different with regard to all other things. They are afraid of mere trifles; they foresee them; they feel them. And this same man who spends so many days and nights in rage and despair for the loss of office, or for some imaginary insult to his honour, is the very one who knows without anxiety and without emotion that he will lose all by death. It is a monstrous thing to see in the same heart and at the same time this sensibility to trifles and this strange insensibility to the greatest objects. It is an incomprehensible enchantment, and a supernatural slumber, which indicates as its cause an all-powerful force.

There must be a strange confusion in the nature of man,

that he should boast of being in that state in which it seems incredible that a single individual should be. However, experience has shown me so great a number of such persons that the fact would be surprising, if we did not know that the greater part of those who trouble themselves about the matter are disingenuous, and not in fact what they say. They are people who have heard it said that it is the fashion to be thus daring. It is what they call shaking off the yoke, and they try to imitate this. But it would not be difficult to make them understand how greatly they deceive themselves in thus seeking esteem. This is not the way to gain it, even I say among those men of the world who take a healthy view of things, and who know that the only way to succeed in this life is to make ourselves appear honourable, faithful, judicious, and capable of useful service to a friend; because naturally men love only what may be useful to them. Now, what do we gain by hearing it said of a man that he has now thrown off the yoke, that he does not believe there is a God who watches our actions, that he considers himself the sole master of his conduct, and that he thinks he is accountable for it only to himself? Does he think that he has thus brought us to have henceforth complete confidence in him, and to look to him for consolation, advice, and help in every need of life? Do they profess to have delighted us by telling us that they hold our soul to be only a little wind and smoke, especially by telling us this in a haughty and self-satisfied tone of voice? Is this a thing to say gaily? Is it not, on the contrary, a thing to say sadly, as the saddest thing in the world.

If they thought of it seriously, they would see that this is so bad a mistake, so contrary to good sense, so opposed to decency, and so removed in every respect from that good breeding which they seek, that they would be more likely to correct than to pervert those who had an inclination to follow them. And indeed, make them give an account of their opinions, and of the reasons which they have for doubting religion, and they will say to you things so feeble and so petty, that they will persuade you of the contrary. The following is what a person one day said to such a one very appositely:

"If you continue to talk in this manner, you will really make me religious." And he was right, for who would not have a horror of holding opinions in which he would have such contemptible persons as companions!

Thus those who only feign these opinions would be very unhappy, if they restrained their natural feelings in order to make themselves the most conceited of men. If, at the bottom of their heart, they are troubled at not having more light, let them not disguise the fact; this avowal will not be shameful. The only shame is to have none. Nothing reveals more an extreme weakness of mind than not to know the misery of a godless man. Nothing is more indicative of a bad disposition of heart than not to desire the truth of eternal promises. Nothing is more dastardly than to act with bravado before God. Let them then leave these impieties to those who are sufficiently ill-bred to be really capable of them. Let them at least be honest men, if they cannot be Christians. Finally, let them recognise that there are two kinds of people one can call reasonable; those who serve God with all their heart because they know Him, and those who seek Him with all their heart because they do not know Him.

But as for those who live without knowing Him and without seeking Him, they judge themselves so little worthy of their own care, that they are not worthy of the care of others; and it needs all the charity of the religion which they despise, not to despise them even to the point of leaving them to their folly. But because this religion obliges us always to regard them, so long as they are in this life, as capable of the grace which can enlighten them, and to believe that they may, in a little time, be more replenished with faith than we are, and that, on the other hand, we may fall into the blindness wherein they are, we must do for them what we would they should do for us if we were in their place, and call upon them to have pity upon themselves, and to take at least some steps in the endeavour to find light. Let them give to reading this some of the hours which they otherwise employ so uselessly; whatever aversion they may bring to the task, they will perhaps gain something, and at least will not lose much. But as for those who bring to the task perfect sincerity and a real desire to meet with truth, those I hope will be satisfied and convinced of the proofs of a religion so divine, which I have here collected, and in which I have followed somewhat after this order . . .

*

Before entering into the proofs of the Christian religion, I find it necessary to point out the sinfulness of those men who live in indifference to the search for truth in a matter which is so important to them, and which touches them so nearly.

Of all their errors, this doubtless is the one which most convicts them of foolishness and blindness, and in which it is easiest to confound them by the first glimmerings of common sense, and by natural feelings.

For it is not to be doubted that the duration of this life is but a moment; that the state of death is eternal, whatever may be its nature; and that thus all our actions and thoughts must take such different directions according to the state of that eternity, that it is impossible to take one step with sense and judgment, unless we regulate our course by the truth of that point which ought to be our ultimate end.

There is nothing clearer than this; and thus, according to the principles of reason, the conduct of men is wholly unreasonable, if they do not take another course.

On this point, therefore, we condemn those who live without thought of the ultimate end of life, who let themselves be guided by their own inclinations and their own pleasures without reflection and without concern, and, as if they could annihilate eternity by turning away their thought from it, think only of making themselves happy for the moment.

Yet this eternity exists, and death, which must open into it, and threatens them every hour, must in a little time infallibly put them under the dreadful necessity of being either annihilated or unhappy for ever, without knowing which of these eternities is for ever prepared for them.

This is a doubt of terrible consequence. They are in peril of eternal woe and thereupon, as if the matter were not worth the trouble, they neglect to inquire whether this is one of those opinions which people receive with too credulous a facility, or one of those which, obscure in themselves, have a very firm, though hidden, foundation. Thus they know not whether there be truth or falsity in the matter, nor whether there be strength or weakness in the proofs. They have them before their eyes; they refuse to look at them; and in that ignorance they choose all that is necessary to fall into this misfortune if it exists, to await death to make trial of it, yet to be very content in this state, to make profession of it, and indeed to boast of it. Can we think seriously on the importance of this subject without being horrified at conduct so extravagant?

This resting in ignorance is a monstrous thing, and they who pass their life in it must be made to feel its extravagance and stupidity, by having it shown to them, so that they may be confounded by the sight of their folly. For this is how men reason, when they choose to live in such ignorance of what they are, and without seeking enlightenment. "I know not," they say . . .

19 ☙ Without this divine knowledge what could men do but either become elated by the inner feeling of their past greatness which still remains to them, or become despondent at the sight of their present weakness? For, not seeing the whole truth, they could not attain to perfect virtue. Some considering nature as incorrupt, others as incurable, they could not escape either pride or sloth, the two sources of all vice; since they cannot but either abandon themselves to it through cowardice, or escape it by pride. For if they knew the excellence of man, they were ignorant of his corruption; so that they easily avoided sloth, but fell into pride. And if they recognised the infirmity of nature, they were ignorant of its dignity; so that they could easily avoid vanity, but it was to fall into despair. Thence arise the different schools of the

Stoics and Epicureans, the Dogmatists, Academicians, etc.

The Christian religion alone has been able to cure these two vices, not by expelling the one through means of the other according to the wisdom of the world, but by expelling both according to the simplicity of the Gospel. For it teaches the righteous that it raises them even to a participation in divinity itself; that in this lofty state they still carry the source of all corruption, which renders them during all their life subject to error, misery, death, and sin; and it proclaims to the most ungodly that they are capable of the grace of their Redeemer. So making those tremble whom it justifies, and consoling those whom it condemns, religion so justly tempers fear with hope through that double capacity of grace and of sin, common to all, that it humbles infinitely more than reason alone can do, but without despair; and it exalts infinitely more than natural pride, but without inflating; thus making it evident that alone being exempt from error and vice, it alone fulfils the duty of instructing and correcting men.

Who then can refuse to believe and adore this heavenly light? For is it not clearer than day that we perceive within ourselves ineffaceable marks of excellence? And is it not equally true that we experience every hour the results of our deplorable condition? What does this chaos and monstrous confusion proclaim to us but the truth of these two states, with a voice so powerful that it is impossible to resist it?

20 ◆§ This is what I see and what troubles me. I look on all sides, and I see only darkness everywhere. Nature presents to me nothing which is not matter of doubt and concern. If I saw nothing there which revealed a Divinity, I would come to a negative conclusion; if I saw everywhere the signs of a Creator, I would remain peacefully in faith. But, seeing too much to deny and too little to be sure, I am in a state to be pitied; wherefore I have a hundred times wished that if a God maintains nature, she should testify to Him unequivocally, and that, if the signs she gives are deceptive, she should

suppress them altogether; that she should say everything or nothing, that I might see which cause I ought to follow. Whereas in my present state, ignorant of what I am or of what I ought to do, I know neither my condition nor my duty. My heart inclines wholly to know where is the true good, in order to follow it; nothing would be too dear to me for eternity.

I envy those whom I see living in the faith with such carelessness, and who make such a bad use of a gift of which it seems to me I would make such a different use.

*

It is incomprehensible that God should exist, and it is incomprehensible that He should not exist; that the soul should be joined to the body, and that we should have no soul; that the world should be created, and that it should not be created, etc.; that original sin should be, and that it should not be.

21 ❧ There are only three kinds of persons; those who serve God, having found Him; others who are occupied in seeking Him, not having found Him; while the remainder live without seeking Him, and without having found Him. The first are reasonable and happy, the last are foolish and unhappy; those between are unhappy and reasonable.

22 ❧ Religion is suited to all kinds of minds. Some pay attention only to its establishment, and this religion is such that its very establishment suffices to prove its truth. Others trace it even to the apostles. The more learned go back to the beginning of the world. The angels see it better still, and from a more distant time.

23 ☙ Words differently arranged have a different meaning, and meanings differently arranged have different effects.

24 ☙ We only consult the ear because the heart is wanting. The rule is uprightness.

Beauty of omission, of judgment.

25 ☙ *Poetical beauty*—As we speak of poetical beauty, so ought we to speak of mathematical beauty and medical beauty. But we do not do so; and the reason is that we know well what is the object of mathematics, and that it consists in proofs, and what is the object of medicine, and that it consists in healing. But we do not know in what grace consists, which is the object of poetry. We do not know the natural model which we ought to imitate; and through lack of this knowledge, we have coined fantastic terms, "The golden age," "The wonder of our times," "Fatal," etc., and call this jargon poetical beauty.

But whoever imagines a woman after this model, which consists in saying little things in big words, will see a pretty girl adorned with mirrors and chains, at whom he will smile; because we know better wherein consists the charm of woman than the charm of verse. But those who are ignorant would admire her in this dress, and there are many villages in which she would be taken for the queen; hence we call sonnets made after this model "Village Queens."

26 ☙ We should not be able to say of a man, "He is a mathematician," or "a preacher," or "eloquent"; but that he is "a gentleman." That universal quality alone pleases me. It is a bad sign when, on seeing a person, you remember his book. I would prefer you to see no quality till you meet it

and have occasion to use it (*Ne quid nimis*), for fear some one quality prevail and designate the man. Let none think him a fine speaker, unless oratory be in question, and then let them think it.

27 ☙ Reason commands us far more imperiously than a master; for in disobeying the one we are unfortunate, and in disobeying the other we are fools.

28 ☙ Man is but a reed, the most feeble thing in nature; but he is a thinking reed. The entire universe need not arm itself to crush him. A vapour, a drop of water suffices to kill him. But, if the universe were to crush him, man would still be more noble than that which killed him, because he knows that he dies and the advantage which the universe has over him; the universe knows nothing of this.

All our dignity consists, then, in thought. By it we must elevate ourselves, and not by space and time which we cannot fill. Let us endeavour, then, to think well; this is the principle of morality.

29 ☙ [*Against the philosophers who believe in God without Jesus Christ.*]

Philosophers—They believe that God alone is worthy to be loved and admired; and they have desired to be loved and admired of men, and do not know their own corruption. If they feel full of feelings of love and admiration, and find therein their chief delight, very well, let them think themselves good. But if they find themselves averse to Him, if they have no inclination but the desire to establish themselves in the esteem of men, and if their whole perfection consists only in making men—but without constraint—find their happiness in loving them, I declare that this perfection is horrible. What! they have known God, and have not desired solely that men should love Him, but that men should stop short at them! They have wanted to be the object of the voluntary delight of men.

30 ☙ We know truth, not only by the reason, but also by the heart, and it is in this last way that we know first principles; and reason, which has no part in it, tries in vain to impugn them. The sceptics, who have only this for their object, labour to no purpose. We know that we do not dream, and however impossible it is for us to prove it by reason, this inability demonstrates only the weakness of our reason, but not, as they affirm, the uncertainty of all our knowledge. For the knowledge of first principles, as space, time, motion, number, is as sure as any of those which we get from reasoning. And reason must trust these intuitions of the heart, and must base them on every argument. (We have intuitive knowledge of the tri-dimensional nature of space, and of the infinity of number, and reason then shows that there are no two square numbers one of which is double of the other. Principles are intuited, propositions are inferred, all with certainty, though in different ways.) And it is as useless and absurd for reason to demand from the heart proofs of her first principles, before admitting them, as it would be for the heart to demand from reason an intuition of all demonstrated propositions before accepting them.

This inability ought, then, to serve only to humble reason, which would judge all, but not to impugn our certainty, as if only reason were capable of instructing us. Would to God, on the contrary, that we had never need of it, and that we knew everything by instinct and intuition! But nature has refused us this boon. On the contrary, she has given us but very little knowledge of this kind; and all the rest can be acquired only by reasoning.

Therefore, those to whom God has imparted religion by

intuition are very fortunate, and justly convinced. But to those who do not have it, we can give it only by reasoning, waiting for God to give them spiritual insight, without which faith is only human, and useless for salvation.

31 ☙ *Order—Against the objection that Scripture has no order.*

The heart has its own order; the intellect has its own, which is by principle and demonstration. The heart has another. We do not prove that we ought to be loved by enumerating in order the causes of love; that would be ridiculous.

32 ☙ It is the heart which experiences God, and not the reason. This, then, is faith: God felt by the heart, not by the reason.

Faith is a gift of God; do not believe that we said it was a gift of reasoning. Other religions do not say this of their faith. They only give reasoning in order to arrive at it, and yet it does not bring them to it.

33 ☙ Thought constitutes the greatness of man.

34 ☙ The heart has its reasons, which reason does not know. We feel it in a thousand things. I say that the heart naturally loves the Universal Being, and also itself naturally, according as it gives itself to them; and it hardens itself against one or the other at its will. You have rejected the one, and kept the other. Is it by reason that you love yourself?

George Berkeley

A TREATISE CONCERNING THE PRINCIPLES OF HUMAN KNOWLEDGE

George Berkeley
[1685–1753]

From Kilkenny, Ireland, where he was born, George Berkeley went to Trinity College, Dublin, as student, fellow and tutor. There he wrote his famous *Treatise Concerning the Principles of Human Knowledge*. After living on the Continent for five years, he returned to England and soon became Dean of Dromore and, later, of Derry in Ireland. He sailed for America in 1728 with the intention of establishing a college in the Bermudas, but remained for three years in Newport, Rhode Island, where he continued with his philosophical writings. Back in England, established as one of the foremost thinkers of the world, he was appointed Bishop of Cloyne. *The Principles of Human Knowledge* created in its own time a revolution in speculative thought and is today the classic essay on the examination of conscious knowledge as evidence of a divine intelligence.

CONCERNING HUMAN KNOWLEDGE

[*Chapters I to VIII*]

GEORGE BERKELEY

Preface

What I here make public has, after a long and scrupulous inquiry, seemed to me evidently true, and not unuseful to be known, particularly to those who are tainted with scepticism, or want a demonstration of the existence and immateriality of God, or the natural immortality of the soul. Whether it be so or no, I am content the reader should impartially examine; since I do not think myself any further concerned for the success of what I have written than as it is agreeable to truth. But to the end this may not suffer, I make it my request that the reader suspend his judgment till he has once, at least, read the whole through with that degree of attention and thought which the subject matter shall seem to deserve. For as there are some passages that, taken by themselves, are very liable (nor could it be remedied) to gross misinterpretation, and to be charged with most absurd consequences, which, nevertheless, upon an entire perusal will appear not to follow from them: so likewise, though the whole should be read over, yet if this be done transiently, it is very probable my sense may be mistaken; but to a thinking reader, I flatter myself, it will be throughout clear and obvious. As for the characters of novelty and singularity, which some of the following notions may seem to bear, it is, I hope, needless to make any apology on that account. He must surely be either very weak, or very little acquainted with the sciences, who shall reject a truth that is capable of demonstration, for no other reason but because it is newly known and contrary to the prejudices of mankind. Thus much I thought fit to premise, in order to prevent, if possible, the hasty censures of a sort of men, who are too apt to condemn an opinion before they rightly comprehend it.

Introduction

Philosophy being nothing else but the study of wisdom and truth, it may with reason be expected that those who have spent most time and pains in it should enjoy a greater calm and serenity of mind, a greater clearness and evidence of knowledge, and be less disturbed with doubts and difficulties than other men. Yet so it is, we see the illiterate bulk of mankind that walk the highroad of plain common sense, and are governed by the dictates of nature, for the most part easy and undisturbed. To them nothing that is familiar appears unaccountable or difficult to comprehend. They complain not of any want of evidence in their senses, and are out of all danger of becoming sceptics. But no sooner do we depart from sense and instinct to follow the light of a superior principle, to reason, meditate, and reflect on the nature of things, but a thousand scruples spring up in our minds concerning those things which before we seemed fully to comprehend. Prejudices and errors of sense do from all parts discover themselves to our view; and, endeavoring to correct these by reason, we are insensibly drawn into uncouth paradoxes, difficulties, and inconsistencies, which multiply and grow upon us as we advance in speculation, till at length, having wandered through many intricate mazes, we find ourselves just where we were, or, which is worse, sit down in a forlorn scepticism.

2 ☙§ The cause of this is thought to be the obscurity of things, or the natural weakness and imperfection of our understandings. It is said the faculties we have are few, and those designed by nature for the support and comfort of life, and not to penetrate into the inward essence and constitution of things. Besides, the mind of man being finite, when it treats of things which partake of infinity it is not to be wondered at if it run into absurdities and contradictions, out of which it is impossible it should ever extricate itself, it being of the nature of infinite not to be comprehended by that which is finite.

3 ☙§ But perhaps we may be too partial to ourselves in placing the fault originally in our faculties, and not rather in the wrong use we make of them. It is a hard thing to suppose that right deductions from true principles should ever end in consequences which cannot be maintained or made consistent. We should believe that God has dealt more bountifully with the sons of men than to give them a strong desire for that knowledge which he had placed quite out of their reach. This were not agreeable to the wonted indulgent methods of Providence, which whatever appetites it may have implanted in the creatures, doth usually furnish them with such means as, if rightly made use of, will not fail to satisfy them. Upon the whole, I am inclined to think that the far greater part, if not all, of those difficulties which have hitherto amused philosophers, and blocked up the way to knowledge, are entirely

owing to ourselves—that we have first raised a dust and then complain we cannot see.

4 ◆§ My purpose therefore is, to try if I can discover what those principles are which have introduced all that doubtfulness and uncertainty, those absurdities and contradictions, into the several sects of philosophy; insomuch that the wisest men have thought our ignorance incurable, conceiving it to arise from the natural dullness and limitation of our faculties. And surely it is a work well deserving our pains to make a strict inquiry concerning the first principles of human knowledge, to sift and examine them on all sides, especially since there may be some grounds to suspect that those lets and difficulties, which stay and embarrass the mind in its search after truth, do not spring from any darkness and intricacy in the objects, or natural defect in the understanding, so much as from false principles which have been insisted on, and might have been avoided.

5 ◆§ How difficult and discouraging soever this attempt may seem, when I consider how many great and extraordinary men have gone before me in the like designs, yet I am not without some hopes, upon the consideration that the largest views are not always the clearest, and that he who is short-sighted will be obliged to draw the object nearer, and may, perhaps, by a close and narrow survey, discern that which had escaped far better eyes.

6 ◆§ In order to prepare the mind of the reader for the easier conceiving what follows, it is proper to premise somewhat, by way of introduction, concerning the nature and abuse of language. But the unraveling this matter leads me in some

measure to anticipate my design, by taking notice of what seems to have had a chief part in rendering speculation intricate and perplexed, and to have occasioned innumerable errors and difficulties in almost all parts of knowledge. And that is the opinion that the mind hath a power of framing *abstract ideas* or notions of things. He who is not a perfect stranger to the writings and disputes of philosophers must needs acknowledge that no small part of them are spent about abstract ideas. These are in a more especial manner thought to be the object of those sciences which go by the name of *logic* and *metaphysics,* and of all that which passes under the notion of the most abstracted and sublime learning, in all which one shall scarce find any question handled in such a manner as does not suppose their existence in the mind, and that it is well acquainted with them.

7 ☙ It is agreed on all hands that the qualities or modes of things do never really exist each of them apart by itself, and separated from all others, but are mixed, as it were, and blended together, several in the same object. But, we are told, the mind being able to consider each quality singly, or abstracted from those other qualities with which it is united, does by that means frame to itself abstract ideas. For example, there is perceived by sight an object extended, colored, and moved: this mixed or compound idea the mind resolving into its simple, constituent parts, and viewing each by itself, exclusive of the rest, does frame the abstract ideas of extension, color, and motion. Not that it is possible for color or motion to exist without extension; but only that the mind can frame to itself by *abstraction* the idea of color exclusive of extension, and of motion exclusive of both color and extension.

8 ☙ Again, the mind having observed that in the particular extensions perceived by sense there is something common

and alike in all, and some other things peculiar, as this or that figure or magnitude, which distinguish them one from another; it considers apart or singles out by itself that which is common, making thereof a most abstract idea of extension, which is neither line, surface, nor solid, nor has any figure or magnitude, but is an idea entirely prescinded from all these. So likewise the mind, by leaving out of the particular colors perceived by sense that which distinguishes them one from another, and retaining that only which is common to all, makes an idea of color in abstract which is neither red, nor blue, nor white, nor any other determinate color. And, in like manner, by considering motion abstractedly not only from the body moved, but likewise from the figure it describes, and all particular directions and velocities, the abstract idea of motion is framed; which equally corresponds to all particular motions whatsoever that may be perceived by sense.

9 ◆ And as the mind frames to itself abstract ideas of qualities or modes, so does it, by the same precision or mental separation, attain abstract ideas of the more compounded beings which include several coexistent qualities. For example, the mind having observed that Peter, James, and John resemble each other in certain common agreements of shape and other qualities, leaves out of the complex or compounded idea it has of Peter, James, and any other particular man, that which is peculiar to each, retaining only what is common to all, and so makes an abstract idea wherein all the particulars equally partake; abstracting entirely from and cutting off all those circumstances and differences which might determine it to any particular existence. And after this manner it is said we come by the abstract idea of man, or, if you please, humanity, or human nature; wherein it is true there is included color, because there is no man but has some color, but then it can be neither white, nor black, nor any particular color,

because there is no one particular color wherein all men partake. So likewise there is included stature, but then it is neither tall stature, nor low stature, nor yet middle stature, but something abstracted from all these. And so of the rest. Moreover, there being a great variety of other creatures that partake in some parts, but not all, of the complex idea of man, the mind, leaving out those parts which are peculiar to men, and retaining those only which are common to all the living creatures, frames the idea of *animal*, which abstracts not only from all particular men, but also all birds, beasts, fishes, and insects. The constituent parts of the abstract idea of animal are body, life, sense, and spontaneous motion. By *body* is meant body without any particular shape or figure, there being no one shape or figure common to all animals, without covering, either of hair, or feathers, or scales, etc., nor yet naked: hair, feathers, scales, and nakedness being the distinguishing properties of particular animals, and for that reason left out of the *abstract idea*. Upon the same account the spontaneous motion must be neither walking, nor flying, nor creeping; it is nevertheless a motion, but what that motion is it is not easy to conceive.

10 ☙ Whether others have this wonderful faculty of abstracting their ideas, they best can tell; for myself, I find indeed I have a faculty of imagining, or representing to myself, the ideas of those particular things I have perceived, and of variously compounding and dividing them. I can imagine a man with two heads, or the upper parts of a man joined to the body of a horse. I can consider the hand, the eye, the nose, each by itself abstracted or separated from the rest of the body. But then whatever hand or eye I imagine, it must have some particular shape and color. Likewise the idea of man that I frame to myself must be either of a white, or a black, or a tawny, a straight, or a crooked, a tall, or a low, or a middle-sized man. I cannot by any effort of thought conceive

the abstract idea above described. And it is equally impossible for me to form the abstract idea of motion distinct from the body moving, and which is neither swift nor slow, curvilinear nor rectilinear; and the like may be said of all other abstract general ideas whatsoever. To be plain, I own myself able to abstract in one sense, as when I consider some particular parts or qualities separated from others, with which, though they are united in some object, yet it is possible they may really exist without them. But I deny that I can abstract from one another, or conceive separately, those qualities which it is impossible should exist so separated; or that I can frame a general notion, by abstracting from particulars in the manner aforesaid—which last are the two proper acceptations of "abstraction." And there are grounds to think most men will acknowledge themselves to be in my case. The generality of men which are simple and illiterate never pretend to abstract notions. It is said they are difficult and not to be attained without pains and study; we may therefore reasonably conclude that, if such there be, they are confined only to the learned.

11 ☙ I proceed to examine what can be alleged in defense of the doctrine of abstraction, and try if I can discover what it is that inclines the men of speculation to embrace an opinion so remote from common sense as that seems to be. There has been a late deservedly esteemed philosopher who, no doubt, has given it very much countenance, by seeming to think the having abstract general ideas is what puts the widest difference in point of understanding betwixt man and beast.

The having of general ideas [saith he] is that which puts a perfect distinction betwixt man and brutes, and is an excellency which the faculties of brutes do by no means attain unto. For, it is evident we observe no footsteps in them of making use of general signs for universal ideas; from which we have reason to imagine that they have not the faculty of abstracting, or making general ideas, since they have no use of words or any other general signs.

And a little after:

> Therefore, I think, we may suppose that it is in this that the species of brutes are discriminated from men, and it is that proper difference wherein they are wholly separated, and which at last widens to so wide a distance. For, if they have any ideas at all, and are not bare machines (as some would have them), we cannot deny them to have some reason. It seems as evident to me that they do, some of them, in certain instances reason as that they have sense; but it is only in particular ideas, just as they receive them from their senses. They are the best of them tied up within those narrow bounds, and have not (as I think) the faculty to enlarge them by any kind of abstraction.[1]

I readily agree with this learned author, that the faculties of brutes can by no means attain to abstraction. But then if this be made the distinguishing property of that sort of animals, I fear a great many of those that pass for men must be reckoned into their number. The reason that is here assigned why we have no grounds to think brutes have abstract general ideas is, that we observe in them no use of words or any other general signs; which is built on this supposition—that the making use of words implies the having general ideas. From which it follows that men who use language are able to abstract or generalize their ideas. That this is the sense and arguing of the author will further appear by his answering the question he in another place puts: "Since all things that exist are only particulars, how come we by general terms?" His answer is: "Words become general by being made the signs of general ideas."[2] But it seems that a word becomes

---

[1] [John Locke] *Essay on* [*concerning*] *Human Understanding*: Book II, Chap. xi, Sec. 10, 11.

[2] *Ibid.*, Book III, Chap. iii, Sec. 6.

general by being made the sign, not of an abstract general idea, but of several particular ideas, any one of which it indifferently suggests to the mind. For example, when it is said "the change of motion is proportional to the impressed force," or that "whatever has extension is divisible," these propositions are to be understood of motion and extension in general; and nevertheless it will not follow that they suggest to my thoughts an idea of motion without a body moved, or any determinate direction and velocity, or that I must conceive an abstract general idea of extension, which is neither line, surface, nor solid, neither great nor small, black, white, nor red, nor of any other determinate color. It is only implied that whatever particular motion I consider, whether it be swift or slow, perpendicular, horizontal, or oblique, or in whatever object, the axiom concerning it holds equally true. As does the other of every particular extension, it matters not whether line, surface, or solid, whether of this or that magnitude or figure.

12 ☙§ By observing how ideas become general we may the better judge how words are made so. And here it is to be noted that I do not deny absolutely there are general ideas, but only that there are any *abstract* general ideas; for in the passages we have quoted wherein there is mention of general ideas, it is always supposed that they are formed by abstraction, after the manner set forth in Sections 8 and 9. Now, if we will annex a meaning to our words, and speak only of what we can conceive, I believe we shall acknowledge that an idea which considered in itself is particular, becomes general by being made to represent or stand for all other particular ideas of the same sort. To make this plain by an example, suppose a geometrician is demonstrating the method of cutting a line in two equal parts. He draws, for instance, a black line of an inch in length: this, which in itself is a particular line, is nevertheless with regard to its signification general, since, as it is there used, it represents all particular lines

whatsoever; so that what is demonstrated of it is demonstrated of all lines, or, in other words, of a line in general. And, as that particular line becomes general by being made a sign, so the *name* "line," which taken absolutely is particular, by being a sign is made general. And as the former owes its generality not to its being the sign of an abstract or general line, but of all particular right lines that may possibly exist, so the latter must be thought to derive its generality from the same cause, namely, the various particular lines which it indifferently denotes.

13 ☙ To give the reader a yet clearer view of the nature of abstract ideas and the uses they are thought necessary to, I shall add one more passage out of the *Essay on Human Understanding*, which is as follows:

Abstract ideas are not so obvious or easy to children or the yet unexercised mind as particular ones. If they seem so to grown men it is only because by constant and familiar use they are made so. For when we nicely reflect upon them, we shall find that general ideas are fictions and contrivances of the mind, that carry difficulty with them, and do not so easily offer themselves as we are apt to imagine. For example, does it not require some pains and skill to form the general idea of a triangle (which is yet none of the most abstract, comprehensive, and difficult); for it must be neither oblique nor rectangle, neither equilateral, equicrural, nor scalenon, but *all and none* of these at once? In effect, it is something imperfect that cannot exist, an idea wherein some parts of several different and *inconsistent* ideas are put together. It is true the mind in this imperfect state has need of such ideas, and makes all the haste to them it can, for the *conveniency of communication and enlargement of knowledge*, to both which it is naturally very much inclined. But yet one has reason to suspect such ideas are marks of our imperfection. At least this is enough to show that the most abstract and general ideas are not those that the mind is first and most easily acquainted with, nor such as its earliest knowledge is conversant about.[3]

If any man has the faculty of framing in his mind such an idea of a triangle as is here described, it is in vain to pretend to dispute him out of it, nor would I go about it. All I desire is that the reader would fully and certainly inform himself whether he has such an idea or no. And this, methinks, can be no hard task for anyone to perform. What is more easy than for anyone to look a little into his own thoughts, and there try whether he has, or can attain to have, an idea that shall correspond with the description that is here given of the general idea of a triangle, which is "neither oblique nor rectangle, equilateral, equicrural nor scalenon, but all and none of these at once"?

14 ◆§ Much is here said of the difficulty that abstract ideas carry with them, and the pains and skill requisite to the forming them. And it is on all hands agreed that there is need of great toil and labor of the mind, to emancipate our thoughts from particular objects, and raise them to those sublime speculations that are conversant about abstract ideas. From all which the natural consequence should seem to be, that so difficult a thing as the forming abstract ideas was not necessary for *communication*, which is so easy and familiar to all sorts of men. But, we are told, if they seem obvious and easy to grown men, it is only because by constant and familiar use they are made so. Now, I would fain know at what time it is men are employed in surmounting that difficulty, and furnishing themselves with those necessary helps for discourse. It cannot be when they are grown up, for then it seems they are not conscious of any such painstaking; it remains therefore to be the business of their childhood. And surely the

[3] Book IV, Chap. vii, Sec. 9.

great and multiplied labor of framing abstract notions will be found a hard task for that tender age. Is it not a hard thing to imagine that a couple of children cannot prate together of their sugar-plums and rattles and the rest of their little trinkets, till they have first tacked together numberless inconsistencies, and so framed in their minds abstract general ideas, and annexed them to every common name they make use of?

15 ☙ Nor do I think them a whit more needful for the enlargement of knowledge than for communication. It is, I know, a point much insisted on, that all knowledge and demonstration are about universal notions, to which I fully agree; but then it does not appear to me that those notions are formed by abstraction in the manner premised: *universality*, so far as I can comprehend, not consisting in the absolute, *positive* nature or conception of anything, but in the *relation* it bears to the particulars signified or represented by it; by virtue whereof it is that things, names, or notions, being in their own nature *particular*, are rendered *universal*. Thus when I demonstrate any proposition concerning triangles, it is to be supposed that I have in view the universal idea of a triangle; which ought not to be understood as if I could frame an idea of a triangle which was neither equilateral, nor scalenon, nor equicrural; but only that the particular triangle I consider, whether of this or that sort it matters not, doth equally stand for and represent all rectilinear triangles whatsoever, and is in that sense *universal*. All which seems very plain and not to include any difficulty in it.

16 ☙ But here it will be demanded how we can know any proposition to be true of all particular triangles, except we have first seen it demonstrated of the abstract idea of a triangle which equally agrees to all? For because a property may be demonstrated to agree to some one particular triangle,

it will not thence follow that it equally belongs to any other triangle which in all respects is not the same with it. For example, having demonstrated that the three angles of an isosceles rectangular triangle are equal to two right ones, I cannot therefore conclude this affection agrees to all other triangles which have neither a right angle nor two equal sides. It seems therefore that, to be certain this proposition is universally true, we must either make a particular demonstration for every particular triangle, which is impossible, or once for all demonstrate it of the abstract idea of a triangle, in which all the particulars do indifferently partake and by which they are all equally represented. To which I answer, that, though the idea I have in view whilst I make the demonstration be, for instance, that of an isosceles rectangular triangle whose sides are of a determinate length, I may nevertheless be certain it extends to all other rectilinear triangles, of what sort or bigness soever. And that because neither the right angle nor the equality nor determinate length of the sides are at all concerned in the demonstration. It is true the diagram I have in view includes all these particulars, but then there is not the least mention made of them in the proof of the proposition. It is not said the three angles are equal to two right ones, because one of them is a right angle, or because the sides comprehending it are of the same length. Which sufficiently shows that the right angle might have been oblique and the sides unequal, and for all that the demonstration have held good. And for this reason it is that I conclude that to be true of any obliquangular or scalenon which I had demonstrated of a particular right-angled equicrural triangle, and not because I demonstrated the proposition of the abstract idea of a triangle. And here it must be acknowledged that a man may consider a figure merely as triangular, without attending to the particular qualities of the angles, or relations of the sides. So far he may abstract; but this will never prove that he can frame an abstract, general, inconsistent idea of a triangle. In like manner we may consider Peter so far forth as man, or so far forth as animal, without framing the forementioned abstract idea, either of man or of animal, inasmuch as all that is perceived is not considered.

17 ☙§ It were an endless as well as an useless thing to trace the schoolmen, those great masters of abstraction, through all the manifold inextricable labyrinths of error and dispute which their doctrine of abstract natures and notions seems to have led them into. What bickerings and controversies, and what a learned dust have been raised about those matters, and what mighty advantage has been from thence derived to mankind, are things at this day too clearly known to need being insisted on. And it had been well if the ill effects of that doctrine were confined to those only who make the most avowed profession of it. When men consider the great pains, industry, and parts that have for so many ages been laid out on the cultivation and advancement of the sciences, and that notwithstanding all this the far greater part of them remains full of darkness and uncertainty, and disputes that are like never to have an end, and even those that are thought to be supported by the most clear and cogent demonstrations contain in them paradoxes which are perfectly irreconcilable to the understandings of men, and that, taking all together, a very small portion of them does supply any real benefit to mankind, otherwise than by being an innocent diversion and amusement—I say the consideration of all this is apt to throw them into a despondency and perfect contempt of all study. But this may perhaps cease upon a view of the false principles that have obtained in the world, amongst all which there is none, methinks, hath a more wide and extended sway over the thoughts of speculative men than this of *abstract* general ideas.

18 ☙§ I come now to consider the *source* of this prevailing notion, and that seems to me to be *language*. And surely noth-

ing of less extent than reason itself could have been the source of an opinion so universally received. The truth of this appears as from other reasons so also from the plain confession of the ablest patrons of abstract ideas, who acknowledge that they are made in order to naming; from which it is a clear consequence that if there had been no such thing as speech or universal signs there never had been any thought of abstraction.[4] Let us examine the manner wherein words have contributed to the origin of that mistake. First, then, it is thought that every name has, or ought to have, one only precise and settled signification, which inclines men to think there are certain abstract, determinate ideas that constitute the true and only immediate signification of each general name; and that it is by the mediation of these abstract ideas that a general name comes to signify any particular thing. Whereas, in truth, there is no such thing as one precise and definite signification annexed to any general name, they all signifying indifferently a great number of particular ideas. All which doth evidently follow from what has been already said, and will clearly appear to anyone by a little reflection. To this it will be objected that every name that has a definition is thereby restrained to one certain signification. For example, a triangle is defined to be "a plane surface comprehended by three right lines," by which that name is limited to denote one certain idea and no other. To which I answer that in the definition it is not said whether the surface be great or small, black or white, nor whether the sides are long or short, equal or unequal, nor with what angles they are inclined to each other; in all which there may be great variety, and consequently there is no one settled idea which limits the signification of the word triangle. It is one thing for to keep a name constantly to the same definition, and another to make it stand everywhere for the same idea; the one is necessary, the other useless and impracticable.

---

[4] See Bk. III, Chap. VI, Sec. 39, and elsewhere of the *Essay on Human Understanding*.

19 ☙ But to give a farther account how words came to produce the doctrine of abstract ideas, it must be observed that it is a received opinion that language has no other end but the communicating our ideas, and that every significant name stands for an idea. This being so and it being withal certain that names which yet are not thought altogether insignificant do not always mark out particular conceivable ideas, it is straightway concluded that they stand for abstract notions. That there are many names in use amongst speculative men which do not always suggest to others determinate, particular ideas, or in truth anything at all, is what nobody will deny. And a little attention will discover that it is not necessary (even in the strictest reasonings) significant names which stand for ideas should, every time they are used, excite in the understanding the ideas they are made to stand for: in reading and discoursing, names being for the most part used as letters are in algebra, in which, though a particular quantity be marked by each letter, yet to proceed right it is not requisite that in every step each letter suggest to your thoughts that particular quantity it was appointed to stand for.

20 ☙ Besides, the communicating of ideas marked by words is not the chief and only end of language, as is commonly supposed. There are other ends, as the raising of some passion, the exciting to or deterring from an action, the putting the mind in some particular disposition; to which the former is in many cases barely subservient, and sometimes entirely omitted, when these can be obtained without it, as I think does not unfrequently happen in the familiar use of language. I entreat the reader to reflect with himself, and see if it doth not often happen, either in hearing or reading a discourse, that the passions of fear, love, hatred, admiration, disdain, and the like, arise immediately in his mind upon the perception of certain words, without any ideas coming between. At first, indeed, the words might have occasioned ideas that were

fitting to produce those emotions; but, if I mistake not, it will be found that when language is once grown familiar, the hearing of the sounds or sight of the characters is oft immediately attended with those passions which at first were wont to be produced by the intervention of ideas that are now quite omitted. May we not, for example, be affected with the promise of a *good thing*, though we have not an idea of what it is? Or is not the being threatened with danger sufficient to excite a dread, though we think not of any particular evil likely to befall us, nor yet frame to ourselves an idea of danger in abstract? If anyone shall join ever so little reflection of his own to what has been said, I believe that it will evidently appear to him that general names are often used in the propriety of language without the speaker's designing them for marks of ideas in his own, which he would have them raise in the mind of the hearer. Even proper names themselves do not seem always spoken with a design to bring into our view the ideas of those individuals that are supposed to be marked by them. For example, when a schoolman tells me "Aristotle hath said it," all I conceive he means by it is to dispose me to embrace his opinion with the deference and submission which custom has annexed to that name. And this effect is often so instantly produced in the minds of those who are accustomed to resign their judgment to authority of that philosopher, as it is impossible any idea either of his person, writings, or reputation should go before. Innumerable examples of this kind may be given, but why should I insist on those things which everyone's experience will, I doubt not, plentifully suggest unto him?

21 § We have, I think, shewn the impossibility of abstract ideas. We have considered what has been said of them by their ablest patrons, and endeavored to show they are of no use for those ends to which they are thought necessary. And lastly, we have traced them to the source from whence they

flow, which appears evidently to be language. It cannot be denied that words are of excellent use, in that by their means all that stock of knowledge which has been purchased by the joint labors of inquisitive men in all ages and nations may be drawn into the view and made the possession of one single person. But at the same time it must be owned that most parts of knowledge have been strangely perplexed and darkened by the abuse of words, and general ways of speech wherein they are delivered. Since therefore words are so apt to impose on the understanding, whatever ideas I consider, I shall endeavor to take them bare and naked into my view, keeping out of my thoughts so far as I am able those names which long and constant use hath so strictly united with them; from which I may expect to derive the following advantages:—

22 ◆§ *First*, I shall be sure to get clear of all controversies *purely verbal;* the springing up of which weeds in almost all the sciences has been a main hindrance to the growth of true and sound knowledge. *Secondly*, this seems to be a sure way to extricate myself out of that fine and subtle net of *abstract ideas* which has so miserably perplexed and entangled the minds of men; and that with this peculiar circumstance, that by now much the finer and more curious was the wit of any man, by so much the deeper was he likely to be ensnared and faster held therein. *Thirdly*, so long as I confine my thoughts to my own ideas divested of words, I do not see how I can easily be mistaken. The objects I consider, I clearly and adequately know. I cannot be deceived in thinking I have an idea which I have not. It is not possible for me to imagine that any of my own ideas are alike or unlike that are not truly so. To discern the agreements or disagreements there are between my ideas, to see what ideas are included in any compound idea and what not, there is nothing more requisite than an attentive perception of what passes in my own understanding.

23 ☙§ But the attainment of all these advantages doth *presuppose an entire deliverance from the deception of words*, which I dare hardly promise myself; so difficult a thing it is to dissolve an union so early begun, and confirmed by so long a habit as that betwixt words and ideas. Which difficulty seems to have been very much increased by the doctrine of *abstraction*. For, so long as men thought abstract ideas were annexed to their words, it doth not seem strange that they should use words for ideas; it being found an impracticable thing to lay aside the word, and retain the abstract idea in the mind, which in itself was perfectly inconceivable. This seems to me the principal cause why those men who have so emphatically recommended to others the laying aside all use of words in their meditations, and contemplating their bare ideas, have yet failed to perform it themselves. Of late many have been very sensible of the absurd opinions and insignificant disputes which grow out of the abuse of words. And, in order to remedy these evils, they advise well that we attend to the ideas signified, and draw off our attention from the words which signify them. But how good soever this advice may be they have given others, it is plain they could not have a due regard to it themselves, so long as they thought the only immediate use of words was to signify ideas, and that the immediate signification of every general name was a determinate abstract idea.

24 ☙§ But these being known to be mistakes, a man may with greater ease prevent his being imposed on by words. He that knows he has no other than particular ideas, will not puzzle himself in vain to find out and conceive the abstract idea annexed to any name. And he that knows names do not always stand for ideas will spare himself the labor of looking for ideas where there are none to be had. It were therefore to be wished that everyone would use his utmost endeavors to obtain a clear view of the ideas he would consider, separating from them all that dress and encumbrance of words which

so much contribute to blind the judgment and divide the attention. In vain do we extend our view into the heavens and pry into the entrails of the earth, in vain do we consult the writings of learned men and trace the dark footsteps of antiquity; we need only draw the curtain of words, to hold the fairest tree of knowledge, whose fruit is excellent and within the reach of our hand.

25 ☙ Unless we take care to clear the first principles of knowledge from the embarrassment and delusion of words. we may make infinite reasonings upon them to no purpose: we may draw consequences from consequences, and be never the wiser. The farther we go, we shall only lose ourselves the more irrecoverably, and be the deeper entangled in difficulties and mistakes. Whoever therefore designs to read the following sheets, I entreat him to make my words the occasion of his own thinking, and endeavor to attain the same train of thoughts in reading that I had in writing them. By this means it will be easy for him to discover the truth or falsity of what I say. He will be out of all danger of being deceived by my words, and I do not see how he can be led into an error by considering his own naked, undisguised ideas.

OF THE PRINCIPLES OF HUMAN KNOWLEDGE

It is evident to anyone who takes a survey of the objects of human knowledge, that they are either ideas (1) actually imprinted on the senses, or else such as are (2) perceived by attending to the passions and operations of the mind, or lastly (3) ideas formed by help of memory and imagination, either compounding, dividing, or barely representing those originally perceived in the aforesaid ways. By sight I have the ideas of lights and colors, with their several degrees and variations. By touch I perceive hard and soft, heat and cold, motion and resistance, and of all these more and less either as to quantity or degree. Smelling furnishes me with odors, the palate with tastes, and hearing conveys sounds to the mind in all their variety of tone and composition. And as several of these are observed to accompany each other, they come to be marked by one name, and so to be reputed as one thing. Thus, for example, a certain color, taste, smell, figure, and consistence, having been observed to go together, are accounted one distinct thing, signified by the name "apple." Other collections of ideas constitute a stone, a tree, a book, and the like sensible things; which, as they are pleasing or disagreeable, excite the passions of love, hatred, joy, grief, and so forth.

2 ☙ But besides all that endless variety of ideas or objects of knowledge, there is likewise something which knows or perceives them, and exercises divers operations, as willing,

imagining, remembering, about them. This perceiving, active being is what I call *mind, spirit, soul,* or *myself*. By which words I do not denote any one of my ideas, but a thing entirely distinct from them wherein they exist, or, which is the same thing, whereby they are perceived; for the existence of an idea consists in being perceived.

3 ◆§ That neither our thoughts, nor passions, nor ideas formed by the imagination, exist without the mind, is what everybody will allow. And it seems no less evident that the various sensations or ideas imprinted on the sense, however blended or combined together (that is, whatever objects they compose), cannot exist otherwise than in a mind perceiving them. I think an intuitive knowledge may be obtained of this by anyone that shall attend to what is meant by the term "exist" when applied to sensible things. The table I write on I say exists—that is, I see and feel it; and if I were out of my study I should say it existed—meaning thereby that if I was in my study I might perceive it, or that some other spirit actually does perceive it. There was an odor, that is, it was smelt; there was a sound, that is, it was heard; a color or figure, and it was perceived by sight or touch. This is all that I can understand by these and the like expressions. For as to what is said of the absolute existence of unthinking things without any relation to their being perceived, that seems perfectly unintelligible. Their *esse* is *percipi*, nor is it possible they should have any existence out of the minds or thinking things which perceive them.

4 ◆§ It is indeed an opinion strangely prevailing amongst men, that houses, mountains, rivers, and in a word all sensible objects, have an existence, natural or real, distinct from their being perceived by the understanding. But with how great an assurance and acquiescence soever this principle may be en-

tertained in the world, yet whoever shall find in his heart to call it in question may, if I mistake not, perceive it to involve a manifest contradiction. For what are the forementioned objects but the things we perceive by sense? and what do we perceive *besides our own ideas or sensations?* and is it not plainly repugnant that any one of these, or any combination of them, should exist unperceived?

5 ◆§ If we thoroughly examine this tenet it will perhaps be found at bottom to depend on the doctrine of *abstract ideas.* For can there be a nicer strain of abstraction than to distinguish the existence of sensible objects from their being perceived, so as to conceive them existing unperceived? Light and colors, heat and cold, extension and figures—in a word the things we see and feel—what are they but so many sensations, notions, ideas, or impressions on the sense? And is it possible to separate, even in thought, any of these from perception? For my part, I might as easily divide a thing from itself. I may, indeed, divide in my thoughts, or conceive apart from each other, those things which perhaps I never perceived by sense so divided. Thus I imagine the trunk of a human body without the limbs, or conceive the smell of a rose without thinking on the rose itself. So far, I will not deny, I can abstract, if that may properly be called abstraction which extends only to the conceiving separately such objects as it is possible may really exist or be actually perceived asunder. But my conceiving or imagining power does not extend beyond the possibility of real existence or perception. Hence, as it is impossible for me to see or feel anything without an actual sensation of that thing, so it is impossible for me to conceive in my thoughts any sensible thing or object distinct from the sensation or perception of it.

6 ◆§ Some truths there are so near and obvious to the mind that a man need only open his eyes to see them. Such I take

this important one to be, to wit, that all the choir of heaven and furniture of the earth, in a word all those bodies which compose the mighty frame of the world, have not any subsistence without a mind, that their *being* is to be perceived or known; that consequently so long as they are not actually perceived by me, or do not exist in my mind or that of any other created spirit, they must either have no existence at all, or else subsist in the mind of some Eternal Spirit; it being perfectly unintelligible, and involving all the absurdity of abstraction, to attribute to any single part of them an existence independent of a spirit. To be convinced of which, the reader need only reflect and try to separate in his own thoughts the *being* of a sensible thing from its *being perceived.*

7 ☙ From what has been said it follows there is not any other substance than *spirit*, or that which perceives. But for the fuller proof of this point, let it be considered the sensible qualities or color, figure, motion, smell, taste, etc.—that is, the ideas perceived by sense. Now, for an idea to exist in an unperceiving thing is a manifest contradiction, for to have an idea is all one as to perceive; that therefore wherein color, figure, and the like qualities exist must perceive them; hence it is clear there can be no unthinking substance or *substratum* of those ideas.

8 ☙ But, say you, though the ideas themselves do not exist without the mind, yet there may be things *like* them, whereof they are copies or resemblances, which things exist without the mind in an unthinking substance. I answer, an idea can be like nothing but an idea; a color or figure can be like nothing but another color or figure. If we look but ever so little into our thoughts, we shall find it impossible for us to conceive a likeness except only between our ideas. Again, I ask

whether those supposed originals or external things, of which our ideas are the pictures or representations, be themselves perceivable or no? If they are, then they are ideas and we have gained our point; but if you say they are not, I appeal to anyone whether it be sense to assert a color is like something which is invisible; hard or soft, like something wbich is intangible; and so of the rest.

9 ☙ Some there are who make a distinction betwixt *primary* and *secondary* qualities. By the former they mean extension, figure, motion, rest, solidity or impenetrability, and number; by the latter they denote all other sensible qualities, as colors, sounds, tastes, and so forth. The ideas we have of these they acknowledge not to be the resemblances of anything existing without the mind, or unperceived, but they will have our ideas of the primary qualities to be patterns or images of things which exist without the mind, in an unthinking substance which they call *matter*. By *matter*, therefore, we are to understand an inert, senseless substance, in which extension, figure, and motion do actually subsist. But it is evident from what we have already shown, that extension, figure, and motion are only ideas existing in the mind, and that an idea can be like nothing but another idea, and that consequently neither they nor their archetypes can exist in an unperceiving substance. Hence, it is plain that the very notion of what is called *matter*, or *corporeal substance*, involves a contradiction in it.

10 ☙ They who assert that figure, motion, and the rest of the primary or original qualities do exist without the mind in unthinking substances, do at the same time acknowledge that color, sounds, heat, cold, and suchlike secondary qualities, do not; which they tell us are sensations existing in the mind

alone, that depend on and are occasioned by the different size, texture, and motion of the minute particles of matter. This they take for an undoubted truth, which they can demonstrate beyond all exception. Now, if it be certain that those original qualities are inseparably united with the other sensible qualities, and not, even in thought, capable of being abstracted from them, it plainly follows that they exist only in the mind. But I desire anyone to reflect and try whether he can, by any abstraction of thought, conceive the extension and motion of a body without all other sensible qualities. For my own part, I see evidently that it is not in my power to frame an idea of a body extended and moving, but I must withal give it some color or other sensible quality which is acknowledged to exist only in the mind. In short, extension, figure, and motion, abstracted from all other qualities, are inconceivable. Where therefore the other sensible qualities are, there must these be also, to wit, in the mind and nowhere else.

11 ☙ Again, *great* and *small*, *swift* and *slow*, are allowed to exist nowhere without the mind, being entirely relative, and changing as the frame or position of the organs of sense varies. The extension therefore which exists without the mind is neither great nor small, the motion neither swift nor slow, that is, they are nothing at all. But, say you, they are extension in general, and motion in general: thus we see how much the tenet of extended movable substances existing without the mind depends on the strange doctrine of *abstract ideas*. And here I cannot but remark how nearly the vague and indeterminate description of matter or corporeal substance, which the modern philosophers are run into by their own principles, resembles that antiquated and so much ridiculed notion of *materia prima*, to be met with in Aristotle and his followers. Without extension solidity cannot be conceived; since therefore it has been shewn that extension exists not in an unthinking substance, the same must also be true of solidity.

12 ☙§ That *number* is entirely the creature of the mind, even though the other qualities be allowed to exist without, will be evident to whoever considers that the same thing bears a different denomination of number as the mind views it with different respects. Thus, the same extension is one, or three, or thirty-six, according as the mind considers it with reference to a yard, a foot, or an inch. Number is so visibly relative, and dependent on men's understanding, that it is strange to think how anyone should give it an absolute existence without the mind. We say one book, one page, one line; all these are equally units, though some contain several of the others. And in each instance, it is plain, the unit relates to some particular combination of ideas arbitrarily put together by the mind.

13 ☙§ *Unity,* I know, some will have to be a simple or uncompounded idea, accompanying all other ideas into the mind. That I have any such idea answering the word "unity" I do not find; and if I had, methinks I could not miss finding it: on the contrary, it should be the most familiar to my understanding, since it is said to accompany all other ideas, and to be perceived by all the ways of sensation and reflection. To say no more, it is an *abstract idea.*

14 ☙§ I shall farther add that, after the same manner as modern philosophers prove certain sensible qualities to have no existence in matter, or without the mind, the same thing may be likewise proved of all other sensible qualities whatsoever. Thus, for instance, it is said that heat and cold are affections only of the mind, and not at all patterns of real beings, existing in the corporeal substances which excite them, for that the same body which appears cold to one hand seems warm to another. Now, why may we not as well argue that figure and extension are not patterns or resemblances of qualities existing

in matter, because to the same eye at different stations, or eyes of a different texture at the same station, they appear various, and cannot therefore be the images of anything settled and determinate without the mind? Again, it is proved that sweetness is not really in the sapid thing, because the thing remaining unaltered the sweetness is changed into bitter, as in case of a fever or otherwise vitiated palate. Is it not as reasonable to say that motion is not without the mind, since if the succession of ideas in the mind become swifter, the motion, it is acknowledged, shall appear slower without any alteration in any external object?

15 ☙ In short, let anyone consider those arguments which are thought manifestly to prove that colors and tastes exist only in the mind, and he shall find they may with equal force be brought to prove the same thing of extension, figure, and motion—though it must be confessed this method of arguing does not so much prove that there is no extension or color in an outward object, as that we do not know by sense which is the true extension or color of the object. But the arguments foregoing plainly show it to be impossible that any color or extension at all, or other sensible quality whatsoever, should exist in an unthinking subject without the mind, or in truth, that there should be any such thing as an outward object.

16 ☙ But let us examine a little the received opinion. It is said extension is a mode or accident of matter, and that matter is the *substratum* that supports it. Now I desire that you would explain to me what is meant by matter's *supporting* extension. Say you, I have no idea of matter and therefore cannot explain it. I answer, though you have no positive, yet, if you have any meaning at all, you must at least have a relative idea of matter; though you know not what it is, yet you must be supposed to know what relation it bears to accidents,

and what is meant by its supporting them. It is evident "support" cannot here be taken in its usual or literal sense—as when we say that pillars support a building; in what sense therefore must it be taken?

17 ☙ If we inquire into what the most accurate philosophers declare themselves to mean by *material substance*, we shall find them acknowledge they have no other meaning annexed to those sounds but the idea of *Being in general*, together with the relative notion of its supporting accidents. The general idea of Being appeareth to me the most abstract and incomprehensible of all other; and as for its supporting accidents, this, as we have just now observed, cannot be understood in the common sense of those words; it must therefore be taken in some other sense, but what that is they do not explain. So that when I consider the two parts or branches which make the signification of the words *material substance*, I am convinced there is no distinct meaning annexed to them. But why should we trouble ourselves any farther, in discussing this material *substratum* or support of figure and motion, and other sensible qualities? Does it not suppose they have an existence without the mind? And is not this a direct repugnancy, and altogether inconceivable?

18 ☙ But though it were possible that solid, figured, movable substances may exist without the mind, corresponding to the ideas we have of bodies, yet how is it possible for us to know this? Either we must know it by sense or by reason. As for our senses, by them we have the knowledge only of our sensations, ideas, or those things that are immediately perceived by sense, call them what you will; but they do not inform us that things exist without the mind, or unperceived, like to those which are perceived. This the materialists themselves acknowledge. It remains therefore that if we have any

knowledge at all of external things, it must be by reason, inferring their existence from what is immediately perceived by sense. But what reason can induce us to believe the existence of bodies without the mind, from what we perceive, since the very patrons of matter themselves do not pretend there is any necessary connection betwixt them and our ideas? I say it is granted on all hands (and what happens in dreams, frenzies, and the like, puts it beyond dispute) that *it is possible we might be affected with all the ideas we have now, though there were no bodies existing without, resembling them.* Hence, it is evident the supposition of external bodies is not necessary for the producing our ideas; since it is granted they are produced sometimes, and might possibly be produced always in the same order we see them in at present, without their concurrence.

19 ☙ But, though we might possibly have all our sensations without them, yet perhaps it may be thought easier to conceive and explain the manner of their production by supposing external bodies in their likeness rather than otherwise; and so it might be at least probable there are such things as bodies that excite their ideas in our minds. But neither can this be said; for though we give the materialists their external bodies, they by their own confession are never the nearer knowing how our ideas are produced, since they own themselves unable to comprehend in what manner body can act upon spirit, or how it is possible it should imprint any idea in the mind. Hence it is evident the production of ideas or sensations in our minds can be no reason why we should suppose matter or corporeal substances, since that is acknowledged to remain equally inexplicable with or without this supposition. If therefore it were possible for bodies to exist without the mind, yet to hold they do so, must needs be a very precarious opinion; since it is to suppose, without any reason at all, that God has created innumerable beings that are entirely useless, and serve to no manner of purpose.

20 ☙ In short, if there were external bodies, it is impossible we should ever come to know it; and if there were not, we might have the very same reasons to think there were that we have now. Suppose (what no one can deny possible) an intelligence without the help of external bodies, to be affected with the same train of sensations or ideas that you are, imprinted in the same order and with like vividness in his mind. I ask whether that intelligence hath not all the reason to believe the existence of corporeal substances, represented by his ideas, and exciting them in his mind, that you can possibly have for believing the same thing? Of this there can be no question; which one consideration were enough to make any reasonable person suspect the strength of whatever arguments he may think himself to have for the existence of bodies without the mind.

21 ☙ Were it necessary to add any farther proof against the existence of matter after what has been said, I could instance several of those errors and difficulties (not to mention impieties) which have sprung from that tenet. It has occasioned numberless controversies and disputes in philosophy, and not a few of far greater moment in religion. But I shall not enter into the detail of them in this place, as well because I think arguments *a posteriori* are unnecessary for confirming what has been, if I mistake not, sufficiently demonstrated *a priori*, as because I shall hereafter find occasion to speak somewhat of them.

22 ☙ I am afraid I have given cause to think I am needlessly prolix in handling this subject. For, to what purpose is it to dilate on that which may be demonstrated with the utmost evidence in a line or two, to anyone that is capable of the least reflection? It is but looking into your own thoughts, and so trying whether you can conceive it possible for a sound, or figure, or motion, or color to exist without the mind or un-

perceived. This easy trial may perhaps make you see that what you contend for is a downright contradiction. Insomuch that I am content to put the whole upon this issue: if you can but conceive it possible for one extended movable substance, or, in general, for any one idea, or anything like an idea, to exist otherwise than in a mind perceiving it, I shall readily give up the cause; and, as for all that compages of external bodies you contend for, I shall grant you its existence, though you cannot either give me any reason why you believe it exists, or assign any use to it when it is supposed to exist. I say, the bare possibility of your opinion's being true shall pass for an argument that it is so.

23 ◆§ But, say you, surely there is nothing easier than for me to imagine trees, for instance, in a park, or books existing in a closet, and nobody by to perceive them. I answer, you may so, there is no difficulty in it; but what is all this, I beseech you, more than framing in your mind certain ideas which you call books and trees, and the same time omitting to frame the idea of anyone that may perceive them? But do not you yourself perceive or think of them all the while? This therefore is nothing to the purpose; it only shews you have the power of imagining or forming ideas in your mind: but it doth not shew that you can conceive it possible the objects of your thought may exist without the mind. To make out this, it is necessary that you conceive them existing unconceived or unthought of, which is a manifest repugnancy. When we do our utmost to conceive the existence of external bodies, we are all the while only contemplating our own ideas. But the mind taking no notice of itself, is deluded to think it can and doth conceive bodies existing unthought of or without the mind, though at the same time they are apprehended by or exist in itself. A little attention will discover to anyone the truth and evidence of what is here said, and make it unnecessary to insist on any other proofs against the existence of *material substance*.

24 ☙§ It is very obvious, upon the least inquiry into our thoughts, to know whether it is possible for us to understand what is meant by the *absolute existence of sensible objects in themselves, or without the mind.* To me it is evident those words mark out either a direct contradiction, or else nothing at all. And to convince others of this, I know no readier or fairer way than to entreat they would calmly attend to their own thoughts; and if by this attention the emptiness or repugnancy of those expressions doth appear, surely nothing more is requisite for the conviction. It is on this therefore that I insist, to wit, that the absolute existence of unthinking things are words without a meaning, or which include a contradiction. This is what I repeat and inculcate, and earnestly recommend to the attentive thoughts of the reader.

25 ☙§ All our ideas, sensations, notions, or the things which we perceive, by whatsoever names they may be distinguished, are visibly inactive: there is nothing of power or agency included in them. So that one idea or object of thought cannot produce or make any alteration in another. To be satisfied of the truth of this, there is nothing else requisite but a bare observation of our ideas. For, since they and every part of them exist only in the mind, it follows that there is nothing in them but what is perceived: but whoever shall attend to his ideas, whether of sense or reflection, will not perceive in them any power or activity; there is, therefore, no such thing contained in them. A little attention will discover to us that the very being of an idea implies passiveness and inertness in it, insomuch that it is impossible for an idea to do anything, or, strictly speaking, to be the cause of anything: neither can it be the resemblance or pattern of any active being, as is evident from Sec. 8. Whence it plainly follows that extension, figure, and motion cannot be the cause of our sensations. To say, therefore, that these are the effects of

powers resulting from the configuration, number, motion, and size of corpuscles, must certainly be false.

26 ⸙§ We perceive a continual succession of ideas, some are anew excited, others are changed or totally disappear. There is therefore some cause of these ideas, whereon they depend, and which produces and changes them. That this cause cannot be any quality or idea or combination of ideas, is clear from the preceding section. It must therefore be a substance; but it has been shewn that there is no corporeal or material substance: it remains therefore that the cause of ideas is an incorporeal active substance or Spirit.

27 ⸙§ A spirit is one simple, undivided, active being: as it perceives ideas it is called the *understanding*, and as it produces or otherwise operates about them it is called the *will*. Hence there can be no *idea* formed of a soul or spirit; for all ideas whatever, being passive and inert (*vide* Sec. 25), they cannot represent unto us, by way of image or likeness, that which acts. A little attention will make it plain to anyone, that to have an idea which shall be like that active principle of motion and change of ideas is absolutely impossible. Such is the nature of *spirit*, or that which acts, that it cannot be of itself perceived, but only by the effects which it produceth. If any man shall doubt of the truth of what is here delivered, let him but reflect and try if he can frame the idea of any power or active being, and whether he hath ideas of two principal powers, marked by the names *will* and *understanding*, distinct from each other as well as from a third idea of substance or being in general, with a relative notion of its supporting or being the subject of the aforesaid powers—which is signified by the same *soul* or *spirit*. This is what some hold; but, so far as I can see, the words *will*, *soul*, *spirit*, do

not stand for different ideas, or, in truth, for any idea at all, but for something which is very different from ideas, and which, being an agent, cannot be like unto, or represented by, any idea whatsoever. Though it must be owned at the same time that we have some *notion* of soul, spirit, and the operations of the mind such as willing, loving, hating; inasmuch as we know or understand the meaning of these words.

28 ☙ I find I can excite ideas in my mind at pleasure, and vary and shift the scene as oft as I think fit. It is no more than willing, and straightway this or that idea arises in my fancy; and by the same power it is obliterated and makes way for another. This making and unmaking of ideas doth very properly denominate the mind active. Thus much is certain and grounded on experience; but when we think of unthinking agents or of exciting ideas exclusive of volition, we only amuse ourselves with words.

29 ☙ But, whatever power I may have over my own thoughts, I find the ideas actually perceived by sense have not a like dependence on my will. When in broad daylight I open my eyes, it is not in my power to choose whether I shall see or no, or to determine what particular objects shall present themselves to my view; and so likewise as to the hearing and other senses, the ideas imprinted on them are not creatures of my will. There is therefore some other will or spirit that produces them.

30 ☙ The ideas of sense are more strong, lively, and distinct than those of the imagination; they have likewise a steadiness, order, and coherence, and are not excited at random, as those which are the effects of human wills often are, but in a regu-

lar train or series, the admirable connection whereof sufficiently testifies the wisdom and benevolence of its Author. Now the set rules or established methods wherein the mind we depend on excites in us the ideas of sense, are called the *laws of nature;* and these we learn by experience, which teaches us that such and such ideas are attended with such and such other ideas, in the ordinary course of things.

31 ☙§ This gives us a sort of foresight which enables us to regulate our actions for the benefit of life. And without this we should be eternally at a loss: we could not know how to act anything that might procure us the least pleasure, or remove the least pain of sense. That food nourishes, sleep refreshes, and fire warms us; that to sow in the seed-time is the way to reap in the harvest; and, in general, that to obtain such or such ends, such or such means are conducive—all this we know, not by discovering any necessary connection between our ideas, but only by the observation of the settled laws of nature, without which we should be all in uncertainty and confusion, and a grown man no more know how to manage himself in the affairs of life than an infant just born.

32 ☙§ And yet this insistent uniform working, which so evidently displays the goodness and wisdom of that governing Spirit whose will constitutes the laws of nature, is so far from leading our thoughts to Him, that it rather sends them wandering after second causes. For, when we perceive certain ideas of sense constantly followed by other ideas and we know this is not of our own doing, we forthwith attribute power and agency to the ideas themselves, and make one the cause of another, than which nothing can be more absurd and unintelligible. Thus, for example, having observed that when we perceive by sight a certain round luminous figure we at the same time perceive by touch the idea or sensation called

heat, we do from thence conclude the sun to be the cause of heat. And in like manner perceiving the motion and collision of bodies to be attended with sound, we are inclined to think the latter the effect of the former.

33 ◈§ The ideas imprinted on the senses by the Author of nature are called *real things;* and those excited in the imagination, being less regular, vivid, and constant, are more properly termed *ideas,* or *images* of *things,* which they copy and represent. But then our sensations, be they never so vivid and distinct, are nevertheless ideas, that is, they exist in the mind, or are perceived by it, as truly as the ideas of its own framing. The ideas of sense are allowed to have more reality in them, that is, to be more strong, orderly, and coherent than the creatures of the mind; but this is no argument that they exist without the mind. They are also less dependent on the spirit, or thinking substance which perceives them, in that they are excited by the will of another and more powerful spirit; yet still they are *ideas,* and certainly no idea, whether faint or strong, can exist otherwise than in a mind perceiving it.

34 ◈§ Before we proceed any farther it is necessary we spend some time in answering objections which may probably be made against the principles we have hitherto laid down. In doing of which, if I seem too prolix to those of quick apprehensions, I hope it may be pardoned, since all men do not equally apprehend things of this nature, and I am willing to be understood by everyone.

First, then, it will be objected that by the foregoing principles all that is real and substantial in nature is banished out of the world, and instead thereof a chimerical scheme of *ideas* takes place. All things that exist, exist only in the mind, that is, they are purely notional. What therefore becomes of the sun, moon, and stars? What must we think of houses, rivers, mountains, trees, stones; nay, even of our own bodies? Are all these but so many chimeras and illusions on the fancy? To all which, and whatever else of the same sort may be objected, I answer that by the principles premised we are not deprived of any one thing in nature. Whatever we see, feel, hear, or anywise conceive or understand remains as secure as ever, and is as real as ever. There is a *rerum natura*, and the distinction between realities and chimeras retains its full force. This is evident from Sec. 29, 30, and 33, where we have shewn what is meant by *real things* in opposition to *chimeras* or ideas of our own framing; but then they both equally exist in the mind, and in that sense they are alike *ideas*.

35 ☙ I do not argue against the existence of any one thing that we can apprehend either by sense or reflection. That the things I see with my eyes and touch with my hands do exist, really exist, I make not the least question. The only thing whose existence we deny is that which *philosophers* call matter or corporeal substance. And in doing of this there is no damage done to the rest of mankind, who, I dare say, will never miss it. The atheist indeed will want the color of an empty name to support his impiety; and the philosophers may possibly find they have lost a great handle for trifling and disputation.

36 ☙ If any man thinks this detracts from the existence or reality of things, he is very far from understanding what hath been premised in the plainest terms I could think of. Take here an abstract of what has been said. There are spiritual substances, minds, or human souls, which will or excite ideas in themselves at pleasure; but these are faint, weak, and unsteady in respect of others they perceive by sense—which, being impressed upon them according to certain rules or laws of nature, speak themselves the effects of a mind more power-

ful and wise than human spirits. These latter are said to have more *reality* in them than the former; by which is meant that they are more affecting, orderly, and distinct, and that they are not fictions of the mind perceiving them. And in this sense the sun that I see by day is the real sun, and that which I imagine by night is the idea of the former. In the sense here given of "reality" it is evident that every vegetable, star, mineral, and in general each part of the mundane system, is as much as a real being by our principles as by any other. Whether others mean anything by the term "reality" different from what I do, I entreat them to look into their own thoughts and see.

37 ☙ It will be urged that thus much at least is true, to wit, that we take away all corporeal substances. To this my answer is that if the word "substance" be taken in the vulgar sense—for a combination of sensible qualities, such as extension, solidity, weight, and the like—this we cannot be accused of taking away. But if it be taken in a philosophic sense—for the support of accidents or qualities without the mind—then indeed I acknowledge that we take it away, if one may be said to take away that which never had any existence, not even in the imagination.

38 ☙ But after all, say you, it sounds very harsh to say we eat and drink ideas, and are clothed with ideas. I acknowledge it does so; the word "idea" not being used in common discourse to signify the several combinations of sensible qualities which are called "things"; and it is certain that any expression which varies from the familiar use of language will seem harsh and ridiculous. But this doth not concern the truth of the proposition, which in other words is no more than to say, we are fed and clothed with those things which we perceive immediately by our senses. The hardness or softness,

the color, taste, warmth, figure, or suchlike qualities, which combined together constitute the several sorts of victuals and apparel, have been shewn to exist only in the mind that perceives them; and this is all that is meant by calling them "ideas"; which word if it was as ordinarily used as "things," would sound no harsher nor more ridiculous than it. I am not for disputing about the propriety, but the truth of the expression. If therefore you agree with me that we eat and drink and are clad with the immediate objects of sense, which cannot exist unperceived or without the mind, I shall readily grant it is more proper or conformable to custom that they should be called things rather than ideas.

39 ☙ If it be demanded why I make use of the word "idea," and do not rather in compliance with custom call them "thing"; I answer, I do it for two reasons:—first, because the term "thing" in contradistinction to "idea," is generally supposed to denote somewhat existing without the mind; secondly, because "thing" hath a more comprehensive signification than "idea," including spirit or thinking things as well as ideas. Since therefore the objects of sense exist only in the mind, and are withal thoughtless and inactive, I chose to mark them by the word "idea," which implies those properties.

40 ☙ But, say what we can, someone perhaps may be apt to reply, he will still believe his senses, and never suffer any arguments, how plausible soever, to prevail over the certainty of them. Be it so; assert the evidence of sense as high as you please, we are willing to do the same. That what I see, hear, and feel doth exist, that is to say, is perceived by me, I no more doubt than I do of my own being. But I do not see how the testimony of sense can be alleged as a proof for the existence of anything which is not perceived by sense. We are not for having any man turn sceptic and disbelieve his senses; on

the contrary, we give them all the stress and assurance imaginable; nor are there any principles more opposite to scepticism than those we have laid down, as shall be hereafter clearly shewn.

41 ❧ *Secondly*, it will be objected that there is a great difference betwixt real fire for instance, and the idea of fire, betwixt dreaming or imagining oneself burnt, and actually being so: if you suspect it to be only the idea of fire which you see, do but put your hand into it and you will be convinced with a witness. This and the like may be urged in opposition to our tenets. To all which the answer is evident from what hath been already said; and I shall only add in this place, that if real fire be very different from the idea of fire, so also is the real pain that it occasions very different from the idea of the same pain, and yet nobody will pretend that real pain either is, or can possibly be, in an unperceiving thing, or without the mind, any more than its idea.

42 ❧ *Thirdly*, it will be objected that we see things actually without or at distance from us, and which consequently do not exist in the mind; it being absurd that those things which are seen at the distance of several miles should be as near to us as our own thoughts. In answer to this, I desire it may be considered that in a dream we do oft perceive things as existing at a great distance off, and yet for all that, those things are acknowledged to have their existence only in the mind.

43 ❧ But, for the fuller clearing of this point, it may be worth while to consider how it is that we perceive distance and things placed at a distance by sight. For, that we should in truth see external space, and bodies actually existing in it,

some nearer, others farther off, seems to carry with it some opposition to what hath been said of their existing nowhere without the mind. The consideration of this difficulty it was that gave birth to my *Essay towards a New Theory of Vision*, which was published not long since, wherein it is shewn that distance or outness is neither immediately of itself perceived by sight, nor yet apprehended or judged of by lines and angles, or anything that hath a necessary connection with it; but that it is only suggested to our thoughts by certain visible ideas and sensations attending vision, which in their own nature have no manner of similitude or relation either with distance or things placed at a distance; but, by a connection taught us by experience, they come to signify and suggest them to us, after the same manner that words of any language suggest the ideas they are made to stand for; insomuch that a man born blind and afterwards made to see, would not, at first sight, think the things he saw to be without his mind, or at any distance from him. (See Sec. 41 of the forementioned treatise.)

44 ☙ The ideas of sight and touch make two species entirely distinct and heterogeneous. *The former are marks and prognostics of the latter*. That the proper objects of sight neither exist without mind, nor are the images of external things, was shewn even in that treatise; though throughout the same the contrary be supposed true of tangible objects—not that to suppose that vulgar error was necessary for establishing the notion therein laid down, but because it was beside my purpose to examine and refute it in a discourse concerning *vision*. So that in strict truth the ideas of sight, when we apprehend by them distance and things placed at a distance, do not suggest or mark out to us things actually existing at a distance, but only admonish us what ideas of touch will be imprinted in our minds at such and such distances of time, and in consequence of such or such actions. It is, I say, evident from what has been said in the foregoing parts of this treatise, and

in Sec. 147 and elsewhere of the essay concerning vision, that visible ideas are the language whereby the governing Spirit on whom we depend informs us what tangible ideas he is about to imprint upon us, in case we excite this or that motion in our own bodies. But for a fuller information in this point I refer to the essay itself.

45 ☙ *Fourthly*, it will be objected that from the foregoing principles it follows things are every moment annihilated and created anew. The objects of sense exist only when they are perceived; the trees therefore are in the garden, or the chairs in the parlor, no longer than while there is somebody by to perceive them. Upon shutting my eyes all the furniture in the room is reduced to nothing, and barely upon opening them it is again created. In answer to all which, I refer the reader to what has been said in Sec. 3, 4, etc., and desire he will consider whether he means anything by the actual existence of an idea distinct from its being perceived. For my part, after the nicest inquiry I could make, I am not able to discover that anything else is meant by those words; and I once more entreat the reader to sound his own thoughts, and not suffer himself to be imposed on by words. If he can conceive it possible either for his ideas or their archetypes to exist without being perceived, then I give up the cause; but if he cannot, he will acknowledge it is unreasonable for him to stand up in defense of he knows not what, and pretend to charge on me as an absurdity the not assenting to those propositions which at bottom have no meaning in them.

46 ☙ It will not be amiss to observe how far the received principles of philosophy are themselves chargeable with those pretended absurdities. It is thought strangely absurd that upon closing my eyelids all the visible objects around me should be reduced to nothing; and yet is not this what philoso-

phers commonly acknowledge, when they agree on all hands that light and colors, which alone are the proper and immediate objects of sight, are mere sensations that exist no longer than they are perceived? Again, it may to some perhaps seem very incredible that things should be every moment creating, yet this very notion is commonly taught in the schools. For the schoolmen, though they acknowledge the existence of matter, and that the whole mundane fabric is framed out of it, are nevertheless of opinion that it cannot subsist without the divine conservation, which by them is expounded to be a continual creation.

47 ◆§ Farther, a little thought will discover to us that though we allow the existence of matter or corporeal substance, yet it will unavoidably follow, from the principles which are now generally admitted, that the particular bodies, of what kind soever, do none of them exist whilst they are not perceived. For, it is evident from Sec. 11 and the following sections, that the matter philosophers contend for is an incomprehensible somewhat, which hath none of those particular qualities whereby the bodies falling under our senses are distinguished one from another. But, to make this more plain, it must be remarked that the infinite divisibility of matter is now universally allowed, at least by the most approved and considerable philosophers, who on the received principles demonstrate it beyond all exception. Hence, it follows there is an infinite number of parts in each particle of matter which are not perceived by sense. The reason therefore that any particular body seems to be of a finite magnitude, or exhibits only a finite number of parts to sense, is, not because it contains no more, since in itself it contains an infinite number of parts, but because the sense is not acute enough to discern them. In proportion therefore as the sense is rendered more acute, it perceives a greater number of parts in the object, that is, the object appears greater, and its figure varies, those parts in its extremities which were before unperceivable ap-

pearing now to bound it in very different lines and angles from those perceived by an obtuser sense. And at length, after various changes of size and shape, when the sense becomes infinitely acute the body shall seem infinite. During all which there is no alteration in the body, but only in the sense. Each body therefore, considered in itself, is infinitely extended, and consequently void of all shape or figure. From which it follows that, though we should grant the existence of matter to be never so certain, yet it is withal as certain, the materialists themselves are by their own principles forced to acknowledge, that neither the particular bodies perceived by sense, nor anything like them, exists without the mind. Matter, I say, and each particle thereof, is according to them infinite and shapeless, and it is the mind that frames all that variety of bodies which compose the visible world, anyone whereof does not exist longer than it is perceived.

48 ☙ If we consider it, the objection proposed in Sec. 45 will not be found reasonably charged on the principles we have premised, so as in truth to make any objection at all against our notions. For, though we hold indeed the objects of sense to be nothing else but ideas which cannot exist unperceived; yet we may not hence conclude they have no existence except only while they are perceived by us, since there may be some other spirit that perceives them though we do not. Wherever bodies are said to have no existence without the mind, I would not be understood to mean this or that particular mind, but all minds whatsoever. It does not therefore allow from the foregoing principles that bodies are annihilated and created every moment, or exist not at all during the intervals between our perception of them.

49 ☙ *Fifthly*, it may perhaps be objected that if extension and figure exist only in the mind, it follows that the mind is extended and figured; since extension is a mode or attribute

which (to speak with the schools) is predicated of the subject in which it exists. I answer, those qualities are in the mind only as they are perceived by it—that is, not by way of *mode* or *attribute*, but only by way of *idea;* and it no more follows the soul or mind is extended, because extension exists in it alone, than it does that it is red or blue, because those colors are on all hands acknowledged to exist in it, and nowhere else. As to what philosophers say of subject and mode, that seems very groundless and unintelligible. For instance, in this proposition, "a die is hard, extended, and square," they will have it that the word "die" denotes a subject or substance, distinct from the hardness, extension, and figure which are predicated of it, and in which they exist. This I cannot comprehend: to me a die seems to be nothing distinct from those things which are termed its modes or accidents. And, to say a die is hard, extended, and square is not to attribute those qualities to a subject distinct from and supporting them, but only an explication of the meaning of the word "die."

50 ❧ *Sixthly*, you will say there have been a great many things explained by matter and motion; take away these and you destroy the whole corpuscular philosophy, and undermine those mechanical principles which have been applied with so much success to account for the phenomena. In short, whatever advances have been made, either by accident or modern philosophers, in the study of nature do all proceed on the supposition that corporeal substance or matter doth really exist. To this I answer that there is not any one phenomenon explained on that supposition which may not as well be explained without it, as might easily be made appear by an induction of particulars. To explain the phenomena, is all one as to shew why, upon such and such occasions, we are affected with such and such ideas. But how matter should operate on a spirit, or produce any idea in it, is what no philosopher will pretend to explain; it is therefore evident there can be no use of matter in natural philosophy. Besides,

they who attempt to account for things do it not by corporeal substance, but by figure, motion, and other qualities, which are in truth no more than mere ideas, and, therefore, cannot be the cause of anything, as hath been already shewn. (See Sec. 25.)

51 ❧ *Seventhly*, it will upon this be demanded whether it does not seem absurd to take away natural causes, and ascribe everything to the immediate operation of spirits? We must no longer say upon these principles that fire heats, or water cools, but that a spirit heats, and so forth. Would not a man be deservedly laughed at, who should talk after this manner? I answer, he would so; in such things we ought to "think with the learned, and speak with the vulgar." They who to demonstration are convinced of the truth of the Copernican system do nevertheless say, "The sun rises," "The sun sets," or "comes to the meridian"; and if they affected a contrary style in common talk it would without doubt appear very ridiculous. A little reflection on what is here said will make it manifest that the common use of language would receive no manner of alteration or disturbance from the admission of our tenets.

52 ❧ In the ordinary affairs of life, any phrases may be retained, so long as they excite in us proper sentiments, or dispositions to act in such a manner as is necessary for our well-being, how false soever they may be if taken in a strict and speculative sense. Nay, this is unavoidable, since, propriety being regulated by custom, language is suited to the received opinions, which are not always the truest. Hence it is impossible, even in the most rigid, philosophic reasonings, so far to alter the bent and genius of the tongue we speak, as never to give a handle for cavilers to pretend difficulties and inconsistencies. But, a fair and ingenuous reader will collect the sense from the scope and tenor and connection of a discourse,

making allowances for those inaccurate modes of speech which use has made inevitable.

53 ☙ As to the opinion that there are no corporeal causes, this has been heretofore maintained by some of the schoolmen, as it is of late by others among the modern philosophers, who though they allow matter to exist, yet will have God alone to be the immediate efficient cause of all things. These men saw that amongst all the objects of sense there was none which had any power or activity included in it; and that by consequence this was likewise true of whatever bodies they supposed to exist without the mind, like unto the immediate objects of sense. But then, that they should suppose an innumerable multitude of created beings, which they acknowledge are not capable of producing any one effect in nature, and which therefore are made to no manner of purpose, since God might have done everything as well without them: this I say, though we should allow it possible, must yet be a very unaccountable and extravagant supposition.

54 ☙ In the *eighth* place, the universal concurrent assent of mankind may be thought by some an invincible argument in behalf of matter, or the existence of external things. Must we suppose the whole world to be mistaken? And if so, what cause can be assigned of so widespread and predominant an error? I answer, first, that, upon a narrow inquiry, it will not perhaps be found so many as is imagined do really believe the existence of matter or things without the mind. Strictly speaking, to believe that which involves a contradiction, or has no meaning in it, is impossible; and whether the foregoing expressions are not of that sort, I refer it to the impartial examination of the reader. In one sense, indeed, men may be said to believe that matter exists, that is, they *act* as if the immediate cause of their sensations, which affects them every moment, and is so nearly present to them, were some sense-

less unthinking being. But, that they should clearly apprehend any meaning marked by those words, and form thereof a settled speculative opinion, is what I am not able to conceive. This is not the only instance wherein men impose upon themselves, by imagining they believe those propositions which they have often heard, though at bottom they have no meaning in them.

55 ☙ But secondly, though we should grant a notion to be never so universally and steadfastly adhered to, yet this is weak argument of its truth to whoever considers what a vast number of prejudices and false opinions are everywhere embraced with the utmost tenaciousness, by the unreflecting (which are the far greater) part of mankind. There was a time when the antipodes and motion of the earth were looked upon as monstrous absurdities even by men of learning: and if it be considered what a small proportion they bear to the rest of mankind, we shall find that at this day those notions have gained but a very inconsiderable footing in the world.

56 ☙ But it is demanded that we assign a cause of this prejudice, and account for its obtaining in the world. To this I answer, that men knowing they perceived several ideas, whereof they themselves were not the authors (as not being excited from within nor depending on the operation of their wills) this made them maintain those ideas, or objects of perception had an existence independent of and without the mind, without ever dreaming that a contradiction was involved in those words. But philosophers having plainly seen that the immediate objects of perception do not exist without the mind, they in some degree corrected the mistake of the vulgar; but at the same time run into another which seems no less absurd, to wit, that there are certain objects really existing without the mind, or having a subsistence distinct from

being perceived, of which our ideas are only images or resemblances, imprinted by those objects on the mind. And this notion of the philosophers owes its origin to the same cause with the former, namely, their being conscious that they were not the authors of their own sensations, which they evidently knew were imprinted from without, and which therefore must have some cause distinct from the minds on which they are imprinted.

57 ◆§ But why they should suppose the ideas of sense to be excited in us by things in their likeness, and not rather have recourse to *spirit*, which alone can act, may be accounted for, first, because they were not aware of the repugnancy there is, as well in supposing things like unto our ideas existing without, as in attributing to them power or activity. Secondly, because the Supreme Spirit, which excites those ideas in our minds, is not marked out and limited to our view by any particular finite collection of sensible ideas, as human agents are by their size, complexion, limbs, and motions. And thirdly, because His operations are regular and uniform. Whenever the course of nature is interrupted by a miracle, men are ready to own the presence of a superior agent. But, when we see things go on in the ordinary course they do not excite in us any reflection; their order and concatenation, though it be an argument of the greatest wisdom, power, and goodness in their creator, is yet so constant and familiar to us that we do not think them the immediate effects of a free spirit; especially since inconsistency and mutability in acting, though it be an imperfection, is looked on as a mark of freedom.

58 ◆§ *Tenthly*, it will be objected that the notions we advance are inconsistent with several sound truths in philosophy and mathematics. For example, the motion of the earth is now universally admitted by astronomers as a truth grounded on

the clearest and most convincing reasons. But, on the foregoing principles, there can be no such thing. For, motion being only an idea, it follows that if it be not perceived it exists not; but the motion of the earth is not perceived by sense. I answer, that tenet, if rightly understood, will be found to agree with the principles we have premised; for, the question whether the earth moves or no amounts in reality to no more than this, to wit, whether we have reason to conclude, from what has been observed by astronomers, that if we were placed in such and such circumstances, and such or such a position and distance both from the earth and sun, we should perceive the former to move among the choir of the planets, and appearing in all respects like one of them; and this, by the established rules of nature which we have no reason to mistrust, is reasonably collected from the phenomena.

59 ☙ We may, from the experience we have had of the train and succession of ideas in our minds, often make, I will not say uncertain conjectures, but sure and well-grounded predictions concerning the ideas we shall be affected with pursuant to a great train of actions, and be enabled to pass a right judgment of what would have appeared to us, in case we were placed in circumstances very different from those we are in at present. Herein consists the knowledge of nature, which may preserve its use and certainty very consistently with what hath been said. It will be easy to apply this to whatever objections of the like sort may be drawn from the magnitude of the stars, or any other discoveries in astronomy or nature.

60 ☙ In the *eleventh* place, it will be demanded to what purpose serves that curious organization of plants, and the animal mechanism in the parts of animals: might not vegetables grow, and shoot forth leaves of blossoms, and animals perform all

their motions as well without as with all that variety of internal parts so elegantly contrived and put together, which, being ideas, have nothing powerful or operative in them, nor have any necessary connection with the effects ascribed to them? If it be a Spirit that immediately produces every effect by a *fiat* or act of His will, we must think all that is fine and artificial in the works, whether of man or nature, to be made in vain. By this doctrine, though an artist hath made the spring and wheels, and every movement of a watch, and adjusted them in such a manner as he knew would produce the motions he designed, yet he must think all this done to no purpose, and that it is an Intelligence which directs the index, and points to the hour of the day. If so, why may not the Intelligence do it, without his being at the pains of making the movements and putting them together? Why does not an empty case serve as well as another? And how comes it to pass that whenever there is any fault in the going of a watch, there is some corresponding disorder to be found in the movements, which being mended by a skillful hand all is right again? The like may be said of all the clockwork of nature, great part whereof is so wonderfully fine and subtle as scarce to be discerned by the best microscope. In short, it will be asked, how, upon our principles, any tolerable account can be given, or any final cause assigned of an innumerable multitude of bodies and machines, framed with the most exquisite art, which in the common philosophy have very apposite uses assigned them, and serve to explain abundance of phenomena?

61 ◆§ To all which I answer, *first*, that though there were some difficulties relating to the administration of Providence, and the uses by it assigned to the several parts of nature, which I could not solve by the foregoing principles, yet this objection could be of small weight against the truth and certainty of those things which may be proved *a priori*, with the utmost evidence and rigor of demonstration. *Secondly*,

but neither are the received principles free from the like difficulties; for, it may still be demanded to what end God should take those roundabout methods of effecting things by instruments and machines, which no one can deny might have been effected by the mere command of His will without all that apparatus; nay, if we narrowly consider it, we shall find the objection may be retorted with greater force on those who hold the existence of those machines without of mind; for it has been made evident that solidity, bulk, figure, motion, and the like have no *activity* or *efficacy* in them, so as to be capable of producing any one effect in nature. (See Sec. 25.) Whoever therefore supposes them to exist (allowing the supposition possible) when they are not perceived does it manifestly to no purpose; since the only use that is assigned to them, as they exist unperceived, is that they produce those perceivable effects which in truth cannot be ascribed to anything but Spirit.

62 ☙ But, to come nigher the difficulty, it must be observed that though the fabrication of all those parts and organs be not absolutely necessary to the producing any effect, yet it is necessary to the producing of things in a constant regular way according to the laws of nature. There are certain general laws that run through the whole chain of natural effects; these are learned by the observation and study of nature, and are by men applied as well to the framing artificial things for the use and ornament of life as to the explaining various phenomena—which explication consists only in shewing the conformity any particular phenomenon hath to the general laws of nature, or, which is the same thing, in discovering the *uniformity* there is in the production of natural effects; as will be evident to whoever shall attend to the several instances wherein philosophers pretend to account for appearances. That there is a great and conspicuous use in these regular constant methods of working observed by the Supreme Agent hath been shewn in Sec. 31. And it is no less

visible that a particular size, figure, motion, and disposition of parts are necessary, though not absolutely to the producing any effect, yet to the producing it according to the standing mechanical laws of nature. Thus, for instance, it cannot be denied that God, or the Intelligence that sustains and rules the ordinary course of things, might if He were minded to produce a miracle, cause all the motions on the dial-plate of a watch, though nobody had ever made the movements and put them in it: but yet, if He will act agreeably to the rules of the mechanism, by Him for wise ends established and maintained in the creation, it is necessary that those actions of the watchmaker, whereby he makes the movements and rightly adjusts them, precede the production of the aforesaid motions; as also that any disorder in them be attended with the perception of some corresponding disorder in the movements, which being once corrected all is right again.

63 ☙ It may indeed on some occasions be necessary that the Author of nature display His overruling power in producing some appearance out of the ordinary series of things. Such exceptions from the general rules of nature are proper to surprise and awe men into an acknowledgment of the Divine Being; but then they are to be used but seldom, otherwise there is a plain reason why they should fail of that effect. Besides, God seems to choose the convincing our reason of His attributes by the works of nature, which discover so much harmony and contrivance in their make, and are such plain indications of wisdom and beneficence in their Author, rather than to astonish us into a belief of His Being by anomalous and surprising events.

64 ☙ To set this matter in a yet clearer light, I shall observe that what has been objected in Sec. 60 amounts in reality to no more than this:—ideas are not anyhow and at random pro-

duced, there being a certain order and connection between them, like to that of cause and effect; there are also several combinations of them made in a very regular and artificial manner, which seem like so many instruments in the hand of nature that, being hid as it were behind the scenes, have a secret operation in producing those appearances which are seen on the theater of the world, being themselves discernible only to the curious eye of the philosopher. But, since one idea cannot be the cause of another, to what purpose is that connection? And, since those instruments, being barely *inefficacious perceptions* in the mind, are not subservient to the production of natural effects, it is demanded why they are made; or, in other words, what reason can be assigned why God should make us, upon a close inspection into His works, behold so great variety of ideas so artfully laid together, and so much according to rule; it not being credible that He would be at the expense (if one may so speak) of all that art and regularity to no purpose.

65 ☙§To all which my answer is, first, that the connection of ideas does not imply the relation of *cause and effect*, but only of a mark or *sign* with the thing *signified*. The fire which I see is not the cause of the pain I suffer upon my approaching it, but the mark that forewarns me of it. In like manner the noise that I hear is not the effect of this or that motion or collision of the ambient bodies, but the sign thereof. Secondly, the reason why ideas are formed into machines, that is, artificial and regular combinations, is the same with that for combining letters into words. That a few original ideas may be made to signify a great number of effects and actions, it is necessary they be variously combined together. And, to the end their use be permanent and universal, these combinations must be made by *rule*, and with *wise contrivance*. By this means abundance of information is conveyed unto us, concerning what we are to expect from such and such actions, and what methods are proper to be taken for the ex-

citing such and such ideas; which in effect is all that I conceive to be distinctly meant when it is said that, by discerning a figure, texture, and mechanism of the inward parts of bodies, whether natural or artificial, we may attain to know the several uses and properties depending thereon, or the nature of the thing.

66 ☙ Hence, it is evident that those things which, under the notion of a cause co-operating or concurring to the production of effects, are altogether inexplicable, and run us into great absurdities, may be very naturally explained, and have a proper and obvious use assigned to them, when they are considered only as marks or signs for our information. And it is the searching after and endeavoring to understand those signs instituted by the Author of Nature, that ought to be the employment of the natural philosopher; and not the pretending to explain things by corporeal causes, which doctrine seems to have too much estranged the minds of men from that active principle, that supreme and wise Spirit "in whom we live, move, and have our being."

67 ☙ In the *twelfth* place, it may perhaps be objected that—though it be clear from what has been said that there can be no such thing as an inert, senseless, extended, solid, figured, movable substance existing without the mind, such as philosophers describe matter—yet, if any man shall leave out of his idea of matter the positive ideas of extension, figure, solidity and motion, and say that he means only by that word an inert, senseless substance, that exists without the mind or unperceived, which is the *occasion of our ideas,* or at the presence whereof God is pleased to excite ideas in us: it doth not appear but that matter taken in this sense may possibly exist. In answer to which I say, first, that it seems no less absurd to suppose a substance without accidents, than it is to sup-

pose accidents without a substance. But secondly, though we should grant this unknown substance may possibly exist, yet where can it be supposed to be? That it exists not in the mind is agreed; and that it exists not in place is no less certain—since all place or extension exists only in the mind, as hath been already proved. It remains therefore that it exists nowhere at all.

68 ◆§ Let us examine a little the description that is here given us of *matter*. It neither acts, nor perceives, nor is perceived; for this is all that is meant by saying it is an inert, senseless, unknown substance: which is a definition entirely made up of negatives, excepting only the relative notion of its standing under or supporting. But then it must be observed that it supports nothing at all, and how nearly this comes to the description of a *nonentity* I desire may be considered. But, say you, it is the *unknown occasion*, at the presence of which ideas are excited in us by the will of God. Now, I would fain know how anything can be present to us, which is neither perceivable by sense nor reflection, nor capable of producing any idea in our minds, nor is at all extended, nor hath any form, nor exists in any place. The words "to be present," when thus applied, must needs be taken in some abstract and strange meaning, and which I am not able to comprehend.

69 ◆§ Again, let us examine what is meant by *occasion*. So far as I can gather from the common use of language, that word signifies either the agent which produces any effect, or else something that is observed to accompany or go before it in the ordinary course of things. But when it is applied to matter as above described, it can be taken in neither of those senses; for matter is said to be passive and inert, and so cannot be an agent or efficient cause. It is also unperceivable, as being

devoid of all sensible qualities, and so cannot be the occasion of our perceptions in the latter sense: as when the burning my finger is said to be the occasion of the pain that attends it. What therefore can be meant by calling matter an *occasion?* The term is either used in no sense at all, or else in some very distant from its received signification.

70 ☙ You will perhaps say that matter, though it be not perceived by us, is nevertheless perceived by God, to whom it is the occasion of exciting ideas in our minds. For, say you, since we observe our sensations to be imprinted in an orderly and constant manner, it is but reasonable to suppose there are certain constant and regular occasions of their being produced. That is to say, that there are certain permanent and distinct parcels of matter, corresponding to our ideas, which, though they do not excite them in our minds, or anywise immediately affect us, as being altogether passive and unperceivable to us, they are nevertheless to God, by whom they are perceived, as it were so many occasions to remind Him when and what ideas to imprint on our minds; that so things may go on in a constant uniform manner.

71 ☙ In answer to this, I observe that, as the notion of matter is here stated, the question is no longer concerning the existence of a thing distinct from *spirit* and *idea*, from perceiving and being perceived; but whether there are not certain ideas of I know not what sort, in the mind of God which are so many marks or notes that direct Him how to produce sensations in our minds in a constant and regular method—much after the same manner as a musician is directed by the notes of music to produce that harmonious train and composition of sound which is called a tune, though they who hear the music do not perceive the notes, and may be entirely ignorant of them. But, this notion of matter seems too ex-

travagant to deserve a confutation. Besides, it is in effect no objection against what we have advanced, to wit, that there is no senseless unperceived substance.

72 ◆§ If we follow the light of reason, we shall, from the constant uniform method of our sensations, collect the goodness and wisdom of the Spirit who excites them in our minds; but this is all that I can see reasonably concluded from thence. To me, I say, it is evident that the being of a spirit infinitely wise, good, and powerful is abundantly sufficient to explain all the appearances ot nature. But as for *inert, senseless matter,* nothing that I perceive has any the least connection with it, or leads to the thoughts of it. And I would fain see anyone explain any the meanest phenomenon in nature by it, or shew any manner of reason, though in the lowest rank of probability, that he can have for its existence, or even make any tolerable sense or meaning of that supposition. For, as to its being an occasion, we have, I think, evidently shewn that with regard to us it is no occasion. It remains therefore that it must be, if at all, the occasion to God of exciting ideas in us; and what this amounts to we have just now seen.

73 ◆§ It is worth while to reflect a little on the motives which inducted men to suppose the existence of *material substance;* that so having observed the gradual ceasing and expiration of those motives or reasons, we may proportionably withdraw the assent that was grounded on them. First, therefore, it was thought that color, figure, motion, and the rest of the sensible qualities or accidents, did really exist without the mind; and for this reason it seemed needful to suppose some unthinking *substratum* or substance wherein they did exist, since they could not be conceived to exist by themselves. Afterwards, in process of time, men being convinced that colors, sounds, and the rest of the sensible, secondary quali-

ties had no existence without the mind, they stripped this *substratum* or material substance of those qualities, leaving only the primary ones, figure, motion, and suchlike, which they still conceived to exist without the mind, and consequently to stand in need of a material support. But, it having been shewn that none even of these can possibly exist otherwise than in a spirit or mind which perceives them, it follows that we have no longer any reason to suppose the being of matter; nay, that it is utterly impossible there should be any such thing, so long as that word is taken to denote an *unthinking substratum* of qualities or accidents wherein they exist without the mind.

74 ☙ But though it be allowed by the materialists themselves that matter was thought of only for the sake of supporting accidents, and, the reason entirely ceasing, one might expect the mind should naturally, and without any reluctance at all, quit the belief of what was solely grounded thereon; yet the prejudice is riveted so deeply in our thoughts, that we can scarce tell how to part with it, and are therefore inclined, since the *thing* itself is indefensible, at least to retain the *name*, which we apply to I know not what abstracted and indefinite notions of being, or occasion, though without any show of reason, at least so far as I can see. For, what is there on our part, or what do we perceive, amongst all the ideas, sensations, notions which are imprinted on our minds, either by sense or reflection, from whence may be inferred the existence of an inert, thoughtless, unperceived occasion? And, on the other hand, on the part of an all-sufficient Spirit, what can there be that should make us believe or even suspect He is directed by an inert occasion to excite ideas in our minds?

75 ☙ It is a very extraordinary instance of the force of prejudice, and much to be lamented, that the mind of man re-

tains so great a fondness, against all the evidence of reason, for a stupid thoughtless *somewhat*, by the interposition whereof it would as it were screen itself from the providenc of God, and remove it farther off from the affairs of the world. But, though we do the utmost we can to secure the belief of *matter*, though, when reason forsakes us, we endeavor to support our opinion on the bare possibility of the thing, and though we indulge ourselves in the full scope of an imagination not regulated by reason to make out that poor possibility, yet the upshot of all is, that there are certain *unknown ideas* in the mind of God; for this, if anything, is all that I conceive to be meant by *occasion* with regard to God. And this at the bottom is no longer contending for the thing, but for the name.

76 § Whether therefore there are such ideas in the mind o God, and whether they may be called by the name "matter," I shall not dispute. But, if you stick to the notion of an unthinking substance or support of extension, motion, and other sensible qualities, then to me it is most evidently impossible there should be any such thing; since it is a plain repugnancy that those qualities should exist in or be supported by an unperceiving substance.

77 § But, say you, though it be granted that there is no thoughtless support of extension and the other qualities or accidents which we perceive, yet there may perhaps be some inert, unperceiving substance or *substratum* of some other qualities, as incomprehensible to us as colors are to a man born blind, because we have not a sense adapted to them. But, if we had a new sense, we should possibly no more doubt of their existence than a blind man made to see does of the existence of light and colors. I answer, first, if what you mean

by the word "matter" be only the unknown support of unknown qualities, it is no matter whether there is such a thing or no, since it no way concerns us; and I do not see the advantage there is in disputing about what we know not *what*, and we know not *why*.

78 ☙§ But, secondly, if we had a new sense it could only furnish us with new ideas or sensations; and then we should have the same reason against their existing in an unperceiving substance that has been already offered with relation to figure, motion, color, and the like. Qualities, as hath been shewn, are nothing else but *sensations* or *ideas*, which exist only in a *mind* perceiving them; and this is true not only of the ideas we are acquainted with at present, but likewise of all possible ideas whatsoever.

79 ☙§ But, you will insist, what if I have no reason to believe the existence of matter? what if I cannot assign any use to it or explain anything by it, or even conceive what is meant by that word? yet still it is no contradiction to say that matter exists, and that this matter is in general a *substance*, or *occasion of ideas;* though indeed to go about to unfold the meaning or adhere to any particular explication of those words may be attended with great difficulties. I answer, when words are used without a meaning, you may put them together as you please without danger of running into a contradiction. You may say, for example, that twice two is equal to seven, so long as you declare you do not take the words of that proposition in their usual acceptation but for marks of you know not what. And, by the same reason, you may say there is an inert thoughtless substance without accidents which is the occasion of our ideas. And we shall understand just as much by one proposition as the other.

80 ☙§ In the *last* place, you will say, what if we give up the cause of material substance, and stand to it that matter is an unknown *somewhat*—neither substance nor accident, spirit nor idea, inert, thoughtless, indivisible, immovable, unextended, existing in no place. For, say you, whatever may be urged against *substance* or *occasion*, or any other positive or relative notion of matter, hath no place at all, so long as this *negative* definition of matter is adhered to. I answer, you may, if so it shall seem good, use the word "matter" in the same sense as other men use "nothing," and so make those terms convertible in your style. For, after all, this is what appears to me to be the result of that definition, the parts whereof when I consider with attention, either collectively or separate from each other, I do not find that there is any kind of effect or impression made on my mind different from what is excited by the term "nothing."

81 ☙§ You will reply, perhaps, that in the foresaid definition is included what doth sufficiently distinguish it from nothing: the positive abstract idea of *quiddity*, *entity*, or *existence*. I own, indeed, that those who pretend to the faculty of framing abstract general ideas do talk as if they had such an idea, which is, say they, the most abstract and general notion of all; that is, to me, the most incomprehensible of all others. That there are a great variety of spirits of different orders and capacities, whose faculties both in number and extent are far exceeding those the Author of my being has bestowed on me, I see no reason to deny. And for me to pretend to determine by my own few, stinted narrow inlets of perception, what ideas the inexhaustible power of the Supreme Spirit may imprint upon them were certainly the utmost folly and presumption—since there may be, for aught that I know, innumerable sorts of ideas or sensations, as different from one another, and from all that I have perceived, as colors are from sounds. But, how ready soever I may be to acknowledge the scantiness of my comprehension with regard to the endless variety of spirits and ideas that may possibly exist, yet for

anyone to pretend to a notion of entity or existence, *abstracted* from *spirit* and *idea*, from perceived and being perceived, is, I suspect, a downright repugnancy and trifling with words.

It remains that we consider the objections which may possibly be made on the part of religion.

82 ❧ Some there are who think that, though the arguments for the real existence of bodies which are drawn from reason be allowed not to amount to demonstration, yet the Holy Scriptures are so clear in the point as will sufficiently convince every good Christian that bodies do really exist, and are something more than mere ideas; there being in Holy Writ innumerable facts related which evidently suppose the reality of timber and stone, mountains and rivers, and cities, and human bodies. To which I answer that no sort of writings whatever, sacred or profane, which use those and the like words in the vulgar acceptation, or so as to have a meaning in them, are in danger of having their truth called in question by our doctrine. That all those things do really exist, that there are bodies, even corporeal substances, when taken in the vulgar sense, has been shewn to be agreeable to our principles; and the difference betwixt *things* and *ideas*, *realities* and *chimeras*, has been distinctly explained. (See Secs. 29, 30, 33, 36, etc.) And I do not think that either what philosophers call *matter*, or the existence of objects without the mind, is anywhere mentioned in Scripture.

83 ❧ Again, whether there can be or be not external things, it is agreed on all hands that the proper use of words is the marking our conceptions, or things only as they are known and perceived by us; whence it plainly follows that in the tenets we have laid down there is nothing inconsistent with the right use and significancy of language, and that discourse, of what kind soever, so far as it is intelligible, remains undis-

turbed. But all this seems so manifest, from what has been largely set forth in the premises, that it is needless to insist any farther on it.

84 ☙§ But, it will be urged that miracles do, at least, lose much of their stress and import by our principles. What must we think of Moses' rod: was it not *really* turned into a serpent; or was there only a change of *ideas* in the minds of the spectators? And, can it be supposed that our Saviour did no more at the marriage-feast in Cana than impose on the sight, and smell, and taste of the guests, so as to create in them the appearance or idea only of wine? The same may be said of all other miracles; which, in consequence of the foregoing principles, must be looked upon only as so many cheats, or illusions of fancy. To this I reply, that the rod was changed into a real serpent, and the water into real wine. That this does not in the least contradict what I have elsewhere said will be evident from Secs. 34 and 35. But this business of *real* and *imaginary* hath been already so plainly and fully explained, and so often referred to, and the difficulties about it are so easily answered from what hath gone before, that it were an affront to the reader's understanding to resume the explication of it in its place. I shall only observe that if at table all who were present should see, and smell, and taste, and drink wine, and find the effects of it, with me there could be no doubts of its reality; so that at bottom the scruple concerning real miracles has no place at all on ours, but only on the received principles, and consequently makes rather for than against what hath been said.

85 ☙§ Having done with the objections, which I endeavored to propose in the clearest light, and gave them all the force and weight I could, we proceed in the next place to take a view of our tenets in their *consequences*. Some of these appear at first sight: as that several difficult and obscure ques-

tions, on which abundance of speculation has been thrown away, are entirely banished from philosophy. "Whether corporeal substance can think," "whether matter be infinitely divisible," and "how it operates on spirit"—these and like inquiries have given infinite amusement to philosophers in all ages; but, depending on the existence of matter, they have no longer any place on our principles. Many other advantages there are, as well with regard to religion as the sciences, which it is easy for anyone to deduce from what has been premised; but this will appear more plainly in the sequel.

86 ☙ From the principles we have laid down it follows human knowledge may naturally be reduced to two heads: that of *ideas* and that of *spirits*. Of each of these I shall treat in order.

And *first* as to ideas or unthinking things. Our knowledge of these hath been very much obscured and confounded, and we have been led into very dangerous errors, by supposing a twofold existence of the objects of sense—the one *intelligible* or in the mind, the other *real* and without the mind; whereby unthinking things are thought to have a natural subsistence of their own distinct from being perceived by spirits. This, which, if I mistake not, hath been shewn to be a most groundless and absurd notion, is the very root of scepticism; for, so long as men thought that real things subsisted without the mind, and that their knowledge was not so far forth *real* as it was conformable to *real things*, it follows they could not be certain they had any real knowledge at all. For how can it be known that the things which are perceived are conformable to those which are not perceived, or exist without the mind?

87 ☙ Color, figure, motion, extension, and the like, considered only as so many *sensations* in the mind, are perfectly known, there being nothing in them which is not perceived.

But, if they are looked on as notes or images, referred to *things* or *archetypes* existing without the mind, then are we involved all in scepticism. We see only the appearances, and not the real qualities of things. What may be the extension, figure, or motion of anything really and absolutely, or in itself, it is impossible for us to know, but only the proportion or relation they bear to our senses. Things remaining the same, our ideas vary, and which of them, or even whether any of them at all, represent the true quality really existing in the thing, it is out of our reach to determine. So that, for aught we know, all we see, hear, and feel may be only phantom and vain chimera, and not at all agree with the real things existing in our *rerum natura.* All this scepticism follows from our supposing a difference between *things* and *ideas,* and that the former have a subsistence without the mind or unperceived. It were easy to dilate on this subject, and show how the arguments urged by sceptics in all ages depend on the supposition of external objects.

88 ☙ So long as we attribute a real existence to unthinking things, distinct from their being perceived, it is not only impossible for us to know with evidence the nature of any real unthinking being, but even that it exists. Hence it is that we see philosophers distrust their senses, and doubt of the existence of heaven and earth, of everything they see or feel, even of their own bodies. And, after all their labor and struggle of thought, they are forced to own we cannot attain to any self-evident or demonstrative knowledge of the existence of sensible things. But, all this doubtfulness, which so bewilders and confounds the mind and makes philosophy ridiculous in the eyes of the world, vanishes if we annex a meaning to our words, and not amuse ourselves with the terms "absolute," "external," "exist," and such like, signifying we know not what. I can as well doubt of my own being as of the being of those things which I actually perceive by sense; it being a manifest contradiction that any sensible object should be

immediately perceived by sight or touch, and at the same time have no existence in nature, since the very *existence* of an unthinking being consists in *being perceived.*

89 ☙ Nothing seems of more importance towards erecting a firm system of sound and real knowledge, which may be proof against the assaults of scepticism, than to lay the beginning in a distinct explication of what is meant by *thing, reality, existence;* for in vain shall we dispute concerning the real existence of things, or pretend to any knowledge thereof, so long as we have not fixed the meaning of those words. *Thing* or *Being* is the most general name of all; it comprehends under it two kinds entirely distinct and heterogeneous, and which have nothing common but the name, to wit, *spirits* and *ideas.* The former are active, indivisible substances: the latter are inert, fleeting, dependent beings, which subsist not by themselves, but are supported by, or exist in minds or spiritual substances. We comprehend our own existence by inward feeling or reflection, and that of other spirits by reason. We may be said to have some knowledge or notion of our own minds, of spirits and active beings, whereof in a strict sense we have not ideas. In like manner we know and have a notion of relations between things or ideas—which relations are distinct from the ideas or things related, inasmuch as the latter may be perceived by us without our perceiving the former. To me it seems that *ideas, spirits,* and *relations* are all in their respective kinds the object of human knowledge and subject of discourse; and that the term "idea" would be improperly extended to signify everything we know or have any notion of.

90 ☙ Ideas imprinted on the senses are real things, or do really exist; this we do not deny, but we deny they can subsist

without the minds which perceive them, or that they are resemblances of any archetypes existing without the mind; since the very being of a sensation or idea consists in being perceived, and an idea can be like nothing but an idea. Again, the things perceived by sense may be termed *external*, with regard to their origin: in that they are not generated from within by the mind itself, but imprinted by a Spirit distinct from that which perceives them. Sensible objects may likewise be said to be "without the mind" in another sense, namely when they exist in some other mind; thus, when I shut my eyes, the things I saw may still exist, but it must be in another mind.

91 ☙ It were a mistake to think that what is here said derogates in the least from the reality of things. It is acknowledged, on the received principles, that extension, motion, and in a word all sensible qualities have need of a support, as not being able to subsist by themselves. But the objects perceived by sense are allowed to be nothing but combinations of those qualities, and consequently cannot subsist by themselves. Thus far it is agreed on all hands. So that in denying the things perceived by sense an existence independent of a substance of support wherein they may exist, we detract nothing from the received opinion of their *reality*, and are guilty of no innovation in that respect. All the difference is that, according to us, the unthinking beings perceived by sense have no existence distinct from being perceived, and cannot therefore exist in any other substance than those unextended indivisible substances or *spirits* which act and think and perceive them; whereas philosophers vulgarly hold that the sensible qualities do exist in an inert, extended, unperceiving substance which they call *matter*, to which they attribute a natural subsistence, exterior to all thinking beings, or distinct from being perceived by any mind whatsoever, even the eternal mind of the Creator, wherein they suppose only ideas of the corporeal

substances created by Him; if indeed they allow them to be at all created.

92 ☙ For, as we have shewn the doctrine of matter or corporeal substance to have been the main pillar and support of scepticism, so likewise upon the same foundation have been raised all the impious schemes of atheism and irreligion. Nay, so great a difficulty hath it been thought to conceive matter produced out of nothing, that the most celebrated among the ancient philosophers, even of those who maintained the being of God, have thought matter to be uncreated and co-eternal with Him. How great a friend *material substance* hath been to atheists in all ages were needless to relate. All their monstrous systems have so visible and necessary a dependence on it that, when this cornerstone is once removed, the whole fabric cannot choose but fall to the ground, insomuch that it is no longer worth while to bestow a particular consideration on the absurdities of every wretched sect of atheists.

93 ☙ That impious and profane persons should readily fall in with those systems which favor their inclinations, by deriding immaterial substance, and supposing the soul to be divisible and subject to corruption as the body; which exclude all freedom, intelligence, and design from the formation of things, and instead thereof make a self-existent, stupid, unthinking substance the root and origin of all beings; that they should hearken to those who deny a Providence, or inspection of a Superior Mind over the affairs of the world, attributing the whole series of events either to blind chance or fatal necessity arising from the impulse of one body or another—all this is very natural. And, on the other hand, when men of better principles observe the enemies of religion lay so great a stress on *unthinking matter*, and all of them use so much

industry and artifice to reduce everything to it, methinks they should rejoice to see them deprived of their grand support, and driven from that only fortress, without which your Epicureans, Hobbists, and the like, have not even the shadow of a pretense, but become the most cheap and easy triumph in the world.

94 ☙ The existence of matter, or bodies unperceived, has not only been the main support of atheists and fatalists, but on the same principle doth idolatry likewise in all its various forms depend. Did men but consider that the sun, moon, and stars, and every other object of the senses are not so many sensations in their minds, which have no other existence but barely being perceived, doubtless they would never fall down and worship their own *ideas*, but rather address their homage to that Eternal Invisible Mind which produces and sustains all things.

95 ☙ The same absurd principle, by mingling itself with the articles of our faith, has occasioned no small difficulties to Christians. For example, about the Resurrection, how many scruples and objections have been raised by Socinians and others? But do not the most plausible of them depend on the supposition that a body is denominated the *same*, with regard not to the form or that which is perceived by sense, but the material substance, which remains the same under several forms? Take away this *material substance*, about the identity whereof all the dispute is, and mean by *body* what every plain ordinary person means by that word, to wit, that which is immediately seen and felt, which is only a combination of sensible qualities or ideas, and then their most unanswerable objections come to nothing.

96 ◆§ Matter being once expelled out of nature drags with it so many sceptical and impious notions, such an incredible number of disputes and puzzling questions, which have been thorns in the sides of divines as well as philosophers, and made so much fruitless work for mankind, that if the arguments we have produced against it are not found equal to demonstration (as to me they evidently seem), yet I am sure all friends to knowledge, peace, and religion have reason to wish they were.

97 ◆§ Beside the external existence of the objects of perception, another great source of errors and difficulties with regard to ideal knowledge is the doctrine of *abstract ideas*, such as it hath been set forth in the Introduction. The plainest things in the world, those we are most intimately acquainted with and perfectly know, when they are considered in an abstract way, appear strangely difficult and incomprehensible. Time, place, and motion, taken in particular or concrete, or what everybody knows, but, having passed through the hands of a metaphysician, they become too abstract and fine to be apprehended by men of ordinary sense. Bid your servant meet you at such a *time* in such a *place*, and he shall never stay to deliberate on the meaning of those words; in conceiving that particular time and place, or the motion by which he is not to get thither, he finds not the least difficulty. But if *time* be taken exclusive of all those particular actions and ideas that diversify the day, merely for the continuation of existence or duration in abstract, then it will perhaps gravel even a philosopher to comprehend it.

98 ◆§ For my own part, whenever I attempt to frame a simple idea of *time*, abstracted from the succession of ideas in my mind, which flows uniformly and is participated by all

beings, I am lost and embrangled in inextricable difficulties. I have no notion of it at all, only I hear others say it is infinitely divisible, and speak of it in such a manner as leads me to entertain odd thoughts of my existence; since that doctrine lays one under an absolute necessity of thinking, either that he passes away innumerable ages without a thought, or else that he is annihilated every moment of his life, both which seem equally absurd. Time therefore being nothing, abstracted from the succession of ideas in our minds, it follows that the duration of any finite spirit must be estimated by the number of ideas or actions succeeding each other in that same spirit or mind. Hence, it is a plain consequence that the soul always thinks; and in truth whoever shall go about to divide in his thoughts, or abstract the *existence* of a spirit from its *cogitation*, will, I believe, find it no easy task.

99 ☙§ So likewise when we attempt to abstract extension and motion from all other qualities, and consider them by themselves, we presently lose sight of them, and run into great extravagances. All which depend on a twofold abstraction; first, it is supposed that extension, for example, may be abstracted from all other sensible qualities; and secondly, that the entity of extension may be abstracted from its being perceived. But, whoever shall reflect, and take care to understand what he says, will, if I mistake not, acknowledge that all sensible qualities are alike *sensations* and alike *real;* that where the extension is, there is the color, too, to wit, in his mind, and that their archetypes can exist only in some other *mind;* and that the objects of sense are nothing but those sensations combined, blended, or (if one may so speak) concreted together; none of all which can be supposed to exist unperceived.

100 ☙§ What it is for a man to be happy, or an object good, everyone may think he knows. But to frame an abstract idea of happiness, prescinded from all particular pleasure, or of

goodness from everything that is good, this is what few can pretend to. So likewise a man may be just and virtuous without having precise ideas of justice and virtue. The opinion that those and the like words stand for general notions, abstracted from all particular persons and actions, seems to have rendered morality very difficult, and the study thereof of small use to mankind. And in effect the doctrine of *abstraction* has not a little contributed towards spoiling the most useful parts of knowledge.

101 ☙§ The two great provinces of speculative science conversant about ideas received from sense, are *natural philosophy* and *mathematics;* with regard to each of these I shall make some observations. And first I shall say somewhat of natural philosophy. On this subject it is that the sceptics triumph. All that stock of arguments they produce to depreciate our faculties and make mankind appear ignorant and low, are drawn principally from this head, namely, that we are under an invincible blindness as to the *true* and *real* nature of things. This they exaggerate, and love to enlarge on. We are miserably bantered, say they, by our senses, and amused only with the outside and show of things. The real essence, the internal qualities and constitution of even the meanest object, is hid from our view; something there is in every drop of water, every grain of sand, which it is beyond the power of human understanding to fathom or comprehend. But it is evident from what has been shewn that all this complaint is groundless, and that we are influenced by false principles to that degree as to mistrust our senses, and think we know nothing of those things which we perfectly comprehend.

102 ☙§ One great inducement to our pronouncing ourselves ignorant of the nature of things is the current opinion that everything includes within itself the cause of its properties; or that there is in each object an inward essence which is the

source whence its discernible qualities flow, and whereon they depend. Some have pretended to account for appearances by occult qualities, but of late they are mostly resolved into mechanical causes, to wit, the figure, motion, weight, and suchlike qualities, of insensible particles; whereas, in truth, there is no other agent or efficient cause than *spirit*, it being evident that motion, as well as all other *ideas*, is perfectly inert. (See Sec. 25.) Hence, to endeavor to explain the production of colors or sounds, by figure, motion, magnitude, and the like, must needs be labor in vain. And accordingly we see the attempts of that kind are not at all satisfactory. Which may be said in general of those instances wherein one idea or quality is assigned for the cause of another. I need not say how many hypotheses and speculations are left out, and how much the study of nature is abridged by this doctrine.

103 ☙ The great mechanical principle now in vogue is *attraction*. That a stone falls to the earth, or the sea swells towards the moon, may to some appear sufficiently explained thereby. But how are we enlightened by being told this is done by attraction? Is it that that word signifies the manner of the tendency, and that it is by the mutual drawing of bodies instead of their being impelled or protruded towards each other? But nothing is determined of the manner or action, and it may as truly (for aught we know) be termed "impulse," or "protrusion," as "attraction." Again, the parts of steel we see cohere firmly together, and this also is accounted for by attraction; but, in this as in the other instances, I do not perceive that anything is signified besides the effect itself; for as to the manner of the action whereby it is produced, or the cause which produces it, these are not so much as aimed at.

104 ☙ Indeed, if we take a view of the several phenomena, and compare them together, we may observe some likeness

and conformity between them. For example, in the falling of a stone to the ground, in the rising of the sea towards the moon, in cohesion, crystallization, etc., there is something alike, namely, an union or mutual approach of bodies. So that any one of these or the like phenomena may not seem strange or surprising to a man who has nicely observed and compared the effects of nature. For that only is thought so which is uncommon, or a thing by itself, and out of the ordinary course of our observation. That bodies should tend towards the center of the earth is not thought strange, because it is what we perceive every moment of our lives. But that they should have a like gravitation towards the center of the moon may seem odd and unaccountable to most men, because it is discerned only in the tides. But a philosopher, whose thoughts take in a larger compass of nature, having observed a certain similitude of appearances, as well in the heavens as the earth, that argue innumerable bodies to have a mutual tendency towards each other, which he denotes by the general name "attraction," whatever can be reduced to that he thinks justly accounted for. Thus he explains the tides by the attraction of the terraqueous globe towards the moon, which to him doth not appear odd or anomalous, but only a particular example of a general rule or law of nature.

105 ◆§ If therefore we consider the difference there is betwixt natural philosophers and other men, with regard to their knowledge of the phenomena, we shall find it consists not in an exacter knowledge of the efficient cause that produces them, for that can be no other than the *will of a spirit;* but only in a greater largeness of comprehension, whereby analogies, harmonies, and agreements are discovered in the works of nature, and the particular effect explained, that is, reduced to general rules (see Sec. 62), which rules, grounded on the analogy and uniformness observed in the production of natural effects, are most agreeable and sought after by the mind; for that they extend our prospect beyond what is pres-

ent and near to us, and enable us to make very probable conjectures touching things that may have happened at very great distances of time and place, as well as to predict things to come; which sort of endeavor towards omniscience is much affected by the mind.

106 ☙ But we shall proceed warily in such things, for we are apt to lay too great stress on analogies, and, to the prejudice of truth, humor that eagerness of the mind whereby it is carried to extend its knowledge into general theorems. For example, in the business of gravitation or mutual attraction, because it appears in many instances, some are straightway for pronouncing it *universal;* and that to attract and be attracted by every other body is an essential quality inherent in all bodies whatsoever. Whereas it is evident the fixed stars have no such tendency towards each other; and, so far is that gravitation from being *essential* to bodies that in some instances a quite contrary principle seems to shew itself; as in the perpendicular growth of plants, and the elasticity of the air. There is nothing necessary or essential in the case, but it depends entirely on the will of the Governing Spirit, who causes certain bodies to cleave together or tend towards each other according to various laws, whilst He keeps others at a fixed distance; and to some He gives a quite contrary tendency to fly asunder just as He sees convenient.

107 ☙ After what has been premised, I think we may lay down the following conclusions. First, it is plain philosophers amuse themselves in vain, when they inquire for any natural efficient cause, distinct from a *mind* or *spirit.* Secondly, considering the whole creation is the workmanship of a *wise and good Agent,* it should seem to become philosophers to employ their thoughts (contrary to what some hold) about the final causes of things; and I confess I see no reason

why pointing out the various ends to which natural things are adapted, and for which they were originally with unspeakable wisdom contrived, should not be thought one good way of accounting for them, and altogether worthy a philosopher. Thirdly, from what hath been premised no reason can be drawn why the history of nature should not still be studied, and observations and experiments made, which, that they are of use to mankind, and enable us to draw any general conclusions, is not the result of any immutable habitudes or relations between things themselves, but only of God's goodness and kindness to men in the administration of the world. (See Secs. 30 and 31.) Fourthly, by a diligent observation of the phenomena within our view, we may discover the general laws of nature, and from them deduce the other phenomena; I do not say *demonstrate*, for all deductions of that kind depend on a supposition that the Author of Nature always operates uniformly, and in a constant observance of those rules we take for principles: which we cannot evidently know.

108 ◆§ Those men who frame general rules from the phenomena and afterwards derive the phenomena from those rules, seem to consider signs rather than causes. A man may well understand natural signs without knowing their analogy, or being able to say by what rule a thing is so or so. And, as it is very possible to write improperly, through too strict an observance of general grammar rules; so, in arguing from general laws of nature, it is not impossible we may extend the analogy too far, and by that means run into mistakes.

109 ◆§ As in reading other books a wise man will choose to fix his thoughts on the sense and apply it to use, rather than lay them out in grammatical remarks on the language; so, in perusing the volume of nature, it seems beneath the dignity

of the mind to affect an exactness in reducing each particular phenomenon to general rules, or shewing how it follows from them. We should propose to ourselves nobler views, namely, to recreate and exalt the mind with a prospect of the beauty, order, extent, and variety of natural things: hence, by proper inferences, to enlarge our notions of the grandeur, wisdom, and beneficence of the Creator; and lastly, to make the several parts of the creation, so far as in us lies, subservient to the ends they were designed for, God's glory, and the sustenation and comfort of ourselves and fellow-creatures.

110 ☙ The best key for the aforesaid analogy or natural science will be easily acknowledged to be a certain celebrated treatise of *mechanics*. In the entrance of which justly admired treatise, time, space, and motion are distinguished into *absolute* and *relative*, *true* and *apparent*, *mathematical* and *vulgar*; which distinction, as it is at large explained by the author,[6] does suppose these quantities to have an existence without the mind; and that they are ordinarily conceived with relation to sensible things, to which nevertheless in their own nature they bear no relation at all.

111 ☙ As for *time*, as it is there taken in an absolute or abstracted sense, for the duration or perseverance of the existence of things, I have nothing more to add concerning it after what has been already said on that subject. (Secs. 97 and 98.) For the rest, this celebrated author holds there is an *absolute space*, which, being unperceivable to sense, remains in itself similar and immovable; and relative space to be the measure thereof, which, being movable and defined by its situation in respect of sensible bodies, is vulgarly taken for immovable space. *Place* he defines to be that part of space which is occu-

[6] Newton.

pied by any body; and according as the space is absolute or relative so also is the place. *Absolute motion* is said to be the translation of a body from absolute place to absolute place, as relative motion is from one relative place to another. And, because the parts of absolute space do not fall under our senses, instead of them we are obliged to use their sensible measures, and so define both place and motion with respect to bodies which we regard as immovable. But, it is said in philosophical matters we must abstract from our senses, since it may be that none of those bodies which seem to be quiescent are truly so, and the same thing which is moved relatively may be really at rest; as likewise one and the same body may be in relative rest and motion, or even moved with contrary relative motions at the same time, according as its place is variously defined. All which ambiguity is to be found in the apparent motions, but not at all in the true or absolute, which should therefore be alone regarded in philosophy. And the true as we are told are distinguished from apparent or relative motions by the following properties. First, in true or absolute motion all parts which preserve the same position with respect of the whole, partake of the motions of the whole. Secondly, the place being moved, that which is placed therein is also moved; so that a body moving in a place which is in motion doth participate the motion of its place. Thirdly, true motion is never generated or changed otherwise than by force impressed on the body itself. Fourthly, true motion is always changed by force impressed on the body moved. Fifthly, in circular motion barely relative there is no centrifugal force, which, nevertheless, in that which is true or absolute, is proportional to the quantity of motion.

112 ◆§ But, notwithstanding what hath been said, I must confess it doth not appear to me that there can be any motion other than *relative;* so that to conceive motion there must be at least conceived two bodies, whereof the distance or position in regard to each other is varied. Hence, if there was

one only body in being it could not possibly be moved. This seems evident, in that the idea I have of motion doth necessarily include relation.

113 ☙§ But, though in every motion it be necessary to conceive more bodies than one, yet it may be that one only is moved, namely, that one which the force causing the change in the distance or situation of the bodies, is impressed. For, however some may define relative motion, so as to term that body *moved* which changes its distance from some other body, whether the force or action causing that change were impressed on it or no, yet as relative motion is that which is perceived by sense, and regarded in the ordinary affairs of life, it should seem that every man of common sense knows what it is as well as the best philosopher. Now, I ask anyone whether, in his sense of motion as he walks along the streets, the stones he passes over may be said to *move*, because they change distance with his feet? To me it appears that though motion includes a relation of one thing to another, yet it is not necessary that each term of the relation be denominated from it. As a man may think of somewhat which does not think, so a body may be moved to or from another body which is not therefore itself in motion.

114 ☙§ As the place happens to be variously defined, the motion which is related to it varies. A man in a ship may be said to be quiescent with relation to the sides of the vessel, and yet move with relation to the land. Or he may move eastward in respect of the one, and westward in respect of the other. In the common affairs of life men never go beyond the earth to define the place of any body; and what is quiescent in respect of that is accounted *absolutely* to be so. But philosophers, who have a greater extent of thought, and juster notions of the system of things, discover even the earth itself to be moved. In order therefore to fix their notions they seem

to conceive the corporeal world as finite, and the utmost unmoved walls or shell thereof to be the place whereby they estimate true motions. If we sound our own conceptions, I believe we may find all the absolute motion we can frame an idea of to be at bottom no other than relative motion thus defined. For, as hath been already observed, absolute motion, exclusive of all external relation, is incomprehensible; and to this kind of relative motion all the above-mentioned properties, causes, and effects ascribed to absolute motion will, if I mistake not, be found to agree. As to what is said of the centrifugal force, that it doth not at all belong to circular relative motion, I do not see how this follows from the experiment which is brought to prove it. (See *Philosophiae Naturalis Principia Mathematica, in Schol. Def. VIII.*) For the water in the vessel at that time wherein it is said to have the greatest relative circular motion, hath, I think, no motion at all; as is plain from the foregoing section.

115 ☙§ For to denominate a body *moved* it is requisite, first, that it change its distance or situation with regard to some other body; and secondly, that the force occasioning that change be applied to it. If either of these be wanting, I do not think that, agreeably to the sense of mankind, or the propriety of language, a body can be said to be in motion. I grant indeed that it is possible for us to think a body which we see change its distance from some other to be moved, though it have no force applied to it (in which sense there may be apparent motion), but then it is because the force causing the change of distance is imagined by us to be applied or impressed on that body thought to move; which indeed shews we are capable of mistaking a thing to be in motion which is not, and that is all.

116 ☙§ From what hath been said it follows that the philosophic consideration of motion doth not imply the being of

an *absolute space*, distinct from that which is perceived of sense and related bodies; which that it cannot exist without the mind is clear upon the same principles that demonstrate the like of all other objects of sense. And perhaps, if we inquire narrowly, we shall find we cannot even frame an idea of *pure space* exclusive of all body. This I must confess seems impossible, as being a most abstract idea. When I excite a motion in some part of my body, if it be free or without resistance, I say there is *space;* but if I find a resistance, then I say there is *body;* and in proportion as the resistance to motion is lesser or greater, I say the space is more or less *pure*. So that when I speak of pure or empty space, it is not to be supposed that the word "space" stands for an idea distinct from or conceivable without body and motion. Though indeed we are apt to think every noun substantive stands for a distinct idea that may be separated from all others; which has occasioned infinite mistakes. When, therefore, supposing all the world to be annihilated besides my own body, I say there still remains *pure space*, thereby nothing else is meant but only that I conceive it possible for the limbs of my body to be moved on all sides without the least resistance, but if that, too, were annihilated then there could be no motion, and consequently no space Some, perhaps, may think the sense of seeing doth furnish them with the idea of pure space; but it is plain from what we have elsewhere shewn, that the ideas of space and distance are not obtained by that sense. (See the Essay concerning Vision.)

117 ☙ What is here laid down seems to put an end to all those disputes and difficulties that have sprung up amongst the learned concerning the nature of *pure space*. But the chief advantage arising from it is that we are freed from that dangerous dilemma, to which several who have employed their thoughts on that subject imagine themselves reduced, to wit, of thinking either that real space is God, or else that there is something beside God which is eternal, uncreated, infinite,

indivisible, immutable. Both which may justly be thought pernicious and absurd notions. It is certain that not a few divines, as well as philosophers of great note, have, from the difficulty they found in conceiving either limits or annihilation of space, concluded it must be divine. And some of late have set themselves particularly to shew the incommunicable attributes of God agree to it. Which doctrine, how unworthy soever it may seem of the Divine Nature, yet I do not see how we can get clear of it, so long as we adhere to the received opinions.

118 ❧ Hitherto of natural philosophy: we come now to make some inquiry concerning that other great branch of speculative knowledge, to wit, mathematics. These, how celebrated soever they may be for their clearness and certainty of demonstration, which is hardly anywhere else to be found, cannot nevertheless be supposed altogether free from mistakes, if in their principles there lurks some secret error which is common to the professors of those sciences with the rest of mankind. Mathematicians, though they deduce their theorems from a great height of evidence, yet their first principles are limited by the consideration of quantity; and they do not ascend into any inquiry concerning those transcendental maxims which influence all the particular sciences, each part whereof, mathematics not excepted, does consequently participate of the errors involved in them. That the principles laid down by mathematicians are true, and their way of deduction from those principles clear and incontestible, we do not deny; but we hold there may be certain erroneous maxims of greater extent than the object of mathematics, and for that reason not expressly mentioned, though tacitly supposed throughout the whole progress of that science; and that the ill effects of those secret unexamined errors are diffused through all the branches thereof. To be plain, we suspect the mathematicians are as well as other men concerned in the errors arising from the doctrine of abstract general ideas, and the existence of objects without the mind.

119 ☙ Arithmetic has been thought to have for its object abstract ideas of *number;* of which to understand the properties and mutual habitudes, is supposed no mean part of speculative knowledge. The opinion of the pure and intellectual nature of numbers in abstract hath made them in esteem with those philosophers who seem to have affected an uncommon fineness and elevation of thought. It hath set a price on the most trifling numerical speculations which in practice are of no use, but serve only for amusement; and hath therefore so far infected the minds of some, that they have dreamed of mighty mysteries involved in numbers, and attempted the explication of natural things by them. But, if we inquire into our own thoughts, and consider what hath been premised, we may perhaps entertain a low opinion of those high flights and abstractions, and look on all inquiries, about numbers only as so many *difficiles nugae,* so far as they are not subservient to practice, and promote the benefit of life.

120 ☙ Unity in abstract we have before considered in Sec. 13, from which and what hath been said in the Introduction, it plainly follows there is not any such idea. But, number being defined a "collection of units," we may conclude that, if there be no such thing as unity or unit in abstract, there are no ideas of number in abstract denoted by the numeral names and figures. The theories therefore in arithmetic, if they are abstracted from the names and figures, as likewise from all use and practice, as well as from the particular things numbered, can be supposed to have nothing at all for their object; hence we may see how entirely the science of numbers is subordinate to practice, and how jejune and trifling it becomes when considered as a matter of mere speculation.

121 ☙ However, since there may be some who, deluded by the specious show of discovering abstracted verities, waste

their time in arithmetical theorems and problems which have not any use, it will not be amiss if we more fully consider and expose the vanity of that pretense; and this will plainly appear by taking a view of arithmetic in its infancy, and observing what it was that originally put men on the study of that science, and to what scope they directed it. It is natural to think that at first, men, for ease of memory and help of computation, made use of counters, or in writing of single strokes, points, or the like, each whereof was made to signify an unit, i.e., some one thing of whatever kind they had occasion to reckon. Afterwards they found out the more compendious ways of making one character stand in place of several strokes or points. And, lastly, the notation of the Arabians or Indians came into use, wherein, by the repetition of a few characters or figures, and varying the significance of each figure according to the place it obtains, all numbers may be most aptly expressed; which seems to have been done in imitation of language, so that an exact analogy is observed betwixt the notation by figures and names, the nine simple figures answering the nine first numeral names and places in the former, corresponding to denominations in the latter. And agreeably to those conditions of the simple and local value of figures, were contrived methods of finding, from the given figures or marks of the parts, what figures and how placed are proper to denote the whole, or *vice versa*. And having found the sought figures, the same rule or analogy being observed throughout, it is easy to read them into words; and so the number becomes perfectly known. For then the number of any particular things is said to be known, when we know the name or figures (with their due arrangement) that according to the standing analogy belong to them. For, these signs being known, we can by the operations of arithmetic know the signs of any part of the particular sums signified by them; and, thus computing in signs (because of the connection established betwixt them and the distinct multitudes of things whereof one is taken for an unit), we may be able rightly to sum up, divide, and proportion the things themselves that we intend to number.

122 ◆§ In arithmetic, therefore, we regard not the *things*, but the *signs*, which nevertheless are not regarded for their own sake, but because they direct us how to act with relation to things, and dispose rightly of them. Now, agreeably to what we have before observed of words in general (Sec. 19, Introd.) it happens here likewise that abstract ideas are thought to be signified by numeral names or characters, while they do not suggest ideas of particular things to our minds. I shall not at present enter into a more particular dissertation on this subject, but only observe that it is evident from what hath been said, those things which pass for abstract truths and theorems concerning numbers, are in reality conversant about no object distinct from particular numeral things, except only names and characters, which originally came to be considered on no other account but their being signs, or capable to represent aptly whatever particular things men had need to compute. Whence it follows that to study them for their own sake would be just as wise, and to as good purpose as if a man, neglecting the true use or original intention and subserviency of language, should spend his time in impertinent criticisms upon words, or reasonings and controversies purely verbal.

123 ◆§ From numbers we proceed to speak of *extension*, which, considered as relative, is the object of geometry. The *infinite* divisibility of *finite* extension, though it is not expressly laid down either as an axiom or theorem in the elements of that science, yet is throughout the same everywhere supposed and thought to have so inseparable and essential a connection with the principles and demonstrations in geometry, that mathematicians never admit it into doubt, or make the least question of it. And, as this notion is the source from whence do spring all those amusing geometrical paradoxes which have such a direct repugnancy to the plain common sense of mankind, and are admitted with so much reluctance into a mind not yet debauched by learning; so it is

the principal occasion of all that nice and extreme subtilty which renders the study of mathematics so difficult and tedious. Hence, if we can make it appear that no finite extension contains innumerable parts, or is infinitely divisible, it follows that we shall at once clear the science of geometry from a great number of difficulties and contradictions which have ever been esteemed a reproach to human reason, and withal make the attainment thereof a business of much less time and pains than it hitherto hath been.

124 ◆§ Every particular finite extension which may possibly be the object of our thought is an *idea* existing only in the mind, and consequently each part thereof must be perceived. If, therefore, I cannot perceive innumerable parts in any finite extension that I consider, it is certain they are not contained in it; but it is evident that I cannot distinguish innumerable parts in any particular line, surface, or solid, which I either perceive by sense, or figure to myself in my mind: wherefore I conclude they are not contained in it. Nothing can be plainer to me than that the extensions I have in view are no other than my own ideas; and it is no less plain that I cannot resolve any one of my ideas into an infinite number of other ideas, that is, that they are not infinitely divisible. If by finite extension be meant something distinct from a finite idea, I declare I do not know what that is, and so cannot affirm or deny anything of it. But if the terms "extension," "parts," etc., are taken in any sense conceivable, that is, for ideas, then to say a finite quantity or extension consists of parts infinite in number is so manifest a contradiction, that everyone at first sight acknowledges it to be so; and it is impossible it should ever gain the assent of any reasonable creature who is not brought to it by gentle and slow degrees, as a converted Gentile to the belief of transubstantiation. Ancient and rooted prejudices do often pass into principles; and those propositions which once obtain the force and credit of a *principle*, are not only themselves, but likewise whatever

is deducible from them, thought privileged from all examination. And there is no absurdity so gross, which, by this means, the mind of man may not be prepared to swallow.

125 ☙§ He whose understanding is possessed with the doctrine of abstract general ideas may be persuaded that (whatever be thought of the ideas of sense) extension in *abstract* is infinitely divisible. And one who thinks the objects of sense exist without the mind will perhaps in virtue thereof be brought to admit that a line but an inch long may contain innumerable parts—really existing, though too small to be discerned. These errors are grafted as well in the minds of geometricians as of other men, and have a like influence on their reasonings; and it were no difficult thing to shew how the arguments from geometry made use of to support the infinite divisibility of extension are bottomed on them. At present we shall only observe in general whence it is the mathematicians are all so fond and tenacious of that doctrine.

126 ☙§ It hath been observed in another place that the theorems and demonstrations in geometry are conversant about universal ideas (Sec. 15, Introd.); where it is explained in what sense this ought to be understood, to wit, the particular lines and figures included in the diagram are supposed to stand for innumerable others of different sizes; or, in other words, the geometer considers them abstracting from their magnitude—which does not imply that he forms an abstract idea, but only that he cares not what the particular magnitude is, whether great or small, but looks on that as a thing different to the demonstration. Hence it follows that a line in the scheme but an inch long must be spoken of as though it contained ten thousand parts, since it is regarded not in itself, but as it is universal; and it is universal only in its significa-

tion, whereby it represents innumerable lines greater than itself, in which may be distinguished ten thousand parts or more, though there may not be above an inch in it. After this manner, the properties of the lines signified are (by a very usual figure) transferred to the sign, and thence, through mistake, thought to appertain to it considered in its own nature.

127 § Because there is no number of parts so great but it is possible there may be a line containing more, the inch-line is said to contain parts more than any assignable number; which is true, not of the inch taken absolutely, but only for the things signified by it. But men, not retaining that distinction in their thoughts, slide into a belief that the small particular line described on paper contains in itself parts innumerable. There is no such thing as the ten-thousandth part of an inch; but there is of a mile or diameter of the earth, which may be signified by that inch. When therefore I delineate a triangle on paper, and take one side not above an inch, for example, in lengths to be the radius, this I consider as divided into ten thousand or an hundred thousand parts or more; for, though the ten-thousandth part of that line considered in itself is nothing at all, and consequently may be neglected without an error or inconveniency, yet these described lines, being only marks standing for greater quantities, whereof it may be the ten-thousandth part is very considerable, it follows that, to prevent notable errors in practice, the radius must be taken of ten thousand parts or more.

128 § From what hath been said the reason is plain why, to the end any theorem become universal in its use, it is necessary we speak of the lines described on paper as though they contained parts which really they do not. In doing of which,

if we examine the matter thoroughly, we shall perhaps discover that we cannot conceive an inch itself as consisting of, or being divisible into, a thousand parts, but only some other line which is far greater than an inch, and represented by it; and that when we say a line is infinitely divisible, we must mean a line which is infinitely great. What we have here observed seems to be the chief cause why, to suppose the infinite divisibility of finite extension hath been thought necessary in geometry.

129 ☙ The several absurdities and contradictions which flowed from this false principle might, one would think, have been esteemed so many demonstrations against it. But, by I know not what logic, it is held that proofs *a posteriori* are not to be admitted against propositions relating to infinity, as though it were not impossible even for an infinite mind to reconcile contradictions; or as if anything absurd and repugnant could have a necessary connection with truth or flow from it. But whoever considers the weakness of this pretense will think it was contrived on purpose to humor the laziness of the mind which had rather acquiesce in an indolent scepticism than be at the pains to go through with a severe examination of those principles it hath ever embraced for true.

130 ☙ Of late the speculations about infinites have run so high, and grown to such strange notions, as have occasioned no scruples and disputes among the geometers of the present age. Some there are of great note who, not content with holding that finite lines may be divided into an infinite number of parts, do yet farther maintain that each of those infinitesimals is itself subdivisible into an infinity of other parts or infinitesimals of a second order, and so on *ad infinitum.* These, I say, assert there are infinitesimals of infinitesimals of infinitesimals, etc., without ever coming to an end! so that

according to them an inch does not barely contain an infinite number of parts, but an infinity of an infinity of an infinity *ad infinitum* of parts. Others there be who hold all orders of infinitesimals below the first to be nothing at all; thinking it with good reason absurd to imagine there is any positive quantity or part of extension which, though multiplied infinitely, can never equal the smallest given extension. And yet on the other hand it seems no less absurd to think the square, cube or other power of a positive real root, should itself be nothing at all; which they who hold infinitesimals of the first order, denying all of the subsequent orders, are obliged to maintain.

131 ☙ Have we not therefore reason to conclude they are *both* in the wrong, and that there is in effect no such thing as parts infinitely small, or an infinite number of parts contained in any finite quantity? But you will say that if this doctrine obtains it will follow the very foundations of geometry are destroyed, and those great men who have raised that science to so astonishing a height, have been all the while building a castle in the air. To this it may be replied that whatever is useful in geometry, and promotes the benefit of human life, does still remain firm and unshaken on our principles; that science considered as practical will rather receive advantage than any prejudice from what has been said. But to set this in a due light may be the proper business of another place. For the rest, though it should follow that some of the more intricate and subtle parts of speculative mathematics may be pared off without any prejudice to truth, yet I do not see what damage will be thence derived to mankind. On the contrary, I think it were highly to be wished that men of great abilities and obstinate application would draw off their thoughts from those amusements, and employ them in the study of such things as lie nearer the concerns of life, or have a more direct influence on the manners.

132 ☙§ If it be said that several theorems undoubtedly true are discovered by methods in which infinitesimals are made use of, which could never have been if their existence included a contradiction in it; I answer that upon a thorough examination it will not be found that in any instance it is necessary to make use of or conceive infinitesimal parts of finite lines, or even quantities less than the *minimum sensible;* nay, it will be evident this is never done, it being impossible.

133 ☙§ By what we have premised, it is plain that very numerous and important errors have taken their rise from those false principles which were impugned in the foregoing parts of this treatise; and the opposites of those erroneous tenets at the same time appear to be most fruitful principles, from whence do flow innumerable consequences highly advantageous to true philosophy, as well as to religion. Particularly *matter*, or *the absolute existence of corporeal objects*, hath been shewn to be that wherein the most avowed and pernicious enemies of all knowledge, whether human or divine, have ever placed their chief strength and confidence. And surely, if by distinguishing the real existence of unthinking things from their being perceived, and allowing them a subsistence of their own out of the minds of spirits, no one thing is explained in nature, but on the contrary a great many inexplicable difficulties arise; if the supposition of matter is barely precarious, as not being grounded on so much as one single reason; if its consequences cannot endure the light of examination and free inquiry, but screen themselves under the dark and general pretense of "infinites being incomprehensible"; if withal the removal of this *matter* be not attended with the least evil consequence; if it be not even missed in the world, but everything as well, nay much easier conceived without it; if, lastly, both sceptics and atheists are forever silenced upon supposing only spirits and ideas, and this scheme of things is perfectly agreeable both to reason and religion: methinks we may expect it should be admitted and firmly em-

braced, though it were proposed only as an *hypothesis*, and the existence of matter had been allowed possible, which yet I think we have evidently demonstrated that it is not.

134 ☙ True it is that, in consequence of the foregoing principles, several disputes and speculations which are esteemed no mean parts of learning, are rejected as useless. But, how great a prejudice soever against our notions this may give to those who have already been deeply engaged, and made large advances in studies of that nature, yet by others we hope it will not be thought any just ground of dislike to the principles and tenets herein laid down, that they abridge the labor of study, and make human sciences far more clear, compendious and attainable than they were before.

135 ☙ Having despatched what we intended to say concerning the knowledge of *ideas*, the method we proposed leads us in the next place to treat of *spirits*—with regard to which, perhaps, human knowledge is not so deficient as is vulgarly imagined. The great reason that is assigned for our being thought ignorant of the nature of spirits is our not having an *idea* of it. But surely it ought not to be looked on as a defect in a human understanding that it does not perceive the idea of spirit, if it is manifestly impossible there should be any such idea. And this if I mistake not has been demonstrated in Section 27; to which I shall here add that a spirit has been shewn to be the only substance or support wherein unthinking beings or ideas can exist; but that this *substance* which supports or perceives ideas should itself be an idea or like an idea is evidently absurd.

136 ☙ It will perhaps be said that we want a sense (as some have imagined) proper to know substances withal, which, if

we had, we might know our own soul as we do a triangle. To this I answer, that, in case we had a new sense bestowed upon us, we could only receive thereby some new sensations or ideas of sense. But I believe nobody will say that what he means by the terms *soul* and *substance* is only some particular sort of idea or sensation. We may therefore infer that, all things duly considered, it is not more reasonable to think our faculties defective, in that they do not furnish us with an idea of spirit or active thinking substance, than it would be if we should blame them for not being able to comprehend a *round square*.

137 § From the opinion that spirits are to be known after the manner of an idea or sensation have risen many absurd and heterodox tenets, and much scepticism about the nature of the soul. It is even probable that this opinion may have produced a doubt in some whether they had any soul at all distinct from their body, since upon inquiry they could not find they had an idea of it. That an *idea*, which is inactive and the existence whereof consists in being perceived, should be the image or likeness of an agent subsisting by itself, seems to need no other refutation than barely attending to what is meant by those words. But perhaps you will say that though an idea cannot resemble a spirit in its thinking, acting, or subsisting by itself, yet it may in some other respects; and it is not necessary that an idea or image be in all respects like the original.

138 § I answer, if it does not in those mentioned, it is impossible it should represent it in any other thing. Do but leave out the power of willing, thinking, and perceiving ideas, and there remains nothing else wherein the idea can be like a spirit. For by the word "spirit" we mean only that which

thinks, wills, and perceives; this, and this alone, constitutes the signification of that term. If therefore it is impossible that any degree of those powers should be represented in an idea, it is evident there can be no idea of a spirit.

139 ◆§ But it will be objected that, if there is no idea signified by the terms "soul," "spirit," and "substance," they are wholly insignificant, or have no meaning in them. I answer, those words do mean or signify a real thing, which is neither an idea nor like an idea, but that which perceives ideas, and wills, and reasons about them. What I am myself, that which I denote by the term "I," is the same with what is meant by "soul" or "spiritual substances." If it be said that this is only quarreling at a word, and that, since the immediate significations of other names are by common consent called "ideas" no reason can be assigned why that which is signified by the name "spirit" or "soul" may not partake in the same appellation: I answer, all the unthinking objects of the mind agree in that they are entirely passive, and their existence consists only in being perceived; whereas a soul or spirit is an active being, whose existence consists, not in being perceived, but in perceiving ideas and thinking. It is therefore necessary, in order to prevent equivocation and confounding natures perfectly disagreeing and unlike, that we distinguish between *spirit* and *idea*. (See Sec. 27.)

140 ◆§ In a large sense, indeed, we may be said to have an idea or rather a notion of *spirit*, that is, we understand the meaning of the word, otherwise we could not affirm or deny anything of it. Moreover, as we conceive the ideas that are in the minds of other spirits by means of our own, which we suppose to be resemblances of them; so we know other spirits by means of our own soul; which in that sense is the image

or idea of them; it having a like respect to other spirits that blueness or heat by me perceived has to those ideas perceived by another.

141 ◆§ It must not be supposed that they who assert the natural immortality of the soul are of opinion that it is absolutely incapable of annihilation even by the infinite power of the Creator who first gave it being, but only that it is not liable to be broken or dissolved by the ordinary laws of nature or motion. They indeed who hold the soul of man to be only a thin vital flame, or system of animal spirits, make it perishing and corruptible as the body; since there is nothing more easily dissipated than such a being, which it is naturally impossible should survive the ruin of the tabernacle wherein it is enclosed. And this notion hath been greedily embraced and cherished by the worst part of mankind, as the most effectual antidote against all impressions of virtue and religion. But it hath been made evident that bodies of what frame or texture soever, are barely passive ideas in the mind, which is more distant and heterogeneous from them than light is from darkness. We have shewn that the soul is indivisible, incorporeal, unextended, and it is consequently incorruptible. Nothing can be plainer than that the motions, changes, decays, and dissolutions which we hourly see befall natural bodies (and which is what we mean by the *course of nature*) cannot possibly affect an active, simple, uncompounded substance; such a being therefore is indissoluble by the force of nature; that is to say, *the soul of man is naturally immortal.*

142 ◆§ After what hath been said, it is, I suppose, plain that our souls are not to be known in the same manner as senseless, inactive objects, or by way of *idea. Spirits* and *ideas* are things so wholly different, that when we say "they exist," "they are

known," or the like, these words must not be thought to signify anything common to both natures. There is nothing alike or common in them: and to expect that by any multiplication or enlargement of our faculties we may be enabled to know a spirit as we do a triangle, seems as absurd as if we should hope to see a sound. This is inculcated because I imagine it may be of moment towards clearing several important questions, and preventing some very dangerous errors concerning the nature of the soul. We may not, I think, strictly be said to have an *idea* of an active being, or of an action, although we may be said to have a *notion* of them. I have some knowledge or notion of my mind, and its acts about ideas, inasmuch as I know or understand what is meant by these words. What I know, that I have some notion of. I will not say that the terms "idea" and "notion" may not be used convertibly, if the world will have it so; but yet it conduceth to clearness and propriety that we distinguish things very different by different names. It is also to be remarked that, all relations including an act of the mind, we cannot so properly be said to have an idea, but rather a notion of the relations and habitudes between things. But if, in the modern way, the word "idea" is extended to spirits, and relations, and acts, this is, after all, an affair of verbal concern.

143 ☙ It will not be amiss to add, that the doctrine of *abstract ideas* hath had no small share in rendering those sciences intricate and obscure which are particularly conversant about spiritual things. Men have imagined they could frame abstract notions of the powers and acts of the mind, and consider them prescinded as well from the mind or spirit itself, as from their respective objects and effects. Hence a great number of dark and ambiguous terms, presumed to stand for abstract notions, have been introduced into metaphysics and morality, and from these have grown infinite distractions and disputes amongst the learned.

144 ◆§ But nothing seems more to have contributed towards engaging men in controversies and mistakes with regard to the nature and operations of the mind, than the being used to speak of those things in terms borrowed from sensible ideas. For example, the will is termed the *motion* of the soul: this infuses a belief that the mind of man is as a ball in motion, impelled and determined by the objects of sense, as necessarily as that is by the stroke of a racket. Hence arise endless scruples and errors of dangerous consequence in morality. All which, I doubt not, may be cleared, and truth appear plain, uniform, and consistent, could but philosophers be prevailed on to retire into themselves, and attentively consider their own meaning.

145 ◆§ From what hath been said, it is plain that we cannot know the existence of other spirits otherwise than by their operations, or the ideas by them excited in us. I perceive several motions, changes, and combinations of ideas, that inform me there are certain particular agents, like myself, which accompany them and concur in their production. Hence, the knowledge I have of other spirits is not immediate, as is the knowledge of my ideas; but depending on the intervention of ideas, by me referred to agents or spirits distinct from myself, as effects or concomitant signs.

146 ◆§ But though there be some things which convince us human agents are concerned in producing them; yet it is evident to everyone that those things which are called the works of nature, that is, the far greater part of the ideas or sensations perceived by us, are not produced by, or dependent on, the wills of men. There is therefore some other Spirit that causes them; since it is repugnant that they should subsist by themselves. (See Sec. 29.) But if we attentively consider the constant regularity, order, and concatenation of natural

things, the surprising magnificence, beauty, and perfection of the larger, and the exquisite contrivance of the smaller parts of creation, together with the exact harmony and correspondence of the whole, but above all the never enough admired laws of pain and pleasure, and the instincts or natural inclinations, appetites, and passions of animals; I say if we consider all these things, and at the same time attend to the meaning and import of the attributes One, Eternal, Infinitely Wise, Good, and Perfect, we shall clearly perceive that they belong to the aforesaid Spirit, "who works all in all," and "by whom all things consist."

147 ☙ Hence, it is evident that God is known as certainly and immediately as any other mind or spirit whatsoever distinct from ourselves. We may even assert that the existence of God is far more evidently perceived than the existence of men; because the effects of nature are infinitely more numerous and considerable than those ascribed to human agents. There is not any one mark that denotes a man, or effect produced by him, which does not more strongly evince the being of that Spirit who is the Author of Nature. For it is evident that in affecting other persons the will of man hath no other object than barely the motion of the limbs of his body; but that such a motion should be attended by, or excite any idea in the mind of another, depends wholly on the will of the Creator. He alone it is who, "upholding all things by the word of His power," maintains that intercourse between spirits whereby they are able to perceive the existence of each other. And yet this pure and clear light which enlightens everyone is itself invisible.

148 ☙ It seems to be a general pretense of the unthinking herd that they cannot *see* God. Could we but see Him, say they, as we see a man, we should believe that He is, and be-

lieving obey *His* commands. But alas, we need only open our eyes to see the Sovereign Lord of all things, with a more full and clear view than we do any one of our fellow-creatures. Not that I imagine we see God (as some will have it) by a direct and immediate view; or see corporeal things, not by themselves, but by seeing that which represents them in the essence of God, which doctrine is, I must confess, to me incomprehensible. But I shall explain my meaning. A human spirit or person is not perceived by sense, as not being an idea; when therefore we see the color, size, figure, and motions of a man, we perceive only certain sensations or ideas excited in our own minds; and these being exhibited to our view in sundry distinct collections, serve to mark out unto us the existence of finite and created spirits like ourselves. Hence it is plain we do not see a man—if by *man* is meant that which lives, moves, perceives, and thinks as we do—but only such a certain collection of ideas as directs us to think there is a distinct principle of thought and motion, like to ourselves, accompanying and represented by it. And after the same manner we see God; all the difference is that, whereas some one finite and narrow assemblage of ideas denotes a particular human mind, whithersoever we direct our view, we do at all times and in all places perceive manifest tokens of the Divinity: everything we see, hear, feel, or anywise perceive by sense being a sign or effect of the power of God; as is our perception of those very motions which are produced by men.

149 ◆§ It is therefore plain that nothing can be more evident to anyone that is capable of the least reflection that the existence of God, or a Spirit who is intimately present to our minds, producing in them all that variety of ideas or sensations which continually affect us, on whom we have an absolute and entire dependence, in short "in whom we live, and move, and have our being." That the discovery of this great truth, which lies so near and obvious to the mind, should

be attained to by the reason of so very few, is a sad instance of the stupidity and inattention of men, who, though they are surrounded with such clear manifestations of the Deity, are yet so little affected by them that they seem, as it were, blinded with excess of light.

150 ☙ But you will say, Hath Nature no share in the production of natural things, and must they be all ascribed to the immediate and sole operation of God? I answer, if by "Nature" is meant only the visible *series* of effects or sensations imprinted on our minds, according to certain fixed and general laws, then it is plain that Nature, taken in this sense, cannot produce anything at all. But, if by "Nature" is meant some being distinct from God, as well as from the laws of nature, and things perceived by sense, I must confess that word is to me an empty sound without any intelligible meaning annexed to it. Nature, in this acceptation, is a vain chimera, introduced by those heathens who had not just notions of the omnipresence and infinite perfection of God. But it is more unaccountable that it should be received among Christians, professing belief in the Holy Scriptures, which constantly ascribe those effects to the immediate hand of God that heathen philosophers are wont to impute to Nature. "The Lord He causeth the vapors to ascend; He maketh lightnings with rain; He bringeth forth the wind out of his treasures." (Jerem. x. 13.) "He turneth the shadow of death into the morning, and maketh the day dark with night." (Amos, v. 8.) "He visiteth the earth, and maketh it soft with showers: He blesseth the springing thereof, and crowneth the year with His goodness; so that the pastures are clothed with flocks, and the valleys are covered over with corn." (See Psalm lxv.) But notwithstanding that this is the constant language of Scripture, yet we have I know not what aversion from believing that God concerns Himself so nearly in our affairs. Fain would we suppose Him at a great distance off, and substitute

some blind unthinking deputy in His stead, though (if we may believe Saint Paul) "He be not far from every one of us."

151 ☙ It will, I doubt not, be objected that the slow and gradual methods observed in the production of natural things do not seem to have for their cause the immediate hand of an Almighty Agent. Besides, monsters, untimely births, fruits blasted in the blossom, rains falling in desert places, miseries incident to human life, and the like, are so many arguments that the whole frame of nature is not immediately actuated and superintended by a Spirit of infinite wisdom and goodness. But the answer to this objection is in a good measure plain from Section 62; it being visible that the aforesaid methods of nature are absolutely necessary, in order to work by the most simple and general rules, and after a steady and consistent manner; which argues both the wisdom and goodness of God. Such is the artificial contrivance of this mighty machine of nature that, whilst its motions and various phenomena strike on our senses, the hand which actuates the whole is itself unperceivable to men of flesh and blood. "Verily," saith the prophet, "thou art a God that hidest thyself." (Isaiah xlv. 15.) But though the Lord conceal Himself from the eyes of the sensual and lazy, who will not be at the least expense of thought, yet to an unbiased and attentive mind nothing can be more plainly legible than the intimate presence of an all-wise Spirit, who fashions, regulates, and sustains the whole system of beings. It is clear, from what we have elsewhere observed, that the operating according to general and stated laws is so necessary for our guidance in the affairs of life, and letting us into the secret of nature, that without it all reach and compass of thought, all human sagacity and design, could serve to no manner of purpose; it were even impossible there should be any such faculties or powers in the mind. (See Sec. 31.) Which one consideration abundantly outbalances whatever particular inconveniences may thence arise.

152 ❧ We should further consider that the very blemishes and defects of nature are not without their use, in that they make an agreeable sort of variety, and augment the beauty of the rest of the creation, as shades in a picture serve to set off the brighter and more enlightened parts. We would likewise do well to examine whether our taxing the waste of seeds and embryos, and accidental destruction of plants and animals, before they come to full maturity, as an imprudence in the Author of nature, be not the effect of prejudice contracted by our familiarity with impotent and saving mortals. In man indeed a thrifty management of those things which he cannot procure without much pains and industry may be esteemed wisdom. But we must not imagine that the inexplicably fine machine of an animal or vegetable costs the great Creator any more pains or trouble in its production than a pebble does; nothing being more evident than that an Omnipotent Spirit can indifferently produce everything by a mere *fiat* or act of His will. Hence, it is plain that the splendid profusion of natural things should not be interpreted weakness or prodigality in the Agent who produces them, but rather be looked on as an argument of the riches of His power.

153 ❧ As for the mixture of pain or uneasiness which is in the world, pursuant to the general laws of nature, and the actions of finite, imperfect spirits, this, in the state we are in at present, is indispensably necessary to our well-being. But our prospects are too narrow. We take, for instance, the idea of some one particular pain into our thoughts and account it *evil;* whereas, if we enlarge our view, so as to comprehend the various ends, connections, and dependencies of things, on what occasions and in what proportions we are affected with pain and pleasure, the nature of human freedom, and the design with which we are put into the world; we shall be forced to acknowledge that those particular things which, considered in themselves, appear to be evil, have the nature

of good, when considered as linked with the whole system of beings.

154 ☙§ From what hath been said, it will be manifest to any considering person, that it is merely for want of attention and comprehensiveness of mind that there are any favorers of atheism or the Manichean heresy to be found. Little and unreflecting souls may indeed burlesque the works of Providence, the beauty and order whereof they have not capacity, or will not be at the pains, to comprehend; but those who are masters of any justness and extent of thought, and are withal used to reflect, can never sufficiently admire the divine traces of wisdom and goodness that shine throughout the economy of nature. But what truth is there which shineth so strongly on the mind that by an aversion of thought, a willful shutting of the eyes, we may not escape seeing it? Is it therefore to be wondered at, if the generality of men, who are ever intent on business or pleasure, and little used to fix or open the eye of their mind, should not have all that conviction and evidence of the Being of God which might be expected in reasonable creatures?

155 ☙§ We should rather wonder that men can be found so stupid as to neglect, than that neglecting they should be unconvinced of such an evident and momentous truth. And yet it is to be feared that too many of parts and leisure, who live in Christian countries, are, merely through a supine and dreadful negligence, sunk into atheism; since it is downright impossible that a soul pierced and enlightened with a thorough sense of the omnipresence, holiness, and justice of that Almighty Spirit should persist in a remorseless violation of His laws. We ought, therefore, earnestly to meditate and dwell on those important points; that so we may attain conviction without all scruple "that the eyes of the Lord are in every

place beholding the evil and the good; that He is with us and keepeth us in all places whither we go, and giveth us bread to eat and raiment to put on;" that He is present and conscious to our innermost thoughts; and that we have a most absolute and immediate dependence on Him. A clear view of which great truths cannot choose but fill our hearts with an awful circumspection and holy fear, which is the strongest incentive to *virtue*, and the best guard against *vice*.

156 ☙ For, after all, what deserves the first place in our studies is the consideration of God and our *duty;* which to promote, as it was the main drift and design of my labors, so shall I esteem them altogether useless and ineffectual if, by what I have said, I cannot inspire my readers with a pious sense of the Presence of God; and, having shewn the falseness or vanity of those barren speculations which make the chief employment of learned men, the better dispose them to reverence and embrace the salutary truths of the Gospel, which to know and to practice is the highest perfection of human nature.

David Hume

AN ENQUIRY CONCERNING HUMAN UNDERSTANDING

David Hume

[1711–1776]

After his graduation from Edinburgh University and after fruitless attempts to make a place for himself in law and in business, David Hume went to France and there wrote his *Treatise on Human Nature*, published in two volumes in 1739, with a third following in 1740. Eight years later his *Philosophical Essays Concerning Human Understanding* included the famous *Treatise*, considerably revised and in a popular vein. His reputation made by this essay, he solidified it in England and on the Continent with *An Enquiry Concerning the Principles of Morals.* Thereafter Hume devoted himself in Edinburgh to the writing of a history of England and his posthumously published *Dialogues Concerning Natural Religion.* His studies of the relationship of impressions and cognitions are fundamental to the entire subject of empirical psychology and philosophy.

AN ENQUIRY CONCERNING HUMAN UNDERSTANDING

DAVID HUME

SECTION I

Of the Different Species of Philosophy

Moral philosophy, or the science of human nature, may be treated after two different manners; each of which has its peculiar merit, and may contribute to the entertainment, instruction, and reformation of mankind. The one considers man chiefly as born for action; and as influenced in his measures by taste and sentiment; pursuing one object, and avoiding another, according to the value which these objects seem to possess, and according to the light in which they present themselves. As virtue, of all objects, is allowed to be the most valuable, this species of philosophers paint her in the most amiable colors; borrowing all helps from poetry and eloquence, and treating their subject in an easy and obvious manner, and such as is best fitted to please the imagination, and engage the affections. They select the most striking observations and instances from common life; place opposite characters in a proper contrast; and alluring us into the paths of virtue by the views of glory and happiness, direct our steps in these paths by the soundest precepts and most illustrious examples. They make us *feel* the difference between vice and virtue; they excite and regulate our sentiments; and so they can but bend our hearts to the love of probity and true honor, they think, that they have fully attained the end of all their labors.

The other species of philosophers consider man in the light of a reasonable rather than an active being, and endeavor to form his understanding more than cultivate his manners. They regard human nature as a subject of speculation; and with a narrow scrutiny examine it, in order to find those principles, which regulate our understanding, excite our sentiments, and make us to approve or blame any particular object, action, or behavior. They think it a reproach to all literature, that philosophy should not yet have fixed, beyond controversy, the foundation of morals, reasoning, and criticism; and should for ever talk of truth and falsehood, vice and virtue, beauty and deformity, without being able to determine the source of these distinctions. While they attempt this arduous task, they are deterred by no difficulties; but proceeding from particular instances to general principles, they still push on their inquiries to principles more general, and rest not satisfied till they arrive at those original principles, by which, in every science, all human curiosity must be bounded. Though their speculations seem abstract, and even unintelligible to common readers, they aim at the approbation of the learned and the wise; and think themselves sufficiently compensated for the labor of their whole lives, if they can discover some hidden truths, which may contribute to the instruction of posterity.

It is certain that the easy and obvious philosophy will always, with the generality of mankind, have the preference above the accurate and abstruse; and by many will be recommended, not only as more agreeable, but more useful than the other. It enters more into common life; molds the heart and affections; and, by touching those principles which actuate men, reforms their conduct, and brings them nearer to that model of perfection which it describes. On the contrary, the abstruse philosophy, being founded on a turn of mind, which cannot enter into business and action, vanishes when the philosopher leaves the shade, and comes into open day; nor can its principles easily retain any influence over our conduct and behavior. The feelings of our heart, the agitation of our passions, the vehemence of our affections, dissipate all its conclusions, and reduce the profound philosopher to a mere plebeian.

This also must be confessed, that the most durable, as well as justest fame, has been acquired by the easy philosophy, and that abstract reasoners seem hitherto to have enjoyed only a momentary reputation, from the caprice or ignorance of their own age, but have not been able to support their renown with more equitable posterity. It is easy for a profound philosopher to commit a mistake in his subtle reasonings; and one mistake is the necessary parent of another, while he pushes on his consequences, and is not deterred from embracing any conclusion, by its unusual appearance, or its contradiction to popular opinion. But a philosopher, who purposes only to represent the common sense of mankind in more beautiful and more engaging colors, if by accident he falls into error, goes no farther; but renewing his appeal to common sense, and the natural sentiments of the mind, returns into the right path, and secures himself from any dangerous illusions. The fame of Cicero flourishes at present; but that of Aristotle is utterly decayed. La Bruyère passes the seas, and still maintains his reputation: But the glory of Malebranche is confined to his own nation, and to his own age. And Addison, perhaps, will be read with pleasure, when Locke shall be entirely forgotten.

The mere philosopher is a character, which is commonly but little acceptable in the world, as being supposed to contribute nothing either to the advantage or pleasure of society; while he lives remote from communication with mankind, and is wrapped up in principles and notions equally remote from their comprehension. On the other hand, the mere ignorant is still more despised; nor is anything deemed a surer sign of an illiberal genius in an age and nation where the sciences flourish, than to be entirely destitute of all relish for those noble entertainments. The most perfect character is supposed to lie between those extremes; retaining an equal ability and taste for books, company, and business; preserving in conversation that discernment and delicacy which arise from polite letters; and in business, that probity and accuracy which are the natural result of a just philosophy. In order to diffuse and cultivate so accomplished a character, nothing can be more useful than compositions of the easy style and manner, which draw not too much from life, require no deep application or retreat to be comprehended, and send back the student among mankind full of noble sentiments and wise precepts, applicable to every exigence of human life. By means of such compositions, virtue becomes amiable, science agreeable, company instructive, and retirement entertaining.

Man is a reasonable being; and as such, receives from science his proper food and nourishment: But so narrow are the bounds of human understanding, that little satisfaction can be hoped for in this particular, either from the extent or security of his acquisitions. Man is a sociable, no less than a reasonable being: But neither can he always enjoy company agreeable and amusing, or preserve the proper relish for them. Man is also an active being; and from that disposition, as well as from the various necessities of human life, must submit to business and occupation: But the mind requires some relaxation, and cannot always support its bent to care and industry. It seems, then, that nature has pointed out a mixed kind of life as most suitable to the human race, and secretly admonished them to allow none of these biases to *draw* too much, so as to incapacitate them for other occupations and entertainments. Indulge your passion for science, says she, but let your science be human, and such as may have a direct reference to action and society. Abstruse thought and profound researches I prohibit, and will severely punish, by the pensive melancholy which they introduce, by the endless uncertainty in which they involve you, and by the cold reception which your pretended discoveries shall meet with, when communicated. Be a philosopher; but, amidst all your philosophy, be still a man.

Were the generality of mankind contented to prefer the easy philosophy to the abstract and profound, without throwing any blame or contempt on the latter, it might not be improper, perhaps, to comply with this general opinion, and allow every man to enjoy, without opposition, his own taste and sentiment. But as the matter is often carried farther, even to the absolute rejecting of all profound reasonings, or what is commonly called *metaphysics*, we shall now proceed to consider what can reasonably be pleaded in their behalf.

We may begin with observing, that one considerable advantage, which results from the accurate and abstract philosophy, is, its subserviency to the easy and humane, which, without the former, can never attain a sufficient degree of exactness in its sentiments, precepts, or reasonings. All polite letters are nothing but pictures of human life in various attitudes and situations; and inspire us with different sentiments, of praise or blame, admiration or ridicule, according to the qualities of the object, which they set before us. An artist must be better qualified to succeed in this undertaking, who, besides a delicate taste and a quick apprehension, possesses an accurate knowledge of the internal fabric, the operations of the understanding, the workings of the passions, and the various species of sentiment which discriminate vice and virtue. How painful soever this inward search or inquiry may appear, it becomes, in some measure, requisite to those, who would describe with success the obvious and outward appearances of life and manners. The anatomist presents to the eye the most hideous and disagreeable objects; but his science is useful to the painter in delineating even a Venus or an Helen. While the latter employs all the richest colors of his art, and gives his figures the most graceful and engaging airs; he must still carry his attention to the inward structure of the human body, the position of the muscles, the fabric of the bones, and the use and figure of every part or organ. Accuracy is, in every case, advantageous to beauty, and just reasoning to delicate sentiment. In vain would we exalt the one by depreciating the other.

Besides, we may observe, in every art or profession, even

those which most concern life or action, that a spirit of accuracy, however acquired, carries all of them nearer their perfection, and renders them more subservient to the interests of society. And though a philosopher may live remote from business, the genius of philosophy, if carefully cultivated by several, must gradually diffuse itself throughout the whole society, and bestow a similar correctness on every art and calling. The politician will acquire greater foresight and subtlety, in the subdividing and balancing of power; the lawyer more method and finer principles in his reasonings; and the general more regularity in his discipline, and more caution in his plans and operations. The stability of modern governments above the ancient, and the accuracy of modern philosophy, have improved, and probably will still improve, by similar gradations.

Were there no advantage to be reaped from these studies, beyond the gratification of an innocent curiosity, yet ought not even this to be despised; as being one accession to those few safe and harmless pleasures, which are bestowed on the human race. The sweetest and most inoffensive path of life leads through the avenues of science and learning; and whoever can either remove any obstructions in this way, or open up any new prospect, ought so far to be esteemed a benefactor to mankind. And though these researches may appear painful and fatiguing, it is with some minds as with some bodies, which being endowed with vigorous and florid health, require severe exercise, and reap a pleasure from what, to the generality of mankind, may seem burdensome and laborious. Obscurity, indeed, is painful to the mind as well as to the eye; but to bring light from obscurity, by whatever labor, must needs be delightful and rejoicing.

But this obscurity in the profound and abstract philosophy, is objected to, not only as painful and fatiguing, but as the inevitable source of uncertainty and error. Here indeed lies the justest and most plausible objection against a considerable part of metaphysics, that they are not properly a science; but arise either from the fruitless efforts of human vanity, which would penetrate into subjects utterly inaccessible to the understanding, or from the craft of popular superstitions, which, being unable to defend themselves on fair ground, raise these entangling brambles to cover and protect their weakness. Chased from the open country, these robbers fly into the forest, and lie in wait to break in upon every unguarded avenue of the mind, and overwhelm it with religious fears and prejudices. The stoutest antagonist, if he remit his watch a moment, is oppressed. And many, through cowardice and folly, open the gates to the enemies, and willingly receive them with reverence and submission, as their legal sovereigns.

But is this a sufficient reason, why philosophers should desist from such researches, and leave superstition still in possession of her retreat? Is it not proper to draw an opposite conclusion, and perceive the necessity of carrying the war into the most secret recesses of the enemy? In vain do we hope, that men, from frequent disappointment, will at last abandon such airy sciences, and discover the proper province of human reason. For, besides, that many persons find too sensible an interest in perpetually recalling such topics; besides this, I say, the motive of blind despair can never reasonably have place in the sciences; since, however unsuccessful former attempts may have proved, there is still room to hope, that the industry, good fortune, or improved sagacity of succeeding generations may reach discoveries unknown to former ages. Each adventurous genius will leap at the arduous prize, and find himself stimulated, rather than discouraged, by the failures of his predecessors; while he hopes that the glory of achieving so hard an adventure is reserved for him alone. The only method of freeing learning, at once, from these abstruse questions, is to inquire seriously into the nature of human understanding, and show, from an exact analysis of its powers and capacity, that it is by no means fitted for such remote and abstruse subjects. We must submit to this fatigue, in order to live at ease ever after: And must cultivate true metaphysics with some care, in order to destroy the false and adulterate. Indolence, which, to some persons, affords a safeguard against this deceitful philosophy, is, with others, overbalanced by curiosity; and despair, which, at some moments, prevails, may give place afterwards to sanguine hopes and expectations. Accurate and just reasoning is the only catholic remedy, fitted for all persons and all dispositions; and is alone able to subvert that abstruse philosophy and metaphysical jargon, which, being mixed up with popular superstition, renders it in a manner impenetrable to careless reasoners, and gives it the air of science and wisdom.

Besides this advantage of rejecting, after deliberate inquiry, the most uncertain and disagreeable part of learning, there are many positive advantages, which result from an accurate scrutiny into the powers and faculties of human nature. It is remarkable concerning the operations of the mind, that, though most intimately present to us, yet, whenever they become the object of reflection, they seem involved in obscurity; nor can the eye readily find those lines and boundaries, which discriminate and distinguish them. The objects are too fine to remain long in the same aspect or situation; and must be apprehended in an instant, by a superior penetration, derived from nature, and improved by habit and reflection. It becomes, therefore, no inconsiderable part of science barely to know the different operations of the mind, to separate them from each other, to class them under their proper heads, and to correct all that seeming disorder, in which they lie involved, when made the object of reflection and inquiry. This talk of ordering and distinguishing, which has no merit, when performed with regard to external bodies, the objects of our senses, rises in its value, when directed towards the operations of the mind, in proportion to the difficulty and labor, which we meet with in performing it. And if we can go no farther than this mental geography, or delineation of the distinct parts and powers of the mind, it is at least a satisfaction to go so far; and the more obvious this science may appear (and it is by no means obvious) the more contemptible still must the ignorance of it be esteemed, in all pretenders to learning and philosophy.

Nor can there remain any suspicion, that this science is uncertain and chimerical; unless we should entertain such a scepticism as is entirely subversive of all speculation, and even action. It cannot be doubted, that the mind is endowed with several powers and faculties, that these powers are distinct from each other, that what is really distinct to the immediate perception may be distinguished by reflection; and consequently, that there is a truth and falsehood in all propositions on this subject, and a truth and falsehood, which lie not beyond the compass of human understanding. There are many obvious distinctions of this kind, such as those between the will and understanding, the imagination and passions, which fall within the comprehension of every human creature; and the finer and more philosophical distinctions are no less real and certain, though more difficult to be comprehended. Some instances, especially late ones, of success in these inquiries, may give us a juster notion of the certainty and solidity of this branch of learning. And shall we esteem it worthy the labor of a philosopher to give us a true system of the planets, and adjust the position and order of those remote bodies; while we affect to overlook those, who, with so much success, delineate the parts of the mind, in which we are so intimately concerned?

But may we not hope, that philosophy, if cultivated with care, and encouraged by the attention of the public, may carry its researches still farther, and discover, at least in some degree, the secret springs and principles, by which the human mind is actuated in its operations? Astronomers had long contented themselves with proving, from the phenomena, the true motions, order, and magnitude of the heavenly bodies: Till a philosopher, at last, arose, who seems, from the happiest reasoning, to have also determined the laws and forces, by which the revolutions of the planets are governed and directed. The like has been performed with regard to other parts of nature. And there is no reason to despair of equal success in our inquiries concerning the mental powers and economy, if prosecuted with equal capacity and caution. It is probable, that one operation and principle of the mind depends on another; which, again, may be resolved into one more general and universal: And how far these researches may possibly be carried, it will be difficult for us, before, or even after, a careful trial, exactly to determine. This is certain, that attempts of this kind are every day made even by those who philosophize the most negligently: And nothing can be more requisite than to enter upon the enterprise with thorough care and attention; that, if it lie within the compass of human understanding, it may at last be happily achieved; if not, it may, however, be rejected with some confidence and security. This last conclusion, surely, is not desirable; nor ought it to be embraced too rashly. For how much must we diminish from the beauty and value of this species of philosophy, upon such a supposition? Moralists have hitherto been accustomed, when they considered the vast multitude and diversity of those actions that excite our approbation or dislike, to search for some common principle, on which this variety of sentiments might depend. And though they have sometimes carried the matter too far, by their passion for some one general principle; it must, however, be confessed, that they are excusable in expecting to find some general principles, into which all the vices and virtues were justly to be resolved. The like has been the endeavor of critics, logicians, and even politicians: Nor have their attempts been wholly unsuccessful; though perhaps longer time, greater accuracy, and more ardent application may bring these sciences still nearer their perfection. To throw up at once all pretensions of this kind may justly be deemed more rash, precipitate, and dogmatical, than even the boldest and most affirmative philosophy, that has ever attempted to impose its crude dictates and principles on mankind.

What though these reasonings concerning human nature seem abstract, and of difficult comprehension? This affords no presumption of their falsehood. On the contrary, it seems impossible, that what has hitherto escaped so many wise and profound philosophers can be very obvious and easy. And whatever pains these researches may cost us, we may think ourselves sufficiently rewarded, not only in point of profit but of pleasure, if, by that means, we can make any addition to our stock of knowledge, in subjects of such unspeakable importance.

But as, after all, the abstractedness of these speculations is no recommendation, but rather a disadvantage to them, and as this difficulty may perhaps be surmounted by care and art, and the avoiding of all unnecessary detail, we have, in the following inquiry, attempted to throw some light upon subjects, from which uncertainty has hitherto deterred the wise, and obscurity the ignorant. Happy, if we can unite the boundaries of the different species of philosophy, by reconciling profound inquiry with clearness, and truth with novelty! And still more happy, if reasoning in this easy manner, we can undermine the foundations of an abstruse philosophy, which seems to have hitherto served only as a shelter to superstition, and a cover to absurdity and error!

SECTION II

Of the Origin of Ideas

Everyone will readily allow that there is a considerable difference between the perceptions of the mind, when a man feels the pain of excessive heat, or the pleasure of moderate warmth, and when he afterwards recalls to his memory this sensation, or anticipates it by his imagination. These faculties may mimic or copy the perceptions of the senses; but they never can entirely reach the force and vivacity of the original sentiment. The utmost we say of them, even when they operate with greatest vigor, is, that they represent their object in so lively a manner, that we could *almost* say we feel or see it: But, except the mind be disordered by disease or madness, they never can arrive at such a pitch of vivacity, as to render these perceptions altogether undistinguishable. All the colors of poetry, however splendid, can never paint natural objects in such a manner as to make the description be taken for a real landscape. The most lively thought is still inferior to the dullest sensation.

We may observe a like distinction to run through all the other perceptions of the mind. A man in a fit of anger, is actuated in a very different manner from one who only thinks of that emotion. If you tell me, that any person is in love, I easily understand your meaning, and form a just conception of his situation; but never can mistake that conception for the real disorders and agitations of the passion. When we reflect on our past sentiments and affections, our thought is a faithful mirror, and copies its objects truly; but the colors which it employs are faint and dull, in comparison of those in which our original perceptions were clothed. It requires no nice discernment or metaphysical head to mark the distinction between them.

Here therefore we may divide all the perceptions of the mind into two classes or species, which are distinguished by their different degrees of force and vivacity. The less forcible and lively are commonly denominated *thoughts* or *ideas*. The other species want a name in our language, and in most others; I suppose, because it was not requisite for any, but philosophical purposes, to rank them under a general term or appellation. Let us, therefore, use a little freedom, and call them *impressions;* employing that word in a sense somewhat different from the usual. By the term *impression*, then, I mean all our more lively perceptions, when we hear, or see, or feel, or love, or hate, or desire, or will. And impressions are distinguished from ideas, which are the less lively perceptions, of which we are conscious, when we reflect on any of those sensations or movements above mentioned.

Nothing, at first view, may seem more unbounded than the thought of man, which not only escapes all human power and authority, but is not even restrained within the limits of nature and reality. To form monsters, and join incongruous shapes and appearances, costs the imagination no more trouble than to conceive the most natural and familiar objects. And while the body is confined to one planet, along which it creeps with pain and difficulty; the thought can in an instant transport us into the most distant regions of the universe; or even beyond the universe, into the unbounded chaos, where nature is supposed to lie in total confusion. What never was seen, or heard of, may yet be conceived; nor is anything beyond the power of thought, except what implies an absolute contradiction.

But though our thought seems to possess this unbounded liberty, we shall find, upon a nearer examination, that it is really confined within very narrow limits, and that all this creative power of the mind amounts to no more than the faculty of compounding, transposing, augmenting, or diminishing the materials afforded us by the senses and experience. When we think of a golden mountain, we only join two consistent ideas, *gold*, and *mountain*, with which we were formerly acquainted. A virtuous horse we can conceive; because, from our own feeling, we can conceive virtue; and this we may unite to the figure and shape of a horse, which is an animal familiar to us. In short, all the materials of thinking are derived either from our outward or inward sentiment: the mixture and composition of these belongs alone to the mind and will. Or, to express myself in philosophical language, all our ideas or more feeble perceptions are copies of our impressions or more lively ones.

To prove this, the two following arguments will, I hope, be sufficient. First, when we analyze our thoughts or ideas, however compounded or sublime, we always find that they resolve themselves into such simple ideas as were copied from a precedent feeling or sentiment. Even those ideas, which, at first view, seem the most wide of this origin, are found, upon a nearer scrutiny, to be derived from it. The idea of God, as meaning an infinitely intelligent, wise, and good Being, arises from reflecting on the operations of our own mind, and augmenting, without limit, those qualities of goodness and wisdom. We may prosecute this inquiry to what length we please; where we shall always find, that every idea which we examine is copied from a similar impression. Those who would assert that this position is not universally true nor without exception, have only one, and that an easy method of refuting it; by producing that idea, which, in their opinion, is not derived from this source. It will then be incumbent on us, if we would maintain our doctrine, to produce the impression, or lively perception, which corresponds to it.

Secondly. If it happen, from a defect of the organ, that a man is not susceptible of any species of sensation, we always find that he is as little susceptible of the correspondent ideas. A blind man can form no notion of colors; a deaf man of sounds. Restore either of them that sense in which he is deficient; by opening this new inlet for his sensations, you also open an inlet for the ideas; and he finds no difficulty in conceiving these objects. The case is the same, if the object, proper for exciting any sensation, has never been applied to the organ. A Laplander or Negro has no notion of the relish of wine. And though there are few or no instances of a like deficiency in the mind, where a person has never felt or is wholly incapable of a sentiment or passion that belongs to his species; yet we find the same observation to take place in a less degree. A man of mild manners can form no idea of inveterate revenge or cruelty; nor can a selfish heart easily conceive the heights of friendship and generosity. It is readily allowed, that other beings may possess many senses of which we can have no conception; because the ideas of them have never been introduced to us in the only manner by which an idea can have access to the mind, to wit, by the actual feeling and sensation.

There is, however, one contradictory phenomenon, which may prove that it is not absolutely impossible for ideas to arise, independent of their correspondent impressions. I believe it will readily be allowed, that the several distinct ideas of color, which enter by the eye, or those of sound, which are conveyed by the ear, are really different from each other; though, at the same time, resembling. Now if this be true of different colors, it must be no less so of the different shades of the same color; and each shade produces a distinct idea, independent of the rest. For if this should be denied, it is possible, by the continual gradation of shades, to run a color insensibly into what is most remote from it; and if you will not allow any of the means to be different, you cannot, without absurdity, deny the extremes to be the same. Suppose, therefore, a person to have enjoyed his sight for thirty years, and to have become perfectly acquainted with colors of all kinds except one particular shade of blue, for instance, which it never has been his fortune to meet with. Let all the different shades of that color, except that single one, be placed before him, descending gradually from the deepest to the lightest; it is plain that he will perceive a blank, where that shade is wanting, and will be sensible that there is a greater distance in that place between the contiguous colors than in any other. Now I ask, whether it be possible for him, from his own imagination, to supply this deficiency, and raise up to himself the idea of that particular shade, though it had never been conveyed to him by his senses? I believe there are few but will be of the opinion that he can: and this may serve as a proof that the simple ideas are not always, in every instance, derived from the correspondent impressions; though this instance is so singular, that it is scarcely worth our observing, and does not merit that for it alone we should alter our general maxim.

Here, therefore, is a proposition, which not only seems, in itself, simple and intelligible; but, if a proper use were made of it, might render every dispute equally intelligible, and banish all that jargon, which has so long taken possession of metaphysical reasonings, and drawn disgrace upon them. All ideas, especially abstract ones, are naturally faint and obscure: the mind has but a slender hold of them: they are apt to be confounded with other resembling ideas; and when we have often employed any term, though without a distinct meaning, we are apt to imagine it has a determinate idea annexed to it. On the contrary, all impressions, that is, all sensations, either outward or inward, are strong and vivid: the limits between them are more exactly determined: nor is it easy to fall into any error or mistake with regard to them. When we entertain, therefore, any suspicion that a philosophical term is employed without any meaning or idea (as is but too frequent), we need but inquire, *from what impression is that supposed idea derived?* And if it be impossible to assign any, this will serve to confirm our suspicion. By bringing ideas into so clear a light we may reasonably hope to remove all dispute, which may arise, concerning their nature and reality.

SECTION III

Of the Association of Ideas

It is evident that there is a principle of connection between the different thoughts or ideas of the mind, and that, in their appearance to the memory or imagination, they introduce each other with a certain degree of method and regularity. In our more serious thinking or discourse this is so observable that any particular thought, which breaks in upon the regular tract or chain of ideas, is immediately remarked and rejected. And even in our wildest and most wandering reveries, nay in our very dreams, we shall find, if we reflect, that the imagination ran not altogether at adventures, but that there was still a connection upheld among the different ideas, which succeeded each other. Were the loosest and freest conversation to be transcribed, there would immediately be observed something which connected it in all its transitions. Or where this is wanting, the person who broke the thread of discourse might still inform you, that there had secretly revolved in his mind a succession of thought, which had gradually led him from the subject of conversation. Among different languages, even where we cannot suspect the least connection or communication, it is found, that the words, expressive of ideas, the most compounded, do yet nearly correspond to each other: a certain proof that the simple ideas, comprehended in the compound ones, were bound together by some universal principle, which had an equal influence on all mankind.

Though it be too obvious to escape observation, that different ideas are connected together; I do not find that any philosopher has attempted to enumerate or class all the principles of association; a subject, however, that seems worthy of curiosity. To me, there appear to be only three principles of connection among ideas, namely, *resemblance*, *contiguity* in time or place, and *cause* or *effect*.

That these principles serve to connect ideas will not, I believe, be much doubted. A picture naturally leads our thoughts to the original: the mention of one apartment in a building naturally introduces an inquiry or discourse concerning the others: and if we think of a wound, we can scarcely forbear reflecting on the pain which follows it. But that this enumeration is complete, and that there are no other principles of association except these, may be difficult to prove to the satisfaction of the reader, or even to a man's own satisfaction. All we can do, in such cases, is to run over several instances, and examine carefully the principle which binds the different thoughts to each other, never stopping till we render the principle as general as possible. The more instances we examine, and the more care we employ, the more assurance shall we acquire, that the enumeration, which we form from the whole, is complete and entire.

SECTION IV

Sceptical Doubts Concerning the Operations of the Understanding

PART I

All the objects of human reason or inquiry may naturally be divided into two kinds, to wit, *relations of ideas*, and *matters of fact*. Of the first kind are the sciences of geometry, algebra, and arithmetic; and in short, every affirmation which is either intuitively or demonstratively certain. *That the square of the hypothenuse is equal to the squares of the two sides*, is a proposition which expresses a relation between these figures. *That three times five is equal to the half of thirty*, expresses a relation between these numbers. Propositions of this kind are discoverable by the mere operation of thought, without dependence on what is anywhere existent in the universe. Though there never were a circle or triangle in nature, the truths demonstrated by Euclid would for ever retain their certainty and evidence.

Matters of fact, which are the second objects of human reason, are not ascertained in the same manner; nor is our evidence of their truth, however great, of a like nature with the foregoing. The contrary of every matter of fact is still possible; because it can never imply a contradiction, and is conceived by the mind with the same facility and distinctness, as if ever so conformable to reality. *That the sun will not rise tomorrow* is no less intelligible a proposition, and implies no more contradiction than the affirmation, *that it will rise.* We should in vain, therefore, attempt to demonstrate its falsehood. Were it demonstratively false, it would imply a contradiction, and could never be distinctly conceived by the mind.

It may, therefore, be a subject worthy of curiosity, to inquire what is the nature of that evidence which assures us of any real existence and matter of fact, beyond the present testimony of our senses, or the records of our memory. This part of philosophy, it is observable, has been little cultivated, either by the ancients or moderns; and therefore our doubts and errors, in the prosecution of so important an inquiry, may be the more excusable; while we march through such difficult paths without any guide or direction. They may even prove useful, by exciting curiosity, and destroying that implicit faith and security, which is the bane of all reasoning and free inquiry. The discovery of defects in the common philosophy, if any such there be, will not, I presume, be a discouragement, but rather an incitement, as is usual, to attempt something more full and satisfactory than has yet been proposed to the public.

All reasonings concerning matter of fact seem to be founded on the relation of *cause and effect.* By means of that relation alone we can go beyond the evidence of our memory and senses. If you were to ask a man, why he believes any matter of fact, which is absent; for instance, that his friend is in the country, or in France; he would give you a reason; and this reason would be some other fact; as a letter received from him, or the knowledge of his former resolutions and promises. A man finding a watch or any other machine in a desert island, would conclude that there had once been men in that island. All our reasonings concerning fact are of the same nature. And here it is constantly supposed that there is a connection between the present fact and that which is inferred from it. Were there nothing to bind them together, the inference would be entirely precarious. The hearing of an articulate voice and rational discourse in the dark assures us of the presence of some person: Why? because these are the effects of the human make and fabric, and closely connected with it. If we anatomize all the other reasonings of this nature, we shall find that they are founded on the relation of cause and effect, and that this relation is either near or remote, direct or collateral. Heat and light are collateral effects of fire, and the one effect may justly be inferred from the other.

If we would satisfy ourselves, therefore, concerning the nature of that evidence, which assures us of matters of fact, we must inquire how we arrive at the knowledge of cause and effect.

I shall venture to affirm, as a general proposition, which admits of no exception, that the knowledge of this relation is not, in any instance, attained by reasonings *a priori;* but arises entirely from experience, when we find that any particular objects are constantly conjoined with each other. Let an object be presented to a man of ever so strong natural reason and abilities; if that object be entirely new to him, he will not be able, by the most accurate examination of its sensible qualities, to discover any of its causes or effects. Adam, though his rational faculties be supposed, at the very first, entirely perfect, could not have inferred from the fluidity and transparency of water that it would suffocate him, or from the light and warmth of fire that it would consume him. No object ever discovers, by the qualities which appear to the senses, either the causes which produced it, or the effects which will arise from it; nor can our reason, unassisted by experience, ever draw any inference concerning real existence and matter of fact.

This proposition, *that causes and effects are discoverable, not by reason but by experience*, will readily be admitted with regard to such objects, as we remember to have once been altogether unknown to us; since we must be conscious of the utter inability, which we then lay under, of foretelling what would arise from them. Present two smooth pieces of marble to a man who has no tincture of natural philosophy; he will never discover that they will adhere together in such a manner as to require great force to separate them in a direct line, while they make so small a resistance to a lateral pressure. Such events, as bear little analogy to the common course of nature, are also readily confessed to be known only by experience; nor does any man imagine that the explosion of gunpowder, or the attraction of a loadstone, could ever be discovered by arguments *a priori*. In like manner, when an effect is supposed to depend upon an intricate machinery or secret structure of parts, we make no difficulty in attributing all our knowledge of it to experience. Who will assert that he can give the ultimate reason, why milk or bread is proper nourishment for a man, not for a lion or a tiger?

But the same truth may not appear, at first sight, to have the same evidence with regard to events, which have become familiar to us from our first appearance in the world, which bear a close analogy to the whole course of nature, and which are supposed to depend on the simple qualities of objects, without any secret structure of parts. We are apt to imagine that we could discover these effects by the mere operation of our reason, without experience. We fancy, that were we brought on a sudden into this world, we could at first have inferred that one billiard ball would communicate motion to another upon impulse; and that we needed not to have waited for the event, in order to pronounce with certainty concerning it. Such is the influence of custom, that, where it is strongest, it not only covers our natural ignorance, but even conceals itself, and seems not to take place, merely because it is found in the highest degree.

But to convince us that all the laws of nature, and all the operations of bodies without exception, are known only by experience, the following reflections may, perhaps, suffice. Were any object presented to us, and were we required to pronounce concerning the effect, which will result from it, without consulting past observation; after what manner, I beseech you, must the mind proceed in this operation? It must invent or imagine some event, which it ascribes to the object as its effect; and it is plain that this invention must be entirely arbitrary. The mind can never possibly find the effect in the supposed cause, by the most accurate scrutiny and examination. For the effect is totally different from the cause, and consequently can never be discovered in it. Motion in the second billiard ball is a quite distinct event from motion in the first: nor is there anything in the one to suggest the smallest hint of the other. A stone or piece of metal raised into the air, and left without any support, immediately falls: but to consider the matter *a priori*, is there anything we discover in this situation which can beget the idea of a downward, rather than an upward, or any other motion, in the stone or metal?

And as the first imagination or invention of a particular effect, in all natural operations, is arbitrary, where we consult not experience; so must we also esteem the supposed tie or connection between the cause and effect, which binds them together, and renders it impossible that any other effect could result from the operation of that cause. When I see, for instance, a billiard ball moving in a straight line towards another; even suppose motion in the second ball should by accident be suggested to me, as the result of their contact or impulse; may I not conceive, that a hundred different events might as well follow from that cause? May not both these balls remain at absolute rest? May not the first ball return in a straight line, or leap off from the second in any line or direction? All these suppositions are consistent and conceivable. Why then should we give the preference to one, which is no more consistent or conceivable than the rest? All our reasonings *a priori* will never be able to show us any foundation for this preference.

In a word, then, every effect is a distinct event from its cause. It could not, therefore, be discovered in the cause, and the first invention or conception of it, *a priori*, must be entirely arbitrary. And even after it is suggested, the conjunction of it with the cause must appear equally arbitrary; since there are always many other effects, which, to reason, must seem fully as consistent and natural. In vain, therefore, should we pretend to determine any single event, or infer any cause or effect, without the assistance of observation and experience.

Hence we may discover the reason why no philosopher, who is rational and modest, has ever pretended to assign the ultimate cause of any natural operation, or to show distinctly the action of that power, which produces any single effect in the universe. It is confessed, that the utmost effort of human reason is to reduce the principles, productive of natural phenomena, to a greater simplicity, and to resolve the many particular effects into a few general causes, by means of reasonings from analogy, experience, and observation. But as to the causes of these general causes, we should in vain attempt their discovery; nor shall we ever be able to satisfy ourselves, by any particular explication of them. These ultimate springs and principles are totally shut up from human curiosity and inquiry. Elasticity, gravity, cohesion of parts, communication of motion by impulse; these are probably the ultimate causes and principles which we ever discover in nature; and we may esteem ourselves sufficiently happy, if, by accurate inquiry and reasoning, we can trace up the particular phenomena to, or near to, these general principles. The most perfect philosophy of the natural kind only staves off our ignorance a little longer: as perhaps the most perfect philosophy of the moral or metaphysical kind serves only to discover larger portions of it. Thus the observation of human blindness and weakness is the result of all philosophy, and meets us at every turn, in spite of our endeavors to elude or avoid it.

Nor is geometry, when taken into the assistance of natural philosophy, ever able to remedy this defect, or lead us into the knowledge of ultimate causes, by all that accuracy of reasoning for which it is so justly celebrated. Every part of mixed mathematics proceeds upon the supposition that certain laws are established by nature in her operations; and abstract reasonings are employed, either to assist experience in the discovery of these laws, or to determine their influence in particular instances, where it depends upon any precise degree of distance and quantity. Thus, it is a law of motion, discovered by experience, that the moment or force of any body in motion is in the compound ratio or proportion of its solid contents and its velocity; and consequently, that a small force may remove the greatest obstacle or raise the greatest weight, if, by any contrivance or machinery, we can increase the velocity of that force, so as to make it an overmatch for its antagonist. Geometry assists us in the application of this law, by giving us the just dimensions of all the parts and figures which can enter into any species of machine; but still the discovery of the law itself is owing merely to experience, and all the abstract reasonings in the world could never lead us one step towards the knowledge of it. When we reason *a priori*, and consider merely any object or cause, as it appears to the mind, independent of all observation, it never could suggest to us the notion of any distinct object, such as its effect; much less, show us the inseparable and inviolable connection between them. A man must be very sagacious who could discover by reasoning that crystal is the effect of heat, and ice of cold, without being previously acquainted with the operation of these qualities.

PART II

But we have not yet attained any tolerable satisfaction with regard to the question first proposed. Each solution still gives rise to a new question as difficult as the foregoing, and leads us on to farther inquiries. When it is asked, *What is the nature of all our reasonings concerning matter of fact?* the proper answer seems to be, that they are founded on the relation of cause and effect. When again it is asked, *What is the foundation of all our reasonings and conclusions concerning that relation?* it may be replied in one word, *experience.* But if we still carry on our sifting humor, and ask, *What is the foundation of all conclusions from experience?* this implies a new question, which may be of more difficult solution and explication. Philosophers, that give themselves airs of superior wisdom and sufficiency, have a hard task when they encounter persons of inquisitive dispositions, who push them from every corner to which they retreat, and who are sure at last to bring them to some dangerous dilemma. The best expedient to prevent this confusion, is to be modest in our pretensions; and even to discover the difficulty ourselves before it is objected to us. By this means, we may make a kind of merit of our very ignorance.

I shall content myself, in this section, with an easy task, and shall pretend only to give a negative answer to the question here proposed. I say then, that, even after we have experience of the operations of cause and effect, our conclusions from that experience are *not* founded on reasoning, or any process of the understanding. This answer we must endeavor both to explain and to defend.

It must certainly be allowed, that nature has kept us at a great distance from all her secrets, and has afforded us only the knowledge of a few superficial qualities of objects; while she conceals from us those powers and principles on which the influence of those objects entirely depends. Our senses inform us of the color, weight, and consistence of bread; but neither sense nor reason can ever inform us of those qualities which fit it for the nourishment and support of a human body. Sight or feeling conveys an idea of the actual motion of bodies; but as to that wonderful force or power, which would carry on a moving body for ever in a continued change of place, and which bodies never lose but by communicating it to others; of this we cannot form the most distant conception. But notwithstanding this ignorance of natural powers and principles, we always presume, when we see like sensible qualities, that they have like secret powers, and expect that effects, similar to those which we have experienced, will follow from them. If a body of like color and consistence with that bread, which we have formerly eaten, be presented to us, we make no scruple of repeating the experiment, and foresee, with certainty, like nourishment and support. Now this is a process of the mind or thought, of which I would willingly know the foundation. It is allowed on all hands that there is no known connection between the sensible qualities and the secret powers; and consequently, that the mind is not led to form such a conclusion concerning their constant and regular conjunction, by anything which it knows of their nature. As to past *experience*, it can be allowed to give *direct* and *certain* information of those precise objects only, and that precise period of time, which fell under its cognizance: but why this experience should be extended to future times, and to other objects, which, for aught we know, may be only in appearance similar; this is the main question on which I would insist. The bread, which I formerly ate, nourished me; that is, a body of such sensible qualities was, at that time, endued with such secret powers: but does it follow, that other bread must also nourish me at another time, and that like sensible qualities must always be attended with like secret powers? The consequence seems no wise necessary. At least, it must be acknowledged that there is here a consequence drawn by the mind; that there is a certain step taken; a process of thought, and an inference, which wants to be explained. These two propositions are far from being the same, *I have found that such an object has always been attended with such an effect*, and *I foresee, that other objects, which are, in appearance, similar, will be attended with similar effects*. I shall allow, if you please, that the one proposition may justly be inferred from the other; I know, in fact, that it always is inferred. But if you insist that the inference is made by a chain of reasoning, I desire you to produce that reasoning. The connection between these propositions is not intuitive. There is required a medium, which may enable the mind to draw such an inference, if indeed it be drawn by reasoning and argument. What that medium is, I must confess, passes my comprehension; and it is incumbent on those to produce it, who assert that it really exists, and is the origin of all our conclusions concerning matter of fact.

This negative argument must certainly, in process of time, become altogether convincing, if many penetrating and able philosophers shall turn their inquiries this way and no one be ever able to discover any connecting proposition or intermediate step, which supports the understanding in this conclusion. But as the question is yet new, every reader may not trust so far to his own penetration, as to conclude, because an argument escapes his inquiry, that therefore it does not really exist. For this reason it may be requisite to venture upon a more difficult task; and enumerating all the branches of human knowledge, endeavor to show that none of them can afford such an argument.

All reasonings may be divided into two kinds, namely demonstrative reasoning, or that concerning relations of ideas, and moral reasoning, or that concerning matter of fact and existence. That there are no demonstrative arguments in the case seems evident; since it implies no contradiction that the course of nature may change, and that an object, seemingly like those which we have experienced, may be attended with different or contrary effects. May I not clearly and distinctly conceive that a body, falling from the clouds, and which, in all other respects, resembles snow, has yet the taste of salt or feeling of fire? Is there any more intelligible proposition than to affirm, that all the trees will flourish in December and January, and decay in May and June? Now whatever is intelligible, and can be distinctly conceived, implies no contradiction, and can never be proved false by any demonstrative argument or abstract reasoning *a priori*.

If we be, therefore, engaged by arguments to put trust in past experience, and make it the standard of our future judgment, these arguments must be probable only, or such as regard matter of fact and real existence, according to the division above mentioned. But that there is no argument of this kind, must appear, if our explication of that species of reasoning be admitted as solid and satisfactory. We have said that all arguments concerning existence are founded on the relation of cause and effect; that our knowledge of that relation is derived entirely from experience; and that all our experimental conclusions proceed upon the supposition that the future will be conformable to the past. To endeavor, therefore, the proof of this last supposition by probable arguments, or arguments regarding existence, must be evidently going in a circle, and taking that for granted, which is the very point in question.

In reality, all arguments from experience are founded on the similarity which we discover among natural objects, and by which we are induced to expect effects similar to those which we have found to follow from such objects. And though none but a fool or madman will ever pretend to dispute the authority of experience, or to reject that great guide of human life, it may surely be allowed a philosopher to have so much curiosity at least as to examine the principle of human nature, which gives this mighty authority to experience, and makes us draw advantage from that similarity which nature has placed among different objects. From causes which appear *similar* we expect similar effects. This is the sum of all our experimental conclusions. Now it seems evident that, if this conclusion were formed by reason, it would be as perfect at first, and upon one instance, as after ever so long a course of experience. But the case is far otherwise. Nothing so like as eggs; yet no one, on account of this appearing similarity, expects the same taste and relish in all of them. It is only after a long course of uniform experiments in any kind, that we attain a firm reliance and security with regard to a particular event. Now where is that process of reasoning which, from one instance, draws a conclusion, so different from that which it infers from a hundred instances that are nowise different from that single one? This question I propose as much for the sake of information, as with an intention of raising difficulties. I cannot find, I cannot imagine any such reasoning. But I keep my mind still open to instruction, if anyone will vouchsafe to bestow it on me.

Should it be said that, from a number of uniform experiments, we *infer* a connection between the sensible qualities and the secret powers; this, I must confess, seems the same difficulty, couched in different terms. The question still recurs, on what process of argument this *inference* is founded? Where is the medium, the interposing ideas, which join propositions so very wide of each other? It is confessed that the color, consistence, and other sensible qualities of bread appear not, of themselves, to have any connection with the secret powers of nourishment and support. For otherwise we could infer these secret powers from the first appearance of these sensible qualities, without the aid of experience; contrary to the sentiment of all philosophers, and contrary to plain matter of fact. Here, then, is our natural state of ignorance with regard to the powers and influence of all objects. How is this remedied by experience? It only shows us a number of uniform effects, resulting from certain objects, and teaches us that those particular objects, at that particular time, were endowed with such powers and forces. When a new object, endowed with similar sensible qualities, is produced, we expect similar powers and forces, and look for a like effect. From a body of like color and consistence with bread we expect like nourishment and support. But this surely is a step or progress of the mind, which wants to be explained. When a man says, *I have found, in all past instances, such sensible qualities conjoined with such secret powers*: And when he says, *Similar sensible qualities will always be conjoined with similar secret powers*, he is not guilty of a tautology, nor are these propositions in any respect the same. You say that the one proposition is an inference from the other. But you must confess that the inference is not intuitive; neither is it demonstrative: Of what nature is it, then? To say it is experimental, is begging the question. For all inferences from experience suppose, as their foundation, that the future will resemble the past, and that similar powers will be conjoined with similar sensible qualities. If there be any suspicion that the course of nature may change, and that the past may be no rule for the future, all experience becomes useless, and can give rise to no inference or conclusion. It is impossible, therefore, that any arguments from experience can prove this resemblance of the past to the future; since all these arguments are founded on the supposition of that resemblance. Let the course of things be allowed hitherto ever so regular; that alone, without some new argument or inference, proves not that, for the future, it will continue so. In vain do you pretend to have learned the nature of bodies from your past experience. Their secret nature, and consequently all their effects and influence, may change, without any change in their sensible qualities. This happens sometimes, and with regard to some objects: Why may it not happen always, and with regard to all objects? What logic, what process of argument secures you against this supposition? My practice, you say, refutes my doubts. But you mistake the purport of my question. As an agent, I am quite satisfied in the point; but as a philosopher, who has some share of curiosity, I will not say scepticism, I want to learn the foundation of this inference. No reading, no inquiry has yet been able to remove my difficulty, or give me satisfaction in a matter of such importance. Can I do better than propose the difficulty to the public, even though, perhaps, I have small hopes of obtaining a solution? We shall, at least, by this means, be sensible of our ignorance, if we do not augment our knowledge.

I must confess that a man is guilty of unpardonable arrogance who concludes, because an argument has escaped his own investigation, that therefore it does not really exist. I must also confess that, though all the learned, for several ages, should have employed themselves in fruitless search upon any subject, it may still, perhaps, be rash to conclude positively that the subject must, therefore, pass all human comprehension. Even though we examine all the sources of our knowledge, and conclude them unfit for such a subject, there may still remain a suspicion, that the enumeration is not complete, or the examination not accurate. But with regard to the present subject, there are some considerations which seem to remove all this accusation of arrogance or suspicion of mistake.

It is certain that the most ignorant and stupid peasants—nay infants, nay even brute beasts—improve by experience, and learn the qualities of natural objects, by observing the effects which result from them. When a child has felt the sensation of pain from touching the flame of a candle, he will be careful not to put his hand near any candle; but will expect a similar effect from a cause which is similar in its sensible qualities and appearance. If you assert, therefore, that the understanding of the child is led into this conclusion by any process of argument or ratiocination, I may justly require you to produce that argument; nor have you any pretense to refuse so equitable a demand. You cannot say that the argument is abstruse, and may possibly escape your inquiry; since you confess that it is obvious to the capacity of a mere infant. If you hesitate, therefore, a moment, or if, after reflection, you produce any intricate or profound argument, you, in a manner, give up the question, and confess that it is not reasoning which engages us to suppose the past resembles the future, and to expect similar effects from causes which are, to appearance, similar. This is the proposition which I intended to enforce in the present section. If I be right, I pretend not to have made any mighty discovery. And if I be wrong, I must acknowledge myself to be indeed a very backward scholar; since I cannot now discover an argument which, it seems, was perfectly familiar to me long before I was out of my cradle.

SECTION V

Sceptical Solution of These Doubts

PART I

The passion for philosophy, like that for religion, seems liable to this inconvenience, that, though it aims at the correction of our manners, and extirpation of our vices, it may only serve, by imprudent management, to foster a predominant inclination, and push the mind, with more determined resolution, towards that side which already *draws* too much, by the bias and propensity of the natural temper. It is certain that, while we aspire to the magnanimous firmness of the philosophic sage, and endeavor to confine our pleasures altogether within our own minds, we may, at last, render our philosophy like that of Epictetus, and other *stoics*, only a more refined system of selfishness, and reason ourselves out of all virtue as well as social enjoyment. While we study with attention the vanity of human life, and turn all our thoughts towards the empty and transitory nature of riches and honors, we are, perhaps, all the while flattering our natural indolence, which, hating the bustle of the world, and drudgery of business, seeks a pretense of reason to give itself a full and uncontrolled indulgence. There is, however, one species of philosophy which seems little liable to this inconvenience, and that because it strikes in with no disorderly passion of the human mind, nor can mingle itself with any natural affection or propensity; and that is the *academic* or *sceptical* philosophy. The academics always talk of doubt and suspense of judgment, of danger in hasty determinations, of confining to very narrow bounds the inquiries of the understanding, and of renouncing all speculations which lie not within the limits of common life and practice. Nothing, therefore, can be more contrary than such a philosophy to the supine indolence of the mind, its rash arrogance, its lofty pretensions, and its superstitious credulity. Every passion is mortified by it, except the love of truth; and that passion never is, nor can be, carried to too high a degree. It is surprising, therefore, that this philosophy, which, in almost every instance, must be harmless and innocent, should be the subject of so much groundless reproach and obloquy. But, perhaps, the very circumstance which renders it so innocent is what chiefly exposes it to the public hatred and resentment. By flattering no irregular passion, it gains few partisans: By opposing so many vices and follies, it raises to itself abundance of enemies, who stigmatize it as libertine, profane, and irreligious.

Nor need we fear that this philosophy, while it endeavors to limit our inquiries to common life, should ever undermine the reasonings of common life, and carry its doubts so far as to destroy all action, as well as speculation. Nature will always maintain her rights, and prevail in the end over any abstract reasoning whatsoever. Though we should conclude, for instance, as in the foregoing section, that, in all reasonings from experience, there is a step taken by the mind which is not supported by any argument or process of the understanding; there is no danger that these reasonings, on which almost all knowledge depends, will ever be affected by such a discovery. If the mind be not engaged by argument to make this step, it must be induced by some other principle of equal weight and authority; and that principle will preserve its influence as long as human nature remains the same. What that principle is may well be worth the pains of inquiry.

Suppose a person, though endowed with the strongest faculties of reason and reflection, to be brought on a sudden into this world; he would, indeed, immediately observe a continual succession of objects, and one event following another; but he would not be able to discover anything farther. He would not, at first, by any reasoning, be able to reach the idea of cause and effect; since the particular powers, by which all natural operations are performed, never appear to the senses; nor is it reasonable to conclude, merely because one event, in one instance, precedes another, that therefore the one is the cause, the other the effect. Their conjunction may be arbitrary and casual. There may be no reason to infer the existence of one from the appearance of the other. And in a word, such a person, without more experience, could never employ his conjecture or reasoning concerning any matter of fact, or be assured of anything beyond what was immediately present to his memory and senses.

Suppose, again, that he has acquired more experience, and has lived so long in the world as to have observed familiar objects or events to be constantly conjoined together; what is the consequence of this experience? He immediately infers the existence of one object from the appearance of the other. Yet he has not, by all his experience, acquired any idea or knowledge of the secret power by which the one object produces the other; nor is it, by any process of reasoning, he is engaged to draw this inference. But still he finds himself determined to draw it: And though he should be convinced that his understanding has no part in the operation, he would nevertheless continue in the same course of thinking. There is some other principle which determines him to form such a conclusion.

This principle is *custom* or *habit.* For wherever the repetition of any particular act or operation produces a propensity to renew the same act or operation, without being impelled by any reasoning or process of the understanding, we always say, that this propensity is the effect of *custom.* By employing that word, we pretend not to have given the ultimate reason of such a propensity. We only point out a principle of human nature, which is universally acknowledged, and which is well known by its effects. Perhaps we can push our inquiries no farther, or pretend to give the cause of this cause; but must rest contented with it as the ultimate principle, which we can assign, of all our conclusions from experience. It is sufficient satisfaction, that we can go so far, without repining at the narrowness of our faculties because they will carry us no farther. And it is certain we here advance a very intelligible proposition at least, if not a true one, when we assert that, after the constant conjunction of two objects—heat and flame, for instance, weight and solidity—we are determined by custom alone to expect the one from the appearance of the other. This hypothesis seems even the only one which explains the difficulty, why we draw, from a thousand instances, an inference which we are not able to draw from one instance, that is, in no respect, different from them. Reason is incapable of any such variation. The conclusions which it draws from considering one circle are the same which it would form upon surveying all the circles in the universe. But no man, having seen only one body move after being impelled by another, could infer that every other body will move after a like impulse. All inferences from experience, therefore, are effects of custom, not of reasoning.

Custom, then, is the great guide of human life. It is that principle alone which renders our experience useful to us, and makes us expect, for the future, a similar train of events with those which have appeared in the past. Without the influence of custom, we should be entirely ignorant of every matter of fact beyond what is immediately present to the memory and senses. We should never know how to adjust means to ends, or to employ our natural powers in the production of any effect. There would be an end at once of all action, as well as of the chief part of speculation.

But here it may be proper to remark, that though our conclusions from experience carry us beyond our memory and senses, and assure us of matters of fact which happened in the most distant places and most remote ages, yet some fact must always be present to the senses or memory, from which we may first proceed in drawing these conclusions. A man, who should find in a desert country the remains of pompous buildings, would conclude that the country had, in ancient times, been cultivated by civilized inhabitants; but did nothing of this nature occur to him, he could never form such an inference. We learn the events of former ages from history; but then we must peruse the volumes in which this instruction is contained, and thence carry up our inferences from one testimony to another, till we arrive at the eyewitnesses and spectators of these distant events. In a word, if we proceed not upon some fact, present to the memory or senses, our reasonings would be merely hypothetical; and however the particular links might be connected with each other, the whole chain of inferences would have nothing to support it, nor could we ever, by its means, arrive at the knowledge of any real existence. If I ask why you believe any particular matter of fact, which you relate, you must tell me some reason; and this reason will be some other fact, connected with it. But as you cannot proceed after this manner, *in infinitum*, you must at last terminate in some fact, which is present to your memory or senses; or must allow that your belief is entirely without foundation.

What, then, is the conclusion of the whole matter? A simple one; though, it must be confessed, pretty remote from the common theories of philosophy. All belief of matter of fact or real existence is derived merely from some object, present to the memory or senses, and a customary conjunction between that and some other object. Or in other words; having found, in many instances, that any two kinds of objects—flame and heat, snow and cold—have always been conjoined together; if flame or snow be presented anew to the senses, the mind is carried by custom to expect heat or cold, and to *believe* that such a quality does exist, and will discover itself upon a nearer approach. This belief is the necessary result of placing the mind in such circumstances. It is an operation of the soul, when we are so situated, as unavoidable as to feel the passion of love, when we receive benefits; or hatred, when we meet with injuries. All these operations are a species of natural instincts, which no reasoning or process of the thought and understanding is able either to produce or to prevent.

At this point, it would be very allowable for us to stop our philosophical researches. In most questions we can never make a single step farther; and in all questions we must terminate here at last, after our most restless and curious inquiries. But still our curiosity will be pardonable, perhaps commendable, if it carry us on to still farther researches, and make us examine more accurately the nature of this *belief*, and of the *customary conjunction*, whence it is derived. By this means we may meet with some explications and analogies that will give satisfaction; at least to such as love the abstract sciences, and can be entertained with speculations, which, however accurate, may still retain a degree of doubt and uncertainty. As to readers of a different taste; the remaining part of this section is not calculated for them, and the following inquiries may well be understood, though it be neglected.

PART II

Nothing is more free than the imagination of man; and though it cannot exceed that original stock of ideas furnished by the internal and external senses, it has unlimited power of mixing, compounding, separating, and dividing these ideas, in all the varieties of fiction and vision. It can feign a train of events, with all the appearance of reality, ascribe to them a particular time and place, conceive them as existent, and paint them out to itself with every circumstance, that belongs to any historical fact, which it believes with the greatest certainty. Wherein, therefore, consists the difference between such a fiction and belief? It lies not merely in any peculiar idea, which is annexed to such a conception as commands our assent, and which is wanting to every known fiction. For as the mind has authority over all its ideas, it could voluntarily annex this particular idea to any fiction, and consequently be able to believe whatever it pleases; contrary to what we find by daily experience. We can, in our conception, join the head of a man to the body of a horse; but it is not in our power to believe that such an animal has ever really existed.

It follows, therefore, that the difference between *fiction* and *belief* lies in some sentiment or feeling, which is annexed to the latter, not to the former, and which depends not on the will, nor can be commanded at pleasure. It must be excited by nature, like all other sentiments; and must arise from the particular situation, in which the mind is placed at any particular juncture. Whenever any object is presented to the memory or senses, it immediately, by the force of custom, carries the imagination to conceive that object, which is usually conjoined to it; and this conception is attended with a feeling or sentiment, different from the loose reveries of the fancy. In this consists the whole nature of belief. For as there is no matter of fact which we believe so firmly that we cannot conceive the contrary, there would be no difference between the conception assented to and that which is rejected, were it not for some sentiment which distinguishes the one from the other. If I see a billiard ball moving towards another, on a smooth table, I can easily conceive it to stop upon contact. This conception implies no contradiction; but still it feels very differently from that conception by which I represent to myself the impulse and the communication of motion from one ball to another.

Were we to attempt a *definition* of this sentiment, we should, perhaps, find it a very difficult, if not an impossible task; in the same manner as if we should endeavor to define the feeling of cold or passion of anger, to a creature who never had any experience of these sentiments. Belief is the true and proper name of this feeling; and no one is ever at a loss to know the meaning of that term; because every man is every moment conscious of the sentiment represented by it. It may not, however, be improper to attempt a *description* of this sentiment; in hopes we may, by that means, arrive at some analogies, which may afford a more perfect explication of it. I say, then, that belief is nothing but a more vivid, lively, forcible, firm, steady conception of an object, than what the imagination alone is ever able to attain. This variety of terms, which may seem so unphilosophical, is intended only to express that act of the mind, which renders realities, or what is taken for such, more present to us than fictions, causes them to weigh more in the thought, and gives them a superior influence on the passions and imagination. Provided we agree about the thing, it is needless to dispute about the terms. The imagination has the command over all its ideas, and can join and mix and vary them, in all the ways possible. It may conceive fictitious objects with all the circumstances of place and time. It may set them, in a manner, before our eyes, in their true colors, just as they might have existed. But as it is impossible that this faculty of imagination can ever, of itself, reach belief, it is evident that belief consists not in the peculiar nature or order of ideas, but in the *manner* of their conception, and in their *feeling* to the mind. I confess, that it is impossible perfectly to explain this feeling or manner of conception. We may make use of words which express something near it. But its true and proper name, as we observed before, is *belief;* which is a term that every one sufficiently understands in common life. And in philosophy, we can go no farther than assert, that *belief* is something felt by the mind, which distinguishes the ideas of the judgment from the fictions of the imagination. It gives them more weight and influence; makes them appear of greater importance; enforces them in the mind; and renders them the governing principle of our actions. I hear at present, for instance, a person's voice, with whom I am acquainted; and the sound comes as from the next room. This impression of my senses immediately conveys my thought to the person, together with all the surrounding objects. I point them out to myself as existing at present, with the same qualities and relations, of which I formerly knew them possessed. These ideas take faster hold of my mind than ideas of an enchanted castle. They are very different to the feeling, and have a much greater influence of every kind, either to give pleasure or pain, joy or sorrow.

Let us, then, take in the whole compass of this doctrine, and allow, that the sentiment of belief is nothing but a conception more intense and steady than what attends the mere fictions of the imagination, and that this *manner* of conception arises from a customary conjunction of the object with something present to the memory or senses: I believe that it will not be difficult, upon these suppositions, to find other operations of the mind analogous to it, and to trace up these phenomena to principles still more general.

We have already observed that nature has established connections among particular ideas, and that no sooner one idea occurs to our thoughts than it introduces its correlative, and carries our attention towards it, by a gentle and insensible movement. These principles of connection or association we have reduced to three, namely *resemblance, contiguity* and *causation;* which are the only bonds that unite our thoughts together, and beget that regular train of reflection or discourse, which, in a greater or less degree, takes place among mankind. Now here arises a question, on which the solution of the present difficulty will depend. Does it happen, in all these relations, that, when one of the objects is presented to the senses or memory, the mind is not only carried to the conception of the correlative, but reaches a steadier and stronger conception of it than what otherwise it would have been able to attain? This seems to be the case with that belief which arises from the relation of cause and effect. And if the case be the same with the other relations or principles of association, this may be established as a general law, which takes place in all the operations of the mind.

We may, therefore, observe, as the first experiment to our present purpose, that, upon the appearance of the picture of an absent friend, our idea of him is evidently enlivened by the resemblance, and that every passion, which that idea occasions, whether of joy or sorrow, acquires new force and vigor. In producing this effect, there concur both a relation and a present impression. Where the picture bears him no resemblance, at least was not intended for him, it never so much as conveys our thought to him: And where it is absent, as well as the person, though the mind may pass from the thought of the one to that of the other, it feels its idea to be rather weakened than enlivened by that transition. We take a pleasure in viewing the picture of a friend, when it is set before us; but when it is removed, rather choose to consider him directly than by reflection in an image, which is equally distant and obscure.

The ceremonies of the Roman Catholic religion may be considered as instances of the same nature. The devotees of that superstition usually plead in excuse for the mummeries, with which they were upbraided, that they feel the good effect of those external motions, and postures, and actions, in enlivening their devotion and quickening their fervor, which otherwise would decay, if directed entirely to distant and immaterial objects. We shadow out the objects of our faith, say they, in sensible types and images, and render them more present to us by the immediate presence of these types, than it is possible for us to do merely by an intellectual view and contemplation. Sensible objects have always a greater influence on the fancy than any other; and this influence they readily convey to those ideas to which they are related, and which they resemble. I shall only infer from these practices, and this reasoning, that the effect of resemblance in enlivening the ideas is very common; and as in every case a resemblance and a present impression must concur, we are abundantly supplied with experiments to prove the reality of the foregoing principle.

We may add force to these experiments by others of a different kind, in considering the effects of *contiguity* as well as of *resemblance*. It is certain that distance diminishes the force of every idea, and that upon our approach to any object; though it does not discover itself to our senses; it operates upon the mind with an influence, which imitates an immediate impression. The thinking on any object readily transports the mind to what is contiguous; but it is only the actual presence of an object, that transports it with a superior vivacity. When I am a few miles from home, whatever relates to it touches me more nearly than when I am two hundred leagues distant; though even at that distance the reflecting on anything in the neighborhood of my friends or family naturally produces an idea of them. But as in this latter case, both the objects of the mind are ideas; notwithstanding there is an easy transition between them; that transition alone is not able to give a superior vivacity to any of the ideas, for want of some immediate impression.

No one can doubt but causation has the same influence as the other two relations of resemblance and contiguity. Superstitious people are fond of the relics of saints and holy men, for the same reason, that they seek after types or images, in order to enliven their devotion, and give them a more intimate and strong conception of those exemplary lives, which they desire to imitate. Now it is evident, that one of the best relics, which a devotee could procure, would be the handiwork of a saint; and if his clothes and furniture are ever to be considered in this light, it is because they were once at his disposal, and were moved and affected by him; in which respect they are to be considered as imperfect effects, and as connected with him by a shorter chain of consequences than any of those, by which we learn the reality of his existence.

Suppose, that the son of a friend, who had been long dead or absent, were presented to us; it is evident, that this object would instantly revive its correlative idea, and recall to our thoughts all past intimacies and familiarities, in more lively colors than they would otherwise have appeared to us. This is another phenomenon, which seems to prove the principle above mentioned.

We may observe, that, in these phenomena, the belief of the correlative object is always presupposed: without which the relation could have no effect. The influence of the picture supposes, that we *believe* our friend to have once existed. Contiguity to home can never excite our ideas of home, unless we *believe* that it really exists. Now I assert, that this belief, where it reaches beyond the memory or senses, is of a similar nature, and arises from similar causes, with the transition of thought and vivacity of conception here explained. When I throw a piece of dry wood into a fire, my mind is immediately carried to conceive, that it augments, not extinguishes the flame. This transition of thought from the cause to the effect proceeds not from reason. It derives its origin altogether from custom and experience. And as it first begins from an object, present to the senses, it renders the idea or conception of flame more strong and lively than any loose, floating reverie of the imagination. That idea arises immediately. The thought moves instantly towards it, and conveys to it all that force of conception, which is derived from the impression present to the senses. When a sword is leveled at my breast, does not the idea of wound and pain strike me more strongly, than when a glass of wine is presented to me, even though by accident this idea should occur after the appearance of the latter object? But what is there in this whole matter to cause such a strong conception, except only a present object and a customary transition to the idea of another object, which we have been accustomed to conjoin with the former? This is the whole operation of the mind, in all our conclusions concerning matter of fact and existence; and it is a satisfaction to find some analogies, by which it may be explained. The transition from a present object does in all cases give strength and solidity to the related idea.

Here, then, is a kind of pre-established harmony between the course of nature and the succession of our ideas; and though the powers and forces, by which the former is governed, be wholly unknown to us; yet our thoughts and conceptions have still, we find, gone on in the same train with the other works of nature. Custom is that principle, by which this correspondence has been effected; so necessary to the subsistence of our species, and the regulation of our conduct, in every circumstance and occurrence of human life. Had not the presence of an object, instantly excited the idea of those objects, commonly conjoined with it, all our knowledge must have been limited to the narrow sphere of our memory and senses; and we should never have been able to adjust means to ends, or employ our natural powers, either to the producing of good, or avoiding of evil. Those, who delight in the discovery and contemplation of *final causes*, have here ample subject to employ their wonder and admiration.

I shall add, for a further confirmation of the foregoing theory, that, as this operation of the mind, by which we infer like effects from like causes, and *vice versa*, is so essential to the subsistence of all human creatures, it is not probable, that it could be trusted to the fallacious deductions of our reason, which is slow in its operations; appears not, in any degree, during the first years of infancy; and at best is, in every age and period of human life, extremely liable to error and mistake. It is more conformable to the ordinary wisdom of nature to secure so necessary an act of the mind, by some instinct or mechanical tendency, which may be infallible in its operations, may discover itself at the first appearance of life and thought, and may be independent of all the labored deductions of the understanding. As nature has taught us the use of our limbs, without giving us the knowledge of the muscles and nerves, by which they are actuated; so has she implanted in us an instinct, which carries forward the thought in a correspondent course to that which she has established among external objects; though we are ignorant of those powers and forces, on which this regular course and succession of objects totally depends.

SECTION VI

Of Probability

Though there by no such thing as *chance* in the world; our ignorance of the real cause of any event has the same influence on the understanding, and begets a like species of belief or opinion.

There is certainly a probability, which arises from a superiority of chances on any side; and according as this superiority increases, and surpasses the opposite chances, the probability receives a proportionable increase, and begets still a higher degree of belief or assent to that side, in which we discover the superiority. If a die were marked with one figure or number of spots on four sides, and with another figure or number of spots on the two remaining sides, it would be more probable, that the former would turn up than the latter; though, if it had a thousand sides marked in the same manner, and only one side different, the probability would be much higher, and our belief or expectation of the event more steady and secure. This process of the thought or reasoning may seem trivial and obvious; but to those who consider it more narrowly, it may, perhaps, afford matter for curious speculation.

It seems evident, that, when the mind looks forward to discover the event, which may result from the throw of such a die, it considers the turning up of each particular side as alike probable; and this is the very nature of chance, to render all the particular events, comprehended in it, entirely equal. But finding a greater number of sides concur in the one event than in the other, the mind is carried more frequently to that event, and meets it oftener, in revolving the various possibilities or chances, on which the ultimate result depends. This concurrence of several views in one particular event begets immediately, by an inexplicable contrivance of nature, the sentiment of belief, and gives that event the advantage over its antagonist, which is supported by a smaller number of views, and recurs less frequently to the mind. If we allow, that belief is nothing but a firmer and stronger conception of an object than what attends the mere fictions of the imagination, this operation may, perhaps, in some measure, be accounted for. The concurrence of these several views or glimpses imprints the idea more strongly on the imagination; gives it superior force and vigor; renders its influence on the passions and affections more sensible; and in a word, begets that reliance or security, which constitutes the nature of belief and opinion.

The case is the same with the probability of causes, as with that of chance. There are some causes, which are entirely uniform and constant in producing a particular effect; and no instance has ever yet been found of any failure or irregularity in their operation. Fire has always burned, and water suffocated every human creature: the production of motion by impulse and gravity is an universal law, which has hitherto admitted of no exception. But there are other causes which have been found more irregular and uncertain; nor has rhubarb always proved a purge, or opium a soporific to everyone, who has taken these medicines. It is true, when any cause fails of producing its usual effect, philosophers ascribe not this to any irregularity in nature; but suppose, that some secret causes, in the particular structure of parts, have prevented the operation. Our reasonings, however, and conclusions concerning the event are the same as if this principle had no place. Being determined by custom to transfer the past to the future, in all our inferences; where the past has been entirely regular and uniform, we expect the event with the greatest assurance, and leave no room for any contrary supposition. But where different effects have been found to follow from causes, which are to *appearance* exactly similar, all these various effects must occur to the mind in transferring the past to the future, and enter into our consideration, when we determine the probability of the event. Though we give the preference to that which has been found most usual, and believe that this effect will exist, we must not overlook the other effects, but must assign to each of them a particular weight and authority, in proportion as we have found it to be more or less frequent. It is more probable, in almost every country of Europe, that there will be frost sometime in January, than that the weather will continue open throughout the whole month; though this probability varies according to the different climates, and approaches to a certainty in the more northern kingdoms. Here then it seems evident, that, when we transfer the past to the future, in order to determine the effect, which will result from any cause, we transfer all the different events, in the same proportion as they have appeared in the past, and conceive one to have existed a hundred times, for instance, another ten times, and another once. As a great number of views do here concur in one event, they fortify and confirm it to the imagination, beget that sentiment which we call *belief*, and give its object the preference above the contrary event, which is not supported by an equal number of experiments, and recurs not so frequently to the thought in transferring the past to the future. Let anyone try to account for this operation of the mind upon any of the received systems of philosophy, and he will be sensible of the difficulty. For my part, I shall think it sufficient, if the present hints excite the curiosity of philosophers, and make them sensible how defective all common theories are in treating of such curious and such sublime subjects.

SECTION VII

Of the Idea of Necessary Connection

PART I

The great advantage of the mathematical sciences above the moral consists in this, that the ideas of the former, being sensible, are always clear and determinate, the smallest distinction between them is immediately perceptible, and the same terms are still expressive of the same ideas, without ambiguity or variation. An oval is never mistaken for a circle, nor an hyperbola for an ellipsis. The isosceles and scalenum are distinguished by boundaries more exact than vice and virtue, right and wrong. If any term be defined in geometry, the mind readily, of itself, substitutes, on all occasions, the definition for the term defined: or even when no definition is employed, the object itself may be presented to the senses, and by that means be steadily and clearly apprehended. But the finer sentiments of the mind, the operations of the understanding, the various agitations of the passions, though really in themselves distinct, easily escape us, when surveyed by reflection; nor is it in our power to recall the original object, as often as we have occasion to contemplate it. Ambiguity, by this means, is gradually introduced into our reasonings: similar objects are readily taken to be the same: and the conclusion becomes at last very wide of the premises.

One may safely, however, affirm, that, if we consider these sciences in a proper light, their advantages and disadvantages nearly compensate each other, and reduce both of them to a state of equality. If the mind, with greater facility, retains the ideas of geometry clear and determinate, it must carry on a much longer and more intricate chain of reasoning, and compare ideas much wider of each other, in order to reach the abstruser truths of that science. And if moral ideas are apt, without extreme care, to fall into obscurity and confusion, the inferences are always much shorter in these disquisitions, and the intermediate steps, which lead to the conclusion, much fewer than in the sciences which treat of quantity and number. In reality, there is scarcely a proposition in Euclid so simple, as not to consist of more parts, than are to be found in any moral reasoning which runs not into chimera and conceit. Where we trace the principles of the human mind through a few steps, we may be very well satisfied with our progress; considering how soon nature throws a bar to all our inquiries concerning causes, and reduces us to an acknowledgment of our ignorance. The chief obstacle, therefore, to our improvement in the moral or metaphysical sciences is the obscurity of the ideas, and ambiguity of the terms. The principal difficulty in the mathematics is the length of inferences and compass of thought, requisite to the forming of any conclusion. And, perhaps, our progress in natural philosophy is chiefly retarded by the want of proper experiments and phenomena, which are often discovered by chance, and cannot always be found, when requisite, even by the most diligent and prudent inquiry. As moral philosophy seems hitherto to have received less improvement than either geometry or physics, we may conclude, that, if there be any difference in this respect among these sciences, the difficulties, which obstruct the progress of the former, require superior care and capacity to be surmounted.

There are no ideas, which occur in metaphysics more obscure and uncertain, than those of *power*, *force*, *energy* or *necessary connection*, of which it is every moment necessary for us to treat in all our disquisitions. We shall, therefore, endeavor, in this section, to fix, if possible, the precise meaning of these terms, and thereby remove some part of that obscurity, which is so much complained of in this species of philosophy.

It seems a proposition, which will not admit of much dispute, that all our ideas are nothing but copies of our impressions, or, in other words, that it is impossible for us to *think* of anything, which we have not antecedently *felt*, either by our external or internal senses. I have endeavored to explain and prove this proposition, and have expressed my hopes, that, by a proper application of it, men may reach a greater clearness and precision in philosophical reasonings, than what they have hitherto been able to attain. Complex ideas may, perhaps, be well known by definition, which is nothing but an enumeration of those parts or simple ideas, that compose them. But when we have pushed up definitions to the most simple ideas, and find still some ambiguity and obscurity; what resource are we then possessed of? By what invention can we throw light upon these ideas, and render them altogether precise and determinate to our intellectual view! Produce the impressions or original sentiments, from which the ideas are copied. These impressions are all strong and sensible. They admit not of ambiguity. They are not only placed in a full light themselves, but may throw light on their correspondent ideas, which lie in obscurity. And by this means, we may, perhaps, attain a new microscope or species of optics, by which, in the moral sciences, the most minute, and most simple ideas may be so enlarged as to fall readily under our apprehension, and be equally known with the grossest and most sensible ideas, that can be the object of our inquiry.

To be fully acquainted, therefore, with the idea of power or necessary connection, let us examine its impression; and in order to find the impression with greater certainty, let us search for it in all the sources, from which it may possibly be derived.

When we look about us towards external objects, and consider the operation of causes, we are never able, in a single instance, to discover any power or necessary connection; any quality, which binds the effect to the cause, and renders the one an infallible consequence of the other. We only find, that the one does actually, in fact, follow the other. The impulse of one billiard ball is attended with motion in the second. This is the whole that appears to the *outward* senses. The mind feels no sentiment or *inward* impression from this succession of objects: consequently there is not, in any single, particular instance of cause and effect, anything which can suggest the idea of power or necessary connection.

From the first appearance of an object, we never can conjecture what effect will result from it. But were the power or energy of any cause discoverable by the mind, we could foresee the effect, even without experience; and might, at first, pronounce with certainty concerning it, by mere dint of thought and reasoning.

In reality, there is no part of matter, that does ever, by its sensible qualities, discover any power or energy, or give us ground to imagine, that it could produce anything, or be followed by any other object, which we could denominate its effect. Solidity, extension, motion; these qualities are all complete in themselves, and never point out any other event which may result from them. The scenes of the universe are continually shifting, and one object follows another in an uninterrupted succession; but the power of force, which actuates the whole machine, is entirely concealed from us, and never discovers itself in any of the sensible qualities of body. We know, that, in fact, heat is a constant attendant of flame; but what is the connection between them, we have no room so much as to conjecture or imagine. It is impossible, therefore, that the idea of power can be derived from the contemplation of bodies, in single instances of their operation; because no bodies ever discover any power, which can be the original of this idea.

Since, therefore, external objects as they appear to the senses, give us no idea of power or necessary connection, by their operation in particular instances, let us see, whether this idea be derived from reflection on the operations of our own minds, and be copied from any internal impression. It may be said, that we are every moment conscious of internal power; while we feel, that, by the simple command of our will, we can move the organs of our body, or direct the faculties of our mind. An act of volition produces motion in our limbs, or raises a new idea in our imagination. This influence of the will we know by consciousness. Hence we acquire the idea of power or energy; and are certain, that we ourselves and all other intelligent beings are possessed of power. This idea, then, is an idea of reflection, since it arises from reflecting on the operations of our own mind, and on the command which is exercised by will, both over the organs of the body and faculties of the soul.

We shall proceed to examine this pretension; and first with regard to the influence of volition over the organs of the body. This influence, we may observe, is a fact, which, like all other natural events, can be known only by experience, and can never be foreseen from any apparent energy or power in the cause, which connects it with the effect, and renders the one an infallible consequence of the other. The motion of our body follows upon the command of our will. Of this we are every moment conscious. But the means, by which this is effected; the energy, by which the will performs so extraordinary an operation; of this we are so far from being immediately conscious, that it must forever escape our most diligent inquiry.

For *first,* Is there any principle in all nature more mysterious than the union of soul with body; by which a supposed spiritual substance acquires such an influence over a material one, that the most refined thought is able to actuate the grossest matter? Were we empowered, by a secret wish, to remove mountains, or control the planets in their orbit; this extensive authority would not be more extraordinary, nor more beyond our comprehension. But if by consciousness we perceived any power or energy in the will, we must know this power; we must know its connection with the effect; we must know the secret union of soul and body, and the nature of both these substances; by which the one is able to operate, in so many instances, upon the other.

Secondly, We are not able to move all the organs of the body with a like authority; though we cannot assign any reason besides experience, for so remarkable a difference between one and the other. Why has the will an influence over the tongue and fingers, not over the heart and liver? This question would never embarrass us, were we conscious of a power in the former case, not in the latter. We should then perceive, independent of experience, why the authority of will over the organs of the body is circumscribed within such particular limits. Being in that case fully acquainted with the power or force, by which it operates, we should also know, why its influence reaches precisely to such boundaries, and no farther.

A man, suddenly struck with palsy in the leg or arm, or who had newly lost those members, frequently endeavors, at first to move them, and employ them in their usual offices. Here he is as much conscious of power to command such limbs, as a man in perfect health is conscious of power to actuate any member which remains in its natural state and condition. But consciousness never deceives. Consequently, neither in the one case nor in the other, are we ever conscious of any power. We learn the influence of our will from experience alone. And experience only teaches us, how one event constantly follows another; without instructing us in the secret connection, which binds them together, and renders them inseparable.

Thirdly, We learn from anatomy, that the immediate object of power in voluntary motion, is not the member itself which is moved, but certain muscles, and nerves, and animal spirits, and, perhaps, something still more minute and more unknown, through which the motion is successfully propagated, ere it reach the member itself whose motion is the immediate object of volition. Can there be a more certain proof that the power, by which this whole operation is performed, so far from being directly and fully known by an inward sentiment or consciousness, is, to the last degree, mysterious and unintelligible? Here the mind wills a certain event: immediately another event, unknown to ourselves, and totally different from the one intended, is produced: this event produces another, equally unknown: till at last, through a long succession, the desired event is produced. But if the original power were felt, it must be known: were it known, its effect also must be known; since all power is relative to its effect. And *vice versa*, if the effect be not known, the power cannot be known nor felt. How indeed can we be conscious of a power to move our limbs, when we have no such power; but only that to move certain animal spirits, which, though they produce at last the motion of our limbs, yet operate in such a manner as is wholly beyond our comprehension?

We may, therefore, conclude from the whole, I hope, without any temerity, though with assurance; that our idea of power is not copied from any sentiment or consciousness of power within ourselves, when we give rise to animal motion, or apply our limbs, to their proper use and office. That their motion follows the command of the will is a matter of common experience, like other natural events: but the power or energy by which this is effected, like that in other natural events, is unknown and inconceivable.

Shall we then assert, that we are conscious of a power or energy in our own minds, when, by an act or command of our will, we raise up a new idea, fix the mind to the contemplation of it, turn it on all sides, and at last dismiss it for some other idea, when we think that we have surveyed it with sufficient accuracy? I believe the same arguments will prove, that even this command of the will gives us no real idea of force or energy.

First, It must be allowed, that, when we know a power, we know that very circumstance in the cause, by which it is enabled to produce the effect: for these are supposed to be synonymous. We must, therefore, know both the cause and effect, and the relation between them. But do we pretend to be acquainted with the nature of the human soul and the nature of an idea, or the aptitude of the one to produce the other? This is a real creation; a production of something out of nothing: which implies a power so great, that it may seem, at first sight, beyond the reach of any being, less than infinite. At least it must be owned, that such a power is not felt, nor known, nor even conceivable by the mind. We only feel the event, namely, the existence of an idea, consequent to a command of the will: but the manner, in which this operation is performed, the power by which it is produced, is entirely beyond our comprehension.

Secondly, The command of the mind over itself is limited, as well as its command over the body; and these limits are not known by reason, or any acquaintance with the nature of cause and effect, but only by experience and observation, as in all other natural events and in the operation of external objects. Our authority over our sentiments and passions is much weaker than that over our ideas; and even the latter authority is circumscribed within very narrow boundaries. Will anyone pretend to assign the ultimate reason of these boundaries, or show why the power is deficient in one case, not in another?

Thirdly, This self-command is very different at different times. A man in health possesses more of it than one languishing with sickness. We are more master of our thoughts in the morning than in the evening; fasting, than after a full meal. Can we give any reason for these variations, except experience? Where then is the power, of which we pretend to be conscious? Is there not here, either in a spiritual or material substance, or both, some secret mechanism or structure of parts, upon which the effect depends, and which, being entirely unknown to us, renders the power or energy of the will equally unknown and incomprehensible?

Volition is surely an act of the mind, with which we are sufficiently acquainted. Reflect upon it. Consider it on all sides. Do you find anything in it like this creative power, by which it raises from nothing a new idea, and with a kind of *fiat*, imitates the omnipotence of its Maker, if I may be allowed so to speak, who called forth into existence all the various scenes of nature? So far from being conscious of this energy in the will, it requires a certain experience as that of which we are possessed, to convince us that such extraordinary effects do ever result from a simple act of volition.

The generality of mankind never find any difficulty in accounting for the more common and familiar operations of nature—such as the descent of heavy bodies, the growth of plants, the generation of animals, or the nourishment of bodies by food; but suppose that, in all these cases, they perceive the very force or energy of the cause, by which it is connected with its effect, and is forever infallible in its operation. They acquire, by long habit, such a turn of mind, that, upon the appearance of the cause, they immediately expect with assurance its usual attendant, and hardly conceive it possible that any other event could result from it. It is only on the discovery of extraordinary phenomena, such as earthquakes, pestilence, and prodigies of any kind, that they find themselves at a loss to assign a proper cause, and to explain the manner in which the effect is produced by it. It is usual for men, in such difficulties, to have recourse to some invisible intelligent principle as the immediate cause of that event which surprises them, and which, they think, cannot be accounted for from the common powers of nature. But philosophers, who carry their scrutiny a little farther, immediately perceive that, even in the most familiar events, the energy of the cause is as unintelligible as in the most unusual, and that we only learn by experience the frequent *conjunction* of objects, without being ever able to comprehend anything like *connection* between them. Here, then, many philosophers think themselves obliged by reason to have recourse, on all occasions, to the same principle, which the vulgar never appeal to but in cases that appear miraculous and supernatural. They acknowledge mind and intelligence to be, not only the ultimate and original cause of all things, but the immediate and sole cause of every event which appears in nature. They pretend that those objects which are commonly denominated *causes*, are in reality nothing but *occasions;* and that the true and direct principle of every effect is not any power or force in nature, but a volition of the Supreme Being, who wills that such particular objects should forever be conjoined with each other. Instead of saying that one billiard ball moves another by a force which it has derived from the author of nature, it is the Deity himself, they say, who, by a particular volition, moves the second ball, being determined to this operation by the impulse of the first ball, in consequence of those general laws which he has laid down to himself in the government of the universe. But philosophers advancing still in their inquiries, discover that, as we are totally ignorant of the power on which depends the mutual operation of bodies, we are no less ignorant of that power on which depends the operation of mind on body, or of body on mind; nor are we able, either from our senses or consciousness, to assign the ultimate principle in one case more than in the other. The same ignorance, therefore, reduces them to the same conclusion. They assert that the Deity is the immediate cause of the union between soul and body; and that they are not the organs of sense, which, being agitated by external objects, produce sensations in the mind; but that it is a particular volition of our omnipotent Maker, which excites such a sensation, in consequence of such a motion in the organ. In like manner, it is not any energy in the will that produces local motion in our members; it is God himself, who is pleased to second our will, in itself impotent, and to command that motion which we erroneously attribute to our own power and efficacy. Nor do philosophers stop at this conclusion. They sometimes extend the same inference to the mind itself, in its internal operations. Our mental vision or conception of ideas is nothing but a revelation made to us by our Maker. When we voluntarily turn our thoughts to any object, and raise up its image in the fancy, it is not the will which creates that idea; it is the universal Creator, who discovers it to the mind, and renders it present to us.

Thus, according to these philosophers, everything is full of God. Not content with the principle, that nothing exists but by his will, that nothing possesses any power but by his concession; they rob nature, and all created beings, of every power, in order to render their dependence on the Deity still more sensible and immediate. They consider not that, by this theory, they diminish, instead of magnifying, the grandeur of those attributes, which they affect so much to celebrate. It argues surely more power in the Deity to delegate a certain degree of power to inferior creatures, than to produce everything by his own immediate volition. It argues more wisdom to contrive at first the fabric of the world with such perfect foresight that, of itself, and by its proper operation, it may serve all the purposes of providence, than if the great Creator were obliged every moment to adjust its parts, and animate by his breath all the wheels of that stupendous machine.

But if we would have a more philosophical confutation of this theory, perhaps the two following reflections may suffice.

First, It seems to me that this theory of the universal energy and operation of the Supreme Being is too bold ever to carry conviction with it to a man, sufficiently apprised of the weakness of human reason, and the narrow limits to which it is confined in all its operations. Though the chain of arguments which conduct to it were ever so logical, there must arise a strong suspicion, if not an absolute assurance, that it has carried us quite beyond the reach of our faculties, when it leads to conclusions so extraordinary, and so remote from common life and experience. We are got into fairy land, long ere we have reached the last steps of our theory; and *there* we have no reason to trust our common methods of argument, or to think that our usual analogies and probabilities have any authority. Our line is too short to fathom such immense abysses. And however we may flatter ourselves that we are guided, in every step which we take, by a kind of verisimilitude and experience, we may be assured that this fancied experience has no authority when we thus apply it to subjects that lie entirely out of the sphere of experience. But on this we shall have occasion to touch afterwards.

Secondly, I cannot perceive any force in the arguments on which this theory is founded. We are ignorant, it is true, of the manner in which bodies operate on each other: their force or energy is entirely incomprehensible: but are we not equally ignorant of the manner or force by which a mind, even the Supreme Mind, operates either on itself or on body? Whence, I beseech you, do we acquire any idea of it? We have no sentiment or consciousness of this power in ourselves. We have no idea of the Supreme Being but what we learn from reflection on our own faculties. Were our ignorance, therefore, a good reason for rejecting anything, we should be led into that principle of denying all energy in the Supreme Being as much as in the grossest matter. We surely comprehend as little the operations of one as of the other. Is it more difficult to conceive that motion may arise from impulse than that it may arise from volition? All we know is our profound ignorance in both cases.

PART II

But to hasten to a conclusion of this argument, which is already drawn out to too great a length: we have sought in vain for an idea of power or necessary connection in all the sources from which we could suppose it to be derived. It appears that, in single instances of the operation of bodies, we never can, by our utmost scrutiny, discover anything but one event following another, without being able to comprehend any force or power by which the cause operates, or any connection between it and its supposed effect. The same difficulty occurs in contemplating the operations of mind on body—where we observe the motion of the latter to follow upon the volition of the former, but are not able to observe or conceive the tie which binds together the motion and volition, or the energy by which the mind produces this effect. The authority of the will over its own faculties and ideas is not a whit more comprehensible: so that, upon the whole, there appears not, throughout all nature, any one instance of connection which is conceivable by us. All events seem entirely loose and separate. One event follows another; but we never can observe any tie between them. They seem *conjoined*, but never *connected*. And as we can have no idea of anything which never appeared to our outward sense or inward sentiment, the necessary conclusion *seems* to be that we have no idea of connection or power at all, and that these words are absolutely without any meaning, when employed either in philosophical reasonings or common life.

But there still remains one method of avoiding this conclusion, and one source which we have not yet examined. When any natural object or event is presented, it is impossible for us, by any sagacity or penetration, to discover, or even conjecture, without experience, what event will result from it, or to carry our foresight beyond that object which is immediately present to the memory and senses. Even after one instance or experiment where we have observed a particular event to follow upon another, we are not entitled to form a general rule, or foretell what will happen in like cases; it being justly esteemed an unpardonable temerity to judge of the whole course of nature from one single experiment, however accurate or certain. But when one particular species of event has always, in all instances, been conjoined with another, we make no longer any scruple of foretelling one upon the appearance of the other, and of employing that reasoning which can alone assure us of any matter of fact or existence. We then call the one object, *cause;* the other, *effect*. We suppose that there is some connection between them; some power in the one, by which it infallibly produces the other, and operates with the greatest certainty and strongest necessity.

It appears, then, that this idea of a necessary connection among events arises from a number of similar instances which occur of the constant conjunction of these events; nor can that idea ever be suggested by any one of these instances, surveyed in all possible lights and positions. But there is nothing in a number of instances, different from every single instance, which is supposed to be exactly similar; except only, that after a repetition of similar instances, the mind is carried by habit, upon the appearance of one event, to expect its usual attendant, and to believe that it will exist. This connection, therefore, which we *feel* in the mind, this customary transition of the imagination from one object to its usual attendant, is the sentiment or impression from which we form the idea of power or necessary connection. Nothing farther is in the case. Contemplate the subject on all sides; you will never find any other origin of that idea. This is the sole difference between one instance, from which we can never receive the idea of connection, and a number of similar instances, by which it is suggested. The first time a man saw the communication of motion by impulse, as by the shock of two billiard balls, he could not pronounce that the one event was *connected;* but only that it was *conjoined* with the other. After he has observed several instances of this nature, he then pronounces them to be *connected.* What alteration has happened to give rise to this new idea of *connection?* Nothing but that he now *feels* these events to be *connected* in his imagination, and can readily foretell the existence of one from the appearance of the other. When we say, therefore, that one object is connected with another, we mean only that they have acquired a connection in our thought, and give rise to this inference, by which they become proofs of each other's existence: a conclusion which is somewhat extraordinary, but which seems founded on sufficient evidence. Nor will its evidence be weakened by any general diffidence of the understanding, or sceptical suspicion concerning every conclusion which is new and extraordinary. No conclusions can be more agreeable to scepticism than such as make discoveries concerning the weakness and narrow limits of human reason and capacity.

And what stronger instance can be produced of the surprising ignorance and weakness of the understanding than the present? For surely, if there be any relation among objects which it imports to us to know perfectly, it is that of cause and effect. On this are founded all our reasonings concerning matter of fact or existence. By means of it alone we attain any assurance concerning objects which are removed from the present testimony of our memory and senses. The only immediate utility of all sciences, is to teach us, how to control and regulate future events by their causes. Our thoughts and inquiries are, therefore, every moment, employed about this relation: yet so imperfect are the ideas which we form concerning it, that it is impossible to give any just definition of cause, except what is drawn from something extraneous and foreign to it. Similar objects are always conjoined with similar. Of this we have experience. Suitably to this experience, therefore, we may define a cause to be *an object, followed by another, and where all the objects similar to the first are followed by objects similar to the second*. Or in other words *where, if the first object had not been, the second never had existed*. The appearance of a cause always conveys the mind, by a customary transition, to the idea of the effect. Of this also we have experience. We may, therefore, suitably to this experience, form another definition of cause, and call it, *an object followed by another, and whose appearance always conveys the thought to that other*. But though both these definitions be drawn from circumstances foreign to the cause, we cannot remedy this inconvenience, or attain any more perfect definition, which may point out that circumstances in the cause, which gives it a connection with its effect. We have no idea of this connection, nor even any distinct notion what it is we desire to know, when we endeavor at a conception of it. We say, for instance, that the vibration of this string is the cause of this particular sound. But what do we mean by that affirmation? We either mean *that this vibration is followed by this sound, and that all similar vibrations have been followed by similar sounds*: Or, *that this vibration is followed by this sound, and that upon the appearance of one the mind anticipates the senses, and forms immediately an idea of the other.* We may consider the relation of cause and effect in either of these two lights; but beyond these, we have no idea of it.

To recapitulate, therefore, the reasonings of this section: every idea is copied from some preceding impression or sentiment; and where we cannot find any impression, we may be certain that there is no idea. In all single instances of the operation of bodies or minds, there is nothing that produces any impression, nor consequently can suggest any idea of power or necessary connection. But when many uniform instances appear, and the same object is always followed by the same event; we then begin to entertain the notion of cause and connection. We then feel a new sentiment or impression, to wit, a customary connection in the thought or imagination between one object and its usual attendant; and this sentiment is the original of that idea which we seek for. For as this idea arises from a number of similar instances, and not from any single instance, it must arise from that circumstance, in which the number of instances differ from every individual instance. But this customary connection or transition of the imagination is the only circumstance in which they differ. In every other particular they are alike. The first instance which we saw of motion communicated by the shock of two billiard balls (to return to this obvious illustration) is exactly similar to any instance that may, at present, occur to us; except only, that we could not, at first, *infer* one event from the other; which we are enabled to do at present, after so long a course of uniform experience. I know not whether the reader will readily apprehend this reasoning. I am afraid that, should I multiply words about it, or throw it into a greater variety of lights, it would only become more obscure and intricate. In all abstract reasonings there is one point of view which, if we can happily hit, we shall go farther towards illustrating the subject than by all the eloquence in the world. This point of view we should endeavor to reach, and reserve the flowers of rhetoric for subjects which are more adapted to them.

SECTION VIII

Of Liberty and Necessity

PART I

It might reasonably be expected in questions which have been canvassed and disputed with great eagerness, since the first origin of science and philosophy, that the meaning of all the terms, at least, should have been agreed upon among the disputants; and our inquiries, in the course of two thousand years, been able to pass from words to the true and real subject of the controversy. For how easy may it seem to give exact definitions of the terms employed in reasoning, and make these definitions, not the mere sound of words, the object of future scrutiny and examination? But if we consider the matter more narrowly, we shall be apt to draw a quite opposite conclusion. From this circumstance alone, that a controversy has been long kept on foot, and remains still undecided, we may presume that there is some ambiguity in the expression, and that the disputants affix different ideas to the terms employed in the controversy. For as the faculties of the mind are supposed to be naturally alike in every individual; otherwise nothing could be more fruitless than to reason or dispute together; it were impossible, if men affix the same ideas to their terms, that they could so long form different opinions of the same subject; especially when they communicate their views, and each party turn themselves on all sides, in search of arguments which may give them the victory over their antagonists. It is true, if men attempt the discussion of questions which lie entirely beyond the reach of human capacity, such as those concerning the origin of worlds, or the economy of the intellectual system or region of spirits, they may long beat the air in their fruitless contests, and never arrive at any determinate conclusion. But if the question regard any subject of common life and experience, nothing, one would think, could preserve the dispute so long undecided but some ambiguous expressions, which keep the antagonists still at a distance, and hinder them from grappling with each other.

This has been the case in the long disputed question concerning liberty and necessity; and to so remarkable a degree that, if I be not much mistaken, we shall find, that all mankind, both learned and ignorant, have always been of the same opinion with regard to this subject, and that a few intelligible definitions would immediately have put an end to the whole controversy. I own that this dispute has been so much canvassed on all hands, and has led philosophers into such a labyrinth of obscure sophistry, that it is no wonder, if a sensible reader indulge his ease so far as to turn a deaf ear to the proposal of such a question, from which he can expect neither instruction nor entertainment. But the state of the argument here proposed may, perhaps, serve to renew his attention; as it has more novelty, promises at least some decision of the controversy, and will not much disturb his ease by any intricate or obscure reasoning.

I hope, therefore, to make it appear that all men have ever agreed in the doctrine both of necessity and of liberty, according to any reasonable sense, which can be put on these terms; and that the whole controversy has hitherto turned merely upon words. We shall begin with examining the doctrine of necessity.

It is universally allowed that matter, in all its operations, is actuated by a necessary force, and that every natural effect is so precisely determined by the energy of its cause that no other effect, in such particular circumstances, could possibly have resulted from it. The degree and direction of every motion is, by the laws of nature, prescribed with such exactness that a living creature may as soon arise from the shock of two bodies as motion in any other degree or direction than what is actually produced by it. Would we, therefore, form a just and precise idea of *necessity*, we must consider whence that idea arises when we apply it to the operation of bodies.

It seems evident that, if all the scenes of nature were continually shifted in such a manner that no two events bore any resemblance to each other, but every object was entirely new, without any similitude to whatever had been seen before, we should never, in that case, have attained the least idea of necessity, or of a connection among these objects. We might say, upon such a supposition, that one object or event has followed another; not that one was produced by the other. The relation of cause and effect must be utterly unknown to mankind. Inference and reasoning concerning the operations of nature would, from that moment, be at an end; and the memory and senses remain the only canals, by which the knowledge of any real existence could possibly have access to the mind. Our idea, therefore, of necessity and causation arises entirely from the uniformity observable in the operations of nature, where similar objects are constantly conjoined together, and the mind is determined by custom to infer the one from the appearance of the other. These two circumstances form the whole of that necessity, which we ascribe to matter. Beyond the constant *conjunction* of similar objects, and the consequent *inference* from one to the other, we have no notion of any necessity or connection.

If it appear, therefore, that all mankind have ever allowed, without any doubt or hesitation, that these two circumstances take place in the voluntary actions of men, and in the operations of mind; it must follow, that all mankind have ever agreed in the doctrine of necessity, and that they have hitherto disputed, merely for not understanding each other.

As to the first circumstance, the constant and regular conjunction of similar events, we may possibly satisfy ourselves by the following considerations. It is universally acknowledged that there is a great uniformity among the actions of men, in all nations and ages, and that human nature remains still the same, in its principles and operations. The same motives always produce the same actions; the same events follow from the same causes. Ambition, avarice, self-love, vanity, friendship, generosity, public spirit: these passions, mixed in various degrees, and distributed through society, have been, from the beginning of the world, and still are, the source of all the actions and enterprises, which have ever been observed among mankind. Would you know the sentiments, inclinations, and course of life of the Greeks and Romans. Study well the temper and actions of the French and English: you cannot be much mistaken in transferring to the former *most* of the observations which you have made with regard to the latter. Mankind are so much the same, in all times and places, that history informs us of nothing new or strange in this particular. Its chief use is only to discover the constant and universal principles of human nature, by showing men in all varieties of circumstances and situations, and furnishing us with materials from which we may form our observations and become acquainted with the regular springs of human action and behavior. These records of wars, intrigues, factions, and revolutions, are so many collections of experiments, by which the politician or moral philosopher fixes the principles of his science, in the same manner as the physician or natural philosopher becomes acquainted with the nature of plants, minerals, and other external objects, by the experiments which he forms concerning them. Nor are the earth, water, and other elements, examined by Aristotle, and Hippocrates, more like to those which at present lie under our observation than the men described by Polybius and Tacitus are to those who now govern the world.

Should a traveler, returning from a far country, bring us an account of men, wholly different from any with whom we were ever acquainted; men, who were entirely divested of avarice, ambition, or revenge; who knew no pleasure but friendship, generosity, and public spirit; we should immediately, from these circumstances, detect the falsehood, and prove him a liar, with the same certainty as if he had stuffed his narration with stories of centaurs and dragons, miracles and prodigies. And if we would explode any forgery in history, we cannot make us of a more convincing argument, than to prove, that the actions ascribed to any person are directly contrary to the course of nature, and that no human motives, in such circumstances, could ever induce him to such a conduct. The veracity of Quintus Curtius is as much to be suspected, when he describes the supernatural courage of Alexander, by which he was hurried on singly to attack multitudes, as when he describes his supernatural force and activity, by which he was able to resist them. So readily and universally do we acknowledge a uniformity in human motives and actions as well as in the operations of body.

Hence likewise the benefit of that experience, acquired by long life and a variety of business and company, in order to instruct us in the principles of human nature, and regulate our future conduct, as well as speculation. By means of this guide, we mount up to the knowledge of men's inclinations and motives, from their actions, expressions, and even gestures; and again descend to the interpretation of their actions from our knowledge of their motives and inclinations. The general observations treasured up by a course of experience, give us the clue of human nature, and teach us to unravel all its intricacies. Pretexts and appearances no longer deceive us. Public declarations pass for the specious coloring of a cause. And though virtue and honor be allowed their proper weight and authority, that perfect disinterestedness, so often pretended to, is never expected in multitudes and parties; seldom in their leaders; and scarcely even in individuals of any rank or station. But were there no uniformity in human actions, and were every experiment which we could form of this kind irregular and anomalous, it were impossible to collect any general observations concerning mankind; and no experience, however accurately digested by reflection, would ever serve to any purpose. Why is the aged husbandman more skillful in his calling than the young beginner but because there is a certain uniformity in the operation of the sun, rain, and earth towards the production of vegetables; and experience teaches the old practitioner the rules by which this operation is governed and directed.

We must not, however, expect that this uniformity of human actions should be carried to such a length as that all men, in the same circumstances, will always act precisely in the same manner, without making any allowance for the diversity of characters, prejudices, and opinions. Such a uniformity in every particular, is found in no part of nature. On the contrary, from observing the variety of conduct in different men, we are enabled to form a greater variety of maxims, which still suppose a degree of uniformity and regularity.

Are the manners of men different in different ages and countries? We learn thence the great force of custom and education, which mold the human mind from its infancy and form it into a fixed and established character. Is the behavior and conduct of the one sex very unlike that of the other? Is it thence we become acquainted with the different characters which nature has impressed upon the sexes, and which she preserves with constancy and regularity? Are the actions of the same person much diversified in the different periods of his life, from infancy to old age? This affords room for many general observations concerning the gradual change of our sentiments and inclinations, and the different maxims which prevail in the different ages of human creatures. Even the characters, which are peculiar to each individual, have a uniformity in their influence; otherwise our acquaintance with the persons and our observation of their conduct could never teach us their dispositions, or serve to direct our behavior with regard to them.

I grant it possible to find some actions, which seem to have no regular connection with any known motives, and are exceptions to all the measures of conduct which have ever been established for the government of men. But if we would willingly know what judgment should be formed of such irregular and extraordinary actions, we may consider the sentiments commonly entertained with regard to those irregular events which appear in the course of nature, and the operations of external objects. All causes are not conjoined to their usual effects with like uniformity. An artificer, who handles only dead matter, may be disappointed of his aim, as well as the politician, who directs the conduct of sensible and intelligent agents.

The vulgar, who take things according to their first appearance, attribute the uncertainty of events to such an uncertainty in the causes as makes the latter often fail of their usual influence; though they meet with no impediment in their operation. But philosophers, observing that, almost in every part of nature, there is contained a vast variety of springs and principles, which are hid, by reason of their minuteness or remoteness, find, that it is at least possible the contrariety of events may not proceed from any contingency in the cause, but from the secret operation of contrary causes. This possibility is converted into certainty by farther observation, when they remark that, upon an exact scrutiny, a contrariety of effects always betrays a contrariety of causes, and proceeds from their mutual opposition. A peasant can give no better reason for the stopping of any clock or watch than to say that it does not commonly go right: but an artist easily perceives that the same force in the spring or pendulum has always the same influence on the wheels; but fails of its usual effect, perhaps by reason of a grain of dust, which puts a stop to the whole movement. From the observation of several parallel instances, philosophers form a maxim that the connection between all causes and effects is equally necessary, and that its seeming uncertainty in some instances proceeds from the secret opposition of contrary causes.

Thus, for instance, in the human body, when the usual symptoms of health or sickness disappoint our expectation; when medicines operate not with their wonted powers; when irregular events follow from any particular cause; the philosopher and physician are not surprised at the matter, nor are ever tempted to deny, in general, the necessity and uniformity of those principles by which the animal economy is conducted. They know that a human body is a mighty complicated machine; that many secret powers lurk in it, which are altogether beyond our comprehension; that to us it must often appear very uncertain in its operations; and that therefore the irregular events, which outwardly discover themselves, can be no proof that the laws of nature are not observed with the greatest regularity in its internal operations and government.

The philosopher, if he be consistent, must apply the same reasoning to the actions and volitions of intelligent agents. The most irregular and unexpected resolutions of men may frequently be accounted for by those who know every particular circumstance of their character and situation. A person of an obliging disposition gives a peevish answer; but he has the toothache, or has not dined. A stupid fellow discovers an uncommon alacrity in his carriage; but he has met with a sudden piece of good fortune. Or even when an action, as something happens, cannot be particularly accounted for, either by the person himself or by others; we know, in general, that the characters of men are, to a certain degree, inconstant and irregular. This is, in a manner, the constant character of human nature; though it be applicable, in a more particular manner, to some persons who have no fixed rule for their conduct, but proceed in a continued course of caprice and inconstancy. The internal principles and motives may operate in a uniform manner, notwithstanding these seeming irregularities; in the same manner as the winds, rain, clouds, and other variations of the weather are supposed to be governed by steady principles; though not easily discoverable by human sagacity and inquiry.

Thus it appears, not only that the conjunction between motives and voluntary actions is as regular and uniform as that between the cause and effect in any part of nature; but also that this regular conjunction has been universally acknowledged among mankind, and has never been the subject of dispute, either in philosophy or common life. Now, as it is from past experience that we draw all inferences concerning the future, and as we conclude that objects will always be conjoined together which we find to have always been conjoined; it may seem superfluous to prove that this experienced uniformity in human actions is a source whence we draw *inferences* concerning them. But in order to throw the argument into a greater variety of lights we shall also insist, though briefly, on this latter topic.

The mutual dependence of men is so great in all societies that scarce any human action is entirely complete in itself, or is performed without some reference to the actions of others, which are requisite to make it answer fully the intention of the agent. The poorest artificer, who labors alone, expects at least the protection of the magistrate, to ensure him the enjoyment of the fruits of his labor. He also expects that, when he carries his goods to market, and offers them at a reasonable price, he shall find purchasers, and shall be able, by the money he acquires, to engage others to supply him with those commodities which are requisite for his subsistence. In proportion as men extend their dealings, and render their intercourse with others more complicated, they always comprehend, in their schemes of life, a greater variety of voluntary actions, which they expect, from the proper motives, to co-operate with their own. In all these conclusions they take their measures from past experience, in the same manner as in their reasonings concerning external objects; and firmly believe that men, as well as all the elements, are to continue, in their operations, the same that they have ever found them. A manufacturer reckons upon the labor of his servants for the execution of any work as much as upon the tools which he employs, and would be equally surprised were his expectations disappointed. In short, this experimental inference and reasoning concerning the actions of others enters so much into human life, that no man, while awake, is ever a moment without employing it. Have we not reason, therefore, to affirm that all mankind have always agreed in the doctrine of necessity according to the foregoing definition and explication of it?

Nor have philosophers ever entertained a different opinion from the people in this particular. For, not to mention that almost every action of their life supposes that opinion, there are even few of the speculative parts of learning to which it is not essential. What would become of *history*, had we not a dependence on the veracity of the historian according to the experience which we have had of mankind? How could *politics* be a science, if laws and forms of government had not a uniform influence upon society? Where would be the foundation of *morals*, if particular characters had no certain or determinate power to produce particular sentiments, and if these sentiments had no constant operation on actions? And with what pretense could we employ our *criticism* upon any poet or polite author, if we could not pronounce the conduct and sentiments of his actors either natural or unnatural to such characters, and in such circumstances? It seems almost impossible, therefore, to engage either in science or action of any kind without acknowledging the doctrine of necessity, and this *inference* from motive to voluntary actions, from characters to conduct.

And indeed, when we consider how aptly *natural* and *moral* evidence link together, and form only one chain of argument, we shall make no scruple to allow that they are of the same nature, and derived from the same principles. A prisoner who has neither money nor interest, discovers the impossibility of his escape, as well when he considers the obstinacy of the gaoler, as the walls and bars with which he is surrounded; and, in all attempts for his freedom, chooses rather to work upon the stone and iron of the one, than upon the inflexible nature of the other. The same prisoner, when conducted to the scaffold, foresees his death as certainly from the constancy and fidelity of his guards, as from the operation of the axe or wheel. His mind runs along a certain train of ideas: the refusal of the soldiers to consent to his escape; the action of the executioner; the separation of the head and body; bleeding, convulsive motions, and death. Here is a connected chain of natural causes and voluntary actions; but the mind feels no difference between them in passing from one link to another. Nor is less certain of the future event than if it were connected with the objects present to the memory or senses, by a train of causes, cemented together by what we are pleased to call a *physical* necessity. The same experienced union has the same effect on the mind, whether the united objects be motives, volition, and actions; or figure and motion. We may change the name of things; but their nature and their operation on the understanding never change.

Were a man, whom I know to be honest and opulent, and with whom I live in intimate friendship, to come into my house, where I am surrounded with my servants, I rest assured that he is not to stab me before he leaves it in order to rob me of my silver standish; and I no more suspect this event than the falling of the house itself, which is new, and solidly built and founded.—*But he may have been seized with a sudden and unknown frenzy.*—So may a sudden earthquake arise, and shake and tumble my house about my ears. I shall therefore change the suppositions. I shall say that I know with certainty that he is not to put his hand into the fire and hold it there till it be consumed: and this event, I think I can foretell with the same assurance, as that, if he throw himself out at the window, and meet with no obstruction, he will not remain a moment suspended in the air. No suspicion of an unknown frenzy can give the least possibility to the former event, which is so contrary to all the known principles of human nature. A man who at noon leaves his purse full of gold on the pavement at Charing Cross, may as well expect that it will fly away like a feather, as that he will find it untouched an hour after. Above one half of human reasonings contain inferences of a similar nature, attended with more or less degrees of certainty proportioned to our experience of the usual conduct of mankind in such particular situations.

I have frequently considered, what could possibly be the reason why all mankind, though they have ever, without hesitation, acknowledged the doctrine of necessity in their whole practice and reasoning, have yet discovered such a reluctance to acknowledge it in words, and have rather shown a propensity, in all ages, to profess the contrary opinion. The matter, I think, may be accounted for after the following manner. If we examine the operations of body, and the production of effects from their causes, we shall find that all our faculties can never carry us farther in our knowledge of this relation than barely to observe that particular objects are *constantly conjoined* together, and that the mind is carried, by a *customary transition*, from the appearance of one to the belief of the other. But though this conclusion concerning human ignorance be the result of the strictest scrutiny of this subject, men still entertain a strong propensity to believe that they penetrate farther into the powers of nature, and perceive something like a necessary connection between the cause and the effect. When again they turn their reflections towards the operations of their own minds, and *feel* no such connection of the motive and the action; they are thence apt to suppose, that there is a difference between the effects which result from material force, and those which arise from thought and intelligence. But being once convinced that we know nothing farther of causation of any kind than merely the *constant conjunction* of objects, and the consequent *inference* of the mind from one to another, and finding that these two circumstances are universally allowed to have place in voluntary actions; we may be more easily led to own the same necessity common to all causes. And though this reasoning may contradict the systems of many philosophers, in ascribing necessity to the determinations of the will, we shall find, upon reflection, that they dissent from it in words only, not in their real sentiment. Necessity, according to the sense in which it is here taken, has never yet been rejected, nor can ever, I think, be rejected by any philosopher. It may only, perhaps, be pretended that the mind can perceive, in the operations of matter, some farther connection between the cause and effect; and connection that has not place in voluntary actions of intelligent beings. Now whether it be so or not, can only appear upon examination; and it is incumbent on these philosophers to make good their assertion, by defining or describing that necessity, and pointing it out to us in the operations of material causes.

It would seem, indeed, that men begin at the wrong end of this question concerning liberty and necessity, when they enter upon it by examining the faculties of the soul, the influence of the understanding, and the operations of the will. Let them first discuss a more simple question, namely, the operations of body and of brute unintelligent matter; and try whether they can there form any idea of causation and necessity, except that of a constant conjunction of objects, and subsequent inference of the mind from one to another. If these circumstances form, in reality, the whole of that necessity, which we conceive in matter, and if these circumstances be also universally acknowledged to take place in the operations of the mind, the dispute is at an end; at least, must be owned to be thenceforth merely verbal. But as long as we will rashly suppose, that we have some farther idea of necessity and causation in the operations of external objects; at the same time, that we can find nothing farther in the voluntary actions of the mind; there is no possibility of bringing the question to any determinate issue, while we proceed upon so erroneous a supposition. The only method of undeceiving us is to mount up higher; to examine the narrow extent of science when applied to material causes; and to convince ourselves that all we know of them is the constant conjunction and inference above mentioned. We may, perhaps, find that it is with difficulty we are induced to fix such narrow limits to human understanding: but we can afterwards find no difficulty when we come to apply this doctrine to the actions of the will. For as it is evident that these have a regular conjunction with motives and circumstances and characters, and as we always draw inferences from one to the other, we must be obliged to acknowledge in words that necessity, which we have already avowed, in every deliberation of our lives, and in every step of our conduct and behavior.

But to proceed in this reconciling project with regard to the question of liberty and necessity; the most contentious question of metaphysics, the most contentious science; it will not require many words to prove, that all mankind have ever agreed in the doctrine of liberty as well as in that of necessity, and that the whole dispute, in this respect also, has been hitherto merely verbal. For what is meant by liberty, when applied to voluntary actions? We cannot surely mean that actions have so little connection with motives, inclinations, and circumstances, that one does not follow with a certain degree of uniformity from the other, and that one affords no inference by which we can conclude the existence of the other. For these are plain and acknowledged matters of fact. By liberty, then, we can only mean *a power of acting or not acting, according to the determinations of the will;* that is, if we choose to remain at rest, we may; if we choose to move, we also may. Now this hypothetical liberty is universally allowed to belong to everyone who is not a prisoner and in chains. Here, then, is no subject of dispute.

Whatever definition we may give of liberty, we should be careful to observe two requisite circumstances; *first*, that it be consistent with plain matter of fact; *secondly*, that it be consistent with itself. If we observe these circumstances, and render our definition intelligible, I am persuaded that all mankind will be found of one opinion with regard to it.

It is universally allowed that nothing exists without a cause of its existence, and that chance, when strictly examined, is a mere negative word, and means not any real power which has anywhere a being in nature. But it is pretended that some causes are necessary, some not necessary. Here then is the advantage of definitions. Let anyone *define* a cause, without comprehending, as a part of the definition, a *necessary connection* with its effect; and let him show distinctly the origin of the idea, expressed by the definition; and I shall readily give up the whole controversy. But if the foregoing explication of the matter be received, this must be absolutely impracticable. Had not objects a regular conjunction with each other, we should never have entertained any notion of cause and effect; and this regular conjunction produces that inference of the understanding, which is the only connection, that we can have any comprehension of. Whoever attempts a definition of cause, exclusive of these circumstances, will be obliged either to employ unintelligible terms or such as are synonymous to the term which he endeavors to define. And if the definition above mentioned be admitted; liberty, when opposed to necessity, not to constraint, is the same thing with chance; which is universally allowed to have no existence.

PART II

There is no method of reasoning more common, and yet none more blamable, than, in philosophical disputes, to endeavor the refutation of any hypothesis, by a pretense of its dangerous consequences to religion and morality. When any opinion leads to absurdities, it is certainly false; but it is not certain that an opinion is false, because it is of dangerous consequence. Such topics, therefore, ought entirely to be forborne; as serving nothing to the discovery of truth, but only to make the person of an antagonist odious. This I observe in general, without pretending to draw any advantage from it. I frankly submit to an examination of this kind, and shall venture to affirm that the doctrines, both of necessity and of liberty, as above explained, are not only consistent with morality, but are absolutely essential to its support.

Necessity may be defined two ways, conformably to the two definitions of *cause*, of which it makes an essential part. It consists either in the constant conjunction of like objects, or in the inference of the understanding from one object to another. Now necessity, in both these senses (which, indeed, are at bottom the same), has universally, though tacitly, in the schools, in the pulpit, and in common life, been allowed to belong to the will of man; and no one has ever pretended to deny that we can draw inferences concerning human actions, and that those inferences are founded on the experienced union of like actions, with like motives, inclinations, and circumstances. The only particular in which anyone can differ, is, that either, perhaps, he will refuse to give the name of necessity to this property of human actions: but as long as the meaning is understood, I hope the word can do no harm; or that he will maintain it possible to discover something farther in the operations of matter. But this, it must be acknowledged, can be of no consequence to morality or religion, whatever it may be to natural philosophy or metaphysics. We may here be mistaken in asserting that there is no idea of any other necessity or connection in the actions of body; but surely we ascribe nothing to the actions of the mind, but what everyone does, and must readily allow of. We change no circumstance in the received orthodox system with regard to the will, but only in that with regard to material objects and causes. Nothing, therefore, can be more innocent, at least, than this doctrine.

All laws being founded on rewards and punishments, it is supposed as a fundamental principle, that these motives have a regular and uniform influence on the mind, and both produce the good and prevent the evil actions. We may give to this influence what name we please; but, as it is usually conjoined with the action, it must be esteemed a *cause*, and be looked upon as an instance of that necessity, which we would here establish.

The only proper object of hatred or vengeance is a person or creature, endowed with thought and consciousness; and when any criminal or injurious actions excite that passion, it is only by their relation to the person, or connection with him. Actions are, by their very nature, temporary and perishing; and where they proceed not from some *cause* in the character and disposition of the person who performed them, they can neither redound to his honor, if good; nor infamy, if evil. The actions themselves may be blamable; they may be contrary to all the rules of morality and religion. But the person is not answerable for them; and as they proceeded from nothing in him that is durable and constant, and leave nothing of that nature behind them, it is impossible he can, upon their account, become the object of punishment or vengeance. According to the principle, therefore, which denies necessity, and consequently causes, a man is as pure and untainted, after having committed the most horrid crime, as at the first moment of his birth, nor is his character anywise concerned in his actions, since they are not derived from it, and the wickedness of the one can never be used as a proof of the depravity of the other.

Men are not blamed for such actions as they perform ignorantly and casually, whatever may be the consequences. Why? but because the principles of these actions are only momentary, and terminate in them alone. Men are less blamed for such actions as they perform hastily and unpremeditately than for such as proceed from deliberation. For what reason? but because a hasty temper, though a constant cause or principle in the mind, operates only by intervals, and infects not the whole character. Again, repentance wipes off every crime, if attended with a reformation of life and manners. How is this to be accounted for? but by asserting that actions render a person criminal merely as they are proofs of criminal principles in the mind; and when, by an alteration of these principles, they cease to be just proofs, they likewise cease to be criminal. But, except upon the doctrine of necessity, they never were just proofs, and consequently never were criminal.

It will be equally easy to prove, and from the same arguments, that *liberty*, according to that definition above mentioned, in which all men agree, is also essential to morality, and that no human actions, where it is wanting, are susceptible of any moral qualities, or can be the objects either of approbation or dislike. For as actions are objects of our moral sentiment, so far only as they are indications of the internal character, passions, and affections; it is impossible that they can give rise either to praise or blame, where they proceed not from these principles, but are derived altogether from external violence.

I pretend not to have obviated or removed all objections to this theory, with regard to necessity and liberty. I can foresee other objections, derived from topics which have not here been treated of. It may be said, for instance, that, if voluntary actions be subjected to the same laws of necessity with the operations of matter, there is a continued chain of necessary causes, pre-ordained and pre-determined, reaching from the original cause of all to every single volition of every human creature. No contingency anywhere in the universe; no indifference; no liberty. While we act, we are, at the same time, acted upon. The ultimate Author of all our volitions is the Creator of the world, who first bestowed motion on this immense machine, and placed all beings in that particular position, whence every subsequent event, by an inevitable necessity, must result. Human actions, therefore, either can have no moral turpitude at all, as proceeding from so good a cause; or if they have any turpitude, they must involve our Creator in the same guilt, while he is acknowledged to be their ultimate cause and author. For as a man, who fired a mine, is answerable for all the consequences whether the train he employed be long or short; so wherever a continued chain of necessary causes is fixed, that Being, either finite or infinite, who produces the first, is likewise the author of all the rest, and must both bear the blame and acquire the praise which belong to them. Our clear and unalterable ideas of morality establish this rule, upon unquestionable reasons, when we examine the consequences of any human action; and these reasons must still have greater force when applied to the volitions and intentions of a Being infinitely wise and powerful. Ignorance or impotence may be pleaded for so limited a creature as man; but these imperfections have no place in our Creator. He foresaw, he ordained, he intended all those actions of men, which we so rashly pronounce criminal. And we must therefore conclude, either that they are not criminal, or that the Deity, not man, is accountable for them. But as either of these positions is absurd and impious, it follows, that the doctrine from which they are deduced cannot possibly be true, as being liable to all the same objections. An absurd consequence, if necessary, proves the original doctrine to be absurd in the same manner as criminal actions render criminal the original cause, if the connection between them be necessary and inevitable.

This objection consists of two parts, which we shall examine separately. *First,* that, if human actions can be traced up, by a necessary chain, to the Deity, they can never be criminal; on account of the infinite perfection of that Being from whom they are derived, and who can intend nothing but what is altogether good and laudable. Or, *Secondly,* if they be criminal, we must retract the attribute of perfection, which we ascribe to the Deity, and must acknowledge him to be the ultimate author of guilt and moral turpitude in all his creatures.

The answer to the first objection seems obvious and convincing. There are many philosophers who, after an exact scrutiny of all the phenomena of nature, conclude, that the *whole,* considered as one system, is, in every period of its existence, ordered with perfect benevolence; and that the utmost possible happiness will, in the end, result to all created beings, without any mixture of positive or absolute ill or misery. Every physical ill, say they, makes an essential part of this benevolent system, and could not possibly be removed, even by the Deity himself, considered as a wise agent, without giving entrance to greater ill, or excluding greater good, which will result from it. From this theory, some philosophers, and the ancient Stoics among the rest, derived a topic of consolation under all afflictions, while they taught their pupils that those ills under which they labored were, in reality, goods to the universe; and that to an enlarged view, which could comprehend the whole system of nature, every event became an object of joy and exultation. But though this topic be specious and sublime, it was soon found in practice weak and ineffectual. You would surely more irritate than appease a man lying under the racking pains of the gout by preaching up to him the rectitude of those general laws, which produced the malignant humors in his body, and led them through the proper canals, to the sinews and nerves, where they now excite such acute torments. These enlarged views may, for a moment, please the imagination of a speculative man, who is placed in ease and security; but neither can they dwell with constancy on his mind, even though undisturbed by the emotions of pain or passion; much less can they maintain their ground when attacked by such powerful antagonists. The affections take a narrower and more natural survey of their object; and by an economy, more suitable to the infirmity of human minds, regard alone the beings around us, and are actuated by such events as appear good or ill to the private system.

The case is the same with *moral* as with *physical* ill. It cannot reasonably be supposed, that those remote considerations, which are found of so little efficacy with regard to one, will have a more powerful influence with regard to the other. The mind of man is so formed by nature that, upon the appearance of certain characters, dispositions, and actions, it immediately feels the sentiment of approbation or blame; nor are there any emotions more essential to its frame and constitution. The characters which engage our approbation are chiefly such as contribute to the peace and security of human society; as the characters which excite blame are chiefly such as tend to public detriment and disturbance: whence it may reasonably be presumed, that the moral sentiments arise, either mediately or immediately, from a reflection of these opposite interests. What though philosophical meditations establish a different opinion or conjecture; that everything is right with regard to the *whole*, and that the qualities, which disturb society, are, in the main, as beneficial, and are as suitable to the primary intention of nature as those which more directly promote its happiness and welfare? Are such remote and uncertain speculations able to counterbalance the sentiments which arise from the natural and immediate view of the objects? A man who is robbed of a considerable sum; does he find his vexation for the loss anywise diminished by these sublime reflections? Why then should his moral resentment against the crime be supposed incompatible with them? Or why should not the acknowledgment of a real distinction between vice and virtue be reconcilable to all speculative systems of philosophy, as well as that of a real distinction between personal beauty and deformity? Both these distinctions are founded in the natural sentiments of the human mind; and these sentiments are not to be controlled or altered by any philosophical theory or speculation whatsoever.

The *second* objection admits not of so easy and satisfactory an answer; nor is it possible to explain distinctly, how the Deity can be the mediate cause of all the actions of men, without being the author of sin and moral turpitude. These are mysteries, which mere natural and unassisted reason is very unfit to handle; and whatever system she embraces, she must find herself involved in inextricable difficulties, and even contradictions, at every step which she takes with regard to such subjects. To reconcile the indifference and contingency of human actions with prescience; or to defend absolute decrees, and yet free the Deity from being the author of sin, has been found hitherto to exceed all the power of philosophy. Happy, if she be thence sensible of her temerity, when she pries into these sublime mysteries; and leaving a scene so full of obscurities and perplexities, return, with suitable modesty, to her true and proper province, the examination of common life; where she will find difficulties enough to employ her inquiries, without launching into so boundless an ocean of doubt, uncertainty, and contradiction!

Immanuel Kant

FROM CRITIQUE OF PURE REASON

Immanuel Kant
[1724–1804]

In the eighty years of his life, Immanuel Kant had never traveled beyond forty miles from his native city of Koenigsberg in Prussia. From his solitary studies as a professor of logic and metaphysics he formulated a system of philosophy which has profoundly revolutionized modern thought. Of his master work, *Critique of Pure Reason* it has been said that he required twelve years to cogitate its principles and only five months to write it. Recondite in the extreme by the very nature of its transcendental ideas and because of the intellectually herculean task of establishing metaphysics as a science, *Critique of Pure Reason* requires the utmost concentration and discipline of mind. The section offered here provides the foundation for the elaborate structure of Kantian thought.

FROM CRITIQUE OF PURE REASON

IMMANUEL KANT

I. Of the Difference Between Pure and Empirical Knowledge

That all our knowledge begins with experience there can be no doubt. For how is it possible that the faculty of cognition should be awakened into exercise otherwise than by means of objects which affect our senses, and partly of themselves produce representations, partly rouse our powers of understanding into activity, to compare, to connect, or to separate these, and so to convert the raw material of our sensuous impressions into a knowledge of objects, which is called experience? In respect of time, therefore, no knowledge of ours is antecedent to experience, but begins with it.

But, though all our knowledge begins with experience, it by no means follows that all arises out of experience. For, on the contrary, it is quite possible that our empirical knowledge is a compound of that which we receive through impressions, and that which the faculty of cognition supplies from itself (sensuous impressions giving merely the *occasion*), an addition which we cannot distinguish from the original element given by sense, till long practice has made us attentive to, and skilful in separating it. It is, therefore, a question which requires close investigation, and is not to be answered at first sight—whether there exists a knowledge altogether independent of experience, and even of all sensuous impressions? Knowledge of this kind is called *a priori*, in contradistinction to empirical knowledge, which has its sources *a posteriori*, that is, in experience.

But the expression, "*a priori*," is not as yet definite enough, adequately to indicate the whole meaning of the question above started. For, in speaking of knowledge which has its sources in experience, we are wont to say that this or that may be known *a priori*, because we do not derive this knowledge immediately from experience, but from a general rule, which, however, we have itself borrowed from experience. Thus, if a man undermined his house, we say, "he might know *a priori* that it would have fallen"; that is, he needed not to have waited for the experience that it did actually fall. But still, *a priori*, he could not know even this much. For, that bodies are heavy, and, consequently, that they fall when their supports are taken away, must have been known to him previously, by means of experience.

By the term "knowledge *a priori*," therefore, we shall in the sequel understand, not such as is independent of this or that kind of experience, but such as is absolutely so of *all* experience. Opposed to this is empirical knowledge, or that which is possible only *a posteriori*, that is, through experience. Knowledge *a priori* is either pure or impure. Pure knowledge *a priori* is that with which no empirical element is mixed up. For example, the proposition, "Every change has a cause," is a proposition *a priori*, but impure, because change is a conception which can only be derived from experience.

II. The Human Intellect, Even in an Unphilosophical State, Is in Possession of Certain Cognitions a Priori

The question now is as to a *criterion*, by which we may securely distinguish a pure from an empirical cognition. Experience no doubt teaches us that this or that object is constituted in such and such a manner, but not that it could not possibly exist otherwise. Now, in the first place, if we have a proposition which contains the idea of necessity in its very conception, it is a judgment *a priori;* if, moreover, it is not derived from any other proposition, unless from one equally involving the idea of necessity, it is absolutely *a priori.* Secondly, an empirical judgment never exhibits strict and absolute, but only assumed and comparative, universality (by induction); therefore, the most we can say is—so far as we have hitherto observed, there is no exception to this or that rule. If, on the other hand, a judgment carries with it strict and absolute universality, that is, admits of no possible exception, it is not derived from experience, but is valid absolutely *a priori.*

Empirical universality is, therefore, only an arbitrary extension of validity, from that which may be predicated of a proposition valid in most cases, to that which is asserted of a proposition which holds good in all; as, for example, in the affirmation, "all bodies are heavy." When, on the contrary, strict universality characterizes a judgment, it necessarily indicates another peculiar source of knowledge, namely, a faculty of cognition *a priori.* Necessity and strict universality, therefore, are infallible tests for distinguishing pure from empirical knowledge, and are inseparably connected with each other. But as in the use of these criteria the empirical limitation is sometimes more easily detected than the contingency of the judgment, or the unlimited universality which we attach to a judgment is often a more convincing proof than its necessity, it may be advisable to use the criteria separately, each being by itself infallible.

Now, that in the sphere of human cognition, we have judgments which are necessary, and in the strictest sense universal, consequently pure *a priori*, it will be an easy matter to show. If we desire an example from the sciences, we need only take any proposition in mathematics. If we cast our eyes upon the commonest operations of the understanding, the proposition, "every change must have a cause," will amply serve our purpose. In the latter case, indeed, the conception of a cause so plainly involves the conception of a necessity of connection with an effect, and of a strict universality of the law, that the very notion of a cause would entirely disappear, were we to derive it, like Hume, from a frequent association of what happens with that which precedes, and the habit thence originating of connecting representations—the necessity inherent in the judgment being therefore merely subjective. Besides, without seeking for such examples of principles existing *a priori* in cognition, we might easily show that such principles are the indispensable basis of the possibility of experience itself, and consequently prove their existence *a priori*. For whence could our experience itself acquire certainty, if all the rules on which it depends were themselves empirical, and consequently fortuitous? No one, therefore, can admit the validity of the use of such rules as first principles. But, for the present, we may content ourselves with having established the fact, that we do possess and exercise a faculty of pure *a priori* cognition; and, secondly, with having pointed out the proper tests of such cognition, namely, universality and necessity.

Not only in judgments, however, but even in conceptions, is an *a priori* origin manifest. For example, if we take away by degrees from our conceptions of a body all that can be referred to mere sensuous experience—color, hardness or softness, weight, even impenetrability—the body will then vanish; but the space which it occupied still remains, and this it is utterly impossible to annihilate in thought. Again, if we take away, in like manner, from our empirical conception of any object, corporeal or incorporeal, all properties which mere experience has taught us to connect with it, still we cannot think away those through which we cogitate it as substance, or adhering to substance, although our conception of substance is more determined than that of an object. Compelled. therefore, by that necessity with which the conception of substance forces itself upon us, we must confess that it has its seat in our faculty of cognition *a priori.*

III. Philosophy Stands in Need of a Science Which Shall Determine the Possibility, Principles, and Extent of Human Knowledge a Priori

Of far more importance than all that has been above said, is the consideration that certain of our cognitions rise completely above the sphere of all possible experience, and by means of conceptions, to which there exists in the whole extent of experience no corresponding object, seem to extend the range of our judgments beyond its bounds. And just in this transcendental or supersensible sphere, where experience affords us neither instruction nor guidance, lie the investigations of *Reason,* which, on account of their importance, we consider far preferable to, and as having a far more elevated aim than, all that the understanding can achieve within the sphere of sensuous phenomena. So high a value do we set upon these investigations, that, even at the risk of error, we persist in following them out, and permit neither doubt nor disregard nor indifference to restrain us from the pursuit. These unavoidable problems of mere pure reason are GOD, FREEDOM (of will) and IMMORTALITY. The science which, with all its preliminaries, has for its especial object the solution of these problems is named metaphysics—a science which is at the very outset dogmatical, that is, it confidently takes upon itself the execution of this task without any previous investigation of the ability or inability of reason for such an undertaking.

Now the safe ground of experience being thus abandoned, it seems nevertheless natural that we should hesitate to erect a building with the cognitions we possess, without knowing whence they come, and on the strength of principles, the origin of which is undiscovered. Instead of thus trying to build without a foundation, it is rather to be expected that we should long ago have put the question, how the understanding can arrive at these *a priori* cognitions, and what is the extent, validity, and worth which they may possess? We say, this is natural enough, meaning by the word natural that which is consistent with a just and reasonable way of thinking; but if we understand by the term, that which usually happens, nothing indeed could be more natural and more comprehensible than that this investigation should be left long unattempted. For one part of our pure knowledge, the science of mathematics, has been long firmly established, and thus leads us to form flattering expectations with regard to others, though these may be of quite a different nature. Besides, when we get beyond the bounds of experience, we are of course safe from opposition in that quarter; and the charm of widening the range of our knowledge is so great, that unless we are brought to a standstill by some evident contradiction, we hurry on undoubtingly in our course. This, however, may be avoided, if we are sufficiently cautious in the construction of our fictions, which are not the less fictions on that account.

Mathematical science affords us a brilliant example, how far, independently of all experience, we may carry our *a priori knowledge*. It is true that the mathematician occupies himself with objects and cognitions only in so far as they can be represented by means of intuition. But this circumstance is easily overlooked, because the said intuition can itself be given *a priori*, and therefore is hardly to be distinguished from a mere pure conception. Deceived by such a proof of the power of reason, we can perceive no limits to the extension of our knowledge. The light dove cleaving in free flight the thin air, whose resistance it feels, might imagine that her movements would be far more free and rapid in airless space. Just in the same way did Plato, abandoning the world of sense, because of the narrow limits it sets to the understanding, venture upon the wings of ideas beyond it, into the void space of pure intellect. He did not reflect that he made no real progress by all his efforts; for he met with no resistance which might serve him for a support, as it were, whereon to rest, and on which he might apply his powers, in order to let the intellect acquire momentum for its progress. It is, indeed, the common fate of human reason in speculation, to finish the imposing edifice of thought as rapidly as possible, and then for the first time to begin to examine whether the foundation is a solid one or no. Arrived at this point, all sorts of excuses are sought after, in order to console us for its want of stability, or rather, indeed, to enable us to dispense altogether with so late and dangerous an investigation. But what frees us during the process of building from all apprehension or suspicion, and flatters us into the belief of its solidity, is this. A great part, perhaps the greatest part, of the business of our reason consists in the analyzation of the conceptions which we already possess of objects. By this means we gain a multitude of cognitions, which although really nothing more than elucidations or explanations of that which (though in a confused manner) was already thought in our conceptions, are, at least in respect of their form, prized as new introspections; while, so far as regards their matter or content, we have really made no addition to our conceptions, but only disinvolved them. But as this process does furnish real *a priori* knowledge,[1] which has a pure progress and useful results, reason, deceived by this, slips in, without being itself aware of it, assertions of a quite different kind; in which, to given conceptions it adds others, *a priori* indeed, but entirely foreign to them, without our knowing how it arrives at these, and, indeed, without such a question ever suggesting itself. I shall therefore at once proceed to examine the difference between these two modes of knowledge.

---

[1] Not synthetical.—*Tr.*

IV. Of the Difference Between Analytical and Synthetical Judgments

In all judgments wherein the relation of a subject to the predicate is cogitated (I mention affirmative judgments only here; the application to negative will be very easy), this relation is possible in two different ways. Either the predicate B belongs to the subject A, as somewhat which is contained (though covertly) in the conception A; or the predicate B lies completely out of the conception A, although it stands in connection with it. In the first instance, I term the judgment analytical, in the second, synthetical. Analytical judgments (affirmative) are therefore those in which the connection of the predicate with the subject is cogitated through identity; those in which this connection is cogitated without identity are called synthetical judgments. The former may be called *explicative*, the latter *augmentative*[2] judgments; because the former add in the predicate nothing to the conception of the subject, but only analyze it into its constituent conceptions, which were thought already in the subject, although in a confused manner; the latter add to our conceptions of the subject a predicate which was not contained in it, and which no analysis could ever have discovered therein. For example, when I say, "all bodies are extended," this is an analytical judgment. For I need not go beyond the conception of *body* in order to find extension connected with it, but merely analyze the conception, that is, become conscious of the manifold properties which I think in that conception, in order to discover this predicate in it: it is therefore an analytical judgment. On the other hand, when I say, "all bodies are heavy," the predicate is something totally different from that which I think in the mere conception of a body. By the addition of such a predicate, therefore, it becomes a synthetical judgment.

---

[2] That is, judgments which really add to, and do not merely analyze or explain the conceptions which make up the sum of our knowledge.—*Tr.*

Judgments of experience, as such, are always synthetical. For it would be absurd to think of grounding an analytical judgment on experience, because, in forming such a judgment, I need not go out of the sphere of my conceptions, and therefore recourse to the testimony of experience is quite unnecessary. That "bodies are extended" is not an empirical judgment, but a proposition which stands firm *a priori.* For before addressing myself to experience, I already have in my conception all the requisite conditions for the judgment, and I have only to extract the predicate from the conception, according to the principle of contradiction, and thereby at the same time become conscious of the necessity of the judgment, a necessity which I could never learn from experience. On the other hand, though at first I do not at all include the predicate of weight in my conception of body in general, that conception still indicates an object of experience, a part of the totality of experience, to which I can still add other parts; and this I do when I recognize by observation that bodies are heavy. I can cognize beforehand by analysis the conception of body through the characteristics of extension, impenetrability, shape, etc., all which are cogitated in this conception. But now I extend my knowledge, and looking back on experience from which I had derived this conception of body, I find weight at all times connected with the above characteristics, and therefore I synthetically add to my conceptions this as a predicate, and say, "all bodies are heavy." Thus it is experience upon which rests the possibility of the synthesis of the predicate of weight with the conception of body, because both conceptions, although the one is not contained in the other, still belong to one another (only contingently, however), as parts of a whole, namely, of experience, which is itself a synthesis of intuitions.

But to synthetical judgments *a priori,* such aid is entirely wanting. If I go out of and beyond the conception A, in order to recognize another B as connected with it, what foundation have I to rest on, whereby to render the synthesis possible? I have here no longer the advantage of looking out in the sphere of experience for what I want. Let us take, for example, the proposition, "everything that happens has a cause."

In the conception of *something that happens*, I indeed think an existence which a certain time antecedes, and from this I can derive analytical judgments. But the conception of a cause lies quite out of the above conception, and indicates something entirely different from "that which happens," and is consequently not contained in that conception. How then am I able to assert concerning the general conception—"that which happens"—something entirely different from that conception, and to recognize the conception of cause although not contained in it, yet as belonging to it, and even necessarily? what is here the unknown = X, upon which the understanding rests when it believes it has found, out of the conception A a foreign predicate B, which it nevertheless considers to be connected with it? It cannot be experience, because the principle adduced annexes the two representations, cause and effect, to the representation existence, not only with universality, which experience cannot give, but also with the expression of necessity, therefore completely *a priori* and from pure conceptions. Upon such synthetical, that is augmentative propositions, depends the whole aim of our speculative knowledge *a priori;* for although analytical judgments are indeed highly important and necessary, they are so, only to arrive at that clearness of conceptions which is requisite for a sure and extended synthesis, and this alone is a real acquisition.

V. In All Theoretical Sciences of Reason, Synthetical Judgments a Priori *Are Contained as Principles*

1 Mathematical judgments are always synthetical. Hitherto this fact, though incontestably true and very important in its consequences, seems to have escaped the analysts of the human mind, nay, to be in complete opposition to all their conjectures. For as it was found that mathematical conclusions all proceed according to the principle of contradiction

(which the nature of every apodictic certainty requires), people became persuaded that the fundamental principles of the science also were recognized and admitted in the same way. But the notion is fallacious; for although a synthetical proposition can certainly be discerned by means of the principle of contradiction, this is possible only when another synthetical proposition precedes, from which the latter is deduced, but never of itself.

Before all, be it observed, that proper mathematical propositions are always judgments *a priori*, and not empirical, because they carry along with them the conception of necessity, which cannot be given by experience. If this be demurred to, it matters not; I will then limit my assertion to *pure* mathematics, the very conception of which implies, that it consists of knowledge altogether non-empirical and *a priori*.

We might, indeed, at first suppose that the proposition, $7 + 5 = 12$, is a merely analytical proposition, following (according to the principle of contradiction) from the conception of a sum of seven and five. But if we regard it more narrowly, we find that our conception of the sum of seven and five contains nothing more than the uniting of both sums into one, whereby it cannot at all be cogitated what this single number is which embraces both. The conception of twelve is by no means obtained by merely cogitating the union of seven and five; and we may analyze our conception of such a possible sum as long as we will, still we shall never discover in it the notion of twelve. We must go beyond these conceptions, and have recourse to an intuition which corresponds to one of the two—our five fingers, for example, or like Segner in his "Arithmetic," five points, and so by degrees add the units contained in the five given in the intuition to the conception of seven. For I first take the number 7, and, for the conception of 5 calling in the aid of the fingers of my hand as objects of intuition, I add the units, which I before took together to make up the number 5, gradually now, by means of the material image my hand, to the number 7, and by this process I at length see the number 12 arise. That 7 should be added to 5, I have certainly cogitated in my conception of a sum $= 7 + 5$, but not that this sum was equal to 12. Arithmetical propositions are therefore always synthetical, of which we may become more clearly convinced by trying large numbers. For it will thus become quite evident, that turn and twist our conceptions as we may, it is impossible, without having recourse to intuition, to arrive at the sum total or product by means of the mere analysis of our conceptions. Just as little is any principle of pure geometry analytical. "A straight line between two points is the shortest," is a synthetical proposition. For my conception of *straight* contains no notion of *quantity*, but is merely *qualitative*. The conception of the *shortest* is therefore wholly an addition, and by no analysis can it be extracted from our conception of a straight line. Intuition must therefore here lend its aid, by means of which, and thus only, our synthesis is possible.

Some few principles preposited by geometricians are, indeed, really analytical, and depend on the principle of contradiction. They serve, however, like identical propositions, as links in the chain of method, not as principles—for example. $a = a$, the whole is equal to itself, or $(a + b)$ 7 a, the whole is greater than its part. And yet even these principles themselves, though they derive their validity from pure conceptions, are only admitted in mathematics because they can be presented in intuition. What causes us here commonly to believe that the predicate of such apodictic judgments is already contained in our conception, and that the judgment is therefore analytical, is merely the equivocal nature of the expression. We must join in thought a certain predicate to a given conception, and this necessity cleaves already to the conception. But the question is, not what we must join in thought to the given conception, but what we really think therein, though only obscurely, and then it becomes manifest, that the predicate pertains to these conceptions, necessarily indeed, yet not as thought in the conception itself, but by virtue of an intuition, which must be added to the conception

2 § The science of Natural Philosophy (Physics) contains in itself synthetical judgments *a priori*, as principles. I shall

adduce two propositions. For instance, the proposition, "in all changes of the material world, the quantity of matter remains unchanged"; or, that, "in all communication of motion, action and reaction must always be equal." In both of these, not only is the necessity, and therefore their origin *a priori* clear, but also that they are synthetical propositions. For in the conception of matter, I do not cogitate its permanency, but merely its presence in space, which it fills. I therefore really go out of and beyond the conception of matter, in order to think on to it something *a priori*, which I did not think in it. The proposition is therefore not analytical, but synthetical, and nevertheless conceived *a priori;* and so it is with regard to the other propositions of the pure part of natural philosophy.

3 ☙ As to Metaphysics, even if we look upon it merely as an attempted science, yet, from the nature of human reason, an indispensable one, we find that it must contain synthetical propositions *a priori.* It is not merely the duty of metaphysics to dissect, and thereby analytically to illustrate the conceptions which we form *a priori* of things; but we seek to widen the range of our *a priori* knowledge. For this purpose, we must avail ourselves of such principles as add something to the original conception—something not identical with, nor contained in it, and, by means of synthetical judgments *a priori*, leave far behind us the limits of experience; for example, in the proposition, "the world must have a beginning," and such like. Thus metaphysics, according to the proper aim of the science, consists merely of synthetical propositions *a priori.*

VI. The Universal Problem of Pure Reason

It is extremely advantageous to be able to bring a number of investigations under the formula of a single problem. For in this manner we not only facilitate our own labor, inasmuch as we define it clearly to ourselves, but also render it more easy for others to decide whether we have done justice to our undertaking. The proper problem of pure reason, then, is contained in the question, "How are synthetical judgments *a priori* possible?"

That metaphysical science has hitherto remained in so vacillating a state of uncertainty and contradiction, is only to be attributed to the fact, that this great problem, and perhaps even the difference between analytical and synthetical judgments, did not sooner suggest itself to philosophers. Upon the solution of this problem, or upon sufficient proof of the impossibility of synthetical knowledge *a priori*, depends the existence or downfall of the science of metaphysics. Among philosophers, David Hume came the nearest of all to this problem; yet it never acquired in his mind sufficient precision, nor did he regard the question in its universality. On the contrary, he stopped short at the synthetical proposition of the connection of an effect with its cause (*principium causalitatis*), insisting that such proposition *a priori* was impossible. According to his conclusions, then, all that we term metaphysical science is a mere delusion, arising from the fancied insight of reason into that which is in truth borrowed from experience, and to which habit has given the appearance of necessity. Against this assertion, destructive to all pure philosophy, he would have been guarded, had he had our problem before his eyes in its universality. For he would then have perceived that, according to his own argument, there likewise could not be any pure mathematical science, which assuredly cannot exist without synthetical propositions *a priori*—an absurdity from which his good understanding must have saved him.

In the solution of the above problem is at the same time comprehended the possibility of the use of pure reason in the foundation and construction of all sciences which contain theoretical knowledge *a priori* of objects, that is to say, the answer to the following questions:

How is pure mathematical science possible?

How is pure natural science possible?

Respecting these sciences, as they do certainly exist, it may with propriety be asked, *how* they are possible?—for that they must be possible, is shown by the fact of their really existing.[3] But as to metaphysics, the miserable progress it has hitherto made, and the fact that of no one system yet brought forward, as far as regards its true aim, can it be said that this science really exists, leaves any one at liberty to doubt with reason the very possibility of its existence.

Yet, in a certain sense, this kind of knowledge must unquestionably be looked upon as *given;* in other words, metaphysics must be considered as really existing, if not as a science, nevertheless as a natural disposition of the human mind (*metaphysica naturalis*). For human reason, without any instigations imputable to the mere vanity of great knowledge, unceasingly progresses, urged on by its own feeling of need, toward such questions as cannot be answered by any empirical application of reason, or principles derived therefrom; and so there has ever really existed in every man some system of metaphysics. It will always exist, so soon as reason awakes to the exercise of its power of speculation. And now the question arises—How is metaphysics, as a natural disposition, possible? In other words, how, from the nature of universal human reason, do those questions arise which pure reason proposes to itself, and which it is impelled by its own feeling of need to answer as well as it can?

But as in all the attempts hitherto made to answer the questions which reason is prompted by its very nature to propose to itself, for example, whether the world had a beginning,

---

[3] As to the existence of pure natural science, or physics, perhaps many may still express doubts. But we have only to look at the different propositions which are commonly treated of at the commencement of proper (empirical) physical science—those, for example, relating to the permanence of the same quantity of matter, the *vis inertiœ*, the equality of action and reaction, etc.—to be soon convinced that they form a science of pure physics (*physica pura*, or *rationalis*), which well deserves to be separately exposed as a special science, in its whole extent, whether that be great or confined.

or has existed from eternity, it has always met with unavoidable contradictions, we must not rest satisfied with the mere natural disposition of the mind to metaphysics, that is, with the existence of the faculty of pure reason, whence, indeed, some sort of metaphysical system always arises; but it must be possible to arrive at certainty in regard to the question whether we know or do not know the things of which metaphysics treats. We must be able to arrive at a decision on the subjects of its questions, or on the ability or inability of reason to form any judgment respecting them; and therefore either to extend with confidence the bounds of our pure reason, or to set strictly defined and safe limits to its action. This last question, which arises out of the above universal problem, would properly run thus: How is metaphysics possible as a science?

Thus the critique of reason leads at last, naturally and necessarily, to science; and, on the other hand, the dogmatical use of reason without criticism leads to groundless assertions, against which others equally specious can always be set, thus ending unavoidably in scepticism.

Besides, this science cannot be of great and formidable prolixity, because it has not to do with objects of reason, the variety of which is inexhaustible, but merely with reason herself and her problems; problems which arise out of her own bosom, and are not proposed to her by the nature of outward things, but by her own nature. And when once reason has previously become able completely to understand her own power in regard to objects which she meets with in experience, it will be easy to determine securely the extent and limits of her attempted application to objects beyond the confines of experience.

We may and must, therefore, regard the attempts hitherto made to establish metaphysical science dogmatically as non-existent. For what of analysis, that is, mere dissection of conceptions, is contained in one or other, is not the aim of, but only a preparation for metaphysics proper, which has for its object the extension, by means of synthesis, of our *a priori* knowledge. And for this purpose, mere analysis is of course useless, because it only shows what is contained in these conceptions, but not how we arrive, *a priori*, at them; and this it is her duty to show, in order to be able afterward to determine their valid use in regard to all objects of experience, to all knowledge in general. But little self-denial, indeed, is needed to give up these pretensions, seeing the undeniable, and in the dogmatic mode of procedure, inevitable contradictions of Reason with herself, have long since ruined the reputation of every system of metaphysics that has appeared up to this time. It will require more firmness to remain undeterred by difficulty from within, and opposition from without, from endeavoring, by a method quite opposed to all those hitherto followed, to further the growth and fruitfulness of a science indispensable to human reason—a science from which every branch it has borne may be cut away, but whose roots remain indestructible.

VII. Idea and Division of a Particular Science, Under the Name of a "Critique of Pure Reason"

From all that has been said, there results the idea of a particular science, which may be called the *Critique of Pure Reason.* For reason is the faculty which furnishes us with the principles of knowledge *a priori.* Hence, pure reason is the faculty which contains the principles of cognizing anything absolutely *a priori.* An Organon of pure reason would be a compendium of those principles according to which alone all pure cognitions *a priori* can be obtained. The completely extended application of such an organon would afford us a system of pure reason. As this, however, is demanding a great deal, and it is yet doubtful whether any extension of our knowledge be here possible, or if so, in what cases, we can regard a science of the mere criticism of pure reason, its sources and limits, as the *propœdeutic* to a system of pure reason. Such a science must not be called a Doctrine, but only a Critique of pure Reason; and its use, in regard to speculation, would be only negative, not to enlarge the bounds of, but to purify our reason, and to shield it against error—which alone is no little gain. I apply the term *transcendental* to all knowledge which is not so much occupied with objects as with the mode of our cognition of these objects, so far as this mode of cognition is possible *a priori*. A system of such conceptions would be called *Transcendental Philosophy*. But this, again, is still beyond the bounds of our present essay. For as such a science must contain a complete exposition not only of our synthetical *a priori*, but of our analytical *a priori* knowledge, it is of too wide a range for our present purpose, because we do not require to carry our analysis any further than is necessary to understand, in their full extent, the principles of synthesis *a priori*, with which alone we have to do. This investigation, which we cannot properly call a doctrine, but only a transcendental critique, because it aims not at the enlargement, but at the correction and guidance of our knowledge, and is to serve as a touchstone of the worth or worthlessness of all knowledge *a priori*, is the sole object of our present essay. Such a critique is consequently, as far as possible, a preparation for an organon; and if this new organon should be found to fail, at least for a canon of pure reason, according to which the complete system of the philosophy of pure reason, whether it extend or limit the bounds of that reason, might one day be set forth both analytically and synthetically. For that this is possible, nay, that such a system is not of so great extent as to preclude the hope of its ever being completed, is evident. For we have not here to do with the nature of outward objects, which is infinite, but solely with the mind, which judges of the nature of objects, and, again, with the mind only in respect of its cognition *a priori*. And the object of our investigations, as it is not to be sought without, but altogether within ourselves, cannot remain concealed, and in all probability is limited enough to be completely surveyed and fairly estimated, according to its worth or worthlessness. Still less let the reader here expect a critique of books and systems of pure reason;

our present object is exclusively a critique of the faculty of pure reason itself. Only when we make this critique our foundation do we possess a pure touchstone for estimating the philosophical value of ancient and modern writings on this subject; and without this criterion, the incompetent historian or judge decides upon and corrects the groundless assertions of others with his own, which have themselves just as little foundation.

Transcendental philosophy is the idea of a science, for which the Critique of Pure Reason must sketch the whole plan architectonically, that is, from principles, with a full guarantee for the validity and stability of all the parts which enter into the building. It is the system of all the principles of pure reason. If this Critique itself does not assume the title of transcendental philosophy, it is only because, to be a complete system, it ought to contain a full analysis of all human knowledge *a priori.* Our Critique must, indeed, lay before us a complete enumeration of all the radical conceptions which constitute the said pure knowledge. But from the complete analysis of these conceptions themselves, as also from a complete investigation of those derived from them, it abstains with reason; partly because it would be deviating from the end in view to occupy itself with this analysis, since this process is not attended with the difficulty and insecurity to be found in the synthesis, to which our Critique is entirely devoted, and partly because it would be inconsistent with the unity of our plan to burden this essay with the vindication of the completeness of such an analysis and deduction, with which, after all, we have at present nothing to do. This completeness of the analysis of these radical conceptions, as well as of the deduction from the conceptions *a priori* which may be given by the analysis, we can, however, easily attain, provided only that we are in possession of all these radical conceptions, which are to serve as principles of the synthesis, and that in respect of this main purpose nothing is wanting.

To the Critique of Pure Reason, therefore, belongs all that constitutes transcendental philosophy; and it is the complete idea of transcendental philosophy, but still not the science itself; because it only proceeds so far with the analysis as is necessary to the power of judging completely of our synthetical knowledge *a priori.*

The principal thing we must attend to, in the division of the parts of a science like this, is: that no conceptions must enter it which contain aught empirical; in other words, that the knowledge *a priori* must be completely pure. Hence, although the highest principles and fundamental conceptions of morality are certainly cognitions *a priori*, yet they do not belong to transcendental philosophy; because, though they certainly do not lay the conceptions of pain, pleasure, desires, inclinations, etc. (which are all of empirical origin), at the foundation of its precepts, yet still into the conception of duty—as an obstacle to be overcome, or as an incitement which should not be made into a motive—these empirical conceptions must necessarily enter, in the construction of a system of pure morality. Transcendental philosophy is consequently a philosophy of the pure and merely speculative reason. For all that is practical, so far as it contains motives, relates to feelings, and these belong to empirical sources of cognition.

If we wish to divide this science from the universal point of view of a science in general, it ought to comprehend, first, a *Doctrine of the Elements*, and, secondly, a *Doctrine of the Method* of pure reason. Each of these main divisions will have its subdivisions, the separate reasons for which we cannot here particularize. Only so much seems necessary, by way of introduction or premonition, that there are two sources of human knowledge (which probably spring from a common, but to us unknown, root), namely, sense and understanding. By the former, objects are *given* to us; by the latter, *thought.* So far as the faculty of sense may contain representations *a priori*, which form the conditions under which objects are given, in so far it belongs to transcendental philosophy. The transcendental doctrine of sense must form the first part of our science of elements, because the conditions under which alone the objects of human knowledge are given must precede those under which they are thought.

Arthur Schopenhauer

THE WORLD AS IDEA

Arthur Schopenhauer

[1788–1860]

The philosopher of disillusion, Arthur Schopenhauer came by his pessimism with almost deliberate intention. He quarreled with his mother, was ignored as a lecturer in philosophy at the University of Berlin, and became a recluse, with a dog as his only companion, to write his major work, *The World As Will and Idea.* It appeared in 1818, and avowed the concept of the external world known to us only through sensation and ideas, and gave new emphasis to the will as "the living principle of reason." Follower of Immanuel Kant and precursor of Friedrich Nietzsche, Arthur Schopenhauer offers, in spite of his pronouncements of doom, a penetrating evaluation of reality and an affirmation of idealism by means of art and stern asceticism.

THE WORLD AS IDEA

ARTHUR SCHOPENHAUER

1 "THE world is my idea":—this is a truth which holds good for everything that lives and knows, though man alone can bring it into reflective and abstract consciousness. If he really does this, he has attained to philosophical wisdom. It then becomes clear and certain to him that what he knows is not a sun and an earth, but only an eye that sees a sun, a hand that feels an earth; that the world which surrounds him is there only as idea, *i.e.*, only in relation to something else, the consciousness, which is himself. If any truth can be asserted *a priori*, it is this: for it is the expression of the most general form of all possible and thinkable experience: a form which is more general than time, or space, or causality, for they all presuppose it; and each of these, which we have seen to be just so many modes of the principle of sufficient reason, is valid only for a particular class of ideas; whereas the antithesis of object and subject is the common form of all these classes, is that form under which alone any idea of whatever kind it may be, abstract or intuitive, pure or empirical, is possible and thinkable. No truth therefore is more certain, more independent of all others, and less in need of proof than this, that all that exists for knowledge, and therefore this whole world, is only object in relation to subject, perception of a perceiver, in a word, idea. This is obviously true of the past and the future, as well as of the present, of what is farthest off, as of what is near; for it is true of time and space them-

selves, in which alone these distinctions arise. All that in any way belongs or can belong to the world is inevitably thus conditioned through the subject, and exists only for the subject. The world is idea.

This truth is by no means new. It was implicitly involved in the skeptical reflections from which Descartes started. Berkeley, however, was the first who distinctly enunciated it, and by this he has rendered a permanent service to philosophy, even though the rest of his teaching should not endure. Kant's primary mistake was the neglect of this principle, as is shown in the appendix. How early again this truth was recognised by the wise men of India, appearing indeed as the fundamental tenet of the Vedânta philosophy ascribed to Vyasa, is pointed out by Sir William Jones in the last of his essays: "On the philosophy of the Asiatics" (Asiatic Researches, vol. iv., p. 164), where he says, "The fundamental tenet of the Vedânta school consisted not in denying the existence of matter, that is, of solidity, impenetrability, and extended figure (to deny which would be lunacy), but in correcting the popular notion of it, and in contending that it has no essence independent of mental perception; that existence and perceptibility are convertible terms." These words adequately express the compatibility of empirical reality and transcendental ideality.

In this first book, then, we consider the world only from this side, only so far as it is idea. The inward reluctance with which any one accepts the world as merely his idea, warns him that this view of it, however true it may be, is nevertheless one-sided, adopted in consequence of some arbitrary abstraction. And yet it is a conception from which he can never free himself. The defectiveness of this view will be corrected in the next book by means of a truth which is not so immediately certain as that from which we start here; a truth at which we can arrive only by deeper research and more severe abstraction, by the separation of what is different and the union of what is identical. This truth, which must be very serious and impressive if not awful to every one, is that a man can also say and must say, "the world is my will."

In this book, however, we must consider separately that aspect of the world from which we start, its aspect as knowable, and therefore, in the meantime, we must, without reserve, regard all presented objects, even our own bodies (as we shall presently show more fully), merely as ideas, and call them merely ideas. By so doing we always abstract from will (as we hope to make clear to every one further on), which by itself constitutes the other aspect of the world. For as the world is in one aspect entirely *idea*, so in another it is entirely *will*. A reality which is neither of these two, but an object in itself (into which the thing in itself has unfortunately dwindled in the hands of Kant), is the phantom of a dream, and its acceptance is an *ignis fatuus* in philosophy.

2 ☙ That which knows all things and is known by none is the subject. Thus it is the supporter of the world, that condition of all phenomena, of all objects which is always presupposed throughout experience; for all that exists, exists only for the subject. Every one finds himself to be subject, yet only in so far as he knows, not in so far as he is an object of knowledge. But his body is object, and therefore from this point of view we call it idea. For the body is an object among objects, and is conditioned by the laws of objects, although it is an immediate object. Like all objects of perception, it lies within the universal forms of knowledge, time and space, which are the conditions of multiplicity. The subject, on the contrary, which is always the knower, never the known, does not come under these forms, but is presupposed by them; it has therefore neither multiplicity nor its opposite unity. We never know it, but it is always the knower wherever there is knowledge.

So then the world as idea, the only aspect in which we consider it at present, has two fundamental, necessary, and inseparable halves. The one half is the object, the forms of which are space and time, and through these multiplicity. The other half is the subject, which is not in space and time, for it is present, entire and undivided, in every percipient being. So that any one percipient being, with the object, constitutes the whole world as idea just as fully as the existing millions could do; but if this one were to disappear, then the whole world as idea would cease to be. These halves are therefore inseparable even for thought, for each of the two has meaning and existence only through and for the other, each appears with the other and vanishes with it. They limit each other immediately; where the object begins the subject ends. The universality of this limitation is shown by the fact that the essential and hence universal forms of all objects, space, time, and causality, may, without knowledge of the object, be discovered and fully known from a consideration of the subject, *i.e.*, in Kantian language, they lie *a priori* in our consciousness. That he discovered this is one of Kant's principal merits, and it is a great one. I however go beyond this, and maintain that the principle of sufficient reason is the general expression for all these forms of the object of which we are *a priori* conscious; and that therefore all that we know purely *a priori* is merely the content of that principle and what follows from it; in it all our certain *a priori* knowledge is expressed. In my essay on the principle of sufficient reason I have shown in detail how every possible object comes under it; that is, stands in a necessary relation to other objects, on the one side as determined, on the other side as determining: this is of such wide application, that the whole existence of all objects, so far as they are objects, ideas and nothing more, may be entirely traced to this their necessary relation to each other, rests only in it, is in fact merely relative; but of this more presently. I have further shown, that the necessary relation which the principle of sufficient reason expresses generally, appears in other forms corresponding to the classes into which objects are divided, according to their possibility; and again that by these forms the proper division of the classes is tested. I take it for granted that what I said in this earlier essay is known and present to the reader, for if it had not been already said it would necessarily find its place here.

3 ☙ The chief distinction among our ideas is that between ideas of perception and abstract ideas. The latter form just one class of ideas, namely concepts, and these are the possession of man alone of all creatures upon earth. The capacity for these, which distinguishes him from all the lower animals, has always been called reason.[1] We shall consider these abstract ideas by themselves later, but, in the first place, we shall speak exclusively of the *ideas of perception.* These comprehend the whole visible world, or the sum total of experience, with the conditions of its possibility. We have always observed that it is a highly important discovery of Kant's, that these very conditions, these forms of the visible world, *i.e.*, the absolutely universal element in its perception, the common property of all its phenomena, space and time, even when taken by themselves and apart from their content, can, not only be thought in the abstract, but also be directly perceived; and that this perception or intuition is not some kind of phantasm arising from constant recurrence in experience, but is so entirely independent of experience that we must rather regard the latter as dependent on it, inasmuch as the qualities of space and time, as they are known in *a priori* perception or intuition, are valid for all possible experience, as rules to which it must invariably conform. Accordingly, in my essay on the principle of sufficient reason, I have treated space and time, because they are perceived as pure and empty of content, as a special and independent class of ideas. This quality of the universal forms of intuition, which was discovered by Kant, that they may be perceived in themselves and apart from experience, and that they may be known as exhibiting those laws on which is founded the infallible science of mathematics, is certainly very important. Not less worthy of remark, however, is this other quality of time and space,

---

[1] Kant is the only writer who has confused this idea of reason, and in this connection I refer the reader to my "Grundprobleme der Ethik": Grundl. dd. Moral. § 6, pp. 148–154, first and second editions.

that the principle of sufficient reason, which conditions experience as the law of causation and of motive, and thought as the law of the basis of judgment, appears here in quite a special form, to which I have given the name of the ground of being. In time, this is the succession of its moments, and in space the position of its parts, which reciprocally determine each other *ad infinitum*.

Any one who has fully understood from the introductory essay the complete identity of the content of the principle of sufficient reason in all its different forms, must also be convinced of the importance of the knowledge of the simplest of these forms, as affording him insight into his own inmost nature. This simplest form of the principle we have found to be time. In it each instant is, only in so far as it has effaced the preceding one, its generator, to be itself in turn as quickly effaced. The past and the future (considered apart from the consequences of their content) are empty as a dream, and the present is only the indivisible and unenduring boundary between them. And in all the other forms of the principle of sufficient reason, we shall find the same emptiness, and shall see that not time only but also space, and the whole content of both of them, *i.e.*, all that proceeds from causes and motives, has a merely relative existence, is only through and for another like to itself, *i.e.*, not more enduring. The substance of this doctrine is old: it appears in Heraclitus when he laments the eternal flux of things; in Plato when he degrades the object to that which is ever becoming, but never being; in Spinoza as the doctrine of the mere accidents of the one substance which is and endures. Kant opposes what is thus known as the mere phenomenon to the thing in itself. Lastly, the ancient wisdom of the Indian philosophers declares, "It is Mâyâ, the veil of deception, which blinds the eyes of mortals, and makes them behold a world of which they cannot say either that it is or that it is not: for it is like a dream; it is like the sunshine on the sand which the traveller takes from afar for water, or the stray piece of rope he mistakes for a snake." (These similes are repeated in innumerable passages of the Vedas and the Puranas.) But what all these mean, and that of which they all speak, is nothing more than what we have just considered—the world as idea subject to the principle of sufficient reason.

4 ◆§ Whoever has recognised the form of the principle of sufficient reason, which appears in pure time as such, and on which all counting and arithmetical calculation rests, has completely mastered the nature of time. Time is nothing more than that form of the principle of sufficient reason, and has no further significance. Succession is the form of the principle of sufficient reason in time, and succession is the whole nature of time. Further, whoever has recognised the principle of sufficient reason as it appears in the presentation of pure space, has exhausted the whole nature of space, which is absolutely nothing more than that possibility of the reciprocal determination of its parts by each other, which is called position. The detailed treatment of this, and the formulation in abstract conceptions of the results which flow from it, so that they may be more conveniently used, is the subject of the science of geometry. Thus also, whoever has recognised the law of causation, the aspect of the principle of sufficient reason which appears in what fills these forms (space and time) as objects of perception, that is to say, matter, has completely mastered the nature of matter as such, for matter is nothing more than causation, as any one will see at once if he reflects. Its true being is its action, nor can we possibly conceive it as having any other meaning. Only as action does it fill space and time; its action upon the immediate objects (which is itself matter) determines that perception in which alone it exists. The consequence of the action of any material object upon any other, is known only in so far as the latter acts upon the immediate object in a different way from that in which it acted before; it consists only of this. Cause and effect thus constitute the whole nature of matter; its true being is its action. (A fuller treatment of this will be found in the essay on the Principle of Sufficient Reason, § 21, p. 77.) The nature of all material things is therefore very appropri-

ately called in German *Wirklichkeit*,[2] a word which is far more expressive than *Realität*. Again, that which is acted upon is always matter, and thus the whole being and essence of matter consists in the orderly change, which one part of it brings about in another part. The existence of matter is therefore entirely relative, according to a relation which is valid only within its limits, as in the case of time and space.

But time and space, each for itself, can be mentally presented apart from matter, whereas matter cannot be so presented apart from time and space. The form which is inseparable from it presupposes space, and the action in which its very existence consists, always imports some change, in other words a determination in time. But space and time are not only, each for itself, presupposed by matter, but a union of the two constitutes its essence, for this, as we have seen, consists in action, *i.e.*, in causation. All the innumerable conceivable phenomena and conditions of things, might be coexistent in boundless space, without limiting each other, or might be successive in endless time without interfering with each other: thus a necessary relation of these phenomena to each other, and a law which should regulate them according to such a relation, is by no means needful, would not, indeed, be applicable: it therefore follows that in the case of all coexistence in space and change in time, so long as each of these forms preserve for itself its condition and its course without any connection with the other, there can be no causation, and since causation constitutes the essential nature of matter, there can be no matter. But the law of causation receives its meaning and necessity only from this, that the essence of change does not consist simply in the mere variation of things, but rather in the fact that at the *same part of space* there is now *one thing* and then *another*, and at *one* and the same point of time there is *here* one thing and *there* another: only this reciprocal limitation of space and time by each other gives meaning, and at the same time necessity, to a law, according

[2] Mira in quibusdam rebus verborum proprietas est, et consuetudo sermonis antiqui quædam efficacissimis notis signat. *Seneca*, epist. 81.

to which change must take place. What is determined by the law of causality is therefore not merely a succession of things in time, but this succession with reference to a definite space, and not merely existence of things in a particular place, but in this place at a different point of time. Change, *i.e.*, variation which takes place according to the law of causality, implies always a determined part of space and a determined part of time together and in union. Thus causality unites space with time. But we found that the whole essence of matter consisted in action, *i.e.*, in causation, consequently space and time must also be united in matter, that is to say, matter must take to itself at once the distinguishing qualities both of space and time, however much these may be opposed to each other, and must unite in itself what is impossible for each of these independently, that is, the fleeting course of time, with the rigid unchangeable perduration of space: infinite divisibility it receives from both. It is for this reason that we find that co-existence, which could neither be in time alone, for time has no contiguity, nor in space alone, for space has no before, after, or now, is first established through matter. But the co-existence of many things constitutes, in fact, the essence of reality, for through it permanence first becomes possible; for permanence is only knowable in the change of something which is present along with what is permanent, while on the other hand it is only because something permanent is present along with what changes, that the latter gains the special character of change, *i.e.*, the mutation of quality and form in the permanence of substance, that is to say, in matter.[3] If the world were in space alone, it would be rigid and immovable, without succession, without change, without action; but we know that with action, the idea of matter first appears. Again, if the world were in time alone, all would be fleeting, without persistence, without contiguity, hence without co-existence, and consequently without permanence; so that in this case also there would be no matter. Only through the union of space and time do we reach matter, and matter is the possibility of co-existence, and, through

[3] It is shown that matter and substance are one.

that, of permanence; through permanence again matter is the possibility of the persistence of substance in the change of its states.[4] As matter consists in the union of space and time, it bears throughout the stamp of both. It manifests its origin in space, partly through the form which is inseparable from it, but especially through its persistence (substance), the *a priori* certainty of which is therefore wholly deducible from that of space[5] (for variation belongs to time alone, but in it alone and for itself nothing is persistent). Matter shows that it springs from time by quality (accidents), without which it never exists, and which is plainly always causality, action upon other matter, and therefore change (a time concept). The law of this action, however, always depends upon space and time together, and only thus obtains meaning. The regulative function of causality is confined entirely to the determination of what must occupy *this time and this space*. The fact that we know *a priori* the unalterable characteristics of matter, depends upon this derivation of its essential nature from the forms of our knowledge of which we are conscious *a priori*.

But as the object in general is only for the subject, as its idea, so every special class of ideas is only for an equally special quality in the subject, which is called a faculty of perception. This subjective correlative of time and space, in themselves as empty forms, has been named by Kant pure sensibility; and we may retain this expression, as Kant was the first to treat of the subject, though it is not exact, for sensibility presupposes matter. The subjective correlative of matter or of causation, for these two are the same, is understanding, which is nothing more than this. To know causality is its one function, its only power; and it is a great one, embracing much, of manifold application, yet of unmistakable identity in all its manifestations. Conversely all causation,

---

[4] This shows the ground of the Kantian explanation of matter, that it is "that which is movable in space," for motion consists simply in the union of space and time.

[5] Not, as Kant holds, from the knowledge of time.

that is to say, all matter, or the whole of reality, is only for the understanding, through the understanding, and in the understanding. The first, simplest, and ever-present example of understanding is the perception of the actual world. This is throughout knowledge of the cause from the effect, and therefore all perception is intellectual. The understanding could never arrive at this perception, however, if some effect did not become known immediately, and thus serve as a starting-point. But this is the affection of the animal body. So far, then, the animal body is the *immediate object* of the subject; the perception of all other objects becomes possible through it. The changes which every animal body experiences, are immediately known, that is, felt; and as these effects are at once referred to their causes, the perception of the latter as *objects* arises. This relation is no conclusion in abstract conceptions; it does not arise from reflection, nor is it arbitrary, but immediate, necessary, and certain. It is the method of knowing of the pure understanding, without which there could be no perception; there would only remain a dull plant-like consciousness of the changes of the immediate object, which would succeed each other in an utterly unmeaning way, except in so far as they might have a meaning for the will either as pain or pleasure. But as with the rising of the sun the visible world appears, so at one stroke, the understanding, by means of its one simple function, changes the dull, meaningless sensation into perception. What the eye, the ear, or the hand feels, is not perception; it is merely its data. By the understanding passing from the effect to the cause, the world first appears as perception extended in space, varying in respect of form, persistent through all time in respect of matter; for the understanding unites space and time in the idea of matter, that is, causal action. As the world as idea exists only through the understanding, so also it exists only for the understanding.

5 ☙ It is needful to guard against the grave error of supposing that because perception arises through the knowledge

of causality, the relation of subject and object is that of cause and effect. For this relation subsists only between the immediate object and objects known indirectly, thus always between objects alone. It is this false supposition that has given rise to the foolish controversy about the reality of the outer world; a controversy in which dogmatism and skepticism oppose each other, and the former appears, now as realism, now as idealism. Realism treats the object as cause, and the subject as its effect. The idealism of Fichte reduces the object to the effect of the subject. Since however, and this cannot be too much emphasized, there is absolutely no relation according to the principle of sufficient reason between subject and object, neither of these views could be proved, and therefore skepticism attacked them both with success. Now, just as the law of causality precedes perception and experience as their condition, and therefore cannot (as Hume thought) be derived from them, so object and subject precede all knowledge, and hence the principle of sufficient reason in general, as its first condition; for this principle is merely the form of all objects, the whole nature and possibility of their existence as phenomena: but the object always presupposes the subject; and therefore between these two there can be no relation of reason and consequent. My essay on the principle of sufficient reason accomplishes just this: it explains the content of that principle as the essential form of every object—that is to say, as the universal nature of all objective existence, as something which pertains to the object as such; but the object as such always presupposes the subject as its necessary correlative; and therefore the subject remains always outside the province in which the principle of sufficient reason is valid. The controversy as to the reality of the outer world rests upon this false extension of the validity of the principle of sufficient reason to the subject also, and starting with this mistake it can never understand itself. On the one side realistic dogmatism, looking upon the idea as the effect of the object, desires to separate these two, idea and object, which are really one, and to assume a cause quite different from the idea, an object in itself, independent of the subject, a thing which is quite inconceivable; for even as object it presupposes subject, and so remains its idea. Opposed to this doctrine is skepticism, which makes the same false presupposition that in the idea we have only the effect, never the cause, therefore never real being; that we always know merely the action of the object. But this object, it supposes, may perhaps have no resemblance whatever to its effect, may indeed have been quite erroneously received as the cause, for the law of causality is first to be gathered from experience, and the reality of experience is then made to rest upon it. Thus both of these views are open to the correction, firstly, that object and idea are the same; secondly, that the true being of the object of perception is its action, that the reality of the thing consists in this, and the demand for an existence of the object outside the idea of the subject, and also for an essence of the actual thing different from its action, has absolutely no meaning, and is a contradiction: and that the knowledge of the nature of the effect of any perceived object, exhausts such an object itself, so far as it is object, *i.e.*, idea, for beyond this there is nothing more to be known. So far then, the perceived world in space and time, which makes itself known as causation alone, is entirely real, and is throughout simply what it appears to be, and it appears wholly and without reserve as idea, bound together according to the law of causality. This is its empirical reality. On the other hand, all causality is in the understanding alone, and for the understanding. The whole actual, that is, active world is determined as such through the understanding, and apart from it is nothing. This, however, is not the only reason for altogether denying such a reality of the outer world as is taught by the dogmatist, who explains its reality as its independence of the subject. We also deny it, because no object apart from a subject can be conceived without contradiction. The whole world of objects is and remains idea, and therefore wholly and for ever determined by the subject; that is to say, it has transcendental ideality. But it is not therefore illusion or mere appearance; it presents itself as that which it is, idea, and indeed as a series of ideas of which the common bond is the principle of sufficient reason. It is according to its inmost meaning quite comprehensible to the healthy understanding, and speaks a language quite intelligible to it. To dispute about its reality can only occur to a mind perverted by over-subtilty, and such discussion always arises from a false application of the principle of sufficient reason, which binds all ideas together of whatever kind they may be, but by no means connects them with the subject, nor yet with a something which is neither subject nor object, but only the ground of the object; an absurdity, for only objects can be and always are the ground of objects. If we examine more closely the source of this question as to the reality of the outer world, we find that besides the false application of the principle of sufficient reason generally to what lies beyond its province, a special confusion of its forms is also involved; for that form which it has only in reference to concepts or abstract ideas, is applied to perceived ideas, real objects; and a ground of knowing is demanded of objects, whereas they can have nothing but a ground of being. Among the abstract ideas, the concepts united in the judgment, the principle of sufficient reason appears in such a way that each of these has its worth, its validity, and its whole existence, here called *truth*, simply and solely through the relation of the judgment to something outside of it, its ground of knowledge, to which there must consequently always be a return. Among real objects, ideas of perception, on the other hand, the principle of sufficient reason appears not as the principle of the ground of *knowing*, but of *being*, as the law of causality: every real object has paid its debt to it, inasmuch as it has come to be, *i.e.*, has appeared as the effect of a cause. The demand for a ground of knowing has therefore here no application and no meaning, but belongs to quite another class of things. Thus the world of perception raises in the observer no question or doubt so long as he remains in contact with it: there is here neither error nor truth, for these are confined to the province of the abstract—the province of reflection. But here the world lies open for sense and understanding; presents itself with naïve truth as that which it really is—ideas of perception which develop themselves according to the law of causality.

6 ☙ For the present, however, in this first book we consider everything merely as idea, as object for the subject. And our own body, which is the starting-point for each of us in our perception of the world, we consider, like all other real objects, from the side of its knowableness, and in this regard it is simply an idea. Now the consciousness of every one is in general opposed to the explanation of objects as mere ideas, and more especially to the explanation of our bodies as such; for the thing in itself is known to each of us immediately in so far as it appears as our own body; but in so far as it objectifies itself in the other objects of perception, it is known only indirectly. But this abstraction, this one-sided treatment, this forcible separation of what is essentially and necessarily united, is only adopted to meet the demands of our argument; and therefore the disinclination to it must, in the meantime, be suppressed and silenced by the expectation that the subsequent treatment will correct the one-sidedness of the present one, and complete our knowledge of the nature of the world.

At present therefore the body is for us immediate object; that is to say, that idea which forms the starting-point of the subject's knowledge; because the body, with its immediately known changes, precedes the application of the law of causality, and thus supplies it with its first data. The whole nature of matter consists, as we have seen, in its causal action. But cause and effect exist only for the understanding, which is nothing but their subjective correlative. The understanding, however, could never come into operation if there were not something else from which it starts. This is simple sensation—the immediate consciousness of the changes of the body, by virtue of which it is immediate object. Thus the possibility of knowing the world of perception depends upon two conditions; the first, *objectively expressed*, is the power of material things to act upon each other, to produce changes in each other, without which common quality of all bodies no perception would be possible, even by means of the sensibility of the animal body. And if we wish to express this condition *subjectively* we say: The understanding first makes perception possible; for the law of causality, the possibility of effect and cause, springs only from the understanding, and is valid only for it, and therefore the world of perception exists only through and for it. The second condition is the sensibility of animal bodies, or the quality of being immediate objects of the subject which certain bodies possess. The mere modification which the organs of sense sustain from without through their specific affections, may here be called ideas, so far as these affections produce neither pain nor pleasure, that is, have no immediate significance for the will, and are yet perceived, exist therefore only for *knowledge*. Thus far, then, I say that the body is immediately *known*, is *immediate object*. But the conception of object is not to be taken here in its fullest sense, for through this immediate knowledge of the body, which precedes the operation of the understanding, and is mere sensation, our own body does not exist specifically as *object*, but first the material things which affect it: for all knowledge of an object proper, of an idea perceived in space, exists only through and for the understanding; therefore not before, but only subsequently to its operation. Therefore the body as object proper, that is, an idea perceived in space, is first known indirectly, like all other objects, through the application of the law of causality to the action of one of its parts upon another, as, for example, when the eye sees the body or the hand touches it. Consequently the form of our body does not become known to us through mere feeling, but only through knowledge, only in idea; that is to say, only in the brain does our own body first come to appear as extended, articulate, organic. A man born blind receives this idea only little by little from the data afforded by touch. A blind man without hands could never come to know his own form; or at the most could infer and construct it little by little from the effects of other bodies upon him. If, then, we call the body an immediate object, we are to be understood with these reservations.

In other respects, then, according to what has been said, all animal bodies are immediate objects; that is, starting-points for the subject which always knows and therefore is never known in its perception of the world. Thus the distinctive characteristic of animal life is knowledge, with movement following on motives, which are determined by knowledge, just as movement following on stimuli is the distinctive characteristic of plant-life. Unorganised matter, however, has no movement except such as is produced by causes properly so called, using the term in its narrowest sense. All this I have thoroughly discussed in my essay on the principle of sufficient reason, § 20, in the "Ethics," first essay, iii., and in my work on Sight and Colour, § 1, to which I therefore refer.

It follows from what has been said, that all animals, even the least developed, have understanding; for they all know objects, and this knowledge determines their movements as motive. Understanding is the same in all animals and in all men; it has everywhere the same simple form; knowledge of causality, transition from effect to cause, and from cause to effect, nothing more; but the degree of its acuteness, and the extension of the sphere of its knowledge varies enormously, with innumerable gradations from the lowest form, which is only conscious of the causal connection between the immediate object and objects affecting it—that is to say, perceives a cause as an object in space by passing to it from the affection which the body feels, to the higher grades of knowledge of the causal connection among objects known indirectly, which extends to the understanding of the most complicated system of cause and effect in nature. For even this high degree of knowledge is still the work of the understanding, not of the reason. The abstract concepts of the reason can only serve to take up the objective connections which are immediately known by the understanding, to make them permanent for thought, and to relate them to each other; but reason never gives us immediate knowledge. Every force and law of nature, every example of such forces and laws, must first be immediately known by the understanding, must be apprehended through perception before it can pass into abstract consciousness for reason. Hooke's discovery of the law of gravitation, and the reference of so many important phenomena to this one law, was the work of immediate apprehension by the understanding; and such also was the proof of Newton's calculations, and Lavoisier's discovery of acids and their important function in nature, and also Goethe's discovery of the origin of physical colours. All these discoveries are nothing more than a correct immediate passage from the effect to the cause, which is at once followed by the recognition of the ideality of the force of nature which expresses itself in all causes of the same kind; and this complete insight is just an example of that single function of the understanding, by which an animal perceives as an object in space the cause which affects its body, and differs from such a perception only in degree. Every one of these great discoveries is therefore, just like perception, an operation of the understanding, an immediate intuition, and as such the work of an instant, an *apperçu*, a flash of insight.

7 ☙ With reference to our exposition up to this point, it must be observed that we did not start either from the object or the subject, but from the idea, which contains and presupposes them both; for the antithesis of object and subject is its primary, universal and essential form. We have therefore first considered this form as such; then (though in this respect reference has for the most part been made to the introductory essay) the subordinate forms of time, space and causality. The latter belong exclusively to the *object*, and yet, as they are essential to the object *as such*, and as the object again is essential to the subject *as such*, they may be discovered from the subject, *i.e.*, they may be known *a priori*, and so far they are to be regarded as the common limits of both. But all these forms may be referred to one general expression, the principle of sufficient reason, as we have explained in the introductory essay.

This procedure distinguishes our philosophical method from that of all former systems. For they all start either from the object or from the subject, and therefore seek to explain the one from the other, and this according to the principle of sufficient reason. We, on the contrary, deny the validity of this principle with reference to the relation of subject and object, and confine it to the object. It may be thought that the philosophy of identity, which has appeared and become generally known in our own day, does not come under either of the alternatives we have named, for it does not start either from the subject or from the object, but from the absolute, known through "intellectual intuition," which is neither object nor subject, but the identity of the two. I will not venture to speak of this revered identity, and this absolute, for I find myself entirely devoid of all "intellectual intuition." But as I take my stand merely on those manifestoes of the "intellectual intuiter" which are open to all, even to profane persons like myself, I must yet observe that this philosophy is not to be excepted from the alternative errors mentioned above. For it does not escape these two opposite errors in spite of its identity of subject and object, which is not thinkable, but only "intellectually intuitable," or to be experienced by a losing of oneself in it. On the contrary, it combines them both in itself; for it is divided into two parts, firstly, transcendental idealism, which is just Fichte's doctrine of the *ego*, and therefore teaches that the object is produced by the subject, or evolved out of it in accordance with the principle of sufficient reason; secondly, the philosophy of nature, which teaches that the subject is produced little by little from the object, by means of a method called construction, about which I understand very little, yet enough to know that it is a process according to various forms of the principle of sufficient reason. The deep wisdom itself which that construction contains, I renounce; for as I entirely lack "intellectual intuition," all those expositions which presuppose it must for me remain as a book sealed with seven seals. This is so truly the case that, strange to say, I have always been unable to find anything at all in this doctrine of profound wisdom but atrocious and wearisome bombast.

The systems starting from the object had always the whole world of perception and its constitution as their problem; yet the object which they take as their starting-point is not always this whole world of perception, nor its fundamental element, matter. On the contrary, a division of these systems may be made, based on the four classes of possible objects set forth in the introductory essay. Thus Thales and the Ionic school, Democritus, Epicurus, Giordano Bruno, and the French materialists, may be said to have started from the first class of objects, the real world: Spinoza (on account of his conception of substance, which is purely abstract, and exists only in his definition) and, earlier, the Eleatics, from the second class, the abstract conception: the Pythagoreans and Chinese philosophy in Y-King, from the third class, time, and consequently number: and, lastly, the schoolmen, who teach a creation out of nothing by the act of will of an extra-mundane personal being, started from the fourth class of objects, the act of will directed by knowledge.

Of all systems of philosophy which start from the object, the most consistent, and that which may be carried furthest, is simple materialism. It regards matter, and with it time and space, as existing absolutely, and ignores the relation to the subject in which alone all this really exists. It then lays hold of the law of causality as a guiding principle or clue, regarding it as a self-existent order (or arrangement) of things, *veritas æterna*, and so fails to take account of the understanding, in which and for which alone causality is. It seeks the primary and most simple state of matter, and then tries to develop all the others from it; ascending from mere mechanism, to chemism, to polarity, to the vegetable and to the animal kingdom. And if we suppose this to have been done, the last link in the chain would be animal sensibility—that is, knowledge—which would consequently now appear as a mere modification or state of matter produced by causality. Now if we had followed materialism thus far with clear ideas, when we reached its highest point we would suddenly be seized with a fit of the inextinguishable laughter of the Olympians. As if waking from a dream, we would all at once become aware that its final result—knowledge, which it reached so laboriously, was presupposed as the indispensable condition of its very starting-point, mere matter; and when we imagined that we thought matter, we really thought only the subject that perceives matter; the eye that sees it, the hand that feels it, the understanding that knows it. Thus the tremendous *petitio principii* reveals itself unexpectedly; for suddenly the last link is seen to be the starting-point, the chain a circle, and the materialist is like Baron Münchausen who, when swimming in water on horseback, drew the horse into the air with his legs, and himself also by his cue. The fundamental absurdity of materialism is that it starts from the *objective*, and takes as the ultimate ground of explanation something *objective*, whether it be matter in the abstract, simply as it is *thought*, or after it has taken form, is empirically given—that is to say, is *substance*, the chemical element with its primary relations. Some such thing it takes, as existing absolutely and in itself, in order that it may evolve organic nature and finally the knowing subject from it, and explain them adequately by means of it; whereas in truth all that is objective is already determined as such in manifold ways by the knowing subject through its forms of knowing, and presupposes them; and consequently it entirely disappears if we think the subject away. Thus materialism is the attempt to explain what is immediately given us by what is given us indirectly. All that is objective, extended, active—that is to say, all that is material—is regarded by materialism as affording so solid a basis for its explanation, that a reduction of everything to this can leave nothing to be desired (especially if in ultimate analysis this reduction should resolve itself into action and reaction). But we have shown that all this is given indirectly and in the highest degree determined, and is therefore merely a relatively present object, for it has passed through the machinery and manufactory of the brain, and has thus come under the forms of space, time and casuality, by means of which it is first presented to us as extended in space and ever active in time. From such an indirectly given object, materialism seeks to explain what is immediately given, the idea (in which alone the object that materialism starts with exists), and finally even the will from which all those fundamental forces, that manifest themselves, under the guidance of causes, and therefore according to law, are in truth to be explained. To the assertion that thought is a modification of matter we may always, with equal right, oppose the contrary assertion that all matter is merely the modification of the knowing subject, as its idea. Yet the aim and ideal of all natural science is at bottom a consistent materialism. The recognition here of the obvious impossibility of such a system establishes another truth which will appear in the course of our exposition, the truth that all science properly so called, by which I understand systematic knowledge under the guidance of the principle of sufficient reason, can never reach its final goal, nor give a complete and adequate explanation: for it is not concerned with the inmost nature of the world, it cannot get beyond the idea; indeed, it really teaches nothing more than the relation of one idea to another.

"No object without a subject," is the principle which renders all materialism for ever impossible. Suns and planets without an eye that sees them, and an understanding that knows them, may indeed be spoken of in words, but for the idea, these words are absolutely meaningless. On the other hand, the law of casuality and the treatment and investigation of nature which is based upon it, lead us necessarily to the conclusion that, in time, each more highly organised state of matter has succeeded a cruder state: so that the lower animals existed before men, fishes before land animals, plants before fishes, and the unorganised before all that is organised; that, consequently, the original mass had to pass through a long series of changes before the first eye could be opened. And yet, the existence of this whole world remains ever dependent upon the first eye that opened, even if it were that of an insect. For such an eye is a necessary condition of the possibility of knowledge, and the whole world exists only in and for knowledge, and without it is not even thinkable. The world is entirely idea, and as such demands the knowing subject as the supporter of its existence. This long course of time itself, filled with innumerable changes, through which matter rose from form to form till at last the first percipient creature appeared,—this whole time itself is only thinkable in the identity of a consciousness whose succession of ideas, whose form of knowing it is, and apart from which, it loses all meaning and is nothing at all. Thus we see, on the one hand, the existence of the whole world necessarily dependent upon the first conscious being, however undeveloped it may be; on the other hand, this conscious being just as necessarily entirely dependent upon a long chain of causes and effects which have preceded it, and in which it itself appears as a small link. These two contradictory points of view, to each of which we are led with the same necessity, we might again call an *antinomy* in our faculty of knowledge, and set it up as the counterpart of that which we found in the first extreme of natural science. The objective world, the world as idea, is not the only side of the world, but merely its outward side; and it has an entirely different side—the side of its inmost nature—its kernel—the thing-in-itself. This we shall consider in the second book, calling it after the most immediate of its objective manifestations—will. But the world as idea, with which alone we are here concerned, only appears with the opening of the first eye. Without this medium of knowledge it cannot be, and therefore it was not before it. But without that eye, that is to say, outside of knowledge, there was also no before, no time. Thus time has no beginning, but all beginning is in time. Since, however, it is the most universal form of the knowable, in which all phenomena are united together through causality, time, with its infinity of past and future, is present in the beginning of knowledge. The phenomenon which fills the first present must at once be known as causally bound up with and dependent upon a sequence of phenomena which stretches infinitely into the past, and this past itself is just as truly conditioned by this first present, as conversely the present is by the past. Accordingly the past out of which the first present arises, is, like it, dependent upon the knowing subject, without which it is nothing. It necessarily happens, however, that this first present does not manifest itself as the first, that is, as having no past for its parent, but as being the beginning of time. It manifests itself rather as the consequence of the past, according to the principle of existence in time. In the same way, the phenomena which fill this first present appear as the effects of earlier phenomena which filled the past, in accordance with the law of causality. Those who like mythological interpretations may take the birth of Kronos (χρονος), the youngest of the Titans, as a symbol of the moment here referred to at which time appears, though indeed it has no beginning; for with him, since he ate his father, the crude productions of heaven and earth cease, and the races of gods and men appear upon the scene.

This explanation at which we have arrived by following the most consistent of the philosophical systems which start from the object, materialism, has brought out clearly the inseparable and reciprocal dependence of subject and object, and at the same time the inevitable antithesis between them. And this knowledge leads us to seek for the inner nature of the world, the thing-in-itself, not in either of the two elements of the idea, but in something quite distinct from it, and which is not encumbered with such a fundamental and insoluble antithesis.

Opposed to the system we have explained, which starts from the object in order to derive the subject from it, is the system which starts from the subject and tries to derive the object from it. The first of these has been of frequent and common occurrence throughout the history of philosophy, but of the second we find only one example, and that a very recent one; the "philosophy of appearance" of J. G. Fichte. In this respect, therefore, it must be considered; little real worth or inner meaning as the doctrine itself had. It was indeed for the most part merely a delusion, but it was delivered with an air of the deepest earnestness, with sustained loftiness of tone and zealous ardour, and was defended with eloquent polemic against weak opponents, so that it was able to present a brilliant exterior and seemed to be something. But the genuine earnestness which keeps truth always steadfastly before it as its goal, and is unaffected by any external influences, was entirely wanting to Fichte, as it is to all philosophers who, like him, concern themselves with questions of the day. In his case, indeed, it could not have been otherwise. A man becomes a philosopher by reason of a certain perplexity, from which he seeks to free himself. This is Plato's θαυμαξειν, which he calls a μαλα ΦιλοσοΦικου παδος. But what distinguishes the false philosopher from the true is this: the perplexity of the latter arises from the contemplation of the world itself, while that of the former results from some book, some system of philosophy which is before him. Now Fichte belongs to the class of the false philosophers. He was made a philosopher by Kant's doctrine of the thing-in-itself, and if it had not been for this he would probably have pursued entirely different ends, with far better results, for he certainly possessed remarkable rhetorical talent. If he had only penetrated somewhat deeply into the meaning of the book that made him a philosopher, "The Critique of Pure Reason," he would have understood that its principal teaching about mind is this. The principle of sufficient reason is not, as all scholastic philosophy maintains, a *veritas æterna*—that is to say, it does not possess an unconditioned validity before, outside of, and above the world. It is relative and conditioned, and valid only in the sphere of phenomena, and thus it may appear as the necessary nexus of space and time, or as the law of causality, or as the law of the ground of knowledge. The inner nature of the world, the thing-in-itself can never be found by the guidance of this principle, for all that it leads to will be found to be dependent and relative and merely phenomenal, not the thing-in-itself. Further, it does not concern the subject, but is only the form of objects, which are therefore not things-in-themselves. The subject must exist along with the object, and the object along with the subject, so that it is impossible that subject and object can stand to each other in a relation of reason and consequent. But Fichte did not take up the smallest fragment of all this. All that interested him about the matter was that the system started from the subject. Now Kant had chosen this procedure in order to show the fallacy of the prevalent systems, which started from the object, and through which the object had come to be regarded as a thing-in-itself. Fichte, however, took this departure from the subject for the really important matter, and like all imitators, he imagined that in going further than Kant he was surpassing him. This philosophy of Fichte, otherwise not worth mentioning, is interesting to us only as the tardy expression of the converse of the old materialism. For materialism was the most consistent system starting from the object, as this is the most consistent system starting from the subject. Materialism overlooked the fact that, with the simplest object, it assumed the subject also; and Fichte overlooked the fact that with the subject (whatever he may call it) he assumed the object also, for no subject is thinkable without an object. Besides this he forgot that all *a priori* deduction, indeed all demonstration in general, must rest upon some necessity, and that all necessity is based on the principle of sufficient reason, because to be necessary, and to follow from given grounds are convertible conceptions.[6] But the principle of sufficient reason is just the universal form of the object as such. Thus it is in the object, but is not valid before and outside of it; it first produces the object and makes it appear in conformity with its regulative principle. We see then that the system which starts from the subject contains the same fallacy as the system, explained above, which starts from the object; it begins by assuming what it proposes to deduce, the necessary correlative of its starting-point.

The method of our own system is *toto genere* distinct from these two opposite misconceptions, for we start neither from the object nor from the subject, but from the *idea*, as the first fact of consciousness. Its first essential, fundamental form, is the antithesis of subject and object. The form of the object again is the principle of sufficient reason in its various forms. Each of these reigns so absolutely in its own class of ideas that, as we have seen, when the special form of the principle of sufficient reason which governs any class of ideas is known, the nature of the whole class is known also: for the whole class, as idea, is no more than this form of the principle of suf-

---

[6] On this see "The Fourfold Root of the Principle of Sufficient Reason," § 49.

ficient reason itself; so that time itself is nothing but the principle of existence in it, *i.e.*, succession; space is nothing but the principle of existence in it, *i.e.*, position; matter is nothing but causality; the concept (as will appear immediately) is nothing but relation to a ground of knowledge. This thorough and consistent relativity of the world as idea, both according to its universal form (subject and object) and according to the form which is subordinate to this (the principle of sufficient reason) warns us, as we said before, to seek the inner nature of the world in an aspect of it which is *quite different and quite distinct from the idea;* and in the next book we shall find this in a fact which is just as immediate to every living being as the idea.

But we must first consider that class of ideas which belongs to man alone. The matter of these is the concept, and the subjective correlative is reason, just as the subjective correlative of the ideas we have already considered was understanding and sensibility, which are also to be attributed to all the lower animals.[7]

8 ☙ As from the direct light of the sun to the borrowed light of the moon, we pass from the immediate idea of perception, which stands by itself and is its own warrant, to reflection, to the abstract, discursive concepts of the reason, which obtain their whole content from knowledge of perception, and in relation to it. As long as we continue simply to perceive, all is clear, firm, and certain. There are neither questions nor doubts nor errors; we desire to go no further, can go no further; we find rest in perceiving, and satisfaction in the present. Perception suffices for itself, and therefore what springs purely from it, and remains true to it, for example, a genuine work of art, can never be false, nor can it be discredited through the lapse of time, for it does not present an opinion but the thing

[7] The first four chapters of the first of the supplementary books belong to these seven paragraphs.

itself. But with abstract knowledge, with reason, doubt and error appear in the theoretical, care and sorrow in the practical. In the idea of perception, illusion may at moments take the place of the real; but in the sphere of abstract thought, error may reign for a thousand years, impose its yoke upon whole nations, extend to the noblest impulses of humanity, and, by the help of its slaves and its dupes, may chain and fetter those whom it cannot deceive. It is the enemy against which the wisest men of all times have waged unequal war, and only what they have won from it has become the possession of mankind. Therefore it is well to draw attention to it at once, as we already tread the ground to which its province belongs. It has often been said that we ought to follow truth even although no utility can be seen in it, because it may have indirect utility which may appear when it is least expected; and I would add to this, that we ought to be just as anxious to discover and to root out all error even when no harm is anticipated from it, because its mischief may be very indirect, and may suddenly appear when we do not expect it, for all error has poison at its heart. If it is mind, if it is knowledge, that makes man the lord of creation, there can be no such thing as harmless error, still less venerable and holy error. And for the consolation of those who in any way and at any time may have devoted strength and life to the noble and hard battle against error, I cannot refrain from adding that, so long as truth is absent, error will have free play, as owls and bats in the night; but sooner would we expect to see the owls and the bats drive back the sun in the eastern heavens, than that any truth which has once been known and distinctly and fully expressed, can ever again be so utterly vanquished and overcome that the old error shall once more reign undisturbed over its wide kingdom. This is the power of truth; its conquest is slow and laborious, but if once the victory be gained it can never be wrested back again.

Besides the ideas we have as yet considered, which, according to their construction, could be referred to time, space, and matter, if we consider them with reference to the object, or to pure sensibility and understanding (*i.e.*, knowledge of causality), if we consider them with reference to the subject, another faculty of knowledge has appeared in man alone of all earthly creatures, an entirely new consciousness, which, with very appropriate and significant exactness, is called *reflection.* For it is in fact derived from the knowledge of perception, and is a reflected appearance of it. But it has assumed a nature fundamentally different. The forms of perception do not affect it, and even the principle of sufficient reason which reigns over all objects has an entirely different aspect with regard to it. It is just this new, more highly endowed, consciousness, this abstract reflex of all that belongs to perception in that conception of the reason which has nothing to do with perception, that gives to man that thoughtfulness which distinguishes his consciousness so entirely from that of the lower animals, and through which his whole behaviour upon earth is so different from that of his irrational fellow-creatures. He far surpasses them in power and also in suffering. They live in the present alone, he lives also in the future and the past. They satisfy the needs of the moment, he provides by the most ingenious preparations for the future, yea for days that he shall never see. They are entirely dependent on the impression of the moment, on the effect of the perceptible motive; he is determined by abstract conceptions independent of the present. Therefore he follows predetermined plans, he acts from maxims, without reference to his surroundings or the accidental impression of the moment. Thus, for example, he can make with composure deliberate preparations for his own death, he can dissemble past finding out, and can carry his secret with him to the grave; lastly, he has an actual choice between several motives; for only in the abstract can such motives, present together in consciousness, afford the knowledge with regard to themselves, that the one excludes the other, and can thus measure themselves against each other with reference to their power over the will. The motive that overcomes, in that it decides the question at issue, is the deliberate determinant of the will, and is a sure indication of its character. The brute, on the other hand, is determined by the present impression; only the fear of present compulsion can constrain its desires, until at last this fear has become custom, and as such continues to determine it; this is called training. The brute feels and perceives; man, in addition to this, *thinks* and *knows*: both *will*. The brute expresses its feelings and dispositions by gestures and sounds; man communicates his thought to others, or, if he wishes, he conceals it, by means of speech. Speech is the first production, and also the necessary organ of his reason. Therefore in Greek and Italian, speech and reason are expressed by the same word; ὁ λογος, *il discorso. Vernunft* is derived from *vernehmen*, which is not a synonym for the verb to hear, but signifies the consciousness of the meaning of thoughts communicated in words. It is by the help of language alone that reason accomplishes its most important achievements,—the united action of several individuals, the planned co-operation of many thousands, civilisation, the state; also science, the storing up of experience, the uniting of common properties in one concept, the communication of truth, the spread of error, thoughts and poems, dogmas and superstitions. The brute first knows death when it dies, but man draws consciously nearer to it every hour that he lives; and this makes life at times a questionable good even to him who has not recognised this character of constant annihilation in the whole of life. Principally on this account man has philosophies and religions, though it is uncertain whether the qualities we admire most in his conduct, voluntary rectitude and nobility of feeling, were ever the fruit of either of them. As results which certainly belong only to them, and as productions of reason in this sphere, we may refer to the marvellous and monstrous opinions of philosophers of various schools, and the extraordinary and sometimes cruel customs of the priests of different religions.

It is the universal opinion of all times and of all nations that these manifold and far-reaching achievements spring from a common principle, from that peculiar intellectual power which belongs distinctively to man and which has been called reason, ὁ λογος, *το λογιστικον*, *το λογιμον*, *ratio*. Besides this, no one finds any difficulty in recognising the manifestations of this faculty, and in saying what is rational and what is irrational, where reason appears as distinguished from the other faculties and qualities of man, or lastly, in pointing out what, on account of the want of reason, we must never expect even from the most sensible brute. The philosophers of all ages may be said to be on the whole at one about this general knowledge of reason, and they have also given prominence to several very important manifestations of it; such as, the control of the emotions and passions, the capacity for drawing conclusions and formulating general principles, even such as are true prior to all experience, and so forth.

The understanding has only one function—immediate knowledge of the relation of cause and effect. Yet the perception of the real world, and all common sense, sagacity, and inventiveness, however multifarious their applications may be, are quite clearly seen to be nothing more than manifestations of that one function. So also the reason has one function; and from it all the manifestations of reason we have mentioned, which distinguish the life of man from that of the brutes, may easily be explained. The application or the non-application of this function is all that is meant by what men have everywhere and always called rational and irrational.[8]

Although concepts are fundamentally different from ideas of perception, they stand in a necessary relation to them, without which they would be nothing. This relation therefore constitutes the whole nature and existence of concepts. Reflection is the necessary copy or repetition of the originally presented world of perception, but it is a special kind of copy in an entirely different material. Thus concepts may quite properly be called ideas of ideas. The principle of sufficient reason has here also a special form. Now we have seen that the form under which the principle of sufficient reason appears in a class of ideas always constitutes and exhausts the whole nature of the class, so far as it consists of ideas, so that time is throughout succession, and nothing more; space is throughout position, and nothing more; matter is throughout causation, and nothing more. In the same way the whole na-

[8] Compare with this paragraph § § 26 and 27 of the third edition of the essay on the principle of sufficient reason.

ture of concepts, or the class of abstract ideas, consists simply in the relation which the principle of sufficient reason expresses in them; and as this is the relation to the ground of knowledge, the whole nature of the abstract idea is simply and solely its relation to another idea, which is its ground of knowledge. This, indeed, may, in the first instance, be a concept, an abstract idea, and this again may have only a similar abstract ground of knowledge; but the chain of grounds of knowledge does not extend *ad infinitum;* it must end at last in a concept which has its ground in knowledge of perception; for the whole world of reflection rests on the world of perception as its ground of knowledge. Hence the class of abstract ideas is in this respect distinguished from other classes; in the latter the principle of sufficient reason always demands merely a relation to another idea of the *same* class, but in the case of abstract ideas, it at last demands a relation to an idea of *another* class.

Those concepts which, as has just been pointed out, are not immediately related to the world of perception, but only through the medium of one, or it may be several other concepts, have been called by preference *abstracta,* and those which have their ground immediately in the world of perception have been called *concreta.* But this last name is only loosely applicable to the concepts denoted by it, for they are always merely *abstracta,* and not ideas of perception. These names, which have originated in a very dim consciousness of the distinctions they imply, may yet, with this explanation, be retained. As examples of the first kind of concepts, *i.e., abstracta* in the fullest sense, we may take "relation," "virtue," "investigation," "beginning," and so on. As examples of the second kind, loosely called *concreta,* we may take such concepts as "man," "stone," "horse," &c. If it were not a somewhat too pictorial and therefore absurd simile, we might very appropriately call the latter the ground floor, and the former the upper stories of the building of reflection.

Reason is feminine in nature; it can only give after it has received. Of itself it has nothing but the empty forms of its operation. There is no absolutely pure rational knowledge except the four principles to which I have attributed metalogical truth; the principles of identity, contradiction, excluded middle, and sufficient reason of knowledge. For even the rest of logic is not absolutely pure rational knowledge. It presupposes the relations and the combinations of the spheres of concepts. But concepts in general only exist after experience of ideas of perception, and as their whole nature consists in their relation to these, it is clear that they presuppose them. No special content, however, is presupposed, but merely the existence of a content generally, and so logic as a whole may fairly pass for pure rational science. In all other sciences reason has received its content from ideas of perception; in mathematics from the relations of space and time, presented in intuition or perception prior to all experience; in pure natural science, that is, in what we know of the course of nature prior to any experience, the content of the science proceeds from the pure understanding, *i.e.*, from the *a priori* knowledge of the law of causality and its connection with those pure intuitions or perceptions of space and time. In all other sciences everything that is not derived from the sources we have just referred to belongs to experience. Speaking generally, *to know rationally* (*wissen*) means to have in the power of the mind, and capable of being reproduced at will, such judgments as have their sufficient ground of knowledge in something outside themselves, *i.e.*, are true. Thus only abstract cognition is *rational knowledge* (*wissen*), which is therefore the result of reason, so that we cannot accurately say of the lower animals that they *rationally know* (*wissen*) anything, although they have apprehension of what is presented in perception, and memory of this, and consequently imagination, which is further proved by the circumstance that they dream. We attribute consciousness to them, and therefore although the word (*bewusstsein*) is derived from the verb to know rationally (*wissen*), the conception of consciousness corresponds generally with that of idea of whatever kind it may be. Thus we attribute life to plants, but not consciousness. *Rational knowledge* (*wissen*) is therefore abstract consciousness, the permanent possession in concepts of the reason, of what has become known in another way.

9 ◆§ *Rational knowledge* (*wissen*) is then all abstract knowledge,—that is, the knowledge which is peculiar to the reason as distinguished from the understanding. Now, as reason only reproduces, for knowledge, what has been received in another way, it does not actually extend our knowledge, but only gives it another form. It enables us to know in the abstract and generally, what first became known in sense-perception, in the concrete. But this is much more important than it appears at first sight when so expressed. For it depends entirely upon the fact that knowledge has become rational or abstract knowledge (*wissen*), that it can be safely preserved, that it is communicable and susceptible of certain and wide-reaching application to practice. Knowledge in the form of sense-perception is valid only of the particular case, extends only to what is nearest, and ends with it, for sensibility and understanding can only comprehend one object at a time. Every enduring, arranged, and planned activity must therefore proceed from principles,—that is, from abstract knowledge, and it must be conducted in accordance with them. Thus, for example, the knowledge of the relation of cause and effect arrived at by the understanding, is in itself far completer, deeper and more exhaustive than anything that can be thought about it in the abstract; the understanding alone knows in perception directly and completely the nature of the effect of a lever, of a pulley, or a cog-wheel, the stability of an arch, and so forth. But on account of the peculiarity of the knowledge of perception just referred to, that it only extends to what is immediately present, the mere understanding can never enable us to construct machines and buildings. Here reason must come in; it must substitute abstract concepts for ideas of perception, and take them as the guide of action; and if they are right, the anticipated result will happen. In the same way we have perfect knowledge in pure perception of

the nature and constitution of the parabola, hyperbola, and spiral; but if we are to make trustworthy application of this knowledge to the real, it must first become abstract knowledge, and by this it certainly loses its character of intuition or perception, but on the other hand it gains the certainty and preciseness of abstract knowledge. The differential calculus does not really extend our knowledge of the curve, it contains nothing that was not already in the mere pure perception of the curve; but it alters the kind of knowledge, it changes the intuitive into an abstract knowledge, which is so valuable for application.

This quality of concepts by which they resemble the stones of a mosaic, and on account of which perception always remains their asymptote, is the reason why nothing good is produced in art by their means. If the singer or the virtuoso attempts to guide his execution by reflection he remains silent. And this is equally true of the composer, the painter, and the poet. The concept always remains unfruitful in art; it can only direct the technical part of it, its sphere is science. We shall consider more fully in the third book, why all true art proceeds from sensuous knowledge, never from the concept. Indeed, with regard to behaviour also, and personal agreeableness in society, the concept has only a negative value in restraining the grosser manifestations of egotism and brutality; so that a polished manner is its commendable production. But all that is attractive, gracious, charming in behaviour, all affectionateness and friendliness, must not proceed from the concepts, for if it does, "we feel intention, and are put out of tune." All dissimulation is the work of reflection; but it cannot be maintained constantly and without interruption: "*nemo potest personam diu ferre fictum*," says Seneca in his book *de clementia;* and so it is generally found out and loses its effect. Reason is needed in the full stress of life, where quick conclusions, bold action, rapid and sure comprehension are required, but it may easily spoil all if it gains the upper hand, and by perplexing hinders the intuitive, direct discovery, and grasp of the right by simple understanding, and thus induces irresolution.

Lastly, virtue and holiness do not proceed from reflection, but from the inner depths of the will, and its relation to knowledge. The exposition of this belongs to another part of our work; this, however, I may remark here, that the dogmas relating to ethics may be the same in the reason of whole nations, but the action of every individual different; and the converse also holds good; action, we say, is guided by *feelings*, —that is, simply not by concepts, but as a matter of fact by the ethical character. Dogmas occupy the idle reason; but action in the end pursues its own course independently of them, generally not according to abstract rules, but according to unspoken maxims, the expression of which is the whole man himself. Therefore, however different the religious dogmas of nations may be, yet in the case of all of them, a good action is accompanied by unspeakable satisfaction, and a bad action by endless remorse. No mockery can shake the former; no priest's absolution can deliver from the latter. Notwithstanding this, we must allow, that for the pursuit of a virtuous life, the application of reason is needful; only it is not its source, but has the subordinate function of preserving resolutions which have been made, of providing maxims to withstand the weakness of the moment, and give consistency to action. It plays the same part ultimately in art also, where it has just as little to do with the essential matter, but assists in carrying it out, for genius is not always at call, and yet the work must be completed in all its parts and rounded off to a whole.

As regards the *content* of the sciences generally, it is, in fact, always the relation of the phenomena of the world to each other, according to the principle of sufficient reason, under the guidance of the *why*, which has validity and meaning only through this principle. *Explanation* is the establishment of this relation. Therefore explanation can never go further than to show two ideas standing to each other in the relation peculiar to that form of the principle of sufficient reason which reigns in the class to which they belong. If this is done we cannot further be asked the question, *why*: for the relation proved is that one which absolutely cannot be imagined as other than it is, *i.e.*, it is the form of all knowledge. Therefore we do not ask why 2 + 2 = 4; or why the equality of the angles of a triangle determines the equality of the sides; or why its effect follows any given cause; or why the truth of the conclusion is evident from the truth of the premises. Every explanation which does not ultimately lead to a relation of which no "why" can further be demanded, stops at an accepted *qualitas occulta;* but this is the character of every original force of nature. Every explanation in natural science must ultimately end with such a *qualitas occulta*, and thus with complete obscurity. It must leave the inner nature of a stone just as much unexplained as that of a human being; it can give as little account of the weight, the cohesion, the chemical qualities, &c., of the former, as of the knowing and acting of the latter. Thus, for example, weight is a *qualitas occulta*, for it can be thought away, and does not proceed as a necessity from the form of knowledge; which, on the contrary, is not the case with the law of inertia, for it follows from the law of causality, and is therefore sufficiently explained if it is referred to that law. There are two things which are altogether inexplicable,—that is to say, do not ultimately lead to the relation which the principle of sufficient reason expresses. These are, first, the principle of sufficient reason itself in all its four forms, because it is the principle of all explanation, which has meaning only in relation to it; secondly, that to which this principle does not extend, but which is the original source of all phenomena; the thing-in-itself, the knowledge of which is not subject to the principle of sufficient reason. We must be content for the present not to understand this thing-in-itself, for it can only be made intelligible by means of the following book, in which we shall resume this consideration of the possible achievements of the sciences. But at the point at which natural science, and indeed every science, leaves things, because not only its explanation of them, but even the principle of this explanation, the principle of sufficient reason, does not extend beyond this point; there philosophy takes them up and treats them after its own method, which is quite distinct from the method of science. In my essay on the principle of sufficient reason, § 51, I have shown how in the different sciences the chief guiding clue is one or other form of that principle; and, in fact, perhaps the most appropriate classification of the sciences might be based upon this circumstance. Every explanation arrived at by the help of this clue is, as we have said, merely relative; it explains things in relation to each other, but something which indeed is presupposed is always left unexplained. In mathematics, for example, this is space and time; in mechanics, physics, and chemistry it is matter, qualities, original forces and laws of nature; in botany and zoology it is the difference of species, and life itself; in history it is the human race with all its properties of thought and will: in all it is that form of the principle of sufficient reason which is respectively applicable. It is peculiar to *philosophy* that it presupposes nothing as known, but treats everything as equally external and a problem; not merely the relations of phenomena, but also the phenomena themselves, and even the principle of sufficient reason to which the other sciences are content to refer everything. In philosophy nothing would be gained by such a reference, as one member of the series is just as external to it as another; and, moreover, that kind of connection is just as much a problem for philosophy as what is joined together by it, and the latter again is just as much a problem after its combination has been explained as before it. For, as we have said, just what the sciences presuppose and lay down as the basis and the limits of their explanation, is precisely and peculiarly the problem of philosophy, which may therefore be said to begin where science ends. It cannot be founded upon demonstrations, for they lead from known principles to unknown, but everything is equally unknown and external to philosophy. There can be no principle in consequence of which the world with all its phenomena first came into existence, and therefore it is not possible to construct, as Spinoza wished, a philosophy which demonstrates *ex firmis principiis*. Philosophy is the most general rational knowledge, the first principles of which cannot therefore be derived from another principle still more general. The principle of contradiction establishes merely the agreement of concepts, but does not itself produce concepts. The principle of sufficient reason explains the connections of phenomena, but not the phenomena themselves; therefore philosophy cannot proceed upon these principles to seek a *causa efficiens* or a *causa finalis* of the whole world. My philosophy, at least, does not by any means seek to know *whence* or *wherefore* the world exists, but merely *what* the world is. But the *why* is here subordinated to the *what*, for it already belongs to the world, as it arises and has meaning and validity only through the form of its phenomena, the principle of sufficient reason. We might indeed say that every one knows what the world is without help, for he is himself that subject of knowledge of which the world is the idea; and so far this would be true. But that knowledge is empirical, is in the concrete; the task of philosophy is to reproduce this in the abstract, to raise to permanent rational knowledge the successive changing perceptions, and in general, all that is contained under the wide concept of feeling and merely negatively defined as not abstract, distinct, rational knowledge. It must therefore consist of a statement in the abstract, of the nature of the whole world, of the whole, and of all the parts. In order then that it may not lose itself in the endless multitude of particular judgments, it must make use of abstraction and think everything individual in the universal, and its differences also in the universal. It must therefore partly separate and partly unite, in order to present to rational knowledge the whole manifold of the world generally, according to its nature, comprehended in a few abstract concepts. Through these concepts, in which it fixes the nature of the world, the whole individual must be known as well as the universal, the knowledge of both therefore must be bound together to the minutest point. Therefore the capacity for philosophy consists just in that in which Plato placed it, the knowledge of the one in the many, and the many in the one. Philosophy will therefore be a sum total of general judgments, whose ground of knowledge is immediately the world itself in its entirety, without excepting anything; thus all that is to be found in human consciousness; it will be *a complete recapitulation, as it were, a reflection, of the world in abstract concepts*, which is only possible by the union of the essentially identical in *one* concept and the relegation of the different to another.

The agreement which all the sides and parts of the world have with each other, just because they belong to a whole, must also be found in this abstract copy of it. Therefore the judgments in this sum-total could to a certain extent be deduced from each other, and indeed always reciprocally so deduced. Yet to make the first judgment possible, they must all be present, and thus implied as prior to it in the knowledge of the world in the concrete, especially as all direct proof is more certain than indirect proof; their harmony with each other virtue of which they come together into the unity of *one* thought, and which arises from the harmony and unity of the world of perception itself, which is their common ground of knowledge, is not therefore to be made use of to establish them, as that which is prior to them, but is only added as a confirmation of their truth. This problem itself can only become quite clear in being solved.

The many-sided view of life as a whole which man, as distinguished from the lower animals, possesses through reason, may be compared to a geometrical, colourless, abstract, reduced plan of his actual life. He, therefore, stands to the lower animals as the navigator who, by means of chart, compass, and quadrant, knows accurately his course and his position at any time upon the sea, stands to the uneducated sailors who see only the waves and the heavens. Thus it is worth noticing, and indeed wonderful, how, besides his life in the concrete, man always lives another life in the abstract. In the former he is given as a prey to all the storms of actual life, and to the influence of the present; he must struggle, suffer, and die like the brute. But his life in the abstract, as it lies before his rational consciousness, is the still reflection of the former, and of the world in which he lives; it is just that reduced chart or plan to which we have referred. Here in the sphere of quiet deliberation, what completely possessed him and moved him intensely before, appears to him cold, colourless, and for the moment external to him; he is merely the spectator, the observer. In respect of this withdrawal into reflection he may be compared to an actor who has played his part in one scene, and who takes his place among the audience till it is time for him to go upon the stage again, and quietly looks on at whatever may happen, even though it be the preparation for his own death (in the piece), but afterwards he again goes on the stage and acts and suffers as he must. From this double life proceeds that quietness peculiar to human beings, so very different from the thoughtlessness of the brutes, and with which, in accordance with previous reflection, or a formed determination, or a recognised necessity, a man suffers or accomplishes in cold blood, what is of the utmost and often terrible importance to him; suicide, execution, the duel, enterprises of every kind fraught with danger to life, and, in general, things against which his whole animal nature rebels. Under such circumstances we see to what an extent reason has mastered the animal nature, and we say to the strong: σιδηρειον νυ τοι ἧτορ! (*ferreum certe tibi cor*), Il. 24, 521.[9] Here we can say truly that reason manifests itself practically, and thus wherever action is guided by reason, where the motives are abstract concepts, wherever we are not determined by particular ideas of perception, nor by the impression of the moment which guides the brutes, there *practical reason* shows itself.

The ideal explained in the *Stoical philosophy* is the most complete development of *practical reason* in the true and genuine sense of the word; it is the highest summit to which man can attain by the mere use of his reason, and in it his difference from the brutes shows itself most distinctly. For the ethics of Stoicism are, originally and essentially, not a doctrine of virtue, but merely a guide to a rational life, the end and aim of which is happiness through peace of mind. Virtuous conduct appears in it as it were merely by accident, as the means, not as the end. Therefore the ethical theory of Stoicism is in its whole nature and point of view fundamentally different from the ethical systems which lay stress directly upon virtue, such as the doctrines of the Vedas, of Plato, of Christianity, and of Kant. Yet the ethics of Stoicism

---

[9] Surely your heart is of iron.

teach that happiness can only be attained with certainty through inward peace and quietness of spirit (ἀταραξία), and that this again can only be reached through virtue; this is the whole meaning of the saying that virtue is the highest good. But if indeed by degrees the end is lost sight of in the means, and virtue is inculcated in a way which discloses an interest entirely different from that of one's own happiness, for it contradicts this too distinctly; this is just one of those inconsistencies by means of which, in every system, the immediately known, or, as it is called, felt truth, leads us back to the right way in defiance of syllogistic reasoning; as, for example, we see clearly in the ethical teaching of Spinoza, which deduces a pure doctrine of virtue from the egoistical *suum utile quœrere* by means of palpable sophisms. According to this, as I conceive the spirit of the Stoical ethics, their source lies in the question whether the great prerogative of man, reason, which, by means of planned action and its results, relieves life and its burdens so much, might not also be capable of freeing him at once, directly, *i.e.*, through mere knowledge, completely, or nearly so, of the sorrows and miseries of every kind of which his life is full. They held that it was not in keeping with the prerogative of reason that the nature given with it, which by means of it comprehends and contemplates an infinity of things and circumstances, should yet, through the present, and the accidents that can be contained in the few years of a life that is short, fleeting, and uncertain, be exposed to such intense pain, to such great anxiety and suffering, as arise from the tempestuous strain of the desires and the antipathies; and they believed that the due application of reason must raise men above them, and can make them invulnerable. Therefore Antisthenes says: Δει κτασθαι νουν, η βροχον (*aut mentem parandam, aut laqueum*,[10] *i.e.*, life is so full of troubles and vexations, that one must either rise above it by means of corrected thoughts, or leave it. It was seen that want and suffering did not directly and of necessity spring from not having, but from desiring to have and not having; that there-

---

[10] Either a prepared mind, or death.

fore this desire to have is the necessary condition under which alone it becomes a privation not to have and begets pain. Men learned also from experience that it is only the hope of what is claimed that begets and nourishes the wish; therefore neither the many unavoidable evils which are common to all, nor unattainable blessings, disquiet or trouble us, but only the trifling more or less of those things which we can avoid or attain; indeed, not only what is absolutely unavoidable or unattainable, but also what is merely relatively so, leaves us quite undisturbed; therefore the ills that have once become joined to our individuality, or the good things that must of necessity always be denied us, are treated with indifference, in accordance with the peculiarity of human nature that every wish soon dies and can no more beget pain if it is not nourished by hope. It followed from all this that happiness always depends upon the proportion between our claims and what we receive. It is all one whether the quantities thus related be great or small, and the proportion can be established just as well by diminishing the amount of the first as by increasing the amount of the second; and in the same way it also follows that all suffering proceeds from the want of proportion between what we demand and expect and what we get. Now this want of proportion obviously lies only in knowledge, and it could be entirely abolished through fuller insight.[11] Therefore Chrysippus says: one ought to live with a due knowledge of the transitory nature of the things of the world. For as often as a man loses self-command, or is struck down by a misfortune, or grows angry, or becomes faint-hearted, he shows that he finds things different from what he expected, consequently that he was caught in error, and did not know the world and life, did not know that the will of the individual is crossed at every step by the chance of inanimate nature and the antagonism of aims and the wickedness of other individuals: he has therefore either not made use of his reason

[11] Omnes perturbationes judicio censent fieri et opinione. Cic. Tusc., 4, 6. *Ταρασσει τους ανθρωπους ου τα πραγματα, αλλα τα περι των πραγματων δογματα* (Perturbant homines non res ipsæ, sed de rebus opiniones). Epictet., c. v.

in order to arrive at a general knowledge of this characteristic of life, or he lacks judgment, in that he does not recognise in the particular what he knows in general, and is therefore surprised by it and loses his self-command.[12] Thus also every keen pleasure is an error and an illusion, for no attained wish can give lasting satisfaction; and, moreover, every possession and every happiness is but lent by chance for an uncertain time, and may therefore be demanded back the next hour. All pain rests on the passing away of such an illusion; thus both arise from defective knowledge; the wise man therefore holds himself equally aloof from joy and sorrow, and no event disturbs his αταραζια.

The ethical system of Stoicism, regarded as a whole, is in fact a very valuable and estimable attempt to use the great prerogative of man, reason, for an important and salutary end; to raise him above the suffering and pain to which all life is exposed, by means of a maxim—

> "Qua ratione queas traducere leniter ævum:
> Ne te semper inops agitet vexetque cupido,
> Ne pavor et rerum mediocriter utilium spes,"

and thus to make him partake, in the highest degree, of the dignity which belongs to him as a rational being, as distinguished from the brutes; a dignity of which, in this sense at any rate, we can speak, though not in any other. It is a consequence of my view of the ethical system of Stoicism that it must be explained at the part of my work at which I consider what reason is and what it can do. But although it may to a certain extent be possible to attain that end through the application of reason, and through a purely rational system of ethics, and although experience shows that the happiest

---

[12] Τουτο γαρ εστι το αιτιρν τοις ανθρωποις παντων των κακων, το τας προληψεις τας κοινας μη δυνασθαι εφαρμοξειν ταις επι μερους (Hæc est causa mortalibus omnium malorum, non posse communes notiones aptare singularibus). Epict. dissert., ii., 26.

Would you learn how to pass your years tranquilly; do not let greedy desire always vex and agitate you, nor fear nor hope of mediocre wealth.

men are those purely rational characters commonly called practical philosophers,—and rightly so, because just as the true, that is, the theoretical philosopher carries life into the concept, they carry the concept into life,—yet it is far from the case that perfection can be attained in this way, and that the reason, rightly used, can really free us from the burden and sorrow of life, and lead us to happiness. Rather, there lies an absolute contradiction in wishing to live without suffering, and this contradiction is also implied in the commonly used expression, "blessed life." This will become perfectly clear to whoever comprehends the whole of the following exposition. In this purely rational system of ethics the contradiction reveals itself thus, the Stoic is obliged in his doctrine of the way to the blessed life (for that is what his ethical system always remains) to insert a recommendation of suicide (as among the magnificent ornaments and apparel of Eastern despots there is always a costly vial of poison) for the case in which the sufferings of the body, which cannot be philosophised away by any principles or syllogistic reasonings, are paramount and incurable; thus its one aim, blessedness, is rendered vain, and nothing remains as a mode of escape from suffering except death; in such a case then death must be voluntarily accepted, just as we would take any other medicine. Here then a marked antagonism is brought out between the ethical system of Stoicism and all those systems referred to above which make virtue in itself directly, and accompanied by the most grievous sorrows, their aim, and will not allow a man to end his life in order to escape from suffering. Not one of them, however, was able to give the true reason for the rejection of suicide, but they laboriously collected illusory explanations from all sides: the true reason will appear in the Fourth Book in the course of the development of our system. But the antagonism referred to reveals and establishes the essential difference in fundamental principle between Stoicism, which is just a special form of endæmonism, and those doctrines we have mentioned, although both are often at one in their results, and are apparently related. And the inner contradiction referred to above, with which the ethical system of

Stoicism is affected even in its fundamental thoughts, shows itself further in the circumstance that its ideal, the Stoic philosopher, as the system itself represents him, could never obtain life or inner poetic truth, but remains a wooden, stiff lay-figure of which nothing can be made. He cannot himself make use of his wisdom, and his perfect peace, contentment, and blessedness directly contradict the nature of man, and preclude us from forming any concrete idea of him. When compared with him, how entirely different appear the overcomers of the world, and voluntary hermits that Indian philosophy presents to us, and has actually produced; or indeed, the holy man of Christianity, that excellent form full of deep life, of the greatest poetic truth, and the highest significance, which stands before us in perfect virtue, holiness, and sublimity, yet in a state of supreme suffering.

Friedrich Nietzsche

THE RELIGIOUS MOOD AND THE NATURAL HISTORY OF MORALS

Friedrich Nietzsche
[1844–1900]

In our own time few concepts have been more violently misrepresented than Friedrich Nietzsche's foreshadowing of the Superman, his insistence upon the need for the transvaluation of all values, his theory of the eternal recurrence, his doctrine of the will to power and his demand for a morality that transcends all accepted moralities, carrying it beyond good and evil. Countless people have been influenced to envisage him as a "blond beast," the anti-Christ, the demophobe and the patron philosopher of Nazism. It is a portrait drawn in fear and prejudice. More poet than philosopher, and more prophet than both, Nietzsche, the idol smasher, finds religion and the state wanting. He proclaims himself with lyric ecstasy as the "yea-sayer" to life and declares himself the destroyer of old values to clear the way for the virtues of strength against meekness, health against decadence, a world polity against chauvinism, and the free spirit against slave morality. "The Religious Mood" and "The Natural History of Morals" are taken from *Beyond Good and Evil.*

THE RELIGIOUS MOOD

FRIEDRICH NIETZSCHE

☙ THE human soul and its limits, the range of man's inner experiences hitherto attained, the heights, depths and distances of these experiences, the entire history of the soul *up to the present time*, and its still unexhausted possibilities: this is the preordained hunting-domain for a born psychologist and lover of a "big hunt." But how often must he say despairingly to himself: "A single individual! alas, only a single individual! and this great forest, this virgin forest!" So he would like to have some hundreds of hunting assistants, and fine trained hounds, that he could send into the history of the human soul, to drive *his* game together. In vain: again and again he experiences, profoundly and bitterly, how difficult it is to find assistants and dogs for all the things that directly excite his curiosity. The evil of sending scholars into new and dangerous hunting-domains, where courage, sagacity, and subtlety in every sense are required, is that they are no longer serviceable just when the "*big hunt*," and also the great danger commences,—it is precisely then that they lose their keen eye and nose. In order, for instance, to divine and determine what sort of history the problem of *knowledge and conscience* has hitherto had in the souls of *homines religiosi*, a person would perhaps himself have to possess as profound, as bruised, as immense an experience as the intellectual conscience of Pascal; and then he would still require that wide-spread heaven of clear, wicked spirituality, which, from above, would be able to oversee, arrange, and effectively formulise this mass of dangerous and painful experiences.—But who could do me this service! And who would have time to wait for such servants!—they evidently appear too rarely, they are so improbable at all times! Eventually one must do everything *oneself* in order to know something; which means that one has *much* to do!—But a curiosity like mine is once for all the most agreeable of vices—pardon me! I mean to say that the love of truth has its reward in heaven, and already upon earth.

☙ Faith, such as early Christianity desired, and not infrequently achieved in the midst of a sceptical and southernly free-spirited world, which had centuries of struggle between philosophical schools behind it and in it, counting besides the education in tolerance which the *imperium Romanum* gave—this faith is *not* that sincere, austere slave-faith by which perhaps a Luther or a Cromwell, or some other northern barbarian of the spirit remained attached to his God and Christianity; it is much rather the faith of Pascal, which resembles in a terrible manner a continuous suicide of reason—a tough, long-lived, wormlike reason, which is not to be slain at once and with a single blow. The Christian faith from the beginning, is sacrifice: the sacrifice of all freedom, all pride, all self-confidence of spirit; it is at the same time subjection, self-derision, and self-mutilation. There is cruelty and religious Phœnicianism in this faith, which is adapted to a tender, many-sided, and very fastidious conscience; it takes for granted that the subjection of the spirit is indescribably *painful*, that all the past and all the habits of such a spirit resist the *absurdissimum*, in the form of which "faith" comes to it. Modern men, with their obtuseness as regards all Christian nomenclature, have no longer the sense for the terribly superlative conception which was implied to an antique taste by the paradox of the formula, "God on the Cross." Hitherto there had never and nowhere been such boldness in inversion, nor anything at once so dreadful, questioning, and questionable as this formula: it promised a transvaluation of all ancient values.—It was the Orient, the *profound* Orient, it was the Oriental slave who thus took revenge on Rome and its noble, light-minded toleration, on the Roman "Catholicism" of non-faith; and it was always, not the faith, but the freedom from the faith, the half-stoical and smiling indifference to the seriousness of the faith, which made the slaves indignant at their masters and revolt against them. "Enlightenment" causes revolt: for the slave desires the unconditioned, he understands nothing but the tyrannous, even in morals; he loves as he hates, without *nuance*, to the very depths, to the point of pain, to the point of sickness—his many *hidden* sufferings make him revolt against the noble taste which seems to *deny* suffering. The scepticism with regard to suffering, fundamentally only an attitude of aristocratic morality, was not the least of the causes, also, of the last great slave-insurrection which began with the French Revolution.

☙§ Wherever the religious neurosis has appeared on the earth so far, we find it connected with three dangerous prescriptions as to regimen: solitude, fasting, and sexual abstinence—but without its being possible to determine with certainty which is cause and which is effect, or *if* any relation at all of cause and effect exists there. This latter doubt is justified by the fact that one of the most regular symptoms among savage as well as among civilised peoples is the most sudden and excessive sensuality; which then with equal suddenness transforms into penitential paroxysms, world-renunciation, and will-renunciation: both symptoms perhaps explainable as disguised epilepsy? But nowhere is it *more* obligatory to put aside explanations: around no other type has there grown such a mass of absurdity and superstition, no other type seems to have been more interesting to men and even to philosophers—perhaps it is time to become just a little indifferent here, to learn caution, or, better still, to look away, *to go away*.—Yet in the background of the most recent philosophy, that of Schopenhauer, we find almost as the problem in itself, this terrible note of interrogation of the religious crisis and awakening. How is the negation of will *possible?* how is the saint possible?—that seems to have been the very question with which Schopenhauer made a start and became a philosopher. And thus it was a genuine Schopenhauerian consequence, that his most convinced adherent (perhaps also his last, as far as Germany is concerned), namely, Richard Wagner, should bring his own life-work to an end just here, and should finally put that terrible and eternal type upon the stage as Kundry, *type vécu,* and as it loved and lived, at the very time that the mad-doctors in almost all European countries had an opportunity to study the type close at hand, wherever the religious neurosis—or as I call it, "the religious mood"—made its latest epidemical outbreak and display as the "Salvation Army."—If it be a question, however, as to what has been so extremely interesting to men of all sorts in all ages, and even to philosophers, in the whole phenomenon of the saint, it is undoubtedly the appearance of the miraculous therein—namely, the immediate *succession of opposites,* of states of the soul regarded as morally antithetical: it was believed here to be self-evident that a "bad man" was all at once turned into a "saint," a good man. The hitherto existing psychology was wrecked at this point; it is not possible it may have happened principally because psychology had placed itself under the dominion of morals, because it *believed* in oppositions of moral values, and saw, read, and *interpreted* these oppositions into the text and facts of the case? What? "Miracle" only an error of interpretation? A lack of philology?

❧ It seems that the Latin races are far more deeply attached to their Catholicism than we Northerners are to Christianity generally, and that consequently unbelief in Catholic countries means something quite different from what it does among Protestants—namely, a sort of revolt against the spirit of the race, while with us it is rather a return to the spirit (or non-spirit) of the race. We Northerners undoubtedly derive our origin from barbarous races, even as regards our talents for religion—we have *poor* talents for it. One may make an exception in the case of the Celts, who have theretofore furnished also the best soil for Christian infection in the north: the Christian ideal blossomed forth in France as much as ever the pale sun of the north would allow it. How strangely pious for our taste are still these later French sceptics, whenever there is any Celtic blood in their origin! How Catholic, how un-German does Auguste Comte's Sociology seem to us, with the Roman logic of its instincts! How Jesuitical, that amiable and shrewd cicerone of Port-Royal, Sainte-Beuve, in spite of all his hostility to Jesuits! And even Ernest Renan: how inaccessible to us Northerners does the language of such a Renan appear, in whom every instant the merest touch of religious thrill throws his refined voluptuous and comfortably couching soul off its balance! Let us repeat after him these fine sentences—and what wickedness and haughtiness is immediately aroused by way of answer in our probably less beautiful but harder souls, that is to say, in our more German souls!—"*Disons donc hardiment que la religion est un produit de l'homme normal, que l'homme est le plus dans le vrai quand il est le plus religieux et le plus assuré d'une destinée infinie. . . . C'est quand il est bon qu'il veut que la virtu corresponde à un order éternal, c'est quand il contemple les choses d'une manière désintéressée qu'il trouve la mort révoltante et absurde. Comment ne pas supposer que c'est dans ces moments là, que l'homme voit le mieux?*" . . . These sentences are so extremely *antipodal* to my ears and habits of thought, that in my first impulse of rage on finding them, I wrote on the margin, "*la niaiserie religieuse par excellence!*" —until in my later rage I even took a fancy to them, these sentences with their truth absolutely inverted! It is so nice and such a distinction to have one's own antipodes!

§ That which is so astonishing in the religious life of the ancient Greeks is the irrestrainable stream of *gratitude* which it pours forth—it is a very superior kind of man who takes *such* an attitude towards nature and life.—Later on, when the populace got the upper hand in Greece, *fear* became rampant also in religion; and Christianity was preparing itself.

☙§ The passion for God: there are churlish, honest-hearted, and importunate kinds of it, like that of Luther—the whole of Protestantism lacks the southern *delicatezza*. There is an Oriental exaltation of the mind in it, like that of an undeservedly favoured or elevated slave, as in the case of St. Augustine, for instance, who lacks in an offensive manner, all nobility in bearing and desires. There is a feminine tenderness and sensuality in it, which modestly and unconsciously longs for a *unio mystica et physica*, as in the case of Madame de Guyon. In many cases it appears, curiously enough, as the disguise of a girl's or youth's puberty; here and there even as the hysteria of an old maid, also as her last ambition. The Church has frequently canonised the woman in such a case.

☙§ The mightiest men have hitherto always bowed reverently before the saint, as the enigma of self-subjugation and utter voluntary privation—why did they thus bow? They divined in him—and as it were behind the questionableness of his frail and wretched appearance—the superior force which wished to test itself by such a subjugation; the strength of will, in which they recognized their own strength and love of power, and knew how to honour it: they honoured something in themselves when they honoured the saint. In addition to this, the contemplation of the saint suggested to them a suspicion: such an enormity of self-negation and anti-naturalness will not have been coveted for nothing—they have said, inquiringly. There is perhaps a reason for it, some very great danger, about which the ascetic might wish to be more accurately informed through his secret interlocutors and visitors? In a word, the mighty ones of the world learned to have a new fear before him, they divined a new power, a strange, still unconquered enemy:—it was the "Will to Power" which obliged them to halt before the saint. They had to question him.

❧ In the Jewish "Old Testament," the book of divine justice, there are men, things, and sayings on such an immense scale, that Greek and Indian literature has nothing to compare with it. One stands with fear and reverence before those stupendous remains of what man was formerly, and one has sad thoughts about old Asia and its little out-pushed peninsula Europe, which would like, by all means, to figure before Asia as the "Progress of Mankind." To be sure, he who is himself only a slender, tame house-animal, and knows only the wants of a house-animal (like our cultured people of today, including the Christians of "cultured" Christianity), need neither be amazed nor even sad amid those ruins—the taste for the Old Testament is a touchstone with respect to "great" and "small": perhaps he will find that the New Testament, the book of grace, still appeals more to his heart (there is much of the odour of the genuine, tender, stupid beadsman and petty soul in it). To have bound up this New Testament (a kind of *rococo* of taste in every respect) along with the Old Testament into one book, as the "Bible," as "The Book in Itself," is perhaps the greatest audacity and "sin against the Spirit" which literary Europe has upon its conscience.

❧ Why Atheism nowadays? "The father" in God is thoroughly refuted; equally so "the judge," "the rewarder." Also his "free will": he does not hear—and even if he did, he would not know how to help. The worst is that he seems incapable of communicating himself clearly; is he uncertain?—This is what I have made out (by questioning and listening at a variety of conversations) to be the cause of the decline of European theism; it appears to me that though the religious instinct is in vigorous growth,—it rejects the theistic satisfaction with profound distrust.

❧ What does all modern philosophy mainly do? Since Descartes—and indeed more in defiance of him than on the the basis of his procedure—an *attentat* has been made on the part of all philosophers on the old conception of the soul, under the guise of a criticism of the subject and predicate conception—that is to say, an *attentat* on the fundamental presupposition of Christian doctrine. Modern philosophy, as epistemological scepticism, is secretly or openly *anti-Christian*, although (for keener ears, be it said) by no means anti-religious. Formerly, in effect, one believed in "the soul" as one believed in grammar and the grammatical subject: one said, "I" is the condition, "think" is the predicate and is conditioned—to think is an activity for which one *must* suppose a subject as cause. The attempt was then made, with marvellous tenacity and subtlety, to see if one could not get out of this net,—to see if the opposite was not perhaps true: "think" the condition, and "I" the conditioned; "I," therefore, only a synthesis which has been *made* by thinking itself. *Kant* really wished to prove that, starting from the subject, the subject could not be proved—nor the object either: the possibility of an *apparent existence* of the subject, and therefore of "the soul," may not always have been strange to him,—the thought which once had an immense power on earth as the Vedanta philosophy.

§ There is a great ladder of religious cruelty, with many rounds; but three of these are the most important. Once on a time men sacrificed human beings to their God, and perhaps just those they loved the best—to this category belong the firstling sacrifices of all primitive religions, and also the sacrifice of the Emperor Tiberius in the Mithra-Grotto on the Island of Capri, that most terrible of all Roman anachronisms. Then, during the moral epoch of mankind, they sacrificed to their God the strongest instincts they possessed, their "nature"; *this* festal joy shines in the cruel glances of ascetics and "anti-natural" fanatics. Finally, what still remained to be sacrificed? Was it not necessary in the end for men to sacrifice everything comforting, holy, healing, all hope, all faith in hidden harmonies, in future blessedness and justice? Was it not necessary to sacrifice God himself, and out of cruelty to themselves to worship stone, stupidity, gravity, fate, nothingness? To sacrifice God for nothingness—this paradoxical mystery of the ultimate cruelty has been reserved for the rising generation; we all know something thereof already.

☙ Whoever, like myself, prompted by some enigmatical desire, has long endeavoured to go to the bottom of the question of pessimism and free it from the half-Christian, half-German narrowness and stupidity in which it has finally presented itself to this century, namely, in the form of Schopenhauer's philosophy; whoever, with an Asiatic and super-Asiatic eye, has actually looked inside, and into the most world-renouncing of all possible modes of thought—beyond good and evil, and no longer like Buddha and Schopenhauer, under the dominion and delusion of morality,—whoever has done this, has perhaps just thereby, without really desiring it, opened his eyes to behold the opposite ideal: the ideal of the most world-approving, exuberant and vivacious man, who has not only learned to compromise and arrange with that which was and is, but wishes to have it again *as it was and is*, for all eternity, insatiably calling out *de capo*, not only to himself, but to the whole piece and play; and not only the play, but actually to him who requires the play—and makes it necessary; because he always requires himself anew—and makes himself necessary.—What? And this would not be—*circulus vitiosus deus?*

☙ The distance, and as it were the space around man, grows with the strength of his intellectual vision and insight: his world becomes profounder; new stars, new enigmas, and notions are ever coming into view. Perhaps everything on which the intellectual eye has exercised its acuteness and profundity has just been an occasion for its exercise, something of a game, something for children and childish minds. Perhaps the most solemn conceptions that have caused the most fighting and suffering, the conceptions "God" and "sin," will one day seem to us of no more importance than a child's plaything or a child's pain seems to an old man;—and perhaps another plaything and another pain will then be necessary once more for "the old man"—always childish enough, an eternal child!

☙ Has it been observed to what extent outward idleness, or semi-idleness, is necessary to a real religious life (alike for its favourite microscopic labour of self-examination, and for its soft placidity called "prayer," the state of perpetual readiness for the "coming of God"), I mean the idleness with a good conscience, the idleness of olden times and of blood, to which the aristocratic sentiment that work is *dishonouring*—that it vulgarises body and soul—is not quite unfamiliar? And that consequently the modern, noisy, time-engrossing, conceited, foolishly proud laboriousness educates and prepares for "unbelief" more than anything else? Amongst these, for instance, who are at present living apart from religion in Germany, I find "free-thinkers" of diversified species and origin, but above all a majority of those in whom laboriousness from generation to generation has dissolved the religious instincts; so that they no longer know what purpose religions serve, and only note their existence in the world with a kind of dull astonishment. They feel themselves already fully occupied, these good people, be it by their business or by their pleasures, not to mention the "Fatherland," and the newspapers, and their "family duties"; it seems that they have no time whatever left for religion; and above all, it is not obvious to them whether it is a question of a new business or a new pleasure—for it is impossible, they say to themselves, that people should go to church merely to spoil their tempers. They are by no means enemies of religious customs; should certain circumstances, State affairs perhaps, require their participation in such customs, they do what is required, as so many things are done—with a patient and unassuming seriousness, and without much curiosity or discomfort;—they live too much apart and outside to feel even the necessity for a *for* or *against* in such matters. Among those indifferent persons may be reckoned nowadays the majority of German Protestants of the middle classes, especially in the great laborious centres of trade and commerce; also the majority of laborious scholars, and the entire University personnel (with the exception of the theologians, whose existence and possibility there always give psychologists new and more subtle puzzles to solve). On the part of pious, or merely church-going people, there is seldom any idea of *how much* good will, one might say arbitrary will, is now necessary for a German scholar to take the problem of religion seriously; his whole profession (and as I have said, his whole workmanlike laboriousness, to which he is compelled by his modern conscience) inclines him to a lofty and almost charitable serenity as regards religion, with which is occasionally mingled a slight disdain for the "uncleanliness" of spirit which he takes for granted wherever any one still professes to belong to the Church. It is only with the help of history (*not* through his own personal experience, therefore) that the scholar succeeds in bringing himself to a respectful seriousness, and to a certain timid deference in presence of religions; but even when his sentiments have reached the stage of gratitude towards them, he has not personally advanced one step nearer to that which still maintains itself as Church or as piety; perhaps even the contrary. The practical indifference to religious matters in the midst of which he has been born and brought up, usually sublimates itself in his case into circumspection and cleanliness, which shuns contact with religious men and things; and it may be just the depth of his tolerance and humanity which prompts him to avoid the delicate trouble which tolerance itself brings with it.—Every age has its own divine type of naïveté, for the discovery of which other ages may envy it: and how much naïveté—adorable, childlike, and boundlessly foolish naïveté is involved in this belief of the scholar in his superiority, in the good conscience of his tolerance, in the unsuspecting, simple certainty with which his instinct treats the religious man as a lower and less valuable type, beyond, before, and *above* which he himself has developed—he, the little arrogant dwarf and mob-man, the sedulously alert, head-and-hand drudge of "ideas," of "modern ideas"!

§ Whoever has seen deeply into the world has doubtless divined what wisdom there is in the fact that men are superficial. It is their preservative instinct which teaches them to be flighty, lightsome, and false. Here and there one finds a passionate and exaggerated adoration of "pure forms" in philosophers as well as in artists: it is not to be doubted that whoever has *need* of the cult of the superficial to that extent, has at one time or another made an unlucky dive *beneath* it. Perhaps there is even an order of rank with respect to those burnt children, the born artists who find the enjoyment of life only in trying to *falsify* its image (as if taking wearisome revenge on it); one might guess to what degree life has disgusted them, by the extent to which they wish to see its image falsified, attenuated, ultrafied, and deified;—one might reckon the *homines religiosi* amongst the artists, as their *highest* rank. It is the profound, suspicious fear of an incurable pessimism which compels whole centuries to fasten their teeth into a religious interpretation of existence: the fear of the instinct which divines that truth might be attained *too soon,* before man has become strong enough, hard enough, artist enough. . . . Piety, the "Life in God," regarded in this light, would appear as the most elaborate and ultimate product of the *fear* of truth, as artist-adoration and artist-intoxication in presence of the most logical of all falsifications, as the will to the inversion of truth, to untruth at any price. Perhaps there has hitherto been no more effective means of beautifying man than piety; by means of it man can become so artful, so superficial, so iridescent, and so good, that his appearance no longer offends.

§ To love mankind *for God's sake*—this has so far been the noblest and remotest sentiment to which mankind has attained. That love to mankind, without any redeeming intention in the background, is only an *additional* folly and brutishness, that the inclination to this love has first to get its proportion, its delicacy, its grain of salt and sprinkling of ambergris from a higher inclination:—whoever first perceived and "experienced" this, however his tongue may have stammered as it attempted to express such a delicate matter, let him for all time be holy and respected, as the man who has so far flown highest and gone astray in the finest fashion!

☙ The philosopher, as *we* free spirits understand him—as the man of the greatest responsibility, who has the conscience for the general development of mankind,—will use religion for his disciplining and educating work, just as he will use the contemporary political and economic conditions. The selecting and disciplining influence—destructive, as well as creative and fashioning—which can be exercised by means of religion is manifold and varied, according to the sort of people placed under its spell and protection. For those who are strong and independent, destined and trained to command, in whom the judgment and skill of a ruling race is incorporated, religion is an additional means for overcoming resistance in the exercise of authority—as a bond which binds rulers and subjects in common, betraying and surrendering to the former the conscience of the latter, their inmost heart, which would fain escape obedience. And in the case of the unique natures of noble origin, if by virtue of superior spirituality they should incline to a more retired and contemplative life, reserving to themselves only the more refined forms of government (over chosen disciples or members of an order), religion itself may be used as a means for obtaining peace from the noise and trouble of managing *grosser* affairs, and for securing immunity from the *unavoidable* filth of all political agitation. The Brahmins, for instance, understood this fact. With the help of a religious organisation, they secured to themselves the power of nominating kings for the people, while their sentiments prompted them to keep apart and outside, as men with a higher and super-regal mission. At the same time religion gives inducement and opportunity to some of the subjects to qualify themselves for future ruling and commanding: the slowly ascending ranks and classes, in which, through fortunate marriage customs, volitional power and delight in self-control are on the increase. To them religion offers sufficient incentives and temptations to aspire to higher intellectuality, and to experience the sentiments of authoritative self-control, of silence, and of solitude. Asceticism and Puritanism are almost indispensable means of educating and ennobling a race which seeks to rise above its hereditary baseness and work itself upward to future supremacy. And finally, to ordinary men, to the majority of the people, who exist for service and general utility, and are only so far entitled to exist, religion gives invaluable contentedness with their lot and condition, peace of heart, ennoblement of obedience, additional social happiness and sympathy, with something of transfiguration and embellishment, something of justification of all the commonplaceness, all the meanness, all the semi-animal poverty of their souls. Religion, together with the religious significance of life, sheds sunshine over such perpetually harassed men, and makes even their own aspect endurable to them; it operates upon them as the Epicurean philosophy usually operates upon sufferers of a higher order, in a refreshing and refining manner, almost *turning* suffering *to account*, and in the end even hallowing and vindicating it. There is perhaps nothing so admirable in Christianity and Buddhism as their art of teaching even the lowest to elevate themselves by piety to a seemingly higher order of things, and thereby to retain their satisfaction with the actual world in which they find it difficult enough to live—this very difficulty being necessary.

☙§ To be sure—to make also the bad counter-reckoning against such religions, and to bring to light their secret dangers—the cost is always excessive and terrible when religions do *not* operate as an educational and disciplinary medium in the hands of the philosopher, but rule voluntarily and *paramountly*, when they wish to be the final end, and not a means along with other means. Among men, as among all other animals, there is a surplus of defective, diseased, degenerating, infirm, and necessarily suffering individuals; the successful cases, among men also, are always the exception; and in view of the fact that man is *the animal not yet properly adapted to his environment*, the rare exception. But worse still. The higher the type a man represents, the greater is the improbability that he will *succeed;* the accidental, the law of irrationality in the general constitution of mankind, manifests itself most terribly in its destructive effect on the higher orders of men, the conditions of whose lives are delicate, diverse, and difficult to determine. What, then, is the attitude of the two greatest religions above-mentioned to the *surplus* of failures in life? They endeavour to preserve and keep alive whatever can be preserved; in fact, as the religions *for sufferers*, they take the part of these upon principle; they are always in favour of those who suffer from life as from a disease, and they would fain treat every other experience of life as false and impossible. However highly we may esteem this indulgent and preservative care (inasmuch as in applying to others, it has applied, and applies also to the highest and usually the most suffering type of man), the hitherto *paramount religions*—to give a general appreciation of them—are among the principal causes which have kept the type of "man" upon a lower level—they have preserved too much *that which should have perished.* One has to thank them for invaluable services; and who is sufficiently rich in gratitude not to feel poor at the contemplation of all that the "spiritual men" of Christianity have done for Europe hitherto! But when they had given comfort to the sufferers, courage to the oppressed and despairing, a staff and support to the helpless, and when they had allured from society into convents and spiritual penitentiaries the broken-hearted and distracted: what else had they to do in order to work systematically in that fashion, and with a good conscience, for the preservation of all the sick and suffering, which means, in deed and in truth, to work for *the deterioration of the European race?* To *reverse* all estimates of value—*that* is what they had to do! And to shatter the strong, to spoil great hopes, to cast suspicion on the delight in beauty, to break down everything autonomous, manly, conquering, and imperious—all instincts which are natural to the highest and most successful type of "man"—into uncertainty, distress of conscience, and self-destruction; forsooth, to invert all love of the earthly and of supremacy over the earth, into hatred of the earth and earthly things—*that* is the task the Church imposed on itself, and was obliged to impose, until, according, to its standard of value, "unworldliness," "unsensuousness," and "higher man" fused into one sentiment. If one could observe the strangely painful, equally coarse and refined comedy of European Christianity with the derisive and impartial eye of an Epicurean god, I should think one would never cease marvelling and laughing; does it not actually seem that some single will has ruled over Europe for eighteen centuries in order to make a *sublime abortion* of man? He, however, who, with opposite requirements (no longer Epicurean) and with some divine hammer in his hand, could approach this almost voluntary degeneration and stunting of mankind, as exemplified in the European Christian (Pascal, for instance), would he not have to cry aloud with rage, pity, and horror: "Oh, you bunglers, presumptuous pitiful bunglers, what have you done! Was that a work for your hands? How you have hacked and botched my finest stone! What have *you* presumed to do!"—I should say that Christianity has hitherto been the most portentous of presumptions. Men, not great enough, nor hard enough to be entitled as artists to take part in fashioning *man;* men, not sufficiently strong and far-sighted to *allow,* with sublime self-constraint, the obvious law of the thousandfold failures and perishings to prevail; men, not sufficiently noble to see the radically different grades of rank and intervals of rank that separate man from man:—*such* men, with their "equality before God," have hitherto swayed the destiny of Europe; until at last a dwarfed, almost ludicrous species has been produced, a gregarious animal, something obliging, sickly, mediocre, the European of the present day.

THE NATURAL HISTORY OF MORALS

FRIEDRICH NIETZSCHE

☙ THE moral sentiment in Europe at present is perhaps as subtle, belated, diverse, sensitive, and refined, as the "Science of Morals" belonging thereto is recent, initial, awkward, and coarse-fingered:—an interesting contrast, which sometimes becomes incarnate and obvious in the very person of a moralist. Indeed, the expression, "Science of Morals" is, in respect to what is designated thereby, far too presumptuous and counter to *good* taste,—which is always a foretaste of more modest expressions. One ought to avow with the utmost fairness *what* is still necessary here for a long time, *what* is alone proper for the present: namely, the collection of material, the comprehensive survey and classification of an immense domain of delicate sentiments of worth, and distinctions of worth, which live, grow, propagate, and perish—and perhaps attempts to give a clear idea of the recurring and more common forms of these living crystallisations—as preparation for a *theory of types* of morality. To be sure, people have not hitherto been so modest. All the philosophers, with a pedantic and ridiculous seriousness, demanded of themselves something very much higher, more pretentious, and ceremonious, when they concerned themselves with morality as a science: they wanted to *give a basis* to morality—and every philosopher hitherto has believed that he has given it a basis; morality itself, however, has been regarded as something "given." How far from their awkward pride was the seemingly insignificant problem—left in dust and decay—of a description of forms of morality, notwithstanding that the finest hands and senses could hardly be fine enough for it! It was precisely owing to moral philosophers knowing the moral facts imperfectly, in an arbitrary epitome, or an accidental abridgement—perhaps as the morality of their environment, their position, their church, their *Zeitgeist*, their climate and zone—it was precisely because they were badly instructed with regard to nations, eras, and past ages, and were by no means eager to know about these matters, that they did not even come in sight of the real problems of morals—problems which only disclose themselves by a comparison of *many* kinds of morality. In every "Science of Morals" hitherto, strange as it may sound, the problem of morality itself has been *omitted;* there has been no suspicion that there was anything problematic there! That which philosophers called "giving a basis to morality," and endeavoured to realise, has, when seen in a right light, proved merely a learned form of good *faith* in prevailing morality, a new means of its *expression*, consequently just a matter-of-fact within the sphere of a definite morality, yea, in its ultimate motive, a sort of denial that it is *lawful* for this morality to be called in question—and in any case the reverse of the testing, analysing, doubting, and vivisecting of this very faith. Hear, for instance, with what innocence—almost worthy of honour —Schopenhauer represents his own task, and draw your conclusions concerning the scientificalness of a "Science" whose latest master still talks in the strain of children and old wives: "The principle," he says (page 136 of the *Grund probleme der Ethik*), "the axiom about the purport of which all moralists are *practically* agreed: *neminem laede, immo omnes quantum potes juva*—is *really* the proposition which all moral teachers strive to establish, . . . the *real* basis of ethics which has been sought, like the philosopher's stone, for centuries."—The difficulty of establishing the proposition referred to may indeed be great—it is well known that Schopenhauer also was unsuccessful in his efforts; and whoever has thoroughly realised how absurdly false and sentimental this proposition is, in a world whose essence is Will to Power, may be reminded that Schopenhauer, although a pessimist, *actually*—played the flute . . . daily after dinner: one may read about the matter in his biography. A question by the way: a pessimist, a repudiator of God and of the world, who *makes a halt* at morality—who assents to morality, and plays the flute to *laede-neminem* morals, what? Is that really—a pessimist?

☙ Apart from the value of such assertions as "there is a categorical imperative in us," one can always ask: What does such an assertion indicate about him who makes it? There are systems of morals which are meant to justify their author in the eyes of other people; other systems of morals are meant to tranquillise him, and make him self-satisfied; with other systems he wants to crucify and humble himself; with others he wishes to take revenge; with others to conceal himself; with others to glorify himself and gain superiority and distinction; —this system of morals helps its author to forget, that system makes him, or something of him, forgotten; many a moralist would like to exercise power and creative arbitrariness over mankind; many another, perhaps, Kant especially, gives us to understand by his morals that "what is estimable in me, is that I know how to obey—and with you it *shall* not be otherwise than with me!" In short, systems of morals are only a *sign-language of the emotions.*

☙ In contrast to *laisser-aller*, every system of morals is a sort of tyranny against "nature" and also against "reason"; that is, however, no objection, unless one should again decree by some system of morals, that all kinds of tyranny and unreasonableness are unlawful. What is essential and invaluable in every system of morals, is that it is a long constraint. In order to understand Stoicism, or Port-Royal, or Puritanism, one should remember the constraint under which every language has attained to strength and freedom—the metrical constraint, the tyranny of rhyme and rhythm. How much trouble have the poets and orators of every nation given themselves!—not excepting some of the prose writers of to-day, in whose ear dwells an inexorable conscientiousness—"for the sake of a folly," as utilitarian bunglers say, and thereby deem themselves wise—"from submission to arbitrary laws," as the anarchists say, and thereby fancy themselves "free," even free-spirited. The singular fact remains, however, that everything of the nature of freedom, elegance, boldness, dance, and masterly certainty, which exists or has existed, whether it be in thought itself, or in administration, or in speaking and persuading, in art just as in conduct, has only developed by means of the tyranny of such arbitrary law; and in all seriousness, it is not at all improbable that precisely this is "nature" and "natural"—and *not laisser-aller!* Every artist knows how different from the state of letting himself go, is his "most natural" condition, the free arranging, locating, disposing, and constructing in the moments of "inspiration"—and how strictly and delicately he then obeys a thousand laws, which, by their very rigidness and precision, defy all formulation by means of ideas (even the most stable idea has, in comparison therewith, something floating, manifold, and ambiguous in it). The essential thing "in heaven and in earth" is, apparently (to repeat it once more), that there should be long *obedience* in the same direction; there thereby results, and has always resulted in the long run, something which has made life worth living; for instance, virtue, art, music, dancing, reason, spirituality—anything whatever that is transfiguring, refined, foolish, or divine. The long bondage of the spirit, the distrustful constraint in the communicability of ideas, the discipline which the thinker imposed on himself to think in accordance with the rules of a church or a court, or conformable to Aristotelian premises, the persistent spiritual will to interpret everything that happened according to a Christian scheme, and in every occurrence to rediscover and justify the Christian God:—all this violence, arbitrariness, severity, dreadfulness, and unreasonableness, has proved itself the disciplinary means whereby the European spirit has attained its strength, its remorseless curiosity and subtle mobility; granted also that much irrecoverable strength and spirit had to be stifled, suffocated, and spoiled in the process (for here, as everywhere, "nature" shows herself as she is, in all her extravagant and *indifferent* magnificence, which is shocking, but nevertheless noble). That for centuries European thinkers only thought in order to prove something—nowadays, on the contrary, we are suspicious of every thinker who "wishes to prove something"—that it was always settled beforehand what *was to be* the result of their strictest thinking, as it was perhaps in the Asiatic astrology of former times, or as it is still at the present day in the innocent, Christian-moral explanation of immediate personal events "for the glory of God," or "for the good of the soul":—this tyranny, this arbitrariness, this severe and magnificent stupidity, has *educated* the spirit; slavery, both in the coarser and the finer sense, is apparently an indispensable means even of spiritual education and discipline. One may look at every system of morals in this light: it is "nature" therein which teaches to hate the *laisser-aller*, the too great freedom, and implants the need for limited horizons, for immediate duties—it teaches the *narrowing of perspectives*, and thus, in a certain sense, that stupidity is a condition of life and development. "Thou must obey some one, and for a long time; *otherwise* thou wilt come to grief, and lose all respect for thyself"—this seems to me to be the moral imperative of nature, which is certainly neither "categorical," as old Kant wished (consequently the "otherwise"), nor does it address itself to the individual (what does nature care for the individual!), but to nations, races, ages, and ranks, above all, however, to the animal "man" generally, to *mankind*.

☙ Industrious races find it a great hardship to be idle: it was a master stroke of *English* instinct to hallow and begloom Sunday to such an extent that the Englishman unconsciously hankers for his week- and work-day again:—as a kind of cleverly devised, cleverly intercalated *fast*, such as is also frequently found in the ancient world (although, as is appropriate in southern nations, not precisely with respect to work). Many kinds of fasts are necessary; and wherever powerful influences and habits prevail, legislators have to see that intercalary days are appointed, on which such impulses are fettered, and learn to hunger anew. Viewed from a higher standpoint, whole generations and epochs, when they show themselves infected with any moral fanaticism, seem like those intercalated periods of restraint and fasting, during which an impulse learns to humble and submit itself—at the same time also to *purify* and *sharpen* itself; certain philosophical sects likewise admit of a similar interpretation (for instance, the Stoa, in the midst of Hellenic culture, with the atmosphere rank and overcharged with Aphrodisiacal odours).—Here also is a hint for the explanation of the paradox, why it was precisely in the most Christian period of European history, and in general only under the pressure of Christian sentiments, that the sexual impulse sublimated into love (*amour-passion*).

There is something in the morality of Plato which does not really belong to Plato, but which only appears in his philosophy, one might say, in spite of him: namely, Socratism, for which he himself was too noble. "No one desires to injure himself, hence all evil is done unwittingly. The evil man inflicts injury on himself; he would not do so, however, if he knew that evil is evil. The evil man, therefore, is only evil through error; if one free him from error one will necessarily make him—good."—This mode of reasoning savours of the *populace*, who perceive only the unpleasant consequences of evil-doing, and practically judge that "it is *stupid* to do wrong"; while they accept "good" as identical with "useful and pleasant," without further thought. As regards every system of utilitarianism, one may at once assume that it has the same origin, and follow the scent: one will seldom err.—Plato did all he could to interpret something refined and noble into the tenets of his teacher, and above all to interpret himself into them—he, the most daring of all interpreters, who lifted the entire Socrates out of the street, as a popular theme and song, to exhibit him in endless and impossible modifications—namely, in all his own disguises and multiplicities. In jest, and in Homeric language as well, what is the Platonic Socrates, if not—

πρόσθε Πλατων οπισθεν τε Πλατων μεσση τε Χι μαιρα.

§ The old theological problem of "Faith" and "Knowledge," or more plainly, of instinct and reason—the question whether, in respect to the valuation of things, instinct deserves more authority than rationality, which wants to appreciate and act according to motives, according to a "Why," that is to say, in conformity to purpose and utility—it is always the old moral problem that first appeared in the person of Socrates, and had divided men's minds long before Christianity. Socrates himself, following, of course, the taste of his talent—that of a surpassing dialectician—took first the side of reason; and, in fact, what did he do all his life but laugh at the awkward incapacity of the noble Athenians, who were men of instinct, like all noble men, and could never give satisfactory answers concerning the motives of their actions? In the end, however, though silently and secretly, he laughed also at himself: with his finer conscience and introspection, he found in himself the same difficulty and incapacity. "But why"—he said to himself—" should one on that account separate oneself from the instincts! One must set them right, and the reason *also*—one must follow the instincts, but at the same time persuade the reason to support them with good arguments." This was the real *falseness* of that great and mysterious ironist; he brought his conscience up to the point that he was satisfied with a kind of self-outwitting: in fact, he perceived the irrationality in the moral judgment.—Plato, more innocent in such matters, and without the craftiness of the plebeian, wished to prove to himself, at the expenditure of all his strength—the greatest strength a philosopher had ever expended—that reason and instinct lead spontaneously to one goal, to the good, to "God"; and since Plato, all theologians and philosophers have followed the same path—which means that in matters of morality, instinct (or as Christians call it, "Faith," or as I call it, "the herd") has hitherto triumphed. Unless one should make an exception in the case of Descartes, the father of rationalism (and consequently the grandfather of the Revolution), who recognised only the authority of reason: but reason is only a tool, and Descartes was superficial.

❧ Whoever has followed the history of a single science, finds in its development a clue to the understanding of the oldest and commonest processes of all "knowledge and cognisance": there, as here, the premature hypotheses, the fictions, the good stupid will to "belief," and the lack of distrust and patience are first developed—our senses learn late, and never learn completely, to be subtle, reliable, and cautious organs of knowledge. Our eyes find it easier on a given occasion to produce a picture already often produced, than to seize upon the divergence and novelty of an impression: the latter requires more force, more "morality." It is difficult and painful for the ear to listen to anything new; we hear strange music badly. When we hear another language spoken, we involuntarily attempt to form the sounds into words with which we are more familiar and conversant—it was thus, for example, that the Germans modified the spoken word *arcubalista* into *armbrust* (crossbow). Our senses are also hostile and averse to the new; and generally, even in the "simplest" processes of sensation, the emotions *dominate*—such as fear, love, hatred, and the passive emotion of indolence.—As little as a reader nowadays reads all the single words (not to speak of syllables) of a page—he rather takes about five out of every twenty words at random, and "guesses" the probably appropriate sense to them—just as little do we see a tree correctly and completely in respect to its leaves, branches, colour, and shape; we find it so much easier to fancy the chance of a tree. Even in the midst of the most remarkable experiences, we still do just the same; we fabricate the greater part of the experience, and can hardly be made to contemplate any event, *except* as "inventors" thereof. All this goes to prove that from our fundamental nature and from remote ages we have been—*accustomed to lying*. Or, to express it more politely and hypocritically, in short, more pleasantly—one is much more of an artist than one is aware of.—In an animated conversation, I often see the face of the person with whom I am speaking so clearly and sharply defined before me, according to the thought he expresses, or which I believe to be evoked in his mind, that the degree of distinctness far exceeds the *strength* of my visual faculty—the delicacy of the play of the muscles and of the expression of the eyes *must* therefore be imagined by me. Probably the person put on quite a different expression, or none at all.

☙§ *Quidquid luce fuit, tenebris agit*: but also contrariwise. What we experience in dreams, provided we experience it often, pertains at last just as much to the general belongings of our soul as anything "actually" experienced; by virtue thereof we are richer or poorer, we have a requirement more or less, and finally, in broad daylight, and even in the brightest moments of our waking life, we are ruled to some extent by the nature of our dreams. Supposing that some one has often flown in his dreams, and that at last, as soon as he dreams, he is conscious of the power and art of flying as his privilege and his peculiarly enviable happiness; such a person, who believes that on the slightest impulse, he can actualise all sorts of curves and angles, who knows the sensation of a certain divine levity, an "upwards" without effort or constraint, a "downwards" without descending or lowering—without *trouble!*—how could the man with such dream-experiences and dream-habits fail to find "happiness" differently coloured and defined, even in his waking hours! How could he fail—to long *differently* for happiness? "Flight," such as is described by poets, must, when compared with his own "flying," be far too earthly, muscular, violent, far too "troublesome" for him.

☙§ The difference among men does not manifest itself only in the difference of their lists of desirable things—in their regarding different good things as worth striving for, and being disagreed as to the greater or less value, the order of rank, of the commonly recognised desirable things:—it manifests itself much more in what they regard as actually *having* and *possessing* a desirable thing. As regards a woman, for instance, the control over her body and her sexual gratification serves as an amply sufficient sign of ownership and possession to the more modest man; another with a more suspicious and ambitious thirst for possession, sees the "questionableness," the mere apparentness of such ownership, and wishes to have finer tests in order to know especially whether the woman not only gives herself to him, but also gives up for his sake what she has or would like to have—only *then* does he look upon her as "possessed." A third, however, has not even here got to the limit of his distrust and his desire for possession: he asks himself whether the woman, when she gives up everything for him, does not perhaps do so for a phantom of him; he wishes first to be thoroughly, indeed, profoundly well known; in order to be loved at all he ventures to let himself be found out. Only then does he feel the beloved one fully in his possession, when she no longer deceives herself about him, when she loves him just as much for the sake of his devilry and concealed insatiability, as for his goodness, patience, and spirituality. One man would like to possess a nation, and he finds all the higher arts of Cagliostro and Catalina suitable for his purpose. Another, with a more refined thirst for possession, says to himself: "One may not deceive where one desires to possess"—he is irritated and impatient at the idea that a mask of him should rule in the hearts of the people: "I must, therefore, *make* myself known, and first of all learn to know myself!" Amongst helpful and charitable people, one almost always finds the awkward craftiness which first gets up suitably him who has to be helped, as though, for instance, he should "merit" help, seek just *their* help, and would show himself deeply grateful, attached, and subservient to them for all help. With these conceits, they take control of the needy as a property, just as in general they are charitable and helpful out of a desire for property. One finds them jealous when they are crossed or forestalled in their charity. Parents involuntarily make something like themselves out of their children—they call that "education"; no mother doubts at the bottom of her heart that the child she has born is thereby her property, no father hesitates about his right to *his own* ideas and notions of worth. Indeed, in former times fathers deemed it right to use their discretion concerning the life or death of the newly born (as amongst the ancient Germans). And like the father, so also do the teacher, the class, the priest, and the prince still see in every new individual an unobjectionable opportunity for a new possession. The consequence is . . .

The Jews—a people "born for slavery," as Tacitus and the whole ancient world say of them; "the chosen people among the nations," as they themselves say and believe—the Jews performed the miracle of the inversion of valuations, by means of which life on earth obtained a new and dangerous charm for a couple of millenniums. Their prophets fused into one the expressions "rich," "godless," "wicked," "violent," "sensual," and for the first time coined the word "world" as a term of reproach. In this inversion of valuations (in which is also included the use of the word "poor" as synonymous with "saint" and "friend") the significance of the Jewish people is to be found; it is with *them* that the *slave-insurrection in morals* commences.

It is to be *inferred* that there are countless dark bodies near the sun—such as we shall never see. Amongst ourselves, this is an allegory; and the psychologist of morals reads the whole star-writing merely as an allegorical and symbolic language in which much may be unexpressed.

❧ The beast of prey and the man of prey (for instance, Cæsar Borgia) are fundamentally misunderstood, "nature" is misunderstood, so long as one seeks a "morbidness" in the constitution of these healthiest of all tropical monsters and growths, or even an innate "hell" in them—as almost all moralists have done hitherto. Does it not seem that there is a hatred of the virgin forest and of the tropics among moralists? And that the "tropical man" must be discredited at all costs, whether as disease and deterioration of mankind, or as his own hell and self-torture? And why? In favour of the "temperate zones"? In favour of the temperate men? The "moral"? The mediocre?—This for the chapter: "Morals as Timidity."

❧ All the systems of morals which address themselves with a view to their "happiness," as it is called—what else are they but suggestions for behaviour adapted to the degree of *danger* from themselves in which the individuals live; recipes for their passions, their good and bad propensities, in so far as such have the Will to Power and would like to play the master; small and great expediences and elaborations, permeated with the musty odour of old family medicines and old-wife wisdom; all of them grotesque and absurd in their form—because they address themselves to "all," because they generalise where generalisation is not authorised; all of them speaking unconditionally, and taking themselves unconditionally; all of them flavoured not merely with one grain of salt, but rather endurable only, and sometimes even seductive, when they are over-spiced and begin to smell dangerously, especially of "the other world?" That is all of little value when estimated intellectually, and is far from being "science," much less "wisdom"; but, repeated once more, and three times repeated, it is expediency, expediency, expediency, mixed with stupidity, stupidity, stupidity—whether it be the indifference and statuesque coldness towards the heated folly of the emotions, which the Stoics advised and fostered; or the no-more-laughing and no-more-weeping of Spinoza, the destruction of the emotions by their analysis and vivisection, which he recommended so naïvely; or the lowering of the emotions to an innocent mean at which they may be satisfied, the Aristotelianism of morals; or even morality as the enjoyment of the emotions in a voluntary attenuation and spiritualisation by the symbolism of art, perhaps as music, or as love of God, and of mankind for God's sake—for in religion the passions are once more enfranchised, provided that . . . ; or, finally, even the complaisant and wanton surrender to the emotions, as has been taught by Hafis and Goethe, the bold letting-go of the reins, the spiritual and corporeal *licentia morum* in the exceptional cases of wise old codgers and drunkards, with whom it "no longer has much danger."—This also for the chapter: "Morals as Timidity."

☙ Inasmuch as in all ages, as long as mankind has existed, there have also been human herds (family alliances, communities, tribes, peoples, states, churches), and always a great number who obey in proportion to the small number who command—in view, therefore, of the fact that obedience has been most practised and fostered among mankind hitherto, one may reasonably suppose that, generally speaking, the need thereof is now innate in every one, as a kind of *formal conscience* which gives the command: "Thou shalt unconditionally do something, unconditionally refrain from something"; in short, "Thou shalt." This need tries to satisfy itself and to fill its form with a content; according to its strength, impatience, and eagerness, it at once seizes as an omnivorous appetite with little selection, and accepts whatever is shouted into its ear by all sorts of commanders—parents, teachers, laws, class prejudices, or public opinion. The extraordinary limitation of human development, the hesitation, protractedness, frequent retrogression, and turning thereof, is attributable to the fact that the herd-instinct of obedience is transmitted best, and at the cost of the art of command. If one imagine this instinct increasing to its greatest extent, commanders and independent individuals will finally be lacking altogether; or they will suffer inwardly from a bad conscience, and will have to impose a deception on themselves in the first place in order to be able to command: just as if they also were only obeying. This condition of things actually exists in Europe at present—I call it the moral hypocrisy of the commanding class. They know no other way of protecting themselves from their bad conscience than by playing the role of executors of older and higher orders (of predecessors, of the constitution, of justice, of the law, or of God himself), or they even justify themselves by maxims from the current opinions of the herd, as "first servants of their people," or "instruments of the public weal." On the other hand, the gregarious European man nowadays assumes an air as if he were the only kind of man that is allowable; he glorifies his qualities, such as public spirit, kindness, deference, industry, temperance, modesty, indulgence, sympathy, by virtue of which he is gentle, endurable, and useful to the herd, as the peculiarly human virtues. In cases, however, where it is believed that the leader and bellwether cannot be dispensed with, attempt after attempt is made nowadays to replace commanders by the summing together of clever gregarious men: all representative constitutions, for example, are of this origin. In spite of all, what a blessing, what a deliverance from a weight becoming unendurable, is the appearance of an absolute ruler for these gregarious Europeans—of this fact the effect of the appearance of Napoleon was the last great proof: the history of the influence of Napoleon is almost the history of the higher happiness to which the entire century has attained in its worthiest individuals and periods.

The man of an age of dissolution which mixes the races with one another, who has the inheritance of a diversified descent in his body—that is to say, contrary, and often not only contrary, instincts and standards of value, which struggle with one another and are seldom at peace—such a man of late culture and broken lights, will, on an average, be a weak man. His fundamental desire is that the war which is *in him* should come to an end; happiness appears to him in the character of a soothing medicine and mode of thought (for instance, Epicurean or Christian); it is above all things the happiness of repose, of undisturbedness, of repletion, of final unity—it is the "Sabbath of Sabbaths," to use the expression of the holy rhetorician, St. Augustine, who was himself such a man.—Should, however, the contrariety and conflict in such natures operate as an *additional* incentive and stimulus to life—and if, on the other hand, in addition to their powerful and irreconcilable instincts, they have also inherited and indoctrinated into them a proper mastery and subtlety for carrying on the conflict with themselves (that is to say, the faculty of self-control and self-deception), there then arise those marvellously incomprehensible, and inexplicable beings, those enigmatical men, predestined for conquering and circumventing others, the finest examples of which are Alcibiades and Cæsar (with whom I should like to associate the *first* of Europeans according to my taste, the Hohenstaufen, Frederick the Second), and amongst artists, perhaps Leonardo da Vinci. They appear precisely in the same periods when that weaker type, with its longing for repose, comes to the front; the two types are complementary to each other, and spring from the same causes.

As long as the utility which determines moral estimates is only gregarious utility, as long as the preservation of the community is only kept in view, and the immoral is sought precisely and exclusively in what seems dangerous to the maintenance of the community, there can be no "morality of love to one's neighbour." Granted even that there is already a little constant exercise of consideration, sympathy, fairness, gentleness, and mutual assistance, granted that even in this condition of society all those instincts are already active which are latterly distinguished by honourable names as "virtues," and eventually almost coincide with the conception "morality": in that period they do not as yet belong to the domain of moral valuations—they are still *ultra-moral.* A sympathetic action, for instance, is neither called good nor bad, moral nor immoral, in the best period of the Romans; and should it be praised, a sort of resentful disdain is compatible with this praise, even at the best, directly the sympathetic action is compared with one which contributes to the welfare of the whole, to the *res publica.* After all, "love to our neighbour" is always a secondary matter, partly conventional and arbitrarily manifested in relation to our *fear of our neighbour.* After the fabric of society seems on the whole established and secured against external dangers, it is this fear of our neighbour which again creates new perspectives of moral valuation. Certain strong and dangerous instincts, such as the love of enterprise, foolhardiness, revengefulness, astuteness, rapacity, and love of power, which up till then had not only to be honoured from the point of view of general utility—under other names, of course, than those here given—but had to be fostered and cultivated (because they were perpetually required in the common danger against the common enemies), are now felt in their dangerousness to be doubly strong—when the outlets for them are lacking—and are gradually branded as immoral and given over to calumny. The contrary instincts and inclinations now attain to moral honour; the gregarious instinct gradually draws its conclusions. How much or how little dangerous to the community or to equality is contained in an opinion, a condition, an emotion, a disposition, or an endowment—that is now the moral perspective; here again fear is the mother of morals. It is by the loftiest and strongest instincts, when they break out passionately and carry the individual far above and beyond the average, and the low level of the gregarious conscience, that the self-reliance of the community is destroyed; its belief in itself, its backbone, as it were, breaks; consequently these very instincts will be most branded and defamed. The lofty independent spirituality, the will to stand alone, and even the cogent reason, are felt to be dangers; everything that elevates the individual above the herd, and is a source of fear to the neighbour, is henceforth called *evil;* the tolerant, unassuming, self-adapting, self-equalising disposition, the *mediocrity* of desires, attains to moral distinction and honour. Finally, under very peaceful circumstances, there is always less opportunity and necessity for training the feelings to severity and rigour; and now every form of severity, even in justice, begins to disturb the conscience; a lofty and rigourous nobleness and self-responsibility almost offends, and awakens distrust, "the lamb," and still more "the sheep," wins respect. There is a point of diseased mellowness and effeminacy in the history of society, at which society itself takes the part of him who injures it, the part of the *criminal*, and does so, in fact, seriously and honestly. To punish, appears to it to be somehow unfair—it is certain that the idea of "punishment" and "the obligation to punish" are then painful and alarming to people. "Is it not sufficient if the criminal be rendered *harmless?* Why should we still punish? Punishment itself is terrible!"—with these questions gregarious morality, the morality of fear, draws its ultimate conclusion. If one could at all do away with danger, the cause of fear, one would have done away with this morality at the same time, it would no longer be necessary, it *would not consider itself* any longer necessary!—Whoever examines the conscience of the present-day European, will always elicit the same imperative from its thousand moral folds and hidden recesses, the imperative of the timidity of the herd: "we wish that some time or other there may be *nothing more to fear!*" Some time or other—the will and the way *thereto* is nowadays called "progress" all over Europe.

Let us at once say again what we have already said a hundred times, for people's ears nowadays are unwilling to hear such truths—*our* truths. We know well enough how offensively it sounds when any one plainly, and without metaphor, counts man amongst the animals; but it will be accounted to us almost a *crime*, that it is precisely in respect to men of "modern ideas" that we have constantly applied the terms "herd." "herd-instincts," and such like expressions. What avail is it? We cannot do otherwise, for it is precisely here that our new insight is. We have found that in all the principal moral judgments Europe has become unanimous, including likewise the countries where European influence prevails: in Europe people evidently *know* what Socrates thought he did not know, and what the famous serpent of old once promised to teach—they "know" to-day what is good and evil. It must then sound hard and be distasteful to the ear, when we always insist that that which here thinks it knows, that which here glorifies itself with praise and blame, and calls itself good, is the instinct of the herding human animal: the instinct which has come and is ever coming more and more to the front, to preponderance and supremacy over other instincts, according to the increasing physiological approximation and resemblance of which it is the symptom. *Morality in Europe at present is herding-animal morality;* and therefore, as we understand the matter, only one kind of human morality, besides which, before which, and after which many other moralities, and above all *higher* moralities, are or should be possible. Against such a "possibility," against such a "should be," however, this morality defends itself with all its strength; it says obstinately and inexorably: "I am morality itself and nothing else is morality!" Indeed, with the help of a religion which has humoured and flattered the sublimest desires of the herding-animal, things have reached such a point that we always find a more visible expression of this morality even in political and social arrangements: the *democratic* movement is the inheritance of the Christian movement. That its *tempo*, however, is much too slow and sleepy for the more impatient ones, for those who are sick and distracted by the herding-instinct, is indicated by the increasingly furious howling, and always less disguised teeth-gnashing of the anarchist dogs, who are now roving through the highways of European culture. Apparently in opposition to the peacefully industrious democrats and Revolution-ideologues, and still more so to the awkward philosophasters and fraternity-visionaries who call themselves Socialists and want a "free society," those are really at one with them all in their thorough and instinctive hostility to every form of society other than that of the *autonomous* herd (to the extent even of repudiating the notions "master" and "servant"—*ni Dieu ni maître*, says a socialist formula); at one in their tenacious opposition to every special claim, every special right and privilege (this means ultimately opposition to *every* right, for when all are equal, no one needs "rights" any longer); at one in their distrust of punitive justice (as though it were a violation of the weak, unfair to the *necessary* consequences of all former society); but equally at one in their religion of sympathy, in their compassion for all that feels, lives, and suffers (down to the very animals, up even to "God"—the extravagance of "sympathy for God" belongs to a democratic age); altogether at one in the cry and impatience of their sympathy, in their deadly hatred of suffering generally, in their almost feminine incapacity for witnessing it or *allowing* it; at one in their involuntary beglooming and heart-softening, under the spell of which Europe seems to be threatened with a new Buddhism; at one in their belief in the morality of *mutual* sympathy, as though it were morality in itself, the climax, the *attained* climax of mankind, the sole hope of the future, the consolation of the present, the great discharge from all the obligations of the past; altogether at one in their belief in the community as the *deliverer*, in the herd, and therefore in "themselves."

§ We, who hold a different belief—we, who regard the democratic movement, not only as a degenerating form of political organisation, but as equivalent to a degenerating, a waning type of man, as involving his mediocrising and depreciation: where have *we* to fix our hopes? In *new philosophers*—there is no other alternative: in minds strong and original enough to initiate opposite estimates of value, to transvalue and invert "eternal valuations"; in forerunners, in men of the future, who in the present shall fix the constraints and fasten the knots which will compel millenniums to take *new* paths. To teach man the future of humanity as his *will*, as depending on human will, and to make preparation for vast hazardous enterprises and collective attempts in rearing and educating, in order thereby to put an end to the frightful rule of folly and chance which has hitherto gone by the name of "history" (the folly of the "greatest number" is only its last form)—for that purpose a new type of philosophers and commanders will some time or other be needed, at the very idea of which everything that has existed in the way of occult, terrible, and benevolent beings might look pale and dwarfed. The image of such leaders hovers before *our* eyes:—is it lawful for me to say it aloud, ye free spirits? The conditions which one would partly have to create and partly utilise for their genesis; the presumptive methods and tests by virtue of which a soul should grow up to such an elevation and power as to feel a *constraint* to these tasks; a transvaluation of values, under the new pressure and hammer of which a conscience should be steeled and a heart transformed into brass, so as to bear the weight of such responsibility; and on the other hand the necessity for such leaders, the dreadful danger that they might be lacking, or miscarry and degenerate:—these are *our* real anxieties and glooms, ye know it well, ye free spirits! these are the heavy distant thoughts and storms which sweep across the heaven of *our* life. There are few pains so grievous as to have seen, divined, or experienced how an exceptional man has missed his way and deteriorated; but he who has the rare eye for the universal danger of "man" himself *deteriorating*, he who like us has recognised the extraordinary fortuitousness which has hitherto played its game in respect to the future of mankind—a game in which neither the hand, nor even a "finger of God" has participated!—he who divines the fate that is hidden under the idiotic unwariness and blind confidence of "modern ideas," and still more under the whole of Christo-European morality—suffers from an anguish with which no other is to be compared. He sees at a glance all that could still *be made out of man* through a favourable accumulation and augmentation of human powers and arrangements; he knows with all the knowledge of his conviction how unexhausted man still is for the greatest possibilities, and how often in the past the type man has stood in presence of mysterious decisions and new paths:—he knows still better from his painfulest recollections on what wretched obstacles promising developments of the highest rank have hitherto usually gone to pieces, broken down, sunk, and become contemptible. The *universal degeneracy of mankind* to the level of the "man of the future"—as idealised by the socialistic fools and shallow-pates—this degeneracy and dwarfing of man to an absolutely gregarious animal (or as they call it, to a man of "free society"), this brutalising of man into a pigmy with equal rights and claims, is undoubtedly possible! He who has thought out this possibility to its ultimate conclusion knows *another* loathing unknown to the rest of mankind—and perhaps also a new *mission!*

William James

PHILOSOPHY

William James

[1842–1910]

If there is an American school of philosophy, its founder and apostle was William James. Pragmatism, the test by practical consequences, owes its existence to the challenging qualities of James's mind. Son of Henry James, the Swedenborgian theologian, the psychologist who wrote like a novelist was the brother of Henry, the novelist who wrote like a psychologist. During a youth beset with illness, William James studied in America and Europe, dabbled in painting and science and attended Harvard University. Medicine was also in his curriculum, but, again because of his invalidism, was abandoned for the study of psychology and philosophy. In 1890, the publication of his *Principles of Psychology* brought him the acknowledged leadership in the field of functional psychology. Chosen to deliver the Gifford Lectures at the University of Edinburgh, he selected as his subject the psychology of religion. Collected in book form under the title *The Varieties of Religious Experience*, these essays summarize and analyze the evidence concerning belief in the supernatural and its diversified manifestations. The chapter following, "Philosophy," is offered in its entirety from this penetrating book.

PHILOSOPHY*

WILLIAM JAMES

The subject of Saintliness left us face to face with the question, Is the sense of divine presence a sense of anything objectively true? We turned first to mysticism for an answer, and found that although mysticism is entirely willing to corroborate religion, it is too private (and also too various) in its utterances to be able to claim a universal authority. But philosophy publishes results which claim to be universally valid if they are valid at all, so we now turn with our question to philosophy. Can philosophy stamp a warrant of veracity upon the religious man's sense of the divine?

I imagine that many of you at this point begin to indulge in guesses at the goal to which I am tending. I have undermined the authority of mysticism, you say, and the next thing I shall probably do is to seek to discredit that of philosophy. Religion, you expect to hear me conclude, is nothing but an affair of faith, based either on vague sentiment, or on that vivid sense of the reality of things unseen of which in my second lecture and in the lecture on Mysticism I gave so many examples. It is essentially private and individualistic; it always exceeds our powers of formulation; and although attempts to pour its contents into a philosophic mould will probably always go on, men being what they are, yet these attempts are always secondary processes which in no way add to the au-

* From *The Varieties of Religious Experience.*

thority, or warrant the veracity, of the sentiments from which they derive their own stimulus and borrow whatever glow of conviction they may themselves possess. In short, you suspect that I am planning to defend feeling at the expense of reason, to rehabilitate the primitive and unreflective, and to dissuade you from the hope of any Theology worthy of the name.

To a certain extent I have to admit that you guess rightly. I do believe that feeling is the deeper source of religion, and that philosophic and theological formulas are secondary products, like translations of a text into another tongue. But all such statements are misleading from their brevity, and it will take the whole hour for me to explain to you exactly what I mean.

When I call theological formulas secondary products, I mean that in a world in which no religious feeling had ever existed, I doubt whether any philosophic theology could ever have been framed. I doubt if dispassionate intellectual contemplation of the universe, apart from inner unhappiness and need of deliverance on the one hand and mystical emotion on the other, would ever have resulted in religious philosophies such as we now possess. Men would have begun with animistic explanations of natural fact, and criticised these away into scientific ones, as they actually have done. In the science they would have left a certain amount of "psychical research," even as they now will probably have to re-admit a certain amount. But high-flying speculations like those of either dogmatic or idealistic theology, these they would have had no motive to venture on, feeling no need of commerce with such deities. These speculations must, it seems to me, be classed as over-beliefs, buildings-out performed by the intellect into directions of which feeling originally supplied the hint.

But even if religious philosophy had to have its first hint supplied by feeling, may it not have dealt in a superior way with the matter which feeling suggested? Feeling is private and dumb, and unable to give an account of itself. It allows that its results are mysteries and enigmas, declines to justify them rationally, and on occasion is willing that they should even pass for paradoxical and absurd. Philosophy takes just the opposite attitude. Her aspiration is to reclaim from mystery and paradox whatever territory she touches. To find an escape from obscure and wayward personal persuasion to truth objectively valid for all thinking men has ever been the intellect's most cherished ideal. To redeem religion from unwholesome privacy, and to give public status and universal right of way to its deliverances, has been reason's task.

I believe that philosophy will always have opportunity to labor at this task.[1] We are thinking beings, and we cannot exclude the intellect from participating in any of our functions. Even in soliloquizing with ourselves, we construe our feelings intellectually. Both our personal ideals and our religious and mystical experiences must be interpreted congruously with the kind of scenery which our thinking mind inhabits. The philosophic climate of our time inevitably forces its own clothing on us. Moreover, we must exchange our feelings with one another, and in doing so we have to speak, and to use general and abstract verbal formulas. Conceptions and constructions are thus a necessary part of our religion; and as moderator amid the clash of hypotheses, and mediator among the criticisms of one man's constructions by another, philosophy will always have much to do. It would be strange if I disputed this, when these very lectures which I am giving are (as you will see more clearly from now onwards) a laborious attempt to extract from the privacies of religious experience some general facts which can be defined in formulas upon which everybody may agree.

Religious experience, in other words, spontaneously and inevitably engenders myths, superstitions, dogmas, creeds, and metaphysical theologies, and criticisms of one set of these by the adherents of another. Of late, impartial classifications and comparisons have become possible, alongside of the denunciations and anathemas by which the commerce between creeds used exclusively to be carried on. We have the beginnings of

---

[1] Compare Professor W. WALLACE's Gifford Lectures, in Lectures and Essays, Oxford, 1898, pp. 17 ff.

a "Science of Religions," so-called; and if these lectures could ever be accounted a crumb-like contribution to such a science, I should be made very happy.

But all these intellectual operations, whether they be constructive or comparative and critical, presuppose immediate experiences as their subject-matter. They are interpretative and inductive operations, operations after the fact, consequent upon religious feeling, not coördinate with it, not independent of what it ascertains.

The intellectualism in religion which I wish to discredit pretends to be something altogether different from this. It assumes to construct religious objects out of the resources of logical reason alone, or of logical reason drawing rigorous inference from non-subjective facts. It calls its conclusions dogmatic theology, or philosophy of the absolute, as the case may be; it does not call them science of religions. It reaches them in an *a priori* way, and warrants their veracity.

Warranted systems have ever been the idols of aspiring souls. All-inclusive, yet simple; noble, clean, luminous, stable, rigorous, true;—what more ideal refuge could there be than such a system would offer to spirits vexed by the muddiness and accidentality of the world of sensible things? Accordingly, we find inculcated in the theological schools of to-day, almost as much as in those of the fore-time, a disdain for merely possible or probable truth, and of results that only private assurance can grasp. Scholastics and idealists both express this disdain. Principal John Caird, for example, writes as follows in his Introduction to the Philosophy of Religion:—

"Religion must indeed be a thing of the heart; but in order to elevate it from the region of subjective caprice and waywardness, and to distinguish between that which is true and false in religion, we must appeal to an objective standard. That which enters the heart must first be discerned by the intelligence to be *true*. It must be seen as having in its own nature a *right* to dominate feeling, and as constituting the principle by which feeling must be judged.[2] In estimating the religious character of individuals, nations, or races, the first question is, not how they feel, but what they think and believe—not whether their religion is one which manifests itself in emotions, more or less vehement and enthusiastic, but what are the *conceptions* of God and divine things by which these emotions are called forth. Feeling is necessary in religion, but it is by the *content* or intelligent basis of a religion, and not by feeling, that its character and worth are to be determined."[3]

Cardinal Newman, in his work, The Idea of a University, gives more emphatic expression still to this disdain for sentiment.[4] Theology, he says, is a science in the strictest sense of the word. I will tell you, he says, what it is not—not "physical evidences" for God, not "natural religion," for these are but vague subjective interpretations:—

"If," he continues, "the Supreme Being is powerful or skillful, just so far as the telescope shows power, or the microscope shows skill, if his moral law is to be ascertained simply by the physical processes of the animal frame, or his will gathered from the immediate issues of human affairs, if his Essence is just as high and deep and broad as the universe and no more; if this be the fact, then will I confess that there is no specific science about God, that theology is but a name, and a protest in its behalf an hypocrisy. Then, pious as it is to think of Him, while the pageant of experiment or abstract reasoning passes by, still such piety is nothing more than a poetry of thought, or an ornament of language, a certain view taken of Nature which one man has and another has not, which gifted minds strike out, which others see to be admirable and ingenious, and which all would be the better for adopting. It is but the theology of Nature, just as we talk of

---

[2] Op. cit., p. 174, abridged.
[3] Ibid., p. 186, abridged and italicized.
[4] Discourse II. § 7.

the *philosophy* or the *romance* of history, or the *poetry* of childhood, or the picturesque or the sentimental or the humorous, or any other abstract quality which the genius or the caprice of the individual, or the fashion of the day, or the consent of the world, recognizes in any set of objects which are subjected to its contemplation. I do not see much difference between avowing that there is no God, and implying that nothing definite can be known for certain about Him."

What I mean by Theology, continues Newman, is none of these things: "I simply mean the *Science of God*, or the truths we know about God, put into a system, just as we have a science of the stars and call it astronomy, or of the crust of the earth and call it geology."

In both these extracts we have the issue clearly set before us: Feeling valid only for the individual is pitted against reason valid universally. The test is a perfectly plain one of fact. Theology based on pure reason must in point of fact convince men universally. If it did not, wherein would its superiority consist? If it only formed sects and schools, even as sentiment and mysticism form them, how would it fulfill its programme of freeing us from personal caprice and waywardness? This perfectly definite practical test of the pretensions of philosophy to found religion on universal reason simplifies my procedure to-day. I need not discredit philosophy by laborious criticism of its arguments. It would suffice if I show that as a matter of history it fails to prove its pretension to be "objectively" convincing. In fact, philosophy does so fail. It does not banish differences; it founds schools and sects just as feeling does. I believe, in fact, that the logical reason of man operates in this field of divinity exactly as it has always operated in love, or in patriotism, or in politics, or in any other of the wider affairs of life, in which our passions or our mystical intuitions fix our beliefs beforehand. It finds arguments for our conviction, for indeed it *has* to find them. It amplifies and defines our faith, and dignifies it and lends it words and plausibility. It hardly ever engenders it; it cannot now secure it.[5]

§ Lend me your attention while I run through some of the points of the older systematic theology. You find them in both Protestant and Catholic manuals, best of all in the innumerable text-books published since Pope Leo's Encyclical recommending the study of Saint Thomas. I glance first at the arguments by which dogmatic theology establishes God's existence, after that at those by which it establishes his nature.[6]

The arguments for God's existence have stood for hundreds of years with the waves of unbelieving criticism breaking against them, never totally discrediting them in the ears of the faithful, but on the whole slowly and surely washing out the mortar from between their joints. If you have a God already whom you believe in, these arguments confirm you. If you are atheistic, they fail to set you right. The proofs are various. The "cosmological" one, so-called, reasons from the contingence of the world to a First Cause which must contain whatever perfections the world itself contains. The "argument from design" reasons, from the fact that Nature's

---

[5] As regards the secondary character of intellectual constructions, and the primacy of feeling and instinct in founding religious beliefs, see the striking work of H. FIELDING, The Hearts of Men, London, 1902, which came into my hands after my text was written. "Creeds," says the author, "are the grammar of religion, they are to religion what grammar is to speech. Words are the expression of our wants; grammar is the theory formed afterwards. Speech never proceeded from grammar, but the reverse. As speech progresses and changes from unknown causes, grammar must follow" (p. 313). The whole book, which keeps unusually close to concrete facts, is little more than an amplification of this text.

[6] For convenience' sake, I follow the order of A. STÖCKL's Lehrbuch der Philosophie, 5te Auflage, Mainz, 1881, Band ii. B. BOEDDER's Natural Theology, London, 1891, is a handy English Catholic Manual; but an almost identical doctrine is given by such Protestant theologians as C. HODGE: Systematic Theology, New York, 1873, or A. H. STRONG: Systematic Theology, 5th edition, New York, 1896.

laws are mathematical, and her parts benevolently adapted to each other, that this cause is both intellectual and benevolent. The "moral argument" is that the moral law presupposes a lawgiver. The "argument *ex consensu gentium*" is that the belief in God is so widespread as to be grounded in the rational nature of man, and should therefore carry authority with it.

As I just said, I will not discuss these arguments technically. The bare fact that all idealists since Kant have felt entitled either to scout or to neglect them shows that they are not solid enough to serve as religion's all-sufficient foundation. Absolutely impersonal reasons would be in duty bound to show more general convincingness. Causation is indeed too obscure a principle to bear the weight of the whole structure of theology. As for the argument from design, see how Darwinian ideas have revolutionized it. Conceived as we now conceive them, as so many fortunate escapes from almost limitless processes of destruction, the benevolent adaptations which we find in Nature suggest a deity very different from the one who figured in the earlier versions of the argument.[7]

---

[7] It must not be forgotten that any form of *dis*order in the world might, by the design argument, suggest a God for just that kind of disorder. The truth is that any state of things whatever that can be named is logically susceptible of teleological interpretation. The ruins of the earthquake at Lisbon, for example: the whole of past history had to be planned exactly as it was to bring about in the fullness of time just that particular arrangement of debris of masonry, furniture, and once living bodies. No other train of causes would have been sufficient. And so of any other arrangement, bad or good, which might as a matter of fact be found resulting anywhere from previous conditions. To avoid such pessimistic consequences and save its beneficent designer, the design argument accordingly invokes two other principles, restrictive in their operation. The first is physical: Nature's forces tend of their own accord only to disorder and destruction, to heaps of ruins, not to architecture. This principle, though plausible at first sight, seems, in the light of recent biology, to be more and more improbable. The second principle is one of anthropomorphic interpretation. No arrangement that for *us* is "disorderly" can possibly have been an object of design at all. This principle is of course a mere assumption in the interests of anthropomorphic Theism.

The fact is that these arguments do but follow the combined suggestions of the facts and of our feeling. They prove nothing rigorously. They only corroborate our preëxistent partialities.

If philosophy can do so little to establish God's existence, how stands it with her efforts to define his attributes? It is worth while to look at the attempts of systematic theology in this direction.

When one views the world with no definite theological bias one way or the other, one sees that order and disorder, as we now recognize them, are purely human inventions. We are interested in certain types of arrangement, useful, æsthetic, or moral—so interested that whenever we find them realized, the fact emphatically rivets our attention. The result is that we work over the contents of the world selectively. It is overflowing with disorderly arrangements from our point of view, but order is the only thing we care for and look at, and by choosing, one can always find some sort of orderly arrangement in the midst of any chaos. If I should throw down a thousand beans at random upon a table, I could doubtless, by eliminating a sufficient number of them, leave the rest in almost any geometrical pattern you might propose to me, and you might then say that that pattern was the thing prefigured beforehand, and that the other beans were mere irrelevance and packing material. Our dealings with Nature are just like this. She is a vast *plenum* in which our attention draws capricious lines in innumerable directions. We count and name whatever lies upon the special lines we trace, whilst the other things and the untraced lines are neither named nor counted. There are in reality infinitely more things "unadapted" to each other in this world than there are things "adapted"; infinitely more things with irregular relations than with regular relations between them. But we look for the regular kind of thing exclusively, and ingeniously discover and preserve it in our memory. It accumulates with other regular kinds, until the collection of them fills our encyclopædias. Yet all the while between and around them lies an infinite anonymous chaos of objects that no one ever thought of together, of relations that never yet attracted our attention.

The facts of order from which the physico-theological argument starts are thus easily susceptible of interpretation as arbitrary human products. So long as this is the case, although of course no argument against God follows, it follows that the argument for him will fail to constitute a knockdown proof of his existence. It will be convincing only to those who on other grounds believe in him already.

☙ Since God is First Cause, this science of sciences says, he differs from all his creatures in possessing existence *a se*. From this "a-se-ity" on God's part, theology deduces by mere logic most of his other perfections. For instance, he must be both *necessary* and *absolute*, cannot not be, and cannot in any way be determined by anything else. This makes Him absolutely unlimited from without, and unlimited also from within; for limitation is non-being; and God is being itself. This unlimitedness makes God infinitely perfect. Moreover, God is *One*, and *Only*, for the infinitely perfect can admit no peer. He is *Spiritual*, for were He composed of physical parts, some other power would have to combine them into the total, and his aseity would thus be contradicted. He is therefore both simple and non-physical in nature. He is *simple metaphysically* also, that is to say, his nature and his existence cannot be distinct, as they are in finite substances which share their formal natures with one another, and are individual only in their material aspect. Since God is one and only, his *essentia* and his *esse* must be given at one stroke. This excludes from his being all those distinctions, so familiar in the world of finite things, between potentiality and actuality, substance and accidents, being and activity, existence and attributes. We can talk, it is true, of God's powers, acts, and attributes, but these discriminations are only "virtual," and made from the human point of view. In God all these points of view fall into an absolute identity of being.

This absence of all potentiality in God obliges Him to be *immutable*. He is actuality, through and through. Were there anything potential about Him, He would either lose or gain by its actualization, and either loss or gain would contradict his perfection. He cannot, therefore, change. Furthermore, He is *immense, boundless;* for could He be outlined in space, He would be composite, and this would contradict his indivisibility. He is therefore *omnipresent*, indivisibly there, at every point of space. He is similarly wholly present at every point of time—in other words *eternal*. For if He began in time, He would need a prior cause, and that would contradict his aseitv. If He ended, it would contradict his necessity.

If He went through any succession, it would contradict his immutability.

He has *intelligence* and *will* and every other creature-perfection, for *we* have them, and *effectus nequit superare causam*. In Him, however, they are absolutely and eternally in act, and their *object*, since God can be bounded by naught that is external, can primarily be nothing else than God himself. He knows himself, then, in one eternal indivisible act, and wills himself with an infinite self-pleasure.[8] Since He must of logical necessity thus love and will himself, He cannot be called "free" *ad intra*, with the freedom of contrarieties that characterizes finite creatures. *Ad extra*, however, or with respect to his creation, God is free. He cannot *need* to create, being perfect in being and in happiness already. He *wills* to create, then, by an absolute freedom.

Being thus a substance endowed with intellect and will and freedom, God is a *person;* and a *living* person also, for He is both object and subject of his own activity, and to be this distinguishes the living from the lifeless. He is thus absolutely *self-sufficient*: his *self-knowledge* and *self-love* are both of them infinite and adequate, and need no extraneous conditions to perfect them.

He is *omniscient*, for in knowing himself as Cause He knows all creature things and events by implication. His knowledge is *previsive*, for He is present to all time. Even our free acts are known beforehand to Him, for otherwise his wisdom would admit of successive moments of enrichment, and this would contradict his immutability. He is *omnipotent* for everything that does not involve logical contradiction. He can make *being*—in other words his power includes *creation*. If what He creates were made of his own substance, it would have to be infinite in essence, as that substance is; but it is finite; so it must be non-divine in substance. If it were made of a substance, an eternally existing matter, for example, which God found there to his hand, and to which He simply gave its form, that would contradict God's definition as First

[8] For the scholastics the *facultas appetendi* embraces feeling, desire, and will.

Cause, and make Him a mere mover of something caused already. The things he creates, then, He creates *ex nihilo*, and gives them absolute being as so many finite substances additional to himself. The forms which he imprints upon them have their prototypes in his ideas. But as in God there is no such thing as multiplicity, and as these ideas for us are manifold, we must distinguish the ideas as they are in God and the way in which our minds externally imitate them. We must attribute them to Him only in a *terminative* sense, as differing aspects, from the finite point of view, of his unique essence. God of course is holy, good, and just. He can do no evil, for He is positive being's fullness, and evil is negation. It is true that He has created physical evil in places, but only as a means of wider good, for *bonum totius præeminet bonum partis.* Moral evil He cannot will, either as end or means, for that would contradict his holiness. By creating free beings He *permits* it only, neither his justice nor his goodness obliging Him to prevent the recipients of freedom from misusing the gift.

As regards God's purpose in creating, primarily it can only have been to exercise his absolute freedom by the manifestation to others of his glory. From this it follows that the others must be rational beings, capable in the first place of knowledge, love, and honor, and in the second place of happiness, for the knowledge and love of God is the mainspring of felicity. In so far forth one may say that God's secondary purpose in creating is *love.*

I will not weary you by pursuing these metaphysical determinations farther, into the mysteries of God's Trinity, for example. What I have given will serve as a specimen of the orthodox philosophical theology of both Catholics and Protestants. Newman, filled with enthusiasm at God's list of perfections, continues the passage which I began to quote to you by a couple of pages of a rhetoric so magnificent that I can hardly refrain from adding them, in spite of the inroad they would make upon our time.[9] He first enumerates God's

---

[9] Op. cit., Discourse III. § 7.

attributes sonorously, then celebrates his ownership of everything in earth and Heaven, and the dependence of all that happens upon his permissive will. He gives us scholastic philosophy "touched with emotion," and every philosophy should be touched with emotion to be rightly understood. Emotionally, then, dogmatic theology is worth something to minds of the type of Newman's. It will aid us to estimate what it is worth intellectually, if at this point I make a short digression.

⁂ What God hath joined together, let no man put asunder. The Continental schools of philosophy have too often overlooked the fact that man's thinking is organically connected with his conduct. It seems to me to be the chief glory of English and Scottish thinkers to have kept the organic connection in view. The guiding principle of British philosophy has in fact been that every difference must *make* a difference, every theoretical difference somewhere issue in a practical difference, and that the best method of discussing points of theory is to begin by ascertaining what practical difference would result from one alternative or the other being true. What is the particular truth in question *known as?* In what facts does it result? What is its cash-value in terms of particular experience? This is the characteristic English way of taking up a question. In this way, you remember, Locke takes up the question of personal identity. What you mean by it is just your chain of particular memories, says he. That is the only concretely verifiable part of its significance. All further ideas about it, such as the oneness or manyness of the spiritual substance on which it is based, are therefore void of intelligible meaning; and propositions touching such ideas may be indifferently affirmed or denied. So Berkeley with his "matter." The cash-value of matter is our physical sensations. That is what it is known as, all that we concretely verify of its conception. That, therefore, is the whole meaning of the term "matter"—any other pretended meaning is mere wind of words. Hume does the same thing with causation. It is known as habitual antecedence, and as tendency on our part to look for something definite to come. Apart from this practical meaning it has no significance whatever, and books about it may be committed to the flames, says Hume. Dugald Stewart and Thomas Brown, James Mill, John Mill, and Professor Bain, have followed more or less consistently the same method; and Shadworth Hodgson has used the principle with full explicitness. When all is said and done, it was English and Scotch writers, and not Kant, who introduced "the critical method" into philosophy, the one method fitted to make philosophy a study worthy of serious men. For what seriousness can possibly remain in debating philosophic propositions that will never make an appreciable difference to us in action? And what could it matter, if all propositions were practically indifferent, which of them we should agree to call true or which false?

An American philosopher of eminent originality, Mr. Charles Sanders Peirce, has rendered thought a service by disentangling from the particulars of its application the principle by which these men were instinctively guided, and by singling it out as fundamental and giving to it a Greek name. He calls it the principle of *pragmatism*, and he defends it somewhat as follows: [10]—

Thought in movement has for its only conceivable motive the attainment of belief, or thought at rest. Only when our thought about a subject has found its rest in belief can our action on the subject firmly and safely begin. Beliefs, in short, are rules for action; and the whole function of thinking is but one step in the production of active habits. If there were any part of a thought that made no difference in the thought's practical consequences, then that part would be no proper element of the thought's significance. To develop a thought's meaning we need therefore only determine what conduct it is fitted to produce; that conduct is for us its sole significance; and the tangible fact at the root of all our thought-distinctions

---

[10] In an article, How to make our Ideas Clear, in the Popular Science Monthly for January, 1878, vol. xii. p. 286.

is that there is no one of them so fine as to consist in anything but a possible difference of practice. To attain perfect clearness in our thoughts of an object, we need then only consider what sensations, immediate or remote, we are conceivably to expect from it, and what conduct we must prepare in case the object should be true. Our conception of these practical consequences is for us the whole of our conception of the object, so far as that conception has positive significance at all.

This is the principle of Peirce, the principle of pragmatism. Such a principle will help us on this occasion to decide, among the various attributes set down in the scholastic inventory of God's perfections, whether some be not far less significant than others.

If, namely, we apply the principle of pragmatism to God's metaphysical attributes, strictly so called, as distinguished from his moral attributes, I think that, even were we forced by a coercive logic to believe them, we still should have to confess them to be destitute of all intelligible significance. Take God's aseity, for example; or his necessariness; his immateriality; his "simplicity" or superiority to the kind of inner variety and succession which we find in finite beings, his indivisibility, and lack of the inner distinctions of being and activity, substance and accident, potentiality and actuality, and the rest; his repudiation of inclusion in a genus; his actualized infinity; his "personality," apart from the moral qualities which it may comport; his relations to evil being permissive and not positive; his self-sufficiency, self-love, and absolute felicity in himself:—candidly speaking, how do such qualities as these make any definite connection with our life? And if they severally call for no distinctive adaptations of our conduct, what vital difference can it possibly make to a man's religion whether they be true or false?

For my own part, although I dislike to say aught that may grate upon tender associations, I must frankly confess that even though these attributes were faultlessly deduced, I cannot conceive of its being of the smallest consequence to us religiously that any one of them should be true. Pray, what specific act can I perform in order to adapt myself the better to God's simplicity? Or how does it assist me to plan my behavior, to know that his happiness is anyhow absolutely complete? In the middle of the century just past, Mayne Reid was the great writer of books of out-of-door adventure. He was forever extolling the hunters and field-observers of living animals' habits, and keeping up a fire of invective against the "closet-naturalists," as he called them, the collectors and classifiers, and handlers of skeletons and skins. When I was a boy, I used to think that a closet-naturalist must be the vilest type of wretch under the sun. But surely the systematic theologians are the closet-naturalists of the deity, even in Captain Mayne Reid's sense. What is their deduction of metaphysical attributes but a shuffling and matching of pedantic dictionary-adjectives, aloof from morals, aloof from human needs, something that might be worked out from the mere word "God" by one of those logical machines of wood and brass which recent ingenuity has contrived as well as by a man of flesh and blood. They have the trail of the serpent over them. One feels that in the theologians' hands, they are only a set of titles obtained by a mechanical manipulation of synonyms; verbality has stepped into the place of vision, professionalism into that of life. Instead of bread we have a stone; instead of a fish, a serpent. Did such a conglomeration of abstract terms give really the gist of our knowledge of the deity, schools of theology might indeed continue to flourish, but religion, vital religion, would have taken its flight from this world. What keeps religion going is something else than abstract definitions and systems of concatenated adjectives, and something different from faculties of theology and their professors. All these things are after-effects, secondary accretions upon those phenomena of vital conversation with the unseen divine, of which I have shown you so many instances, renewing themselves *in sæcula sæculorum* in the lives of humble private men.

So much for the metaphysical attributes of God! From the point of view of practical religion, the metaphysical monster which they offer to our worship is an absolutely worthless invention of the scholarly mind.

☙ What shall we now say of the attributes called moral? Pragmatically, they stand on an entirely different footing. They positively determine fear and hope and expectation, and are foundations for the saintly life. It needs but a glance at them to show how great is their significance.

God's holiness, for example: being holy, God can will nothing but the good. Being omnipotent, he can secure its triumph. Being omniscient, he can see us in the dark. Being just, he can punish us for what he sees. Being loving, he can pardon too. Being unalterable, we can count on him securely. These qualities enter into connection with our life, it is highly important that we should be informed concerning them. That God's purpose in creation should be the manifestation of his glory is also an attribute which has definite relations to our practical life. Among other things it has given a definite character to worship in all Christian countries. If dogmatic theology really does prove beyond dispute that a God with characters like these exists, she may well claim to give a solid basis to religious sentiment. But verily, how stands it with her arguments?

It stands with them as ill as with the arguments for his existence. Not only do post-Kantian idealists reject them root and branch, but it is a plain historic fact that they never have converted any one who has found in the moral complexion of the world, as he experienced it, reasons for doubting that a good God can have framed it. To prove God's goodness by the scholastic argument that there is no non-being in his essence would sound to such a witness simply silly.

No! the book of Job went over this whole matter once for all and definitively. Ratiocination is a relatively superficial and unreal path to the deity: "I will lay mine hand upon my mouth; I have heard of Thee by the hearing of the ear, but now mine eye seeth Thee." An intellect perplexed and baffled, yet a trustful sense of presence—such is the situation of the man who is sincere with himself and with the facts, but who remains religious still.[11]

---

[11] Pragmatically, the most important attribute of God is his puni-

We must therefore, I think, bid a definitive good-by to dogmatic theology. In all sincerity our faith must do without that warrant. Modern idealism, I repeat, has said good-by to this theology forever. Can modern idealism give faith a better warrant, or must she still rely on her poor self for witness?

☙§ The basis of modern idealism is Kant's doctrine of the Transcendental Ego of Apperception. By this formidable term Kant merely meant the fact that the consciousness "I think them" must (potentially or actually) accompany all our objects. Former skeptics had said as much, but the "I" in question had remained for them identified with the personal individual. Kant abstracted and depersonalized it, and made it the most universal of all his categories, although for Kant himself the Transcendental Ego had no theological implications.

It was reserved for his successors to convert Kant's notion of *Bewusstsein überhaupt*, or abstract consciousness, into an infinite concrete self-consciousness which is the soul of the world, and in which our sundry personal self-consciousnesses have their being. It would lead me into technicalities to show you even briefly how this transformation was in point of fact effected. Suffice it to say that in the Hegelian school, which to-day so deeply influences both British and American thinking, two principles have borne the brunt of the operation.

The first of these principles is that the old logic of identity never gives us more than a post-mortem dissection of *disjecta membra*, and that the fullness of life can be construed to

---

tive justice. But who, in the present state of theological opinion on that point, will dare maintain that hell fire or its equivalent in some shape is rendered certain by pure logic? Theology herself has largely based this doctrine upon revelation; and, in discussing it, has tended more and more to substitute conventional ideas of criminal law for *a priori* principles of reason. But the very notion that this glorious universe, with planets and winds, and laughing sky and ocean, should have been conceived and had its beams and rafters laid in technicalities of criminality, is incredible to our modern imagination. It weakens a religion to hear it argued upon such a basis.

thought only by recognizing that every object which our thought may propose to itself involves the notion of some other object which seems at first to negate the first one.

The second principle is that to be conscious of a negation is already virtually to be beyond it. The mere asking of a question or expression of a dissatisfaction proves that the answer or the satisfaction is already imminent; the finite, realized as such, is already the infinite *in posse.*

Applying these principles, we seem to get a propulsive force into our logic which the ordinary logic of a bare, stark self-identity in each thing never attains to. The objects of our thought now act within our thought, act as objects act when given in experience. They change and develop. They introduce something other than themselves along with them; and this other, at first only ideal or potential, presently proves itself also to be actual. It supersedes the thing at first supposed, and both verifies and corrects it, in developing the fullness of its meaning.

The program is excellent; the universe *is* a place where things are followed by other things that both correct and fulfill them; and a logic which gave us something like this movement of fact would express truth far better than the traditional school-logic, which never gets of its own accord from anything to anything else, and registers only predictions and subsumptions, or static resemblances and differences. Nothing could be more unlike the methods of dogmatic theology than those of these new logic. Let me quote in illustration some passages from the Scottish transcendentalist whom I have already named.

"How are we to conceive," Principal Caird writes, "of the reality in which all intelligence rests?" He replies: "Two things may without difficulty be proved, viz., that this reality is an absolute Spirit, and conversely that it is only in communion with this absolute Spirit or Intelligence that the finite Spirit can realize itself. It is absolute; for the faintest movement of human intelligence would be arrested, if it did not presuppose the absolute reality of intelligence, of thought itself. Doubt or denial themselves presuppose and indirectly affirm it. When I pronounce anything to be true, I pronounce it, indeed, to be relative to thought, but not to be relative to my thought, or to the thought of any other individual mind. From the existence of all individual minds as such I can abstract; I can think them away. But that which I cannot think away is thought or self-consciousness itself, in its independence and absoluteness, or, in other words, an Absolute Thought or Self-Consciousness."

Here, you see, Principal Caird makes the transition which Kant did not make: he converts the omnipresence of consciousness in general as a condition of "truth" being anywhere possible, into an omnipresent universal consciousness which he identifies with God in his concreteness. He next proceeds to use the principle that to acknowledge your limits is in essence to be beyond them; and makes the transition to the religious experience of individuals in the following words:—

"If [Man] were only a creature of transient sensations and impulses, of an ever coming and going succession of intuitions, fancies, feelings, then nothing could ever have for him the character of objective truth or reality. But it is the prerogative of man's spiritual nature that he can yield himself up to a thought and will that are infinitely larger than his own. As a thinking, self-conscious being, indeed, he may be said, by his very nature, to live in the atmosphere of the Universal Life. As a thinking being, it is possible for me to suppress and quell in my consciousness every movement of self-assertion, every notion and opinion that is merely mine, every desire that belongs to me as this particular Self, and to become the pure medium of a thought that is universal—in one word, to live no more my own life, but let my consciousness be possessed and suffused by the Infinite and Eternal life of spirit. And yet it is just in this renunciation of self that I truly gain myself, or realize the highest possibilities of my own nature. For whilst in one sense we give up self to live the universal and absolute life of reason, yet that to which we thus surrender ourselves is in reality our truer self. The life of absolute reason is not a life that is foreign to us."

Nevertheless, Principal Caird goes on to say, so far as we are able outwardly to realize this doctrine, the balm it offers remains incomplete. Whatever we may be *in posse*, the very best of us *in actu* falls very short of being absolutely divine. Social morality, love, and self-sacrifice even, merge our Self only in some other finite self or selves. They do not quite identify it with the Infinite. Man's ideal destiny, infinite in abstract logic, might thus seem in practice forever unrealizable.

"Is there, then," our author continues, "no solution of the contradiction between the ideal and the actual? We answer, There is such a solution, but in order to reach it we are carried beyond the sphere of morality into that of religion. It may be said to be the essential characteristic of religion as contrasted with morality, that it changes aspiration into fruition, anticipation into realization; that instead of leaving man in the interminable pursuit of a vanishing ideal, it makes him the actual partaker of a divine or infinite life. Whether we view religion from the human side or the divine—as the surrender of the soul to God, or as the life of God in the soul—in either aspect it is of its very essence that the Infinite has ceased to be a far-off vision, and has become a present reality. The very first pulsation of the spiritual life, when we rightly apprehend its significance, is the indication that the division between the Spirit and its object has vanished, that the ideal has become real, that the finite has reached its goal and become suffused with the presence and life of the Infinite.

"Oneness of mind and will with the divine mind and will is not the future hope and aim of religion, but its very beginning and birth in the soul. To enter on the religious life is to terminate the struggle. In that act which constitutes the beginning of the religious life—call it faith, or trust, or self-surrender, or by whatever name you will—there is involved the identification of the finite with a life which is eternally realized. It is true indeed that the religious life is progressive;

but understood in the light of the foregoing idea, religious progress is not progress *towards*, but *within* the sphere of the Infinite. It is not the vain attempt by endless finite additions or increments to become possessed of infinite wealth, but it is the endeavor, by the constant exercise of spiritual activity, to appropriate that infinite inheritance of which we are already in possession. The whole future of the religious life is given in its beginning, but it is given implicitly. The position of the man who has entered on the religious life is that evil, error, imperfection, do not really belong to him: they are excrescences which have no organic relation to his true nature: they are already virtually, as they will be actually, suppressed and annulled, and in the very process of being annulled they become the means of spiritual progress. Though he is not exempt from temptation and conflict, [yet] in that inner sphere in which his true life lies, the struggle is over, the victory already achieved. It is not a finite but an infinite life which the spirit lives. Every pulse-beat of its [existence] is the expression and realization of the life of God." [12]

You will readily admit that no description of the phenomena of the religious consciousness could be better than these words of your lamented preacher and philosopher. They reproduce the very rapture of those crises of conversion of which we have been hearing; they utter what the mystic felt but was unable to communicate; and the saint, in hearing them, recognizes his own experience. It is indeed gratifying to find the content of religion reported so unanimously. But when all is said and done, has Principal Caird—and I only use him as an example of that whole mode of thinking—transcended the sphere of feeling and of the direct experience of the individual, and laid the foundations of religion in impartial reason? Has he made religion universal by coercive reasoning, transformed it from a private faith into a public

---

[12] John Caird: An Introduction to the Philosophy of Religion, London and New York, 1880, pp. 243–250, and 291–299, much abridged.

certainty? Has he rescued its affirmations from obscurity and mystery?

I believe that he has done nothing of the kind, but that he has simply reaffirmed the individual's experiences in a more generalized vocabulary. And again, I can be excused from proving technically that the transcendentalist reasonings fail to make religion universal, for I can point to the plain fact that a majority of scholars, even religiously disposed ones, stubbornly refuse to treat them as convincing. The whole of Germany, one may say, has positively rejected the Hegelian argumentation. As for Scotland, I need only mention Professor Fraser's and Professor Pringle-Pattison's memorable criticisms, with which so many of you are familiar.[13] Once more, I ask, if transcendental idealism were as objectively and absolutely rational as it pretends to be, could it possibly fail so egregiously to be persuasive?

---

[13] A. C. FRASER: Philosophy of Theism, second edition, Edinburgh and London, 1899, especially part ii, chaps. vii and viii.; A. SETH [PRINGLE-PATTISON]: Hegelianism and Personality, Ibid., 1890, passim.

The most persuasive arguments in favor of a concrete individual Soul of the world, with which I am acquainted, are those of my colleague, Josiah Royce, in his Religious Aspect of Philosophy, Boston, 1885; in his Conception of God, New York and London, 1897; and lately in his Aberdeen Gifford Lectures, The World and the Individual, 2 vols., New York and London, 1901–02. I doubtless seem to some of my readers to evade the philosophic duty which my thesis in this lecture imposes on me, by not even attempting to meet Professor Royce's arguments articulately. I admit the momentary evasion. In the present lectures, which are cast throughout in a popular mould, there seemed no room for subtle metaphysical discussion, and for tactical purposes it was sufficient, the contention of philosophy being what it is (namely, that religion can be transformed into a universally convincing science), to point to the fact that no religious philosophy has actually convinced the mass of thinkers. Meanwhile let me say that I hope that the present volume may be followed by another, if I am spared to write it, in which not only Professor Royce's arguments, but others for monistic absolutism shall be considered with all the technical fullness which their great importance calls for. At present I resign myself to lying passive under the reproach of superficiality.

What religion reports, you must remember, always purports to be a fact of experience: the divine is actually present, religion says, and between it and ourselves relations of give and take are actual. If definite perceptions of fact like this cannot stand upon their own feet, surely abstract reasoning cannot give them the support they are in need of. Conceptual processes can class facts, define them, interpret them; but they do not produce them, nor can they reproduce their individuality. There is always a *plus*, a *thisness*, which feeling alone can answer for. Philosophy in this sphere is thus a secondary function, unable to warrant faith's veracity, and so I revert to the thesis which I announced at the beginning of this lecture.

In all sad sincerity I think we must conclude that the attempt to demonstrate by purely intellectual processes the truth of the deliverances of direct religious experience is absolutely hopeless.

☙§ It would be unfair to philosophy, however, to leave her under this negative sentence. Let me close, then, by briefly enumerating what she *can* do for religion. If she will abandon metaphysics and deduction for criticism and induction, and frankly transform herself from theology into science of religions, she can make herself enormously useful.

The spontaneous intellect of man always defines the divine which it feels in ways that harmonize with its temporary intellectual prepossessions. Philosophy can by comparison eliminate the local and the accidental from these definitions. Both from dogma and from worship she can remove historic incrustations. By confronting the spontaneous religious constructions with the results of natural science, philosophy can also eliminate doctrines that are now known to be scientifically absurd or incongruous.

Sifting out in this way unworthy formulations, she can leave a residuum of conceptions that at least are possible. With these she can deal as *hypotheses*, testing them in all the manners, whether negative or positive, by which hypotheses are ever tested. She can reduce their number, as some are found more open to objection. She can perhaps become the champion of one which she picks out as being the most closely verified or verifiable. She can refine upon the definition of this hypothesis, distinguishing between what is innocent over-belief and symbolism in the expression of it, and what is to be literally taken. As a result, she can offer mediation between different believers, and help to bring about consensus of opinion. She can do this the more successfully, the better she discriminates the common and essential from the individual and local elements of the religious beliefs which she compares.

I do not see why a critical Science of Religions of this sort might not eventually command as general a public adhesion as is commanded by a physical science. Even the personally non-religious might accept its conclusions on trust, much as blind persons now accept the facts of optics—it might appear as foolish to refuse them. Yet as the science of optics has to be fed in the first instance, and continually verified later, by facts experienced by seeing persons; so the science of religions would depend for its original material on facts of personal experience, and would have to square itself with personal experience through all its critical reconstructions. It could never get away from concrete life, or work in a conceptual vacuum. It would forever have to confess, as every science confesses, that the subtlety of nature flies beyond it, and that its formulas are but approximations. Philosophy lives in words, but truth and fact well up into our lives in ways that exceed verbal formulation. There is in the living act of perception always something that glimmers and twinkles and will not be caught, and for which reflection comes too late. No one knows this as well as the philosopher. He must fire his volley of new vocables out of his conceptual shotgun, for his profession condemns him to this industry, but he secretly knows the hollowness and irrelevancy. His formulas are like stereoscopic or kinetoscopic photographs seen outside the instrument; they lack the depth, the motion, the vitality. In the religious sphere, in particular, belief that formulas are true can never wholly take the place of personal experience.